General Benjamin Smith

ALSO BY ALAN D. WATSON

Wilmington, North Carolina, to 1861
(McFarland, 2003)

General Benjamin Smith

*A Biography of the
North Carolina Governor*

ALAN D. WATSON

McFarland & Company, Inc., Publishers
Jefferson, North Carolina, and London

LIBRARY OF CONGRESS CATALOGUING-IN-PUBLICATION DATA

Watson, Alan D., 1942–
    General Benjamin Smith : a biography of the North Carolina governor / Alan D. Watson.
      p.   cm.
    Includes bibliographical references and index.

    ISBN 978-0-7864-6156-1
    softcover : 50# alkaline paper ∞

    1. Smith, Benjamin, 1756–1826. 2. North Carolina — Politics and government —1776–1865. 3. Governors — North Carolina — Biography. I. Title.
    F258.S64W37   2011
    975.6'03092 — dc22   2010054290
    [B]

BRITISH LIBRARY CATALOGUING DATA ARE AVAILABLE

© 2011 Alan D. Watson. All rights reserved

No part of this book may be reproduced or transmitted in any form or by any means, electronic or mechanical, including photocopying or recording, or by any information storage and retrieval system, without permission in writing from the publisher.

Cover image: portrait of Benjmain Smith (courtesy of State Archives, Office of Archives and History, Raleigh, North Carolina)

Manufactured in the United States of America

McFarland & Company, Inc., Publishers
   Box 611, Jefferson, North Carolina 28640
     www.mcfarlandpub.com

Contents

Acknowledgments vi
Introduction 1

1. South Carolinian 5
2. Wilmington and the Lower Cape Fear 24
3. North Carolinian 34
4. Benefactor 47
5. Smithville 61
6. General 74
7. Speaker 88
8. Francophobe 100
9. Planter 115
10. Republican 127
11. Duelist 138
12. Adjutant General 146
13. Governor 162
14. Denouement and Death 181
15. Remembrance and Rehabilitation 198

Notes 207
Bibliography 233
Index 243

Acknowledgments

In pursuing Benjamin Smith I have been aided by many who have generously offered their time and effort to bring this project to fruition. The staffs at archival repositories at East Carolina University, Duke University, the University of North Carolina at Chapel Hill, and the University of South Carolina have been immensely helpful. I must also thank Robert G. Anthony of the North Carolina Collection at the University of North Carolina at Chapel Hill, Michael Hill of the Research Branch of the Office of Archives and History, Department of Cultural Resources, Raleigh, N.C., Chris Fonvielle of the Department of History, UNC Wilmington, Vann Evans, Gregory King-Owen, Steve McAlister, and Joseph Shepard for their valuable aid.

Special thanks are extended to Sue Cody, Randall Library, UNC Wilmington, and Beverly Tetterton, North Carolina Room, New Hanover Public Library, Wilmington, N.C., for their indispensable assistance in the production of this volume and for their inestimable help over many years.

Portions of the following articles have been used with permission: "Benjamin Smith: North Carolina's Education Governor," *Brunswick Gazette* 5 (October/November/December 2006): 1–7; "Benjamin Smith: Remembrance and Rehabilitation," *The Bulletin* (a Publication of the Historical Society of the Lower Cape Fear) 53 (October 2009): [1]–7; "Benjamin Smith: Brunswick County 'General' and North Carolina Governor," *North Carolina Historical Review* 87 (January 2010): 28–56.

Introduction

The story of Benjamin Smith (1757–1826), contemporaneously known as "General," unfolds in several layers. On a personal level, it is ultimately a pathetic tale of a young, ambitious scion of a distinguished South Carolina family, who by a fortunate marriage, speculation, and leveraging, amassed an enormous estate centered in Brunswick County, North Carolina. Several plantations, including Belvedere and Orton, Smith's principal seats, lined the Cape Fear River. Fine town residences in Wilmington and eponymous Smithville (present Southport) offered respite from plantation life. Additional property dotted the North Carolina landscape from New Bern to Hillsborough and encompassed holdings in Kentucky, Tennessee, and South Carolina. He became a lowcountry South Carolina nabob transplanted to the Cape Fear region of North Carolina.

Yet Smith died in abject poverty. Poor judgment, evidenced in speculative ventures and unwise sureties, together with an always risky dependence upon rice cultivation led to increasing indebtedness and ignominious downfall. Briefly Smith spent time in a debtor's prison. At the end the General was completely dependent upon the charity of a few remaining friends. Yet even death failed to end his troubles. According to local folklore, creditors tried to claim his body in order to force Smith's family and friends to make restitution for outstanding debts. Smith's life, in effect, seemed the reverse of that of Horatio Alger.

Beyond the General's eventful personal life, a journey through North Carolina's history with Benjamin Smith presents an entrée into the evolution of the United States and North Carolina from the aftermath of the Revolution to the War of 1812. Coming of age during the war for American independence and quickly moving into the public arena, Smith joined others across the country and state in rejecting the hapless government of the Articles of Confederation and endorsing its replacement by that of the federal Constitution. At the same time, his maturation and service during the Revolution produced a desire to achieve recognition for martial exploits and a militant opposition to any intrusion by Great Britain or France upon American sovereignty. That attitude led Smith to warn of calamity and rattle sabers on more than one occasion.

Smith's rise to prominence also coincided with the appearance of political parties in the United States. Unsurprisingly, he found a home with the Federalists, given their predilection for wealth and a powerful, active national government to protect and promote moneyed interests. Yet, Smith, an egotistical man who needed votes to sustain his political ambitions, appeared to be a political trimmer, not unlike other Federalists in North Carolina. After 1800, when the Jeffersonian Republicans dominated the political scene in state and nation, Smith switched sides. In the process he helped to ensure a continuation of his legislative career and later a successful candidacy for the governorship of North Carolina.

More than national affairs, Smith's activities in the public sphere illumine North Carolina politics, government, and education in the early national era. For a quarter century the General represented Brunswick County in the state legislature, all the while serving on prestigious committees and in deliberations that churned out numerous laws of major and minor significance. More progressive than most, certainly in North Carolina, Smith sought to foster domestic manufacturing, banking, penal reform and a penitentiary, improvements to transportation, and particularly militia reform, the last evidencing a sense of military grandeur that early characterized the young man of the Revolution.

Following Smith permits a look into the development of education in North Carolina, particularly the University of North Carolina, the first state aided institution of higher education in the country. The story of the General cannot be told without considering the travails of the university in its early years. As an original trustee and the first benefactor of the university, the General evidenced an unstinting support for an institution that was not always so gracious in return. All the while Smith recognized the need to promote secondary education in the form of academies and endorsed the rather radical proposal of public schools for all white children.

Smith capped his career in state politics by serving a single term as governor of the state, a position that seemingly offered the incumbent little authority at that time but which the General exploited to the utmost. Smith better defined the bounds of gubernatorial clemency, relied more for advice on his executive council, and, as commander in chief, worked mightily to place North Carolina's militia on a sound footing. He particularly used the office as a bully pulpit to present a broad, compelling, progressive program for legislative consideration, in all trying to render the governor's office a more formidable, engaged part of the political process.

Pursuing the General also affords insight into local government, specifically the Brunswick County Court, which was representative of county courts in North Carolina. Those courts, exercising judicial and administrative powers, were the organs of government that most affected the everyday lives of the people of the state. As a justice of the peace who helped to compose the county court, Smith proved conscientious in attending to county affairs, in the process illustrating the functions of the court which ranged from overseeing fiscal matters, public buildings, and transportation to licensing grist mills, caring for orphans, and appointing slave patrols. Along the way the General was responsible for moving the county seat to Smithville, where it remained for over a century and a half.

Beyond his endeavors in politics and government, Smith offers a glimpse into the economic life and travails of the planter class in North Carolina. As expected of gentlemen planters, he experimented with various crops and embraced advanced agricultural techniques. However, the General depended principally upon the cultivation of rice, contending with the weather, market fluctuations, and a recalcitrant labor force to produce the seed. At one time he was the largest slave owner in North Carolina, a man whose conscience seemed unbothered by buying, selling, and gifting humans. Conversely, his restive bondsmen constantly challenged his authority, evidencing the age-old struggle between slave owner and slave. Representative of men of his class, Smith realized the need to diversify his economic operations and constantly explored other avenues of revenue that ranged from ferry keeping to shipbuilding.

In its broadest perspective, however, the life of Benjamin Smith reflected post–Revolutionary gendered expectations of elite, white Southern males. Masculinity meant autonomy, self-assertion, and boldness to individuals who were convinced of their own superiority but simultaneously were imbued with a sense of civic obligation and the need to perpetuate the principles of the Revolution in the young republic of America. However, the personal independence of elite males, which enabled charitable endeavors, permitted a disinterested ability to work on behalf of the public, and often contributed to a domineering demeanor, rested upon the mastery of others.

Beyond the independence, self-confidence, and arrogance engendered by slave ownership and privilege, masculinity entailed a certain self-promotion, or "acting the part of a gentleman." That in turn led to a conscious concern for reputation, which ultimately depended upon recognition and approval by one's community. As Smith and white southern males knew, a man's reputation equated with honor, a construct that has been compellingly put forward to explain the lives and culture of privileged Southern men. An intangible, unlike dress or education, honor was exclusivist, elitist, and protected in the extreme by dueling, a ritualized ceremony designed to resolve conflicts among peers. Any perceived slight was taken seriously, for honor at all times was prized. Protection of reputation forced many in North Carolina to personal confrontations on the field of honor, including Smith on at least one occasion.

Benjamin Smith presents an exciting, sometimes poignant, look into life in North Carolina two centuries ago, principally from the perspective of an elite Southern planter and public servant. Despite his lamentable demise local historians later began to rehabilitate his reputation so that the General became a folk hero by the early twentieth century. Yet, even after eliminating the fiction and embellishments from his story, Smith stands as an apt representative of a social class of a bygone era and a major contributor to the development of North Carolina in the early days of the Republic.

CHAPTER 1

SOUTH CAROLINIAN

The year 1757, immodestly but arguably, proved one of the most consequential in modern Western history. Reeling from French successes in America during the course of the French and Indian War, Great Britain elevated William Pitt, the Great Commoner, to Parliamentary leadership. The young P.M. in 1757 reorganized and redirected the British war effort in Europe and America, reversing British fortunes in the struggle for supremacy in North America. During the ensuing four years the British and their colonials routed the enemy and then waited for the Treaty of Paris in 1763 to evict the French from their long presence on the continent. That victory in turn paved the way for subsequent colonial resistance to British rule along the coast of North America that eventuated in the appearance of an independent United States.[1]

Charles Town, South Carolina, buzzing with excitement in 1757 over the French and Indian War and the threat of the Cherokee to the west, reflected the hurly-burly of urban life in a center of increasing wealth and sophistication. The provincial governor reviewed the muster of the local militia. Doubtlessly he was encouraged by the martial enthusiasm of the town as evidenced by the formation of an artillery company — "to be of real Utility and not for Parade" — and a military club, both for gentlemen.[2] The Charles-Town Library Society convened in the tavern of John Gordon, perhaps for more than intellectual stimulation, to receive news of the king's approval of a 1754 South Carolina statute incorporating the organization.[3] And in their peregrinations about town all must have appreciated the efforts of the municipal commissioners, however problematic, to improve the regulation of traffic and the collection of trash along the streets.[4]

The year 1757 also marked the birth of Benjamin Smith. Born on January 10,[5] to Thomas Smith (of Broad Street) and Sarah Moore Smith in Charles Town, Benjamin was the seventh of twelve children of that union. A previous son of the same name had died in infancy as had several other children. But seven of the twelve survived to legal majority — three brothers, Roger (1745–

1805), Peter (1754–1821), and James (1761–1835) and three sisters — Sarah (1752–?), Mary (1764–1839), and Ann (1765–1799?). Only younger siblings James and Mary outlived Benjamin, who died in 1826.[5] In July 1757, Thomas and Sarah took Benjamin to St. Philip's Church in Charles Town for baptism by the Rev. Richard Clarke. Rector of St. Philip's from 1755 to 1759, the Rev. Clarke "was admired as a preacher, both in Charles town and London," according to early South Carolina historian David Ramsay. No doubt Thomas and Sarah Smith appreciated his eloquence and serious preaching which filled that Anglican church and "reformed [the] lives of many of his hearers."[6]

An impeccable pedigree. That was the immediate inheritance of Benjamin Smith. Among his paternal ancestors was great-great-grandfather first landgrave Thomas Smith (1648–1694), and great-grandfather second landgrave Thomas Smith (1664?-1738). Their distinguished titles derived from the Fundamental Constitutions of 1669, a document by which the Lords Proprietors of Carolina hoped to impose some semblance of English society upon the wilderness of (South) Carolina that was destined to be settled the next year along the Ashley River. The Fundamental Constitutions, written by Anthony Ashley Cooper and John Locke, was a remarkably liberal document for its time, but recreating the hierarchical class structure of England in America required an aristocracy in America — hence the titles of landgrave and cacique, whose recipients obtained substantial grants of land to justify their eminent status.[7]

Father and son immigrated to South Carolina in 1684, where they contributed to the political turmoil of the proprietary years of the province. The first landgrave, an English dissenter, supported the proprietors in their effort to institute reforms in the colony and briefly served as governor of the province. The second landgrave followed closely in the footsteps of his father. Early in the eighteenth century he led the dissenters in the colony in opposition to attempts to impose an Anglican religious establishment on the province. Two decades later, while a member of the governor's council, Smith advocated the emission of large quantities of paper currency, an issue that also badly divided the colony and led to the landgrave's arrest for treason, charged as he was with plotting a rebellion against the government. Though never formally tried, Smith subsequently lost his seat on the council. A new gubernatorial administration brought a measure of tranquility to South Carolina. At the same it thwarted Smith's attempts to speculate in land, and thereafter he played but a minor role in public affairs.[8]

The second landgrave Smith married twice. His first wife was Anna Cornelia Van Myddagh. Among their ten children (there were ten by the second marriage as well) was Sabina (1694?–1735), who married (another) Thomas Smith (1691–1724). That Smith's father, the captain of a merchant vessel, died at sea before Thomas was born. Obtaining property from his father-in-law and grandfather, Thomas, husband of Sabina, eventually settled in Goose Creek, St. James Parish, where incidentally the landgraves had also made their principal residences. During his relatively brief life Smith accumulated a 350-acre plantation with twenty-five slaves and property scattered throughout the province. He served in the provincial legislature and held numerous local offices. His marriage produced three children: Benjamin, Anne, and Thomas (1720–1790), the last the father of our subject.[9]

On his maternal side Benjamin Smith likewise claimed distinguished forebears, among them two governors, one of the first permanent settlers of the Lower Cape Fear in North Carolina, and perhaps the most flamboyant character in the proprietary history of South Carolina. Great-grandfather James Moore (d. 1706), like so many early South Carolinians, emigrated from Barbados to the mainland colony, certainly by 1675. A self-made planter in the Goose Creek area, he married Margaret Berringer, step-daughter of Gov. Sir John Yeamans (1672–1674), the step-great-great grandfather of Benjamin. The propitious union, plus successful agricultural and mercantile pursuits, augmented by illicit commerce with pirates and engagement in the forbidden Indian slave trade, led to fortune and political fame. After navigating the perilous course of politics in the late seventeenth century, Moore received a proprietary appointment as governor from 1700 to 1703, during which time he led an unsuccessful expedition to capture the Spanish fortress of St. Augustine in Florida. Before his death Moore recouped some prestige when he commanded a foray to the south that virtually wiped out the pro–Spanish Apalache Indians.[10]

Among the ten children sired by James was Roger Moore (1694–1751), grandfather of Benjamin. Also a politically active and wealthy planter in Goose Creek, St. James Parish, Moore initially opposed proprietary efforts to regain control of South Carolina following the rebellion in 1719. However, after his marriage to Catherine Rhett in 1721, he joined the proprietary faction. Unsuccessful in his support of the proprietors, Moore and others left South Carolina during the turmoil of the 1720s. Obtaining grants of land along the Cape Fear River in North Carolina in 1726, he became one of the pioneering settlers of the Lower Cape Fear region with his brothers Maurice and Nathaniel. He developed two plantations, Kendal and Orton, along the river. Accumulating almost 60,000 acres of land and 250 slaves, he became "King Roger" in North Carolina. The plantation house at Orton, perhaps the first brick residence in the region, still stands, though transformed over the years from a modest dwelling to an impressive Greek Revival mansion overlooking the Cape Fear River.[11]

Moore's wife, Catherine Rhett, daughter of William Rhett (1666–1723),

"King" Roger Moore's Tomb at Orton Plantation. Courtesy of New Hanover Public Library.

linked Benjamin Smith to one of the most powerful men in South Carolina during the proprietary era. Rhett arrived in South Carolina from England in 1694, after which he led a tumultuous life. He spurned the proprietors, once denouncing an appointment as receiver general of the quit rents by claiming publicly, "I wou'd wipe my arse with the Commission." Yet he *accepted* the office, only to fail to fulfill the duties required of him. Still, the proprietors continued to support him, and in turn Rhett reciprocated, becoming the only casualty (wounded by gunfire) in a coup in 1719, by which South Carolinians overturned proprietary government. Over the years Rhett reputedly engaged in illicit trade with the Spanish, French, and perhaps pirates (though under commission from South Carolina he captured the buccaneer Stede Bonnet in North Carolina in 1718). Just prior to his death, Rhett incurred the scorn of two South Carolina governors. One claimed that he was an enemy "to his country & detestable reviler of mankind"; the other, that he was "a haughty, proud, insolent fellow and a cheating scoundrel." Perhaps his death by apoplexy should have been anticipated. At any rate, among the four children of Roger and Catherine Rhett Moore was Sarah, mother of our subject, who married Thomas Smith of Broad Street in 1744.[12]

Thomas Smith of Broad Street (to distinguish him from Thomas Smith who lived on the Bay in Charles Town), and his brother, Benjamin, forsook plantation agriculture to engage in the mercantile trade. Benjamin, prominent in politics, including his service as speaker of the Commons House, accumulated a fortune "vast enough to establish his family as one of the first families of South Carolina," according to historian George C. Rogers, Jr. Thomas entered the world of commerce in 1742 as a junior partner of Hopton & Smith, a company that specialized in the Indian trade, and thereafter expanded his horizons to overseas shipping. Except for shares in several ships with Benjamin, Thomas followed an independent career that brought him an equally comfortable estate, the result of a disciplined work ethic and a "calculating and materialistic way of life." Those attributes, associated with a rising middle class in Britain, according to historian Richard Hofstadter, might translate into elitist status in America. Befitting a man of his stature, Thomas held numerous positions of public trust in Charles Town and St. Philip's Parish, and in the Berkeley County militia. He also sat in the South Carolina Commons House from 1769 to 1772.[13]

After working for twenty years Thomas contemplated retirement in 1762. He returned from a voyage to England to find that two of his "hands" had left to go into business for themselves, forcing Smith "to attend more to my Business than I hope I shall ever do again." However, he had achieved a "Competancy" by that time, and wanted to consider "retiring in some measure from this busy World." His eldest son, Roger, almost seventeen at the time, had chosen to follow in his father's footsteps, but was in England, so Thomas felt "under a kind of necessity of Plodding on." The following year Roger was ordered home, and Thomas hoped that in three years, when Roger became twenty years of age, "I shall be released." By May 1764, Roger was by his father's side in the "Compting House." Subsequently Thomas turned the business over to his son, who, under his father's aegis, prospered.[14]

Thomas Smith, claiming to have "Sufficient [assets] to Answer all the reasonable Purposes of life (allowing for an increase of family whom it was never my intention to bring up in Idleness)," began to ease into retirement, more or less. In 1765 he inherited Broom Hall plantation, a 640 acre tract on Goose Creek some nineteen miles from Charles Town, in a "good neighbourhood," at which he hoped to reside from May through July. The house presented "a neat outside appearance," wrote a visitor, "but a better inward appearance, being comfortably and neatly furnished [with] all Conveniences." Smith did not intend to work the plantation for profit, but to maintain it as a country retreat. Hence he kept only *thirty* slaves at Broom Hall, meaning for the plantation to afford him "some employment and amusement" without the anxiety of depending upon producing a profitable crop for market. Nonetheless, as he contemplated retirement, Smith realistically observed, "Not that I expect then to be free from business, for the necessary care of a large family and raising an income from what Estate I have acquired (money loaned at interest and the rental of tenements and warehouses) with some services to the Public will engross a good deal of my time while I am in Town w[hi]ch will be two thirds of my time."[15]

Thus young Benjamin Smith spent his first dozen years mostly in Charles Town, punctuated by sojourns to the country. The town meanwhile grew ever more resplendent in its wealth, urbanity, and ostentation. As South Carolina switched from the export of deerskins and foodstuffs to rice and indigo, the economy of the province boomed. And Charles Town, a fine port situated at the confluence of the Ashley and Cooper rivers, became a center of international trade. Vessels leaving England and Europe for America picked up the trade winds by sailing past the Azores on their way to the West Indies, making Charles Town a destination on the continent before returning home in circular fashion via a northerly crossing of the Atlantic. Packet boats, established by the British Post Office, regularly sailed the Atlantic for the West Indies and Charles Town by the mid–1760s, placing the colonials in closer touch with England and the continent, and reinforcing an obvious attachment to their mother country that remained compelling to many to the eve of the Revolution, and, for some, beyond.[16]

By the mid–1760s, Charles Town was a thriving, vibrant place, basking in its golden age of commerce at the time of Benjamin's youth. Blacks and whites equally inhabited the port. Open to the world, Charles Town was an entrepot for slaves, whether brought directly from Africa or from the West Indies, and for whites from all over the western world who sought to advance their fortunes. The Exchange, built in the 1760s and 1770s, was the most imposing public structure in the town, resembling its counterpart in London, Liverpool, and Bristol. Merchants, who served as factors for plantation nabobs and lesser sorts, and the shipping economy required an extensive support staff of artisans and servants. Opportunity begot opportunity. Wealth begot wealth. Fortunes ballooned. But life had to be lived to its fullest, and quickly, for the vicissitudes of hurricanes, fires, and disease undermined wealth and shortened life spans. Young Benjamin fortunately escaped the smallpox epidemic of 1760 that carried away 650 people of a population approximating 8,000. It was not uncommon to see most men and women in mourning apparel at public events.[17]

When not beset by epidemic or other calamity, Charles Town presented a handsome appearance and inviting atmosphere to strangers. "Pleasantly Seated," the town reflected a rectilinear platting. Streets intersected one another at right angles. The principal thoroughfares, Bay, Broad (whereon the Smiths lived), and Meeting, were "Straight, broad and Airy." Visitors, at least of some social pretension, found the "Inhabitants ... courteous, polite and affable, the most hospitable and attentive to Strangers." Sandy streets, swarms of flies and mosquitoes, and hot, humid weather might prove troublesome to the uninitiated but received little consideration from townspeople who had long grown inured to those and other inconveniences. Single horse riding chairs were commonplace on the streets, though the wealthier kept four-wheeled carriages imported from England together with attendant coachmen and liverymen.[18]

The riding conveyances, the erection of elegant homes, a devotion to the arts, and an often extravagant lifestyle attested to a growing affluence. A visitor to Charles Town in 1773 dined with Thomas Smith, Benjamin's father, in company with "several gentlemen and ladies." The repast featured "a plenteous table of meats" and "Excellent wines." Two days later he dined with Roger Smith, Benjamin's older brother, with a "good deal of company (which included two recently appointed assistant justices from Great Britain), [an] elegant table, and the best provisions I have seen in this town. Once the cloth was removed, a handsome des[s]ert of most kinds of knickknacks [appeared]. Good wines and much festivity." The Charles Town theater, the St. Cecilia Society, the oldest music society in the United States, and the Charles-Town Library Society reflected an appreciation of the arts. More popular perhaps were the races where one might view "a prodigious fine collection of excellent, though very high-priced horses," and witness two thousand pounds sterling change hands during a single competition.[19]

Red-haired and freckled-faced Benjamin Smith spent his impressionable early years amid the luxury of his large family circle and the tumult of Charles Town life and politics. A "good natured[,] passionate little fellow," according to his father, the boy witnessed the emotion of colonial politics as the English provinces along the North Atlantic coast reacted, sometimes violently, to attempts by their mother country to impose a greater degree of control over the colonies after the conclusion of the French and Indian War. The Sugar Act of 1764 alarmed the mercantile community particularly, but news of an intended stamp duty was more ominous. Indeed, when the Stamp Act became effective on November 1, not only was the legislation deemed inimical to American liberties — no taxation without representation — but the port of Charles Town was closed, dealing a potential deathblow the economy of the region. Mobs seemed to rule the streets for a time, and later in the year a Christmastime slave insurrection scare added to the general apprehension.[20]

The Stamp Act crisis proved brief but eventful in South Carolina. While British officials in the colony determined to uphold the Stamp Act, merchants, planters, and lawyers evidenced their opposition by petitions and support of the Stamp Act Congress in New York in October 1765. Charles Town artisans or mechanics, aided by sailors, took to the streets in riotous fashion, even ransacking the home of prominent merchant Henry Laurens. The colonials organized nonimportation agreements to exert economic pressure upon

England to force the repeal of the Stamp Act. Meanwhile, the lieutenant governor of the province relented sufficiently to allow the port to open for business. Then in the spring of 1766 news that Parliament had rescinded the Stamp Act brought jubilation and relief to Charles Town, reflected in the observation of Benjamin Smith, brother of Thomas and uncle of young Benjamin, to his cousin in Boston, "With what pleasure & satisfaction must every true lover his Country receive the late most interesting and agreable intelligence, 'The Repeal of the Stamp Act'.... [H]ad the colonys submitted, they would soon have been carried on from one degree of Slavery to another."[21]

Nevertheless, the crisis only temporarily abated, for political reality in England demanded that Parliament impose additional taxes upon the American colonies. Those levies took the form of the Townshend duties, which in turn were accompanied by a determined effort by the British to enforce the laws regulating colonial trade. That change in regulatory policy led to "customs racketeering," according to historian Oliver M. Dickerson. South Carolinians belatedly followed the lead of Boston and organized another nonimportation agreement, but some merchants, particularly those like Roger Smith who were engaged in the slave trade, were reluctant to support it. Benjamin and Thomas Smith again appeared among the more conservative in the planter-merchant-lawyer triumvirate in their opposition to the crown. Still, late in 1769 his brother Benjamin wrote appreciatively to his Boston cousin Isaac Smith, "The whole Continent of America have great reason to speak the praises of your Country Men ... [who] have shewn a Manly behaviour consistent with the true Sons of Liberty." He had no doubt that nonimportation would lead to relief "from all unconstitutional Acts of Parl[iamen]t."[22]

Amid the excitement and turmoil of politics in Charles Town, Benjamin, deemed by his father to have a "good Capacity" for learning, must have pursued his early education. At age twelve he prepared to embark for Philadelphia for advanced training. Thomas, his father, sailed in August 1769 on the *Prince of Wales* with seven young men from the province, including his sons, Peter and Benjamin. According to the *South-Carolina Gazette*, "'Till this Year ... [the boys] were usually sent to *England* and *Scotland*; but now that the Mother Country seems unfriendly to us, they are destined for the College at Philadelphia." A total of nine from South Carolina were entered that year, apparently the first from South Carolina to attend the Philadelphia academy. Thomas declined to take the usual letters of recommendation with him in order to avoid obligatory meetings and preserve more time to conduct business. However, Henry Laurens notified a correspondent in Philadelphia of Smith's arrival, writing that "he is a friend of mine & that if you happen to be acquainted with him you will not be displeased thereby."[23]

Some South Carolinians regretted the need to send their boys to Pennsylvania or anywhere else for a finishing education. Opined the *Gazette* at the departure of Benjamin and the others, "Nothing so strikingly proves the Want of a proper Seminary of Learning in this Province [South Carolina], as the Number of Lads that are continually sending *abroad* to be qualified for the learned Professions." Late in 1769 prominent South Carolinians launched a movement to establish a college, formulated plans for the institution by 1770, and presented their proposals to the Commons House. Political disagreement between the governor and the legislature prevented the enactment of a law to establish the college. However, from those and other efforts eventually emerged the College of Charleston in 1785, of which Roger Smith, Benjamin's older brother, was one of the original trustees. The conjunction of his Philadelphia experience, the need for a local university, and Roger's interest in the College of Charleston doubtlessly was not lost on Benjamin, who later exhibited unflagging support for higher education, though in North Carolina.[24]

As suggested by the *Gazette*, Benjamin originally may have been destined for study in England. In 1760, Thomas took his eldest son, Roger, age fourteen, to England for a finishing education. Roger spent several years in the mother country. Noteworthy was Thomas's decision to place Roger under the care of an admitted dissenter. Thomas was a professed "Established Church Man," and pious in his spiritual life, even more so, apparently, in his later years. At the same time, he felt that "all Sensible Men are of the same generous Sentiment. For my part I look on the difference [between Churchman and Dissenter as] of so little consequence that ... I ... [could] conveniently communicate with the one [as] I should with the other." Perhaps in casting about the colonies for a suitable college for Benjamin, Thomas chose the College of Philadelphia because it was nonsectarian, a trait owed to Benjamin Franklin, one of its founders.[25]

While in Philadelphia for approximately three years Benjamin enjoyed an urban environment similar to that of Charles Town but on a grander scale. Boasting some thirty, perhaps as many as forty, thousand residents by the time of the Revolution, the Pennsylvania capital not only surpassed its North American rivals but constituted one of the most populous towns in the British empire. It was the principal commercial entrepot and financial center of the American colonies, and even more polyglot than Charles Town. Although Franklin infrequently resided in the town during the years before the Revolution, Philadelphia bore the imprint of his early civic promotions — well-paved avenues accompanied by brick sidewalks, streetlights, some five hundred public water pumps, a fire department, etc. Philadelphia's extraordinary wealth fueled the arts as well. And as befitted Franklin, the town was North America's principal conduit of the Enlightenment from the Old World to the New.

Young Benjamin Smith must have been a mite overwhelmed as he walked the streets to the continuous tune of noisy coaches, chariots, wagons, and drays.[26]

When Thomas Smith and his entourage arrived in 1769, Philadelphians supported an ongoing and successful boycott of Townshend-taxed items, principally tea. News of the Boston Massacre arrived in March 1770. Though alarming, the significance of that event was confined mostly to Massachusetts. Still, the British attempted to mollify the colonials in the aftermath of the massacre by repealing the Townshend levies except, ominously, the tax on tea. Nonimportation movements along the coast, including that in Pennsylvania, began to collapse, giving way to widespread evasion by some merchants who "think it no crime to cheat the King of his Duties." All the while Philadelphia politics, internecine or anti–British, was hard fought. Well organized factions offered slates of candidates for local offices, and political campaigns using the newspapers, pamphlets, pulpits, and soapbox harangues obtruded upon the public consciousness. For Benjamin, the scene was reminiscent of Charles Town, only writ on a grander scale.[27]

In Philadelphia Thomas Smith intended for his sons Peter and Benjamin to study under the Rev. Jacob Duche. Scion of the one of the wealthiest families in the Pennsylvania capital, Duche graduated in the first class of the College of Philadelphia in 1757 after which he studied in Clare College, Cambridge, before being ordained into the clergy of the Church of England. Returning to Philadelphia in 1759, Duche obtained an appointment as professor of oratory at the college. At the same time he served as rector of the parishes of Christ Church and St. Peter's, achieving recognition for his elegant sermons and literary compositions. Duche's initial zeal for liberty won him appointments as chaplain to the first and second Continental Congresses. But Duche resigned from the latter in 1776, renouncing the Revolution and going in exile to England in 1778, where he fell under the influence of the doctrines of the mystic Emmanuel Swedenborg. He returned the United States in 1792 to enjoy the freedom he once rejected.[28]

After two years in Philadelphia, Benjamin became the subject of correspondence between his father and Laurens. The latter visited Philadelphia and the young men at the college on his way to England in 1771. Thomas had brought Peter home to work with his elder brother, Roger, but Benjamin remained in Philadelphia. According to Laurens, Benjamin was "reputed [to be] an advancing Scholar, and I think him a very promising Youth." If Thomas intended for him "to go forward in the Study of Language and Science, in order to qualify him for one of the learned professions," Laurens suggested that the following year would be a propitious time to send Benjamin to England to attend Winchester, Westminster, or Eaton. Otherwise, according to Laurens, "If Ben is design'd for Trade, ... the first Rudiments may be gain'd in as great Degree of Certainty and Clearness, in Charles Town, as can be acquir'd in any Counting House in London." Other factors also commended the South Carolina port—a knowledge of local customs, an acquaintance with the people of the province, and "the difference of Expence of Money and Morals." Laurens and others readily and rightly feared the corrupting influence of England.[29]

Ultimately Benjamin may have been destined for the bar rather than trade, for in 1774, the year of his mother's death, he was entered into Middle Temple, one of the four Inns of Court in London to which young colonial gentlemen were dispatched for a legal education. Before the Revolution, Southerners, especially South Carolinians, more than Northerners, patronized the Inns, and Middle Temple appeared to be the institution of choice for South Carolinians. Middle Temple, located between the Thames Embankment and the Strand, dated from the mid-fourteenth century. Still, by the eighteenth century, Middle Temple, like the other Inns, had abandoned a systematic program of instruction for its students. Study was informal, and as rigorous or as leisurely as suited the student. Requirements often might be commuted by a monetary stipend. The Inns only mandated that students be twenty-one years of age, establish a residence, however nominal, for three years at one of the institutions, and wait for five years to elapse after their enrollment before being called to the bar.[30]

Actually many of the young men who entered the Inns of Court, including half of the South Carolinians, never intended seriously to practice law. But if they did, attendance at the Inns conferred a prestige that immediately separated them from the home-grown attorneys. More generally, however, knowledge of the law simply proved highly useful to gentlemen of affairs. Additionally, travel abroad was deemed part of a gentleman's education, broadening his horizons, establishing valuable personal contacts, and acquainting him with "the attraction of the English cultural scene."[31]

Therein lay the rub. As the Revolution approached, Thomas Smith began to harbor strong misgivings about the mother country. He wrote in 1772 to his cousin in Boston, who had just returned from a two-year sojourn in the British Isles:

> I ... Sincerely congratulate you on your safe return to your native & I dare say most agreeable Country for notwithstanding these old Countrys you have visited have the advantage of us in some respects I think we may enjoy more Solid happiness in America where I hope there is more innocency. I am convinced you've seen those places without being infected with any of their vices or follies as most of our Youth are too apt to be.... We are in this Country so unfortunate as to be growing rich too fast, the natural consequences of which are the introduction of Luxury, Vice and immorality.[32]

When Benjamin returned to Charles Town from Philadelphia in 1772 or 1773, his father no doubt preferred that he remain in the colony, where life's temptations already were too enticing, as opposed to going to England. Thus Benjamin pursued his law studies in South Carolina. In 1774, he became the first law student of Edward Rutledge, who had returned to South Carolina in early 1773 after studying, coincidentally, at Middle Temple.[33]

Benjamin prepared for the usual apprenticeship of some five years to qualify for the bar, but the deteriorating relationship between England and the colonies negated his plans. Studying under the supervision of Rutledge, who became one of the leading opponents of Britain in South Carolina, encouraged the anti–British predilections of Benjamin. At the same time the teenager no doubt joined the Charles Town militia which numbered approximately 1,600 men in 1774. The militia included companies of grenadiers, artillery, and light infantry. The eighty-man roster of each company was filled by volunteers from the well-to-do in town (doubtlessly numbering Benjamin), who looked quite handsome in their fine uniforms, while "the rest of the common town militia[,] if possible[,] make a worse figure than the train bands of London," according to an English traveler. Thus, as a member of the local militia in his late teens, Benjamin witnessed the rush of events that led to independence in South Carolina.[34]

A new crisis loomed in the colonies after Parliament passed the Tea Act in 1773, legislation that favored the East India Company with a virtual monopoly on the sale of that potable in America. Of course the hated tax on tea remained to bedevil the South Carolinians, who in the aftermath of the Townshend duties continued to adhere to nonimportation to protest the taxation. Roger Smith, to "his lasting honour," according to the *Gazette*, had "determined some Weeks before the tea arrived, not to have any concern in a business, which his countrymen conceived to have so fatal a tendency" to American interests.[35] Although more restrained than the Boston Tea Party later in December 1773, the Charles Town protest against the importation of tea was equally effective. The following year the Intolerable Acts and the closing of the port of Boston gave impetus to the radical leadership in Charles Town.

News of the conflict at Lexington and Concord in Massachusetts, which reached Charles Town on May 8, 1775, fueled the flames of colonial resentment, making a separation with the mother country (in hindsight) nigh inevitable. In September, Lord William Campbell, governor of South Carolina, fled Charles Town for the safety of the British man-of-war *Tamar*, which was anchored in the harbor. December found hostilities commencing in the backcountry as loyalists attacked rebels at Ninety-Six, only to be repulsed. In March 1776, South Carolina's Second Provincial Congress adopted a constitution to form a temporary government which shouldered the responsibility of repulsing a British attack on Charles Town. In the Battle of Sullivan's Island in June, a British invasion force of eleven ships and 2,900 regulars and marines ignominiously failed to capture the port. Within days the Continental Congress declared independence on behalf of the colonies, a decision in which South Carolina concurred.[36]

Throughout those proceedings, the precise whereabouts of Benjamin Smith are moot, though given his almost rabid anti–British sentiments in later life it might be fair to say that he was not oblivious to his surroundings and the exhortations of the radicals in Charles Town. Virtually all accounts of his military career insist that he was in New York in mid–1776, where he served as an aide-de-camp to Gen. George Washington in the ill-fated Battle of Long Island on August 27. After failing to capture to Charles Town in June, the British sailed northward to join the Howe brothers (Gen. William and Adm. Richard) in their assault on New York. Washington and the Continental Army, including perhaps Smith, were unable to withstand the British attack and retreated to safety, largely as a result of the ultra cautiousness of Gen. Howe.[37]

Yet doubts must be entertained about the engagement of Smith at Long Island. No one has explained how the nineteen year old with no military service except, perhaps, a year or so of militia training, came to the attention of Washington, or merited an appointment as an aide to His Excellency. Extant records do not record his presence with Washington or at the battle. Smith never presented a certificate of his involvement. When President Washington undertook his famed Southern Tour in 1791, he lodged at Smith's plantation along Cape Fear River across from Wilmington, but that visit may well have reflected Smith's enormous wealth, the custom of hospitality (and who would shun the opportunity to house the president?), and the location of the plantation which was on the road leading directly to South Carolina, Washington's next destination. According to a later critic of Smith, who reflected adversely upon various facets of Smith's life, the president at the time "did not know Mr. Smith, and seemed never to have heard of him." Smith responded to his adversary, but never mentioned Washington and the Battle of Long Island.[38]

Whether or not Smith was in New York for the Battle of Long Island, he certainly had been to North Carolina, and no doubt often. Rather than martial, his intentions were marital. Shunning the belles of Charles Town, Smith wooed his cousin Sarah Dry, daughter of William and Mary Jane Dry of Brunswick County. Hopefully Smith did not share the opinion of a visitor to Charles Town in 1774, who wrote, "the ladies (in Charles Town) in general ... are not tolerably handsome, for most of them have pale sickish languid complections and are commonly ill shaped, their shoulders seeming to have a longing desire to rise high enough to hide their ears." On November 18,

Ruins of St. Philip's Church. Courtesy of New Hanover Public Library.

1777, the twenty-year-old Benjamin wed Sarah in St. Philip's Church in Charles Town, a more gracious and certainly safer setting (at the time, at least, from British threats) than the St. Philip's Church in North Carolina, which lay in ruins several miles from the Drys' plantation in mostly abandoned Brunswick Town.[39]

Sarah Dry, like Benjamin, sported a distinguished ancestry, ultimately sharing with her husband two great-grandfathers, James Moore (d. 1706) and William Rhett (1666–1723), which rendered the couple second cousins via two bloodlines. The progenitor of the Dry family in Carolina was Robert Dry(e), who immigrated to South Carolina about 1680. His son, William I (d. 1699?), and grandson William II (d. 1740) were merchants, though the latter, who married Rebecca Moore, daughter of Gov. James Moore and brother of Roger, purchased a plantation near Goose Creek Bridge. He also owned lots in Beaufort. His marriage to Rebecca Moore allied Dry with the Goose Creek Moores not only in family but also in politics. Representing St. James Goose Creek Parish in the Commons House, three times as speaker, Dry demanded that the council respect the rights of the lower house, and as a leader of the Goose Creek militia was prepared to resort to military muscle to make his point. Instead, Dry sold his properties in South Carolina and in

1736 moved his family to Brunswick County, North Carolina, where he joined Roger Moore and his brothers, who had been instrumental in opening the area.[40]

Dry's only son, William III (1720–1781), pursued a prominent and profitable career in his adopted colony. He burst on the public scene in September 1748, when the Spanish beset and plundered Brunswick Town along the Cape Fear River during the last year of King George's War. Dry led townspeople, farmers, sailors, and slaves in a counterattack that drove off the invaders. Along with manifold public positions, including commissioner of roads, commissioner of pilotage for the Cape Fear River, surveyor of the North Carolina–South Carolina boundary, commissioner of the Brunswick Town, and alderman of the borough of Wilmington, Dry evidenced an interest in politics. He served briefly in the Lower House of the legislature, and received an appointment to the Royal Council in 1763, where he was characterized by Gov. Arthur Dobbs as "a Gentlemen of Great Worth and Fortune and zealous in Supporting his Majesty's Rights." And wealthy Dry was, having acquired plantations in Brunswick County and property throughout the colony.[41]

Dry's public career began its denouement during the Stamp Act crisis of 1765–1766. As customs collector of the Port of Brunswick, he witnessed the wrath of angry men who objected to the stoppage of commerce on the Cape Fear River, rifled his office, and forced him to forswear the enforcement of the Stamp Act. Dry refused to allow his royal offices to draw him into the orbit of the crown, and eventually became a leading advocate of republican principles, who "talks treason by the hour," according to a visitor to the area. The governor suspended him from his seat on the council, noting that by "his notorious unreserved and frequent avowals of his inclinations and favour to the present unprincipled revolt in America, ... I am sure that he has astonished even the foremost Leaders of sedition." Despite Dry's protestations of support for the American cause, he retired to his home in Brunswick County with his wife and daughter and took no active part in the Revolution.[42]

From her maternal perspective Sarah Dry looked back to great-grandfathers William Rhett (1666–1723) and the almost equally notorious Nicholas Trott (1663–1740), son of a London merchant who arrived in Charles Town by 1699 and was destined for a tumultuous career in the province. Presaging his stormy life in South Carolina, almost as soon as he disembarked Trott criticized Governor Joseph Blake, who responded by suspending Trott's commission as attorney general and naval officer and ordering his imprisonment. Trott, having the favor of the Lords Proprietors, quickly rebounded, and with Rhett wielded great influence in South Carolina's government. Trott's daughter, Mary, married William Rhett (1695–1729). Mary Jane (1729–1795), one of their daughters, in turn married William Dry III. The assets of Mary Jane

Rhett, "a lady of great fortune and merit," supplemented Dry's inheritance and acquisitions to render the family one of the wealthiest in the most affluent region of North Carolina, the Lower Cape Fear.[43]

Given the unsettled times, it appears that the newlyweds, Sarah and Benjamin, remained in North Carolina, no doubt with the Drys. To entice Benjamin, a young man who had neither mercantile nor legal training, to remain in the northern state, the Drys in December 1778 gave the couple Blue Banks plantation, a 3,840 tract along the Northwest Cape Fear River in Brunswick County, and another 960 acres of land in Brunswick County, along with 57 slaves to Sarah. Benjamin, however, was loath to sever his ties with his family and Charles Town. Leaving Sarah with her family, he spent a good deal of time in South Carolina where his presence soon was needed to rebuff the British.[44]

A relative calm prevailed in South Carolina after 1776, until the British turned their attention again to the southern states (or colonies in the estimation of the British). The British had achieved little permanent success in the northern and middle states. Assuming the presence of a large number of loyalists in Georgia and the Carolinas, and presuming to work with Native American allies, the British decided to focus on Georgia, pacify South Carolina, and extend their influence northward. To that end a successful amphibious attack on Savannah in December 1778 was followed by the capture of Augusta, a backcountry rallying point for loyalists.

As the British worked their way up the Savannah River, they probed Port Royal Sound in the vicinity of Beaufort, South Carolina, an action that led to the Battle of Port Royal Island, the initial British foray into South Carolina. Fort Lyttelton, containing twenty-one cannon and a garrison of nine Continental troops, protected Port Royal Island. When a small British naval flotilla which carried two hundred regular infantry appeared, the commander of Fort Lyttelton ordered the cannon spiked and the bastion destroyed in order that they not fall into the hands of the enemy. Within hours Brig. Gen. William Moultrie arrived with reinforcements — one hundred and fifty Charles Town militia, including Lt. Benjamin Smith, plus a detachment of Charles Town Artillery — to save the fort. But it was too late, according to Moultrie, "the business being done in too-great a hurry and the people moved off." Moultrie relocated his Charles Town militia, other local militia, and Continentals to Beaufort.[45]

Two days later, on February 3, 1779, the British landed their forces and the Battle of Port Royal Island was joined. Moultrie rushed his men to meet the enemy. A smart fire from the militia, the two field pieces of the Charles Town Artillery, and the Continentals and their brass two-pounder forced the British to retreat — "precipitately" according to the Americans. The British did not realize that at the same time the Americans, almost destitute of ammunition for their field pieces, had begun a slow withdrawal, or they might have reconsidered. Doubly inspiring to the Americans was the subsequent action by the Beaufort militia and light horse that nearly turned the British retreat into a rout. South Carolinians were jubilant and the militia basked in the praises of the people and press. There was even the prediction of "another Burgoyne in the southern quarter of America." The Battle of Port Royal Island may have boosted local morale but the British accomplished their principal objective — the destruction of Fort Lyttelton — which would ease their future invasion of South Carolina.[46]

Although the Battle of Port Royal Island little affected the course of the American Revolution, it certainly impacted the life of Lt. Benjamin Smith. The conflict fanned his resentment against the British, buttressed his claim to military distinction, and elevated his interest in martial matters. In the aftermath of the battle Gen. Moultrie sent Smith to the British vessels anchored off Port Royal to obtain the effects of the seven prisoners taken by the Americans. Upon the completion of his mission, Smith carefully reported on the location and movement of the British ships and other information that might be deemed useful. His observations reflected an appreciation for the need to gather data, however insignificant, that might help the military cause.[47]

On the other hand, the following year Smith, by that time apparently a major in the Berkeley County regiment of militia, was responsible for an egregious blunder that undermined the patriot effort to hold Charles Town in the face of a British siege in 1780. Early in the year a large British fleet with Gen. Henry Clinton, commander of British forces in America, and eight thousand troops, sailed from New York to Charles Town, intending to rectify the embarrassment of 1776. Gen. Benjamin Lincoln took charge of the defense of the port, but was badly outnumbered, having less than sixteen hundred Continental soldiers, South and North Carolina militia, and a naval squadron of four vessels. Continental military strategy dictated that the army should opt "to cover the Country, and leave the City to its fate," or retreat in order to fight another day, but South Carolina Governor John Rutledge insisted upon protecting Charles Town, and assured Lincoln that adequate reinforcements were forthcoming. By mid–April, however, Clinton had surrounded the town and reinforcement or evacuation became impossible.[48]

Charles Town and its garrison settled in for a siege, though the outcome appeared inevitable. Lincoln opened surrender negotiations with Clinton, though still held out hopes for reinforcements. Governor Rutledge maintained a correspondence with Lincoln through messengers who slipped through British lines. On May 1, Lincoln sent Edward Rutledge to plead with his brother, the governor, for immediate relief. Rutledge indiscreetly carried a letter from Benjamin Smith to his wife in North Carolina. When Rutledge and his party were captured, the letter was discovered.

> Charlestown, April 30, 1780
>
> "Having never had an opportunity of writing ... since the enemy began to act with vigor, and knowing that a thousand evil reports will prevail to increase [your] uneasiness — mine I have supported pretty well until last night, when I really almost sunk under the load. Nothing remains around to comfort me but a probability of saving my life.... After going through many difficulties, our affairs are daily declining, and not a ray of hope remains to us of success. The enemy have turned the siege into a blockade, which in a short time must have the desired effect, and the most sanguine do not now entertain the smallest hope of the town being saved.... When I wrote last it was the general opinion that we could evacuate the town at pleasure; but a considerable reenforcement having arrived to the enemy, has enabled them to strengthen their ports so effectually as to prevent that measure.... You will see by the inclosed summons that the persons and properties of the inhabitants will be saved; and consequently I expect to have the liberty of soon returning to you; but the army must be made prisoners of war. This will give a rude shock to the independence of America; and a Lincolnade will become as common as a Burgoynade.... This letter will run great risqué, as it will be surrounded on all sides, but I know the person to whose care it is committed, and feel [ing] for your uneasy situation I could not but trust. Assure yourself that I shall shortly see you, as nothing prevents Lincoln's surrender but a point of honor in holding out to the last extremity. This is nearly at hand, as our provisions will soon fail.[49]

The British quickly realized the propaganda value of the letter. They printed copies of the missive and lobbed them into Charles Town in unloaded bomb shells. Nonetheless, morale was already low — obviously in the case of Smith — and the outcome was foreordained by that juncture. Lincoln indeed was seeking terms of surrender. The letter had no material effect on the course of events but the embarrassment caused by its disclosure dogged Smith for many years. He defended the indefensible by explaining that the missive contained nothing of which the British were unaware (through defectors) and was intercepted shortly before the surrender of the garrison. Moreover, the British had "garbled and published it so [that it] appear [ed] very differently from the original." Perhaps, but one suspects that the letter required very little editorial work by the British to serve their purposes. The garrison surrendered on May 12.[50]

By the time that the British initiated their siege of Charles Town, Thomas Smith had retired to his plantation at Goose Creek with his wife, a daughter, and the family of his son Roger, but his four sons remained in the garrison. Peter, who had married Mary Middleton in 1776, became ill and joined his wife and father-in-law at their plantation in the backcountry. After the fall of Charles Town, both Thomas and Peter may have accepted British protection.

The former purportedly subscribed money to raise a troop of British horse in Charles Town. Peter, in early 1782 was "still with the Enemy, or at Goosecreek, which is nearly the same Thing," according to Edward Rutledge. Thomas probably hoped to protect his extensive property holdings. As he later wrote, he was "in the way of both parties," for Goose Creek lay between the British in Charles Town and the guerilla bands of patriots Francis Marion and Thomas Sumter in the swamps. Although Thomas apparently suffered little actual reprisal, even for his seeming sympathy for the British, the staggering inflation that beset the state during the war cut deeply into his pecuniary returns.[51]

Citizens and militia in Charles Town at the time of the surrender, including Roger, James, and Benjamin Smith, became prisoners of war on parole, pledged to retire to their homes and take no further active role in the war. Roger, the oldest son, remained in Charles Town to care for his business, though he was deemed a rebel sympathizer by the British. James, the youngest, aged 19, was dispatched by his father to London in March 1781, where he enrolled at Middle Temple. According to Thomas, "he could not accomplish himself in the Law here as we were then circumstanced and it was a pity that he should be loosing his time." Perhaps the vices and luxuries of England no longer troubled the elder Smith. Certainly he had little difficulty adjusting to the British occupation of Charles Town and vicinity. Ultimately, it is probable that he simply sought to advance the career of a son.[52]

Within two months of the fall of Charles Town, Benjamin, on parole, returned to "his family in the Country," according to his brother-in-law Thomas Bee, perhaps in a reference to Thomas Smith's Broom Hall plantation in Goose Creek, or, more likely, to Benjamin Smith's Blue Banks plantation in Brunswick County, North Carolina. Smith subsequently traveled both to Wilmington and Charles Town, thus occasioning some question about the observance of his parole. He justified his action by claiming that he went to Wilmington to seek runaway slaves, "which instead of asking for as a favour, I demanded as a right under the capitulation." As for Charles Town, he obtained permission from the British to return to the South Carolina port in order to recover from "a very severe indisposition." The evacuation of Charles Town by the British in December 1782, after more than two and a half years of occupation, freed Smith from the strictures of his parole. Although he retained close ties to South Carolina, and felt himself but a "sojourner" in North Carolina, Smith was destined to remain permanently in the northern state.[53]

CHAPTER 2

WILMINGTON AND THE LOWER CAPE FEAR

Although Benjamin Smith may have intended to return to South Carolina as he indicated to a kinsman in 1783, circumstances conspired to commit him irrevocably to Brunswick County, which together with New Hanover County, comprised the heart of the Lower Cape Fear region in North Carolina. Cape Fear (early known also as Cape Fair) constitutes the southernmost of North Carolina's three capes that jut into the Atlantic — Hatteras, Lookout, and Fear. The designation, Lower Cape Fear, refers to a nebulous area of present southeastern North Carolina near or adjacent to the lower Cape Fear River and its tributaries. The region, originally denominated New Hanover Precinct, splintered into several counties in the wake of a growing populace that needed more proximate organs of local government in the face of the difficulties of traveling in early America. By the time of the Revolution, the Lower Cape Fear subsumed New Hanover, Brunswick, and (at least parts of) Onslow, Duplin, and Bladen counties.[1]

The Cape Fear River, North Carolina's most majestic river and the only one that empties directly into the Atlantic Ocean, provided the enticement for settlement. The river originates in the interior of North Carolina in two widely separated places. The more important of its sources, the Northwest or simply Cape Fear River, begins at the confluence of the Deep and Haw in present Chatham County and travels southeast about 150 miles to join the Northeast Cape Fear. The Northeast rises in present Wayne County and meanders its way some 100 miles to meet the Northwest at the forks or southern tip of Great Island, usually called Eagles Island after the mid-eighteenth century. Linking the two rivers along the northern edge of Eagles Island was a channel called the Thoroughfare.[2] The Cape Fear flows as a single stream about 30 miles from the forks to the Atlantic Ocean. Several tributaries, large and small, feed the main rivers, which together drain over a quarter of North

Carolina's present one hundred counties. Although the grand extent of the river system was unknown in the early eighteenth century, the possibilities were obvious.

The permanent occupation of the Lower Cape Fear by Europeans proceeded from the efforts of the brothers Maurice and Roger Moore of South Carolina together with the connivance of proprietary governor George Burrington of North Carolina. Attempts by New Englanders and Barbadians in the 1660s to plant settlements along the Cape Fear River had failed, and the subsequent inattention derived largely from contention between the governments of North and South Carolina over the ownership of the region. Burrington, ignoring express instructions from the proprietors of the Carolinas, began to issue land grants along the Cape Fear River in the mid–1720s to prospective settlers and speculators, including Maurice Moore. Political unrest in South Carolina in the late 1720s, "the most serious political crisis in [the] sixty-year history" of the colony, according to historian M. Eugene Sirmans, prompted an exodus from the southern province to the Lower Cape Fear. In fact, the South Carolinians simply extended the northern bounds of their province as they moved to North Carolina, much like the seventeenth century Virginians who had pushed south into the Albemarle region of future North Carolina.[3]

Although the significance of the South Carolina presence in the early settlement of the Lower Cape Fear has been well documented, recent investigation downplays the number of immigrants from the southern province as opposed to those from the Albemarle region of North Carolina, the middle colonies, and even from England and Scotland. Still, low country South Carolinians mostly spearheaded the movement to the Lower Cape Fear and provided the region "with initiative, capital, resources, settlers, and perhaps most important, an example of how to create a prosperous and stable colonial society."[4] That charter group included Roger Moore, William Dry, and allied cousins, forbears of Benjamin Smith and his wife, Sarah Dry.

Those early settlers crossed the (then undefined) boundary of North and South Carolina in the mid– to late–1720s to plant themselves along the west bank of the Cape Fear River in what became New Hanover, and subsequently Brunswick, County. The colonials, at least some of them, were not unaware that their reigning monarchs in England came from the House of Brunswick-Hanover. Maurice Moore quickly established Brunswick Town some twelve miles from the bar or mouth of the river to serve as a center of government and commerce, in effect to replicate the role played by Charles Town in South Carolina. The area was organized governmentally as New Hanover Precinct (later County) in 1729, with Brunswick Town as the seat. However, the upriver town of Wilmington, sited more or less at the junction of the Thoroughfare and Northeast branch of the Cape Fear on the east side of the river, appeared in the next decade, and eventually not only supplanted Brunswick Town as the county seat but relegated the latter to little more than a village.[5]

Wilmington, touted by Gov. Gabriel Johnston, North Carolina's second royal executive, early appeared as the village of Carthage or Newton in the 1730s. At the instigation of the governor and by a most dubious political ploy, Newton obtained incorporation as Wilmington in 1739/40. The name honored Johnston's political patron, Spencer Compton, Earl of Wilmington, who succeeded Sir Robert Walpole as England's second prime minister in 1742. Wilmington fairly soon eclipsed Brunswick Town as the nucleus of trade in the Lower Cape Fear, drawing as it did upon the hinterlands of the two branches of the Cape Fear River. Moreover, despite the Flats, or shoals in the Cape Fear below the town, which impeded river commerce, Wilmington became North Carolina's principal deepwater port. By the time of the Revolution, Wilmington shared billing with Edenton and New Bern as the most populous towns in North Carolina, housing perhaps a thousand souls — as opposed to twelve thousand in Charles Town, South Carolina.

For ambitious men, Wilmington clearly offered potential. No matter that its original grid plat succumbed to structural encroachments and alley-bisected blocks. The riverfront, with its noisy and noisome wharves, stevedores, and carts and drays, was the centerpiece of town. The Cape Fear River was the lifeline of the town and region. Via the river naval stores and wood products along with some foodstuffs left North Carolina. Manufactured goods from England and the northern colonies, and tropical produce from the West Indies, arrived in port. Understandably Wilmington attracted a motley array of nationals from the British Isles as well as adventurers from the northern colonies who shared the town almost equally with Africans, mostly enslaved. Dedicated to the dollar, or as it were, the British pound sterling, Wilmington lacked the haut couteur found in, say, New Bern, some eighty-five miles to the north, which not only was a port of consequence, but was on its way to staking a claim as the "Athens of North Carolina."

The Africans or African Americans in Wilmington manifested the omnipresence and importance of slavery throughout the Lower Cape Fear. The first settlers of the region, the South Carolinians and those from the Albemarle, brought bondsmen with them. The number and percentage of Africans rose, both by natural increase and by forced immigration, the latter facilitated by the port of Wilmington. The consequent increase in slaves both reflected and contributed to the enormous wealth of the region. The Lower Cape Fear exhibited a pattern of slave ownership that differed remarkably from the rest of North Carolina. Slaves composed 25 percent of the population of the colony in 1767, but 62 percent to 70 percent of the population of New

Hanover and Brunswick counties. The concentration of 2.49 bondsmen per square miles was the highest of any area of North Carolina, in which .94 per square mile was the average. According to the lieutenant governor of the colony in 1765, "When a man marries his Daughters[,] he never talks of the fortune in Money[,] but 20[,] 30[,] or 40 slaves is her Portion."[6] Dry's gift of 57 bondsmen to his daughter Sarah upon her marriage to Smith attested to the lieutenant governor's observation.

And in Wilmington, as in most North Carolina towns (and Charles Town), slaves seemed to enjoy a great deal of latitude of action, if not actual liberty. To the consternation of whites, bondsmen easily evaded legislation and town ordinances meant to minimize their mobility, discourage commercial and social relations with whites, and reduce the possibility of slave violence. In addition to the blacks who managed the homes of absentee planters, the ability of slaves to rent houses and tenements reflected their independent income, derived from engaging in sundry trades by hiring themselves out, either with their approval of masters or in their spare time. Neither provincial laws nor town ordinances greatly discouraged the "pernicious practice of dealing with Negroes."[7]

Wilmington dominated New Hanover County, but accessing the seat of county government proved difficult for the growing number of people living west of the Cape Fear River. Thus the legislature in 1764 decided to carve Brunswick County from that part of New Hanover County lying south and west of the Cape Fear River and from neighboring Bladen County. The move gave a new lease on life to Brunswick Town, which again became a county seat — that time logically, at least in nomenclature, of Brunswick County.[8] Sparsely settled communities south of Brunswick Town — Shallotte (Charlotte, after the wife of George II) and Lockwoods Folly — could offer no challenge. But Brunswick Town, "a poor, hungry, unprovided Place" in 1731, had not advanced greatly in 1775, when a visitor found it "very poor — a few scattered houses on the edge of the woods, without street or regularity." British troops in 1776 delivered the coup de grace to Brunswick Town. Failing to capture Wilmington and the region, the soldiers vented their disappointment by pillaging along the lower stretches of the Cape Fear and forcing the residents of Brunswick Town to flee.[9]

Contrary to local lore, Brunswick Town's homes, businesses, and St. Philip's Church probably survived the British assault in 1776 intact, only to fall prey to a second invasion in 1781, when a conflagration destroyed the town. While the enemy controlled Wilmington from January through November of that year, troops under the command of Lord Charles Cornwallis temporarily occupied the village in April. Aided perhaps by slaves of Robert Howe, owner of Kendal plantation which was located along the river above

Brunswick Town and Orton plantation, the soldiers may have been the culprits in the igneous destruction. However, "Tories and other hangers-on," who reputedly engaged in wanton destruction in areas controlled by the British army, offer another possibility.[10]

In any case, shortly after the war Brunswick Town appeared "almost totally demolished and abandoned." Efforts to revive the village, stemming from the construction of a few houses, failed. Actually a comeback had little chance of success. Shipping had gravitated altogether to Wilmington and the state legislature in 1779 had moved the county seat of Brunswick County to the relative safety of Lockwoods Folly. The few river pilots who assumed residence among the ruins of Brunswick Town soon moved to another settlement farther south along the river, where they pitched their humble dwellings and awaited legislative recognition as Smithville (present Southport). In the postwar years one of the ubiquitous taverns in North Carolina opened in Brunswick Town to offer a glimmer of hope for the future, but even the presence of alcohol was insufficient to serve as a nucleus for the rebirth of the town. With the abandonment of Brunswick Town, the county lacked even a village of consequence.[11]

Brunswick County displayed a sparsely settled, agrarian atmosphere, where a few large plantations shared sand, scrub oak, and pine forest with a number of small farms and a few slave hideaways secreted in the swamps. North of a desolate Brunswick Town and overlooking the Cape Fear River lay Orton, surmounted by Kendal, Lilliput, and then Pleasant Oaks. At the juncture of Town Creek and the Cape Fear, Pleasant Oaks gave way to a number of plantation seats along Town Creek which extended into the interior to the northwest. Crossing Town Creek and continuing north along the river brought the traveler to Mallory Plantation; the Forks at the southern tip of Eagles Island, where the Cape Fear divided, which belonged to the Eagles family; Buchoi, owned by Judge Alfred Moore; Belville, and then Belvedere, owned by William Dry. Farther north and bearing west beyond the junction of the Northwest Cape Fear and the Thoroughfare lay Blue Banks, home of the Drys, and a host of additional sites with such enticing names as Prospect, Mulberry, Auburn, and Magnolia.[12]

Following their marriage and appropriate celebratory partying in Charles Town, Benjamin and Sarah Dry Smith made their way to the bucolic wilds of southeastern North Carolina unless they sailed from Charles Town to Wilmington, which was highly unlikely, given the presence of British warships stationed off the Cape Fear to intercept American traffic. The route of the Smiths was entirely predictable. In fact, there was only one road along the Atlantic coast that led from Charles Town to North Carolina. Approximating present U.S. Highway 17 or the Ocean Highway, the King's Highway as it was termed before the Revolution was often little more than a sandy bank. The Smiths passed by Georgetown and then the Boundary House, a domicile and house of entertainment (tavern) that straddled the North Carolina–South Carolina border, before passing through Lockwoods Folly west of the Cape Fear River. Having no reason to deviate to Brunswick Town or to cross Eagles Island to Wilmington, they continued northwest to Blue Banks.[13]

Lengthy journeys in the Lower Cape Fear were not intended for the faint of heart. From the Boundary House a sixty-mile stretch of highway to Wilmington took the traveler along a "labyrinthine woods-road" through the ubiquitous pine barrens of the area in which grass-covered stumps of trees made the journey more perilous. Indeed, after marking the route of a road, the colonials did little more than cut the trees to the requisite width demanded by law and clear the underbrush. Rickety bridges (if they existed at all, given poor workmanship and frequent freshets) and low lands or swamps without adequate causeways or causeys through them added to the traveler's woes. Shortcuts in that vicinity were verboten unless one desired to lose one's the way, spend the night fending off wolves, and climb a tree in the morning to try to find the desired pathway.[14]

By all accounts such journeys were also exceedingly monotonous. Yet breaking the tedium were innumerable snakes, including every poisonous variety known in North Carolina, which slithered across the road to the consternation of horses, hung from trees to harass riders, or dropped into gigs and coaches to amuse the traveler. Nature also provided an extensive variety of insects, most particularly flies and mosquitoes, to torment animals and humans alike. A British postal inspector in 1774 described unflatteringly his travel or travail in the region:

> On the whole, the road from Charles Town to Wilmington is certainly the most tedious and disagreeable of any on the Continent of North America, it is through a poor, sandy, barren, gloomy country without accommodations for travellers. Death is painted in the countenances of those you meet, that indeed happens but seldom on the road. Neither man nor beast can stand a long journey thro' so bad a country where there's much fatigue and no refreshment; what must it be in their violent heats when I found it so bad in the month of January.[15]

The young couple eventually reached Blue Banks, the gift of the Drys, which initially they called home. And young and dependent they were. Benjamin, without craft or trade, or claim to the legal profession, was a footloose, twenty-year-old with pretensions only to military grandeur. He depended upon the largesse of his family in Charles Town or that of his in-laws. But Sarah must have been a naïf comparably. According to her father's will, dated September 21, 1779, she had not yet attained her legal majority, and thus was no more than seventeen at that point.[16] Hence, at her marriage in 1777, she was fifteen at most. Perhaps both sets of parents were desperate. Thomas Smith may have counted on the Drys to support their son-in-law and daughter; the Drys, residing in the wilds of Brunswick County during a war whose outcome was at best uncertain, may have envisioned the prospect of few eligible bachelors at the time.

In addition, precedent favored Sarah. Her mother had wed at seventeen; her sister, even younger. William and Mary Jane Dry had two children, Rebecca and Sarah in that order. Rebecca, born in 1749, married Thomas McGuire (McGwire) in 1763, at age fourteen (possibly fifteen), only to die three years later in 1766. The inscription on the tablet above the grave of Rebecca McGuire at St. Philip's Church in Brunswick Town bears the following curious inscription: Quisquis Mor Sustulerit Ultimus Suorum Moriatur, or "Whosoever disturbs my death (resting-place), may he die as the last of his race."[17]

The marriage age of the Dry sisters was exceptional, even by early American standards. Of course John Brickell had written from the Albemarle region of North Carolina about 1730, women "marry generally very young, some at thirteen or fourteen, and she that continues unmarried until twenty is reckoned a stale Maid, which is a very indifferent character in this country." As subsequent investigation has shown, Brickell clearly overstated the case, though native-born women in seventeenth and early eighteenth century Maryland on average wed at ages from 16.5 to 18.2. The only rigorous study of North Carolina marriages, centering on a sample of 61 in the Albemarle in the late seventeenth and early eighteenth centuries, found two women each marrying at ages fourteen and fifteen, but 51 yet unmarried at age twenty.[18]

Still, the year prior to Rebecca Dry's marriage had witnessed the nuptials of fifteen-year-old Justina Davis to seventy-three-year-old royal governor Arthur Dobbs. Again, that also was extraordinary. Indeed, Miss Davis entertained thoughts of another, but the match proceeded according to the desire of her parents, or so it was alleged, who refused to allow their daughter to ignore the chance to snare the wealth and renown of the governor of the province. Of course salacious quills bled ink, but according to later letters from Justina the union apparently was harmonious.[19]

Admittedly, McGuire did not bring Dobbs's credentials to the marriage table, but his future appeared bright in North Carolina. Irish-born, he was a lawyer who had completed his studies at Gray's Inn in 1754 before arriving in the colony by 1760 to accept an appointment as judge of the vice-admiralty court. He resided in Brunswick County, where in 1764 he represented the county in the House of Commons and received an appointment as justice of the peace. About the time of the death of his wife, McGuire abandoned the judgeship to accept a commission in 1767 as attorney general of North Carolina, and, in 1775, an appointment to the royal council of the colony. McGuire never renounced his allegiance to the crown, though he lived quietly through the Revolution on a plantation on the Northwest Cape Fear in Bladen County, and returned to England in 1785.[20]

Downstream from McGuire, the Smiths moved in with the Drys to occupy Blue Banks. The 640-acre plantation, located on both sides of the Northwest Cape Fear above the Thoroughfare, originally belonged Bath County, North Carolina, merchant Seth Pilkington but was acquired by Roger Moore. He in turn gave the property to his son George in 1746. Dry purchased the property in 1764. The plantation house, no doubt built originally by Roger Moore, commanded a spectacular view from its perch on a high bluff generously estimated by a traveler at one hundred feet above the southwest side river of the Cape Fear. Along the upper stretches of the Northwest Cape Fear the river had scoured the landscape, leaving steep elevations on the southwest to overlook low lands across the way which were subject to flooding. Thus the colonials lined the southwest side of the river with their homes to avoid the freshes that roiled the Cape Fear after rains upriver, but utilized the low, swampy lands for the cultivation of rice and the harvesting of timber.[21]

Blue Banks held its own among the plantations of the Lower Cape Fear. Overlooking the river, the main house was a two-story affair, exhibiting the traditional hall and parlor plan over which lay four rooms. The house included three closets of indeterminate size. For a building of that day, it was a commodious structure. Outbuildings included a kitchen, stable, and brick barn. On the northwest side of the river some 130 acres had been cleared, eighty of which sufficed for rice, and the remainder for corn and indigo. The high land on the southwest side of the river contained two to three hundred cleared acres suitable for corn and two streams bearing sufficient water to power grist mills. Blue Banks was a splendid seat for a planter,[22] though for the Smiths it turned out to be a starter home.

William Dry remained at Blue Banks until his death on June 3, 1781. Like McGuire, Dry was a placeman in the colonial government of North Carolina — collector of customs at Port Brunswick and member of the council, but unlike his son-in-law, a native of America, who accumulated a small fortune in the colony. Dry's personal life remains something of a mystery, but he seems to have been the archetypal country gentleman. In 1771, he added to his extensive property holdings by purchasing the elegant home of Gov. William Tryon, formerly Russellborough, the residence of Gov. Arthur Dobbs, which abutted Brunswick Town to the north along the river. Dry renamed the home Bellfont. Two years later Massachusetts lawyer Josiah Quincy, Jr., visited Bellfont and found that "Dry ['s] is justly called the house of universal hospitality — his table abounds with plenty — his servants excel in cookery —

and his sensible lady exceeds (at least I think equals) Sister Q [uincy] in the pastry and knick-knack way." Like Dry's career of public service, Bellfont fell victim to the British at the beginning of the Revolution.[23]

Death, perhaps, best illuminated of the character of William and Mary Jane Dry. Even allowing for the admiration of a daughter and the usual extolling of the virtues of the deceased, the inscriptions on the tablets above their graves at St. Philip's cemetery in mostly deserted Brunswick Town evoke their admirable character. Upon William's death, after an introductory bio, the inscription concluded:

> This small tribute
> Of Affection, Veneration and Gratitude
> Is paid
> To one of the best of Fathers
> By his beloved & only daughter
> Sarah Smith

Twelve years later Mary Jane Dry was laid to rest beside her husband at St. Philip's. Part of the inscription on the tablet read:

> To say she was a good wife, a tender mother, a warm and
> steady friend, a kind mistress, charitable [,]
> gentle to all below, ... feeling for the sufferings of others
> and ever ready to alleviate them is only
> to do justice to her merits. The Crown of glory
> To all these was her being
> A TRULY CHRISTIAN....
> ....
> This marble is raised by her grateful
> And affectionate son-in-law and daughter
> BENJAMIN & SARAH DRY SMITH[24]

Following William Dry's death in 1781, Smith became the principal executor of Dry's will and via his wife beneficiary of the manifold properties of his deceased father-in-law. Dry had named his wife and daughter executrixes and Cornelius Harnett, Thomas McGuire, and Smith executors. Harnett, the "Samuel Adams of North Carolina," or revolutionary par excellence in the colony, had predeceased Dry by two months[25]; McGuire, given his pro–English feelings, purposely kept a low profile in Bladen County, hoping to avoid any undue retaliation by patriot-rebels. The ladies, in the presence of Smith, deferred of course to the head of the household. Thus by default the twenty-four-year-old assumed the mantle of executor, and set about trying to settle the extensive estate.

In fulfilling the demands of the will and settling debts owed by and to the deceased, Smith may have recalled the experience of his uncle, father, and others in Charles Town, who reportedly found such responsibilities quite lucrative. In the case of Smith, the executor stood to realize little immediate pecuniary gain from handling the accounts of the estate, but he quickly learned a great deal about local geography and people as he ascertained property bounds and make business contacts. In fact, not only was Smith putting Dry's affairs in order, in the process he was preparing for permanent residence in North Carolina. The Lower Cape Fear, with its demographics — the exceptional African American presence; physiography — ocean and river setting, and marshlands; urban center — Wilmington, well populated by slaves; and wealthy planter culture, must have made Smith feel at home. It was low country South Carolina and Charles Town writ on a smaller scale.

CHAPTER 3

NORTH CAROLINIAN

As Benjamin Smith surveyed Blue Banks late in the spring of 1783, he wrote feelingly to a South Carolina relative to express his disappointment that he was "not in the way, of at least offering my Services to the State, & by those efforts becoming more worthy of my friends."[1] Clearly young Smith remembered the manifold civic contributions of his family and reflected the internalization of the values of his class, men of wealth and leisure who used their talents for the benefit of the public. However, the state in question was South Carolina. Smith yearned to return home, as it were, but soon came to realize that home did not coincide with the heart, and that services might be rendered to another state, North Carolina.

Initially Smith viewed his situation quite practically: "Circumstances here [North Carolina] require particular attention, which, if I give them, some hope may reasonably be entertained of their being placed on such footing as to admit of a partial or total Absence, without anxiety or uneasiness." Were he to return immediately to South Carolina, "it would reduce me in a short time either to work, or mortify, by Yearly contracting my present mode of living." Thus he thought it "wiser to suffer now, for a short time, to enable me to enjoy my friends permanently hereafter & then have an opportunity of serving my Country."[2]

Circumstances dictated first the settlement of the estate of his deceased father-in-law, whose properties in North Carolina centered in Brunswick and New Hanover counties but ranged as far as New Bern in Craven County and Hillsborough in Orange County. Of course, accompanying Dry's assets were the debts of the departed. Of the five executors named in the will — Smith, Cornelius Harnett, Thomas McGuire, Mary Jane Dry, and Sarah Smith, Benjamin by default became the principal acting executor.[3] Harnett had died in April 1781, having been captured by the British as he fled Wilmington, reputedly thrown "like a sack of meal" across the back of a horse, returned to the port, and imprisoned in a roofless blockhouse, where exposure to the elements aggravated his deteriorating health.[4] McGuire, ensconced on his plantation above Blue Banks, tried to maintain a low profile due to his loyalist proclivities. Mother-in-law and wife naturally deferred to the male head of the household.

Once Smith probated Dry's will, though he waited until 1783, perhaps due to the exigencies of the Revolution, he began settling the affairs of the estate. In the process he tried to bring some order to the real estate at his command, and at the same time he contemplated a new habitation commensurate with his wealth and rising public stature. Land had to be located, and unregistered deeds held by Dry filed in court. Smith was successful in rearranging properties in the his immediate locale, principally Brunswick County, but experienced difficulty in finding buyers for land in Duplin and Onslow counties and for lots in New Bern and land adjoining that town.[5]

In the midst of his spirited transactions, Smith reacquired property that only recently had been alienated by Dry, namely land in Brunswick County which Smith converted into his principal plantation residence for many years, as well two ferries which promised to be a lucrative source of income. Upon the creation of Brunswick County in 1764, the provincial legislature sought to cut a road through Eagles Island, which lay opposite Wilmington between the Northeast and Northwest Cape Fear rivers, in order to facilitate overland travel from Wilmington south to Brunswick Town and South Carolina, and west to the interior of North Carolina. The next year the legislature mandated the construction of two roads from the ferry landing on the Northwest Cape Fear to join the main highway that led from Georgetown, South Carolina, past Brunswick Town through Bladen County to Cross Creek and Campbellton (later Fayetteville) on the Northwest Cape Fear River in Cumberland County. It was in fact the route taken by the Smiths on their way to Blue Banks following their marriage. Rather than anticipating the travel plans of the Smiths, the General Assembly hoped to stimulate trade between backcountry and Wilmington and Brunswick Town via Cross Creek and Campbellton.[6]

An alluvial morass, Eagles Island posed a formidable obstacle to road construction. Thus the General Assembly invested Dry with the ownership of the two ferries at the ends of the road—from the island to Wilmington across the Northeast Cape Fear and from the island to Brunswick County across the Northwest River—on the condition that he make and maintain the road and all necessary bridges through the island. Dry agreed, but found the task overly demanding (as the modern traveler crossing Eagles Island on U.S. 17, 74, 76 might understand from a glance at the roadside). British postal inspector Hugh Finlay in 1774 excoriated the condition of the road, writing that "every person passing and repassing is in danger of breaking a leg or an arm ... and yearly [it] grows worse." He claimed that Dry had been indicted "more than once" for failure to live up to his bargain, but noted that the attorney general of the colony at the time was his erstwhile son-in-law and friend, Thomas McGuire.[7]

Perhaps feeling the pressure of failure, Dry, in 1777, sold the Ferry Plantation, located across Northwest Cape Fear at the ferry landing in Brunswick County, to Samuel Campbell, partner in the Wilmington mercantile firm of Campbell and (Robert) Hogg, along with the two ferries that connected Eagles Island with Wilmington to the east and Brunswick County to the west. Campbell acquired the property for the benefit of the business. Upon the dissolution of the company in 1778, probably due to the loyalist sympathies of the partners, Campbell sold his share of the plantation and ferry rights to Hogg. At his death two years later, Hogg left his estate to his brother James, who lived in Hillsborough. In 1783, Smith purchased the plantation with its brick tenement and ferry rights for £1,800 sterling, a bargain, crowed young Smith at the time, and so it was according to Archibald Maclaine, a long-time, curmudgeonly, snuff-loving Wilmington attorney, who knew property values in the area better than Smith.[8]

Smith converted the Ferry Plantation into his country seat by the mid–1780s, calling it Belvedere. And, indeed, the two-story, Georgian-inspired plantation house commanded an imposing prospect from a bluff overlooking the Northwest Cape Fear (present Brunswick) River, near but slightly north of present Belville in Brunswick County. Within eyesight on a clear day, beyond the two rivers and Eagles Island, lay Wilmington, two miles distant. A one-and-a-half-story building containing the kitchen, plus numerous outbuildings that included among others a carriage house, stable, wash house, and smokehouse, accompanied the main house. An overseer's house and kitchen stood in the distance.[9]

Plantation operations centered on rice, the cultivation of which occupied many planters along the lower Cape Fear and Northwest rivers. Belvedere boasted some two hundred acres of tidal swamp, much of which was ditched and banked for that purpose. Perhaps the most impressive structures on the plantation were the barns. One was a two-story, brick structure which housed tools and machinery, including a threshing machine, and measured one hundred and ten by forty feet. The other, wooden, stood at the edge of the river and at such a height that rice and other goods might be loaded and unloaded directly from the water. And the depth of the river at that point purportedly was sufficient to admit any ship that could cross the bar at the mouth of the river. The development of the property must have appealed to the ambitious Smith.

Initially Belvedere may have paled compared to some estates found along the Ashley and Cooper Rivers in South Carolina, but Smith's move surely must have succeeded in defining his eminent position in Lower Cape Fear society. By 1786 Smith had relocated from Blue Banks to Belvedere after which he sought but never successfully to sell the former plantation. At their new home Sarah and he lavishly entertained as befitted the station to which Smith had risen in society. One can only imagine the beauty of the lighted house from the river and the festive atmosphere when the Smiths hosted the wedding of Jamaican merchant Francis Brice and Betsy Jones. Brice, a loyalist during the Revolution, who raised a company of more than a hundred men in the service of the king, fled North Carolina with the British army in 1781, but returned years later to claim a patriotic prize.[10]

Probating Dry's estate and registering deeds brought Smith into the public sphere, most particularly introducing him to the court of pleas and quarter sessions in Brunswick County. The county court, composed of justices of the peace or magistrates who were appointed for life by the governor on the recommendation of the county's legislative representatives, exercised both judicial and administrative functions. As an inferior court, its authority was limited in civil and criminal matters, but as an administrative agency, the court was omnipresent. Under the domain of the justices fell fiscal matters (taxation and expenditure); public buildings and structures (courthouses, jails, warehouses); appointments (sheriffs, constables, road overseers, inspectors); transportation (roads, bridges, ferries); licensure (taverns keepers, ferry keepers, grist mill operators); probate (wills, inventories, sales of estates, deeds); orphanage; and aspects of slavery. The magistrates, in effect, controlled practically every aspect of public life within their jurisdiction and many facets of private life as well.

Not only did the county court represent the principal source of governmental authority known to most early North Carolinians, but the quarterly meetings of the justices also offered opportunities for people to gather at the courthouse, or, in the absence of a courthouse, the seat of government, to exchange pleasantries, gossip, and news, to transact personal and public business, and to engage in political harangues and electioneering. Elections and militia musters usually coincided with court meetings and often became rowdy affairs. Decorum outside the courthouse, and occasionally within, degenerated into shouting matches, drinking bouts, and fisticuffs. Weekly gatherings at churches and chapels and chance meetings at taverns that dotted the countryside offered opportunities for social commingling. Still, for better or worse, the heart of the public sphere in Brunswick or any county was the court. Surely Smith aspired to join the gentleman justices on the bench.

The Brunswick County magistrates quickly recognized the potential of Smith. Despite his tender age, the justices appointed Smith to return the tax assessments for the North West District, one of five militia divisions of the county. The court also designated Smith and two others as joint overseers of the North West Road, a highway that led from the Brick House, a recognizable landmark located at the ferry landing on Smith's recently acquired property on the Northwest Cape Fear opposite Wilmington, to the Bladen County line. The young planter was also tabbed for jury service in the Brunswick County court as well as for the Wilmington District Court. Road overseer and jury service, not to mention involvement in tax assessments, were well recognized stepping stones to that most prestigious office, justice of the peace, at least for a select few in the county.[11]

In addition, the Brunswick justices, probably at the suggestion of Smith, undertook to improve the road or causeway through Eagles Island, an enterprise from which the young planter stood to gain after purchasing the rights to the ferries at either end of the road in 1783. Later in that year the Brunswick court exempted for two years the men under Smith's control, mainly his slaves, who were liable to work on the public roads in the county, if Smith used them to labor on the highway through the island. At the same time the justices probably raised the ferriage rates in the county, given the rampant inflation that had beset the state during the revolutionary years, in a move that offered Smith the prospect of greater remuneration from ferry traffic. It was a classic case of using private advantage to advance the commonweal, but a practice common enough in an era in which the resources of government were limited.[12]

Ferry from Market Street in Wilmington to Eagles Island. Courtesy of New Hanover Public Library.

At court and elsewhere Smith from time to time encountered his half brother-in-law, William Dry, Jr., the natural son of William Dry. While "the enjoyment of a negro or mulatto woman" by white males seemed quite common according to a visitor to the Cape Fear region in 1773, an observation echoed two years later by another in the region, planters also directed their attentions to girls or women of their own race. A Jamaican traveler in North Carolina in 1775 downplayed interracial liaisons, remarking, "Dont suppose Fornication is out of Fashion here, more than in other Places, No! the difference only is, that the White Girls monopolize it." Indeed, among others in the Cape Fear area, Cornelius Harnett, the famed revolutionary and friend of Dry, fathered an illegitimate son. Dry apparently had engaged in a dalliance with a not too distant cousin of the Moore family.[13]

Dry acknowledged his paternity. In his will, the father left a 640-acre tract of land and eight slaves to his son on the condition that William not contest the remaining bequests. Before his death, however, Dry learned that the land had been previously patented and that during the war several of the slaves had "gone over to the British and Died." Thus he offered Dry Jr. a tract of land on Town Creek in Brunswick County and five slaves.[14] Though a pygmy of a planter compared to Smith, young Dry looked to a promising future. The county court in 1782 named him entry taker for Brunswick County, a local official who recorded land claims, and, in 1783, a grand juror to represent the county at the Wilmington District Court in 1784. Thereafter Dry maintained a very low public profile, only helping to survey land on which Smith proposed to build a grist mill and proving a deed.[15]

Several years later Smith came to the aid of Dry. The state treasurer in 1790 had sued the Brunswick County entry taker for failing to submit his accounts in a timely fashion. Smith, a state legislator at the time, convinced the General Assembly that Dry had been ill and unable to comply with the request of the treasurer, and had not delayed the settlement of his accounts with any intent to defraud the public. Thus the legislature decided to exonerate Dry. Four years later, however, when Dry's securities as entry taker (those who posted bond to guarantee Dry against malfeasance in office) were questioned, Dry quickly resigned the office and vanished from the public eye.[16]

Meanwhile Smith burst upon the state scene in North Carolina in April 1784, when at the age of twenty-seven and barely a permanent resident of the state, Brunswick voters elected him to represent the county in the senate, the upper house of the legislature or General Assembly. The legislature consisted of a senate and house of commons in which each county was entitled to one and two representatives respectively, regardless of population, hardly indicative of the democratic impulses emanating from the American Revolution. Moreover, in a further rejection of egalitarianism, government remained firmly in the hands of the propertied. The state constitution required that senators own at least three hundred acres of property; commoners, one hundred. As Smith continued to locate and systematize his vast inheritance, no one gave passing thought to his constitutional qualification, though some may have wondered about his political experience and familiarity with North Carolina.

Smith joined a legislative cast, mainly planters and lawyers, whose wealth, erudition, and sophistication were decidedly unrepresentative of the general populace of the state. North Carolina exhibited a large (fourth among the states in 1790) population composed overwhelmingly of small farmers scattered in isolated fashion across an expanse of five hundred miles from the Atlantic Ocean to the Appalachian Mountains and then beyond to include present Tennessee. Slave ownership was restricted; large slaveholdings more so. Professional men were few, mostly lawyers whose presence was necessary in a litigious society but whose reputation was highly suspect. Limited educational opportunities resulted in widespread illiteracy. The "social system," which was "still in its swaddling clothes," according to the famed Latin American adventurer Francisco de Miranda in 1783, found individuals fond of boxing and wrestling, the latter exercise accompanied by the gouge that left many a one-eyed man in North Carolina.[17]
Explained Jedidiah Morse,

> When two boxers are wearied out with fighting and bruising each other, they come, as it is called, to close quarters, and each endeavours to twist his forefingers in the ear-locks of his antagonist. When these are fast clenched, the thumbs are extended each way to the nose, and the eyes are gently turned out of their sockets. The victor, for his expertness, receives shouts of applause from the sportive throng, while his poor eyeless antagonist is laughed at for his misfortune.[18]

Perhaps most distinguishing the legislators was their capacity to absent themselves from plantation and law practice, at least for a month or two of public service, exhibiting leisure time never contemplated by ordinary Carolinians.

The solons gathered in Hillsborough, seat of Orange County in the Piedmont, though during and after the Revolution legislators found their destination problematic. New Bern had been designated the permanent capital of North Carolina in 1766, but the British threat to the coast during the Revolution forced lawmakers to remove to more secure quarters, and that eventuated in a nomadic capital that flitted from Tarboro to Smithfield (Johnston County Courthouse) to Hillsborough among other locations. The public records, exposed to the elements, dutifully followed in carts, wagons, and saddlebags. When Hillsborough resident and Orange County delegate William Hooper conveyed the results of the legislative session to his friend James Iredell in Edenton, he hoped that his missive would arrive safely. He noted, "Its manner of traveling is not very honourable as it has taken its passage in a common cart to Halifax, but the scandal is much alleviated by its having the Publick records for its companions." The state desperately awaited a permanent capital.[19]

In 1784, Hillsborough already boasted a long and tumultuous history, dating from the days of the Regulator Movement prior to the Revolution. Though small, like its urban-village counterparts elsewhere in the state, Hillsborough was a center of trade and social intercourse as well as political upheaval. According to a visitor in 1784, Hillsborough was "a healthy spot, enjoys a good share of commerce for an inland town, and is in a very promising state of improvement." The town contained a church, courthouse, an academy, and some forty houses. Its "genteel society" attracted one of North Carolina's first post–Revolutionary newspapers. Nonetheless, Hooper missed stimulating intellectual companionship, for after the dissolution of the General Assembly and the departure of his friend James Hogg, he lamented, "I have not a Single male [in town] with whom I can converse, and the ladies ... like Pa[r]tridges and other very delicate food one cannot feed upon them always, a little Bacon & Greens now and then by way of Solids makes a pleasing variety."[20]

Smith made the jaunt from Blue Banks to Hillsborough in six days. Taking the main highway that paralleled the Northwest Cape Fear, he arrived in Fayetteville, the seat of Cumberland County and trade entrepot connecting the backcountry with the Lower Cape Fear. After some extended rest and refreshment no doubt, he turned in a more northerly direction, crossing a succession of rivers — Lower Little River, Upper Little River, Rocky River, and finally Haw River, the last requiring a substantial ferriage — before reaching his destination. All was remembered when Smith sought reimbursement (with other legislators) from the state for travel and per diem.[21]

The General Assembly convened on Monday, April 19, in Hillsborough. Smith arrived on Thursday, fashionably late, helping to explain the chagrin of Samuel Johnston, a fellow legislator, on the previous Wednesday, who despaired of finding a quorum because "very few of the members are yet come to Town."[22] For a freshman legislator, the delay was surprising, particularly given the unparalleled opportunity for hob-nobbing among the elite of the state. From Richard Caswell, speaker of the senate and once and future governor of the state, and Samuel Johnston (future governor, United States senator, first grand master of Masons) to Willie Jones (Eton-educated, horse racing and fox hunting devotee, and consummate Halifax politician), Benjamin Williams (future United States congressman and North Carolina governor), James Robertson (pre–Revolutionary settler, sometime land speculator, and politician in present Tennessee), and Griffith Rutherford (Revolutionary military officer of note and subsequent land speculator) among others, Smith met an impressive corps of revolutionaries and politicians. Most importantly, he encountered John Haywood, clerk of the state senate, who served in that capacity from 1781 to 1786, after which he became treasurer of the state for four decades. The two men formed a lifelong friendship that redounded greatly to the benefit of Smith.[23]

If an army marches on its stomach, a legislature advances via its committees, a process to which Smith was quickly initiated. Hardly had he taken his seat on Thursday before he was assigned to a committee to consider the memorial of Samuel Strudwick, an English placeman before the Revolution, who had remained in the state and valiantly sought to protect his property from confiscation. Eight additional committee appointments followed, three of which dealt with various petitions, including that of Robert Rowan and others, who had served as officers in the French and Indian War. Upon the conclusion of the conflict the royal Proclamation of 1763 had instructed colonial governors to reward officers with grants of land beyond the Appalachians commensurate with their rank. Rowan and others, having yet to obtain their grants after twenty years and knowing that the legislature entertained thoughts of transferring the western territory to the national government, sought satisfaction.[24]

Other significant committees on which Smith served included that which considered communications from the governor, a committee on which Smith became a fixture and chairman in later years. In addition, Smith participated on joint committees with the house of commons that toiled over the inspection of state exports, the equitable treatment of state creditors, the definition of taxable property, and the imposition of taxes, which not only resulted in legislation in some instances but introduced Smith to the behind-the-scenes process of drafting statutes and widened his circle of acquaintances and friends among members of the lower house, including brothers John Gray and William Blount.[25]

Together with two other brothers, Thomas and Reading, the Blounts exercised enormous influence in North Carolina during the last quarter of the eighteenth century, both in politics and mercantile trade, shipping, and real estate speculation. William, who became the territorial governor of the area of south of the Ohio in 1790 at the appointment of George Washington, in conjunction with James Robertson, dabbled extensively in western land. John Gray and Thomas ran one of the largest mercantile operations in the state, though the former was not averse to speculating in land, while the latter enjoyed the fray of politics. Reading maintained the lowest profile of the quartet. Of the Blounts, William reputedly was "the shrewdest and most ambitious," a "businessman in politics for business," John Gray, "the smartest and most levelheaded," Thomas, "the most charming," and Reading, "the most daring and spirited."[26]

Committee service also introduced Smith to a long-standing conflict between North Carolina and the government of the French West Indian island of Martinique over compensation for war materiel provided by the governor and intendant of the island during the Revolution. At the end of the war, when a French agent sought compensation, Gov. Alexander Martin turned to the legislature in what had already become a convoluted matter. Smith's joint committee offered the best possible advice under the circumstances for ascertaining and discharging the debt. Yet, not until 1792, when Martin again was governor, was the debt finally extinguished. As historian James R. Morrill has well observed, "the record of the state's spasmodic, ill-informed, costly, and prolonged effort to discharge its one foreign obligation" was "ample illustration of North Carolina's fiscal difficulties and ... the chaos attendant to eighteenth-century public finance."[27]

Of course, as a legislator, Smith represented the wishes of his constituents where possible. Specifically, in the session of 1784, he conveyed the desire of the justices of the peace of the Brunswick to alter the location of the county court. Given the threat posed by the British during the Revolution and virtual abandonment of Brunswick Town, legislation in 1779 had moved the court from Brunswick Town to John Bell's plantation at Lockwoods Folly. However, the money appropriated to build a courthouse and jail had proved insufficient due to inflation and the difficulty of collecting taxes, and son Robert Bell, the current owner of the plantation, deemed the use of his house for court purposes "inconvenient and disagreeable." Thus the General Assembly by law instructed the county justices to use any acceptable dwelling within two miles of the Lockwoods Folly Bridge as a temporary court. Additionally, it appointed a commission to purchase five acres of land within the prescribed geographic bounds and to erect a courthouse, jail, and stocks on the property. As a future magistrate of the county, Smith came to know the locale all too well.[28]

Lockwoods Folly referred not only to a river and inlet in Brunswick County but also to the adjacent land, most particularly the ferry site crossing the river. Despite the unsavory toponyms of its originating waters, the junction of Pinch Gut Creek and Red Run in central Brunswick County, Lockwoods Folly River has been described as the most beautiful river in North Carolina other than the Waccamaw. Several explanations have been offered for the term Lockwoods Folly: a sea captain named Lockwood who mistook the inlet for the entrance of the Cape Fear River and wrecked his vessel; a boat builder named Lockwood who constructed a craft on the river, only to find that it was too large to sail through the inlet to the sea; a Barbadian named Lockwood who had early settled with others in the region and had been driven away by Indians; a clump of firs on a hill ("Lock Wood Folly") after an early meaning of the word "folly"; and, from the French folie, for "delight" or "favorite place."

In Smith's time, however, it was a "lonely part of the world" where the "sand [was] barren" and the "country thinly settled." But the courthouse soon appeared, erected on the west side of the river proximate to the bridge, and the Brunswick justices occupied the structure for the first time apparently in June 1786.[29]

In the legislative session of 1784 Smith also solidified his control over the ferries leading to and from Eagles Island. The Brunswick County court, after urging Smith to pursue the Eagles Island thoroughfare, unanimously recommended that the General Assembly "grant ... [Smith] such encouragement by law as may be necessary to finish a very laborious undertaking, which will be attended with great public utility." The legislature responded with a bill, introduced by Thomas Person of Granville County (to avoid conflict of interest), that recognized the investment of the ferries in Smith and forbade any competitive ferriage to and from Eagles Island, in effect awarding Smith a monopoly on two ferries along the most traveled road in eastern North Carolina. The law also exempted Smith's men from road work in the county for another a year if they labored on the Eagles Island passage. On the downside, the statute reduced the ferriage charges set by the Brunswick County court.[30] Nonetheless, sanctioned by state authority, Smith secured claim to a potentially rewarding investment, the operation or rental of the ferries, one of many possible sources of revenue by which planters sought to diversify their income base.

Smith's ample estate also permitted him to demonstrate a sense of noblesse oblige that simultaneously impressed his fellow legislators as well as benefited indirectly his economic interests. When the General Assembly considered legislation to improve the navigation of the Cape Fear River and to regulate pilotage on the waterway from the Atlantic Ocean to Wilmington, it decided that a lighthouse on Bald Head Island or some other place near to the mouth of the river would be desirable to help ships avoid the Frying Pan Shoals that menaced shipping off the coast. The river, of course, serviced Wilmington, the principal port in the state, a good part of southeastern North Carolina, and specifically Smith, whose many properties, including Belvedere, lined its banks. The statute in question imposed a tonnage duty on ships entering the river to raise moneys to construct a lighthouse.[31]

But, of course, land was needed on Bald Head, which constituted part of the complex originally known as the Cape Island, occasionally Ceder Island, and now Smith or Bald Head Island, and Smith owned the island. William Dry had purchased the property from the heirs of Landgrave Thomas Smith. Thus, ironically, Bald Head or Smith Island returned to the Smith family through Benjamin's marriage to the daughter of Dry. Smith doubtlessly assured his fellow legislators in 1784 that he would donate sufficient land on Bald Head Island to the state on which to erect the lighthouse. Almost two years later, after funds from the tonnage duty had accumulated, Smith, Robert Howe, North Carolina's highest ranking officer in the Continental army and owner of Kendal plantation on the Cape Fear River, and the commissioners of navigation and pilotage of the Cape Fear River visited Bald Head to fix a site for the lighthouse. Soon thereafter construction may have begun.[32] In the process Smith again entwined his interest with that of the public.

Coincidentally, Smith served in the legislative session that first ceded North Carolina's western lands, or present Tennessee, to the national government. The ratification and implementation of the Articles of Confederation had been predicated on the assumption, or at least the hope, that the states that claimed land below the Ohio River would yield their holdings to the United States. Settled before the Revolution in contravention to the royal Proclamation of 1763 by land-hungry farmers, fur trappers, and adventurers, and promoted by speculators, the Tennessee or over-mountain region had been divided into counties and incorporated into North Carolina's government, though the distance separating the western region from the east and the obstacle to communication posed by the Appalachian Mountains led to a most tenuous connection with the mother state. Adding to the confusion was the organization of the Transylvania Company in 1775 (originally the Louisa Company, 1774), led by Richard Henderson, James Hogg, and other influential North Carolinians, which claimed some 350,000 acres of land in Tennessee and present Kentucky. Although Smith voted for the cession in 1784, a minority in the senate, led by Griffith Rutherford, heavily involved in Tennessee speculation, entered a formal protest against the action.[33]

North Carolina larded its cession in 1784 with several provisos, including the protection of grants already made in the region and the retention of the land until Congress accepted the proffer. Even then opposition persisted, emanating from speculators and others genuinely concerned that the state was alienating a valuable asset, land that might be used for bounty payments to Revolutionary soldiers, to redeem specie and certificates, and generally to enhance the credit of the state. Supporting the cession were other speculators who saw a more roseate future under national protection as well as those who hoped to relieve the state of the expense of supporting government and providing protection against the Indians beyond the mountains. In Tennessee, a separatist faction led by John Sevier took advantage of the cession to create an independent state called Franklin (after Benjamin). According to a biographer of Sevier, "grievances against the mother State, [the settlers'] fear of continued domination, the subordination of their interests to those of the eastern part of North Carolina, their apparent abandonment by that government, and their resentment against real and fancied wrongs led them to embark upon a new experiment in self-government."[34]

Yet, a second session of the General Assembly in North Carolina, meeting late in 1784, rescinded the cession, but to no immediate avail. Despite the appearance of a pro-North Carolina faction, Sevier and the Franklinites, whether from democratic impulses, a "lawless thirst for power," or a penchant for speculation, resisted the efforts of North Carolina to reincorporate the territory. A pseudo-civil war darkened Tennessee from 1785 to 1788, when Sevier finally recanted and Franklin collapsed. Then, in 1789, after North Carolina ratified the federal Constitution and joined the new United States, the state once again turned the western territory over to the national authority. At last, wrote Archibald Maclaine, "we are rid of a people who were a pest and a burthen to us."[35]

Smith was more than an interested spectator in shifting tides of western ventures, for he began to dabble in speculative ventures in the Tennessee territory. In 1784, he entered claims for 101,505 acres in western North Carolina (eventually Tennessee) in the land office of John Armstrong in Hillsborough, which handled claims in the transmontane region. Smith immediately paid the necessary fees for 20,000 acres but signed a promissory to Armstrong for the remainder of the purchase. Soon thereafter the land office closed. To Smith's dismay, "astonishment" in his words, he found that his property in Tennessee fell within an area allotted by the federal government to the Chickasaw Indians by the Treaty of Hopewell in 1786. Neither Armstrong nor the secretary of state of North Carolina would void his claims, leaving Smith responsible for paying for land that lay beyond his right to possess or alienate.[36]

The most significant and enduring consequence of Smith's legislative experience in 1784 was his elevation to the bench of the Brunswick County court. Though a paper trail is lacking, Smith's contacts in the General Assembly, and particularly with Gov. Martin, brought him the recognition needed for a gubernatorial appointment as magistrate. Though Smith was not reelected to the state legislature when it next met in October 1784 (the earlier session in 1784 having changed the date of the annual meeting of the General Assembly to October to avoid the conflict with spring planting), in the quarterly session of the Brunswick County court in December, he proudly produced a commission from the state chief executive as a magistrate and took his seat on the bench. Smith wasted no time in announcing his new title, signing himself as esquire in public documents within a month.[37] The occasion marked the beginning of a forty-year stint as a county magistrate that only ended with the death of Smith.

CHAPTER 4

BENEFACTOR

Smith's relocation to North Carolina and rise to prominence took place against the broader backdrop of momentous state and national events. The struggle for independence seemed settled as Smith happily noted in 1783. As he rejoiced in the news of the ratification of the preliminary Treaty of Paris that promised to end the Revolution, Smith opined, "We have long, too long felt the direful effects of cursed War. May Heavenly smiling peace now comfort us for her long absence."[1] Nonetheless the conclusion of the war did little to abate the internal conflict that had beset North Carolina at the onset of the war for independence.

Following the decision of the Continental Congress in July 1776 to separate the colonies from Great Britain, North Carolina moved to draft a constitution for establishing an independent government. In the process the state divided into two political camps, conservatives and radicals. The conservatives, whose leaders included Archibald Maclaine of Wilmington, favored a powerful executive, an independent judiciary, protection for property, and restricted suffrage — an elitist conception of government. The radicals desired a powerful legislature, weak executive, a bill of rights to protect individual liberties, and diminished property requirements for voting and holding office. In essence the radicals represented the socioeconomic forces of democracy unleashed by the colonial rebellion against England, or mass versus class.

The resulting constitution in 1776 reflected compromise, but ultimately represented a more democratic frame of government compared to that of the colonial era. It recognized the principle of popular sovereignty. The executive and judicial departments were distinctly subordinated to the legislature. Property requirements for voting were relaxed. And a declaration (bill) of rights was added to the constitution. Despite equal county representation in the legislature, which discriminated against the more populous western counties, the political disqualification of non–Protestants, and the failure to submit to the document to the people for ratification, the new government was decidedly more democratic in spirit, form, and objectives than the colonial structure which it replaced. And it functioned "as a democracy, militant and assertive, if not always enlightened and judicious."[2]

Meanwhile, as the Revolution proceeded on the military front, the Continental Congress wrestled with a constitution of its own, a framework by which to establish a national government for the thirteen states. North Carolina delegates were leery, bordering on the paranoid, of a powerful central institution that might threaten the liberties of the people and the rights of the states, an understandable reaction in light of a century and more of British rule, but taken to the extreme by some politicians. As the Articles of Confederation emerged from the Congress, the national constitution appeared to offer little threat either to the people or the states, providing as it did for a loose union of thirteen autonomous entities. The North Carolina General Assembly in 1778, under the prodding of Cornelius Harnett, reversed an earlier decision and ratified the Articles of Confederation.[3]

All in all, the Articles, like the North Carolina state constitution, represented the American reaction to English rule and reflected the democratic forces at work. The constitution offered a framework in which relatively powerful state governments dominated a weak central structure that lacked even the power to tax and regulate commerce. Fear of executive dominance led to a government controlled by the legislature or Congress, which in turn exercised executive functions. A unicameral legislature in which each state possessed an equal vote reflected the democratic forces at work. As implied by the term confederation, the national Union was a loose alliance of independent states broadly (and ineffectually) controlled by a national authority. In the inestimable opinion of one historian, it was a "prescription for rigor mortis."[4]

The Articles of Confederation only exacerbated the division between conservatives and radicals in North Carolina politics, as did several war-related issues. Whereas the conservatives preferred lenient treatment of loyalists, protection of private property, and sound money, the radicals, who controlled North Carolina's government during most of the revolutionary and post-revolutionary years, sought the confiscation of loyalist property, fiat emissions of paper money, and a government more responsive to the people. Smith gravitated toward the conservatives as evidenced by his castigation of legislation in 1783 sanctioning the issue of paper currency, "which again is to be forc'd upon people notwithstanding the late & compleat experience of the whole Continent."[5] The national government and the states had notoriously overissued paper currency which had led to a stupendous inflation, and, in effect, flagrant indirect taxation.

In North Carolina the institution of the United States under the Articles of Confederation in 1781 intensified the intra–Whig struggle of the Revolution and proved a source of contention between conservatives and radicals. The former deplored the evident ineptitude of the government, the embarrassments suffered in foreign affairs, including the continuing hostility and denigration of Great Britain, and the failure to protect property rights and guard against popular excesses such as Shays' Rebellion at home. According to Richard Dobbs Spaight, a wealthy young planter from Craven County who represented the state in Congress, "There is no man of reflection, who has maturely considered what must and will result from the weakness of our present Federal Government, and the tyrannical and unjust proceedings of most of the State Governments ... but must sincerely wish for a strong and efficient National Government."[6]

Radicals such as Timothy Bloodworth of Wilmington appreciated the democratic aspects of the national government and the safeguards provided for state autonomy and individuals rights. Reared without formal education in poverty-stricken conditions, Bloodworth was the embodiment of the self-made man. A jack-of-all-trades whose vita included employment as blacksmith, tavern keeper, and ferry keeper, he acquired considerable property and slaves but remained true to his roots. Before, during, and after the Revolution Bloodworth was a proponent of democracy and easily one of the most popular politicians of the late eighteenth century in the Lower Cape Fear.[7]

At the same time Bloodworth was a staunch advocate of state prerogatives. Writing to Governor Richard Caswell in 1786, after Congress had passed an ordinance to regulate Indian affairs, he confided that "after repeated endeavors, we have obliged the Superintendent [of Indian Affairs] for the Southern District, to act in conjunction with the Authority of the State in all matters wherein the Legislative Rights of the States may be concerned." Similarly he helped to undermine the Jay-Gardoqui Treaty of 1786, which threatened to transgress the rights of the states as well as undermine the "loyalties of citizens" and depreciate land values in North Carolina west of the Appalachians (present Tennessee).[8]

Benjamin Smith had an opportunity to represent North Carolina in the Confederation Congress when the General Assembly of which he was member in April 1784 selected the Brunswick planter among others to join Spaight in Philadelphia for that uninspiring task and enacted legislation to *compel* the attendance of appointees. But Smith failed to appear, though he initially accepted £320 from the state treasury, or half the salary designated for congressmen. However, in a cost-cutting measure, the state legislature decided to restrict the number of representatives from the state at any one time to three, and Hugh Williamson, Spaight, and John Sitgreaves outranked Smith in seniority. At its next meeting in October 1784, the General Assembly omitted Smith from the list of delegates to Philadelphia.[9]

Subsequently the young planter had to defend his reputation against allegations in the General Assembly that he had kept the £320 for his own use. The threat of a lawsuit loomed. In a letter to the 1786–1787 session of the legislature Smith explained why he had not attended Congress, and declared that he had returned most of the £320 upon learning that he had not been reelected to Congress. Actually, he waited until April 10, 1786, to refund £300 to the treasury and to December 27, 1786, the day of his written explanation to the General Assembly, to remit the remaining £20 plus the warrants that allowed him to draw upon another £320, or the remainder of his original salary. Clearly Smith was in no hurry to make restitution to the state.[10]

Although the radicals dominated North Carolina politics in the 1780s, zealously guarding the rights of the state against the remotest encroachment of the national government, a minority that included Smith agreed with James Iredell, who lamented "the disordered and distracted" state of affairs in which "our public debts [are] unpaid, the treaty of peace unfulfilled on both sides, our commerce at the very verge of ruin, and all private industry at a stand, for want of a united, vigorous government."[11] Given the radicals' superiority in the state, North Carolina failed to show much enthusiasm for the movement that led to the Constitutional Convention in Philadelphia in 1787. Only the energy and skill of a few conservatives during the last two days of the General Assembly of 1786 ensured the participation of the state in the Philadelphia proceedings in 1787. North Carolina's delegates, Hugh Williamson, Richard Dobbs Spaight, William Blount, William R. Davie, and Alexander Martin, all respectable, wealthy, eastern (except Martin), planter-lawyer-merchant class conservatives, were decidedly unrepresentative of the state's great mass of provincial, lightly-educated, agrarian radicals.

Following the arduous proceedings at Philadelphia, a new constitution emerged, one that reversed the power relationship between the national government and states and threatened to create a commanding central authority. Yet, the task of replacing the Articles was only half finished. A minimum of nine states was required to ratify the Constitution in order to implement the new government. The North Carolina legislature, after heated elections in August 1787, when intimations about the proposed constitution emerged, was controlled by radicals, who nevertheless called for elections in March 1788 for a ratifying convention. Immediately the country and state divided into two political camps—Federalists who favored ratification and Anti-Federalists who preferred the status quo, or, at least, a constitution amended to protect states' and individual rights.

The March elections for delegates to the constitutional convention that was scheduled to meet in Hillsborough in November brought Benjamin Smith

4. Benefactor

again to the state political scene. Although unsuccessful in a bid for the state Senate from Brunswick County in 1787, he had been busy moving from Blue Banks to Belvedere during the winter and spring of 1785–1786, and, with Sarah, converting the property into an appropriate seat of entertainment. At the same he began to develop the potential of the plantation for the cultivation of rice. Emulating many planters, Smith sought in 1785 to erect a grist mill on his property, in part to convert his corn into meal but also to grind the grain of others, collecting the customary toll for compensation, another manifestation of the means by which planters diversified their sources of income. All the while, Smith remained active in the real estate market.[12]

As justice of the peace, Smith attended conscientiously the quarterly meetings of the Brunswick County court, establishing a precedent that he followed to the end of his life. In turn the court depended upon him to take responsibility for the tax list for the North West District, to oversee the maintenance of the road from the Brick House to the interior of the county, and to administer the oath of office to a constable. While at court, Smith conveniently qualified as the executor of the estate of John Rowan and the administrator of the estate of Justice John Haselton, Jr., positions that promised to be lucrative sources of income as he knew from the experience of his father and uncle in South Carolina. Smith also asked the court in 1785 to approve the manumission of a mulatto slave according to the will of William Dry, four years after the death of Dry and two years after the probate of the will — but better late than never.[13]

To the Hillsborough Convention in 1788 Brunswick voters sent five representatives, including Smith, who alone favored ratification. What prompted some to embrace the new constitution and others to oppose is intriguing. Neither wealth nor political experience greatly differentiated Federalist and Anti-Federalist leaders. Yet, Federalists, like Smith, tended to be younger, and thus perhaps more energetic and more impatient with the status quo. They also exhibited a more catholic frame of mind, a broader world view, which in the case of Smith included his youthful educational experience in Philadelphia, his reputed military service in the Continental Army, and his recent immigration from South Carolina, a state with which he maintained close ties and which supported ratification (particularly Charleston where Smith had family ties).[14] Evidence also suggests a Federalist affinity for the Church of England, which became the Protestant Episcopal Church of America after the Revolution, an institution embraced by Smith. Perhaps most importantly, Federalists, again exemplified by Smith, tended to be men of commerce, whether merchants or planters, who stood to benefit from a stronger, more active national government that promoted shipping, protected contracts, and provided sound money.

Smith arrived late by four days in Hillsborough, but given the overwhelming majority of the Antis, whose numbers included the other four members of the Brunswick delegation, he might as well have stayed at home. The opposition, led by Willie Jones of Halifax, charitably agreed that Gov. Samuel Johnston, a Federalist, might preside over the meeting. Then, Jones proposed a quick vote on ratification, in effect, to acknowledge the inevitable and save the taxpayers of the state per diem handouts to the delegates. But the Federalists insisted on a full airing of the Constitution. A week-long, one-sided debate ensued in which Federalists James Iredell and Richard Dobbs Spaight expended their best oratorical ammunition in a futile effort to shatter, or even dent, the cement-hardened minds of their opposition. Smith uttered not a word, at least in public, but he was not alone. Most at the convention were likewise silent. Eventually the Anti-Federalists carried a resolution by a vote of 184 to 84 that neither ratified nor rejected the Constitution.[15]

The decision was audacious, for during the course of the Hillsborough Convention, New York ratified the Constitution, the eleventh state to approve, which meant that the new government was destined to begin in 1789 without North Carolina (and Rhode Island). The Antis in North Carolina were prepared to accept the state's status as an autonomous political entity in order to put pressure on the United States government to adopt a bill of rights. To that end the Hillsborough Convention adopted a series of proposed amendments to check federal power, protect states' rights, and safeguard special interests in North Carolina, and a declaration of rights to secure personal liberties.

Smith and the Federalists may have lost the decision to join the Union, but the convention was not ready to decamp, for the matter of a permanent location for the capital of the state came to the fore. Following the Revolution the General Assembly embarrassingly had been unable to fix a seat for the government. As a result the legislature convened in several locations about the state. Tarboro, Fayetteville, and Hillsborough were the frontrunners in the race to replace the colonial capital of New Bern. But no town commanded a majority of the votes in the legislature, and the uncertainty of the annual meetings and the shifting locations, which jeopardized the public records, led the General Assembly in 1787 to refer the decision to the Hillsborough Convention. Smith was not reticent. He seconded a motion by Joseph McDowell, an Anti-Federalist from Rockingham County, to ballot on a place for the seat of government. The motion carried by a vote of 134 to 117.[16]

The convention spent the following day deliberating a location for the capital. The members gathered at six o'clock in the morning, acknowledging the heat of an August day and the prospect of a long, if not rancorous, session. Several sites received nominations, including New Bern, Fayetteville, Hillsborough,

Tarboro, Smithfield in Johnston County, the junction of the Deep and Haw Rivers, and Isaac Hunter's plantation in Wake County. Local interests aside, Albemarle and western representatives in the Hillsborough Convention sought a location more central than New Bern. Smith and the delegates from the Lower Cape Fear advocated Fayetteville, located on the Northwest Cape Fear River about a hundred miles north of Wilmington.[17]

Originating in the settlements of Cross Creek and Campbellton, which were combined in 1778, and renamed Fayetteville in 1783, the Cape Fear River town was a thriving commercial entrepot whose population of nearly 1,500 rivaled that of Wilmington. Merchants in Wilmington kept agents in Fayetteville to draw trade from the backcountry through the upper Cape Fear to the port. While visiting Wilmington on his Southern Tour in 1791, President George Washington reported that six thousand hogsheads of tobacco were annually sent to Wilmington via Fayetteville. In what was intended to be a satirical description of Fayetteville in 1788, William J. Dawson of Bertie County in the Albemarle region of the state inadvertently spoke to the cultural

Fayetteville City Market. Courtesy of State Archives, Office of Archives and History, Raleigh.

scene of the town, when he mentioned theatrical performances, traveling shows featuring magicians, and annual horse races. The following year a newspaper deserted Wilmington to relocate in Fayetteville.[18]

Residents of Fayetteville unabashedly sought the honor of the capital of the state. During the 1780s the town had erected two "large and elegant buildings," located about twelve hundred yards apart at opposite ends of Green Street, for the accommodation of the Cumberland County court and the anticipated General Assembly respectively. The wooden courthouse stood in the middle of James Square, named for merchant James Hogg who had donated the site to the town. The large, two-story, brick State House, begun in 1787 with private subscriptions, was the more impressive building. At ground level it contained an open arcade suitable for a market, above which were two large chambers within an enclosed upper story that were designed for the accommodation of the General Assembly (senate and house of commons). According to the *Wilmington Centinel*, the edifice aimed to promote Fayetteville "as worthy of being the Capital of an extensive state."[19]

The evident "public spirit" that inspired the construction of the courthouse and statehouse also resulted in the opening of new roads and erecting bridges "to render the communication with the country more easy and convenient" as well as the improvement of the navigability of Cross Creek that led from the Northwest Cape Fear to the heart of town. According the *Centinel*, "considering the situation of Fayette-Ville, so convenient for commanding the trade of an extensive back country, and its other advantages ... it must soon become a place of great consequence." Smith agreed. In July 1788, a month before the meeting of the Hillsborough Convention, he advertised land for sale along the Northwest Cape Fear River, claiming that the location of the property between Wilmington and Fayetteville, "which will probably in a short time become the capital of the state," would doubtlessly lead to its increased value.[20]

The Hillsborough Convention, however, disagreed. On a second ballot a slim majority selected a site within ten miles of Isaac Hunter's plantation in Wake County, leaving to a future legislature the exact location and details of laying out a town. Hunter's plantation seemed a relatively more central location and at the same time a compromise that avoided special interests attached to the various proposed towns. A formal protest ensued, presented by William Barry Gove, representative of Cumberland County (in which Fayetteville was located), and signed by 119, or nearly half the delegates, including Smith. The dissenters claimed that bestowing capital status upon Fayetteville would galvanize commerce in the state by drawing trade to North Carolina that ordinarily went to Virginia and South Carolina. Conversely, establishing the seat of government "in a place unconnected with commerce, and where there is at present no town, will be attended with a heavy expence to the people, and the town when established never can rise above the degree of a village." Though outvoted, the considerable number of dissenters, including Smith, posed problems for Wake County in the future.[21]

While Isaac Hunter must have relished the thought of serving future state legislators a rum punch that was highly popular in his tavern in Wake County, a swift and striking change of opinion occurred in North Carolina. Federalists undertook an educational campaign to reverse the decision at Hillsborough. Among other factors the prospect of discriminatory tariff duties, the desire for federal protection against the Indians in the west, the need for another southern state in the Union to guard against aggressive northern economic interests, and the embarrassing alignment with Rhode Island, with its unsavory reputation as a den of thieves and cesspool of democracy, contributed to the change of heart. Moreover, in 1789 the establishment of an orderly national government headed by the respected George Washington also aided the cause. Though governor and Federalist leader Samuel Johnston harbored reservations about Washington's "Talents" and "Library knowledge," he appreciated the president's imploring "divine benediction and guidance in the councils, which are shortly [to consider] ... the political relation, which is to subsist hereafter, between the state of North-Carolina, and the states now in union under the new general government." Ultimately, as Anti-Federalist William Lenoir admitted, adoption of the Constitution was "an alternative less fatal than absolute severance from the adjoining States."[22]

Thus the General Assembly that met in 1788 issued a call for a second state convention, to meet in Fayetteville, though Anti-Federalists postponed the gathering as long as possible — until November 1789. Elections in August produced a decidedly Federalist majority. Of the five-man Brunswick delegation, only Smith was reelected, and he was accompanied by three other Federalists. The convention opened on Monday, November 16, at which time Smith was placed on the committee of elections to adjudge any disputed electoral contest. On Tuesday, it was the Federalists' turn to opt for a quick vote. The Antis demurred after which the Federalists showed "a degree of patience that astonished every body" while the opposition registered its views. Unlike the Hillsborough Convention, no detailed transcription of the proceedings was kept at Fayetteville. In 1788 the Federalists required a printed record to help effect a subsequent change in public opinion, but in Fayetteville they only needed to muster as large a majority as possible to affirm North Carolina's support for the Constitution.[23]

Finally, on Saturday, the convention reached its anticipated decision. William R. Davie, leading Federalist and member of the Philadelphia convention, moved that the convention ratify the Constitution on "behalf of the freemen, citizens and inhabitants of the State of North Carolina," and Benjamin Smith was accorded the honor of seconding the motion. The Federalists rejoiced in their margin of victory, 194 to 77, for they had worked mightily to reverse the decision in Hillsborough by a greater majority than that achieved by the Antis in 1788.[24]

Nonetheless, the Anti-Federalists in Fayetteville wrung a concession from the Federalists, or perhaps it was a gesture of goodwill by the Federalists that permitted a graceful exit by the Antis. A committee of seven, apparently chaired by Anti-Federalist James Galloway, but including four Federalists, among them Smith, reported eight amendments that North Carolina expected its delegates in the Congress to propose to the national legislature upon admission to the Union. As might be anticipated, the amendments were designed to restrain the power of the national government. The convention unanimously approved the proposed amendments. The Anti-Federalists gave ground grudgingly, clinging to principle to the very end.[25]

A last order of business in the convention was a sop thrown to Fayetteville. To mitigate the slight of placing the state capital in the wilds of Wake County as opposed to the river port, the convention amended the state constitution to allow Fayetteville a representative in the state house of commons. Before the Revolution, the North Carolina General Assembly, using the example of borough representation in England, had permitted nine towns in the colony to send delegates to the lower house of the legislature. Rationalizing borough representation was the need to recognize the interests of urban communities whose peculiar mercantile concerns might be overlooked by a predominantly agrarian society. The constitution of 1776 reduced the number of borough towns to six, but the size and potential of Fayetteville as well as the desire of the convention to placate the town after its abortive effort to seek capital status justified adding a seventh (though one-third of the voting members of the convention disagreed).[26]

Upon the conclusion of the convention Smith and many members of the constitutional convention remained in Fayetteville because they also represented their respective counties in the General Assembly that met in the Cumberland town at the same time. In part the simultaneous meetings represented an economy move, an effort to relieve the state from paying travel and per diem twice to many of the same personnel. In part, too, combining the gatherings was designed to ensure better attendance at all the functions. Adding to the political mix in Fayetteville in 1789 was the annual meeting of the Grand Lodge and Ancient, Free & Accepted Masons of North Carolina, which again embraced many of the politicians.

It was an intimate atmosphere, if intimacy could be construed to embrace some four hundred individuals. The residents of Fayetteville, at least, felt the closeness. The members of the three conventions swelled the town's population by a quarter, but the economic boon to market suppliers, merchants, tavern keepers, and renters of private rooms ameliorated any inconvenience. The new, commodious, brick State House, though short-lived in its original purpose, served well that November in 1789. Nonetheless, the unseasonably cold weather no doubt contributed to drafty quarters, particularly before stoves were fixed and andirons were added.[27]

Smith, elected to the House of Commons from Brunswick County, had arrived ten days after the legislature convened on November 2 (for which tardiness he was later excused by the house). He missed the death and funeral of Richard Caswell, former governor and current speaker of the Senate. The speaker suffered a paralytic stroke while presiding over the upper house, lingered for five days, and died on November 10. An elaborate state funeral followed the next day. Coincidentally, Caswell was also grand master of the Masons, and thus received appropriate recognition from the Grand Lodge at the time of his demise. Perhaps, in retrospect, Smith's delay was fortuitous, for sickness early plagued members of the convention members and legislators, including Governor Samuel Johnston and his brother John. The latter was "dangerously" ill for several days.[28]

After laudations to Caswell, the General Assembly, buttressed by the straggling Smith, recommenced its deliberations. The Federalist ratification victory created a brief hiatus in legislative activity. After kudos passed among the victors the General Assembly incorporated into its business the election of two senators to represent North Carolina in the United States. Smith's name was mentioned but, of course, he could not contend with the cadre of political heavyweights who waited the call, which ultimately went to Samuel Johnston and Benjamin Hawkins. Sufficiently assuaging any regret was Smith's appointment as colonel of the Brunswick County militia, a post no doubt greatly coveted and genuinely cherished, for throughout his life Smith seemed to

Richard Caswell Masonic emblem. Courtesy of State Archives, Office of Archives and History, Raleigh.

suffer from delusions of military grandeur. Thereafter he was Colonel Smith — until later, when he became general.[29]

Committee activity again absorbed much time. In addition to making Smith responsible for the consideration of an array of petitions, memorials, and bills, the house placed him on the committee of propositions and grievances, a standing committee of some clout, and a committee of two to wait upon the newly-elected governor of the state and bring him before the General Assembly to be sworn into office.[30] The last may have been honorific, but it constituted an acknowledgment of the status of the young Brunswick planter as well as recognized perhaps some pomposity of his demeanor that was deemed fitting for the occasion. In any case, Smith was accorded such recognition often in the future, and eventually turned the tables on the legislature when he was elected governor in 1810.

The General Assembly in 1789 returned to the proposed lighthouse on Bald Head Island. Noting that the lighthouse was under construction, the General Assembly added Smith to the commissioners of pilotage and navigation for the Cape Fear River, not that Smith was conversant with licensing and supervising pilots, the principal responsibility of the commissioners, but he had an interest in the need to improve the navigability of the river. Moreover, the legislature offered perfunctory recognition to Smith, perhaps to induce him to "execute a deed [to the state] for the ... ten acres as by him promised" for the erection of the lighthouse, a commitment he had made some three years earlier.[31]

To sweeten the deal, the legislature prohibited anyone but the lighthouse keeper and those under previous agreement with William Dry from keeping livestock and carrying a gun on the island, in effect solidifying Smith's title to Bald Head and converting the island into his personal refuge. That exclusivity evoked the indignation of his (erstwhile) friend Archibald Maclaine of Wilmington, who claimed that the land was "of little consequence" and that the public simply should have purchased it. As a result Smith enjoyed a privilege beyond that of any ordinary Carolinian when demanding that anyone wishing to carry a firearm on the island, whether government officials, hunters, or sightseers, seek his permission. Successful prosecutions of violators, incidentally, meant that half the fines would go to Smith. According to Maclaine, the timber on the island was worth more than the cattle. "Why did he not make it penal to carry an axe on any part of the Island?"[32]

Smith proved less successful in a memorial to the legislature in 1789, which evidenced a boldness of vision that encompassed a mixture of public-spirited citizenship and self-promotion. He contended that much of Green Swamp, a 170-square-mile bog which was located in northwestern Brunswick County and mostly owned by the state, was useless at that time. Thus Smith proposed draining the swamp which would improve the health of the region (then "infected with malignant vapors, rising continually from so large a tract of mire and filthiness") and provide rich land for cultivation which would offer employment to farmers and the prospect of additional tax revenues to the state. Moreover, a canal from Green Swamp might redirect the exportation of produce of the region from Georgetown, South Carolina, to the mouth of Little River in North Carolina, converting the latter into "a port of some consequence." For his part, Smith hoped to swap his entries for land in Tennessee for acreage along the Waccamaw River and tributaries in and about the vicinity of Green Swamp. The Senate approved the proposal by a close margin but the House rejected the memorial by voice vote.[33]

Smith rebounded from the defeat of the Green Swamp venture to assist in thwarting the decision of the Hillsborough Convention in 1788 to locate the permanent state capital in Wake County. The convention in 1788 had left the decision of the exact spot to subsequent legislatures, but the opposition to Wake County lingered and festered. On three occasions in the legislative session of 1789, Smith and those who favored Fayetteville (or some other location) voted down bills to appoint commissioners to pick a spot in Wake, keeping the matter of the state capital in limbo and futilely hoping for a change in opinion.[34]

On a positive note, a signal achievement of the General Assembly of 1789 was the initiation of the University of North Carolina, which in 1795 became the first publicly-supported institution of higher education to open in the United States. The state constitution of 1776 had stipulated that the legislature should establish "a school or schools ... for the convenient instruction of youth, with ... salaries to the masters, paid by the public ... and, [that] all usefull learning ... be encouraged and promoted in one or more universities." William R. Davie, later denominated the "Father of the University," shepherded through the legislature the charter for the University of North Carolina along with a statute that provided the institution with a building fund and endowment consisting of moneys (with some exceptions) "due and owing the public of North Carolina either for arrearages under the former or present government" to January 1, 1783, and past and future property that escheated to the state — the Escheats Act.[35]

The incorporating legislation named the trustees for the university, led by Davie and other luminaries, but included Smith, whose appointment presaged his longstanding and unwavering support for the university, and, more generally, his abiding efforts to promote education at every level throughout his public career. At the same time Smith's trusteeship more pointedly acknowledged his intention to endow the university with 20,000 acres of land that he had earlier acquired in Tennessee by military warrants. The gesture was bold and sincere, though subsequent years revealed that the land was worth far less than originally thought, and that the university encountered such difficulty obtaining title to the land that it was only sold (and the endowment realized) a decade after Smith's death. Nonetheless, those matters must not detract from the munificence of the donation and Smith's legitimate claim as the university's first benefactor, factors to which he adverted later when his desperate financial circumstances required sympathy.[36]

The trustees of the university, many of whom were in Fayetteville as members of the legislature, held an unofficial meeting on December 18 at which Davie informed the members of Smith's gift. The board presented Smith with a resolution of gratitude "for his liberal and generous donation." Three days later the General Assembly followed with a joint resolution of thanks. Smith obtained maximum exposure for his generosity. The legislature voted to publish its resolution in every newspaper in the state — the two sheets that appeared in New Bern and Fayetteville.[37]

The General Assembly concluded its session on December 22, at which time Smith may have been present, though earlier he had obtained permission to leave on December 14. That turned out to be a customary ploy on his part in years to come. On the last day of the session Governor Alexander Martin addressed a joint session of the legislature, begging the members "to reconcile those jarring sentiments ... that seemed unfortunately to prevail in different parts of the State," and hoping that "the Federal and Anti Federal name [might] be heard no more as a reproach." The executive rejoiced that the government of the United States was still in the hands of the people and there it must remain. Regardless of the governor's plea, political conflict in North Carolina abated not at all, but in fact rose to new heights in the decade to follow.[38]

CHAPTER 5

SMITHVILLE

As North Carolina joined the federal Union, the state quickly evidenced its support for the new government. Of some 180 members of the General Assembly in 1789, 148 had been members of the Fayetteville Convention, but only twenty-nine of those had opposed ratification. Both United States senators chosen by the legislature favored the Constitution. The February 1790, popular elections for congressmen, five initially for North Carolina pending the outcome of the federal census of that year, resulted in four who had backed the Constitution. The exception was Timothy Bloodworth in the Cape Fear District. Benjamin Smith offered for that seat, but according to Archibald Maclaine, he "has no popularity," and, as it turned out, certainly not enough to compete with the democratic, if not demagogic, Bloodworth.[1]

Though the seat in Congress eluded him, Col. Smith looked with satisfaction upon his situation as North Carolina embraced statehood. After all, he was the squire of Belvedere, a tract which included the former Ferry Plantation on the west side of the Northwest Cape Fear as well as the land across the way on Eagles Island. "Forming it is believed a plantation combining more advantages as to profit & beauty than any other single one in the States of North Carolina [,] South Carolina [,] or Georgia," according to a contemporary, Smith put 251 acres under cultivation in rice, almost evenly divided between the west and east sides of the river. A combined 288 acres of uncultivated swamp land on both sides of the river in addition to 1,787 acres of high ground on the west side of the river composed the remainder of the plantation. Remuneration from the ferries, the possibility of a tavern operated from the Brick House at the western ferry terminus in Brunswick County, rice mills, and saw mills made Belvedere an enviable investment.[2]

But, of course, critical to the realization of pecuniary gain in the Lower Cape Fear at the end of the eighteenth century as well as the elegant lifestyle to which the Smiths were accustomed was labor, bonded labor, and Smith had it in abundance. The first decennial census conducted by the United

States in 1790 found Smith claiming 221 slaves, more than any slave owner in the state. His nearest rival, Cullen Pollock in the Albemarle region, counted 204. Another eleven slave owners claimed more than a hundred bondsmen (mostly closer to one hundred than two hundred). Although 31 percent of North Carolina's families held slaves, numbers generally were small. Only 804, or 5.5 percent, owned twenty or more. But in Brunswick County the figures were higher, 37 and 17 percent respectively, betokening the wealth of the area. Smith stood at the apex of an elite group.[3]

Accustomed from birth to the institution, Smith had no qualms about trafficking in humans. He bought, sold, and gifted men, women, and children. But bonded labor was restive. Newspaper advertisements reflected numerous runaways among Smith's slave holdings along with the master's determination to reclaim his property. Not surprisingly, Smith opposed restrictions on the importation of slaves into the state. The General Assembly, deeming such importations "productive of evil consequences, and highly impolitic" in 1786, had sought to restrain the practice by means of a stiff tariff, but that law was repealed in 1790. The successful slave insurrection in Sainte-Domingue in 1791 led to a reconsideration of the subject. Although Smith, as a state senator in 1793, helped to block a bill that would have prohibited further importations, the following year he was unable to deny the passage of similar legislation that encompassed slaves and indentured servants of color.[4]

Although subdued in 1790 by the death of his father, whom he apparently admired greatly, Smith must have looked to the future, his own and that of the United States, with sanguinity. Yet enthusiasm in North Carolina for the new nation was short-lived. Anti-Constitution sentiment was only briefly subdued. Even the pro-Constitution forces harbored serious reservations about a powerful, centralized government. Secretary of the Treasury Alexander Hamilton's financial program, particularly the assumption of state debts and the whiskey excise (the latter proposed in 1790 and instituted in 1791) revived Anti-Federalist fears. From Fayetteville, John Sibley, physician and co-publisher of the local newspaper, publicly refuted charges that he had speculated in public securities, declaring that he had no knowledge of the assumption law until he recently received a copy of the statute in a letter from Smith, who then was in Charleston, presumably helping to settle his father's estate. General ignorance allowed speculators in North Carolina (and elsewhere) to fleece the unknowing for a pittance. Sibley's denial evoked another complaint — the failure of Congress to extend the federal postal system to the western part of the state. As for the whiskey excise, no state, not even Pennsylvania, site of the famous Whiskey Rebellion, proved more averse to that imposition than North Carolina.[5]

By the time that the state legislators, including Smith, convened in Fayetteville in November 1790, many North Carolinians wondered about the propriety of their decision to opt for statehood. Governor Alexander Martin, never more than a lukewarm proponent of the federal Constitution since he had left the Philadelphia Convention in 1787, had become alienated. In his address to the General Assembly, the governor spoke of the "new and unexpected precedent" embodied by assumption, and wondered about its impact on the "independent and internal sovereignty of the state." The House of Commons, by a vote of 55 to 26, with Smith in the minority, refused to take an oath of allegiance to federal Constitution, and, agreeing with the governor, passed a resolution condemning assumption as "dangerous to the interests and rights of North Carolina." Additionally, the superior court of the Edenton judicial district in 1790 refused to obey a writ of certiorari from the District Court of the United States, claiming as a court of original jurisdiction that it was not answerable to any other judicature. The house of commons, sans Smith, applauded that act of judicial defiance.[6]

North Carolina's early disaffection from the national government seemed to climax late in 1790, though an undercurrent of suspicion remained. Congressional elections in the state early in 1791 returned a delegation decidedly favoring an active government. In the Cape Fear District, William Barry Grove of Fayetteville easily defeated incumbent Timothy Bloodworth, notorious opponent of the Constitution, and Smith even won a handful of votes in Brunswick County. Nonetheless, closed sessions of the United States Senate, the need for additional federal courts and post roads, and concerns about coastal defense aroused consternation among members of succeeding legislatures, who only slightly relaxed their vigilance toward a threatening or inattentive Congress. Smith's advocacy of the Constitution and support for the new government ultimately placed him in the minority of an incipient political alignment in the state that presaged the formation of political parties.[7]

The opening of the legislative session on November 1, 1790, found Smith in the House of Commons, having enjoyed at least some popularity among the voters of Brunswick, if not elsewhere in his congressional district. His unusual timeliness was rewarded by numerous committee assignments. Among them were appointments to joint (with the senate) committees on public (as opposed to private) bills and finance, both betokening the rising stature of the Brunswick planter. So was the decision of the House to entrust him to prepare several bills or amendments to bills. Assignments to committees considering the establishment and jurisdiction of courts and improving the navigability of Cross Creek reflected Smith's interest in two areas that occupied his attention throughout his public service—the state's judiciary and internal improvements.[8]

In the latter field, North Carolina tentatively began to explore the possibility of improving its transportation system by road and by water. Internal improvements were deemed important to encouraging trade, lowering costs to farmers taking produce to market, and more generally utilizing the bountiful natural resources of the state. At the same time, many hoped to develop the ports along the coast in order to reduce the state's dependence upon neighboring Virginia and South Carolina in which many North Carolinians marketed their crops. Ultimately North Carolinians saw internal improvements as a means to rouse the state from the poverty, despair, indifference, and conservatism that seemed increasingly to afflict its inhabitants, and led to the characterization of North Carolina as the Rip Van Winkle state in years to come.[9]

Following the Revolution, North Carolina continued to depend upon the county courts and local labor to clear waterways and maintain roads and bridges. But Smith as a neophyte legislator had seen Governor Martin's message to the legislature in 1784 in which the executive claimed, "The Trade and navigation of this country is of lasting consequence, and require your immediate interposition and patronage. It is necessary [that] our rivers be rendered more navigable, and our roads opened and supported." Thus the legislature began to incorporate navigation companies that relied mainly upon voluntary contributions by "such public spirited persons as may be inclined to aid [such] laudable undertaking[s]."[10] The mostly unsuccessful efforts of those voluntary companies led to a reliance upon chartered toll companies, which raised capital by the sale of stock and charged a fee for the use of a stream or river whose navigability had been improved by the companies' efforts. Eventually the state found it necessary to invest in the improvement efforts, with problematic results.

In 1790, the legislature entertained a proposal to incorporate a toll company to render Cross Creek navigable from Fayetteville to the Northwest Cape Fear River, a distance of about a mile. Smith chaired the committee in the House of Commons that considered the bill. Among the incorporators were his friend James Hogg, influential Fayetteville legislator William Barry Grove, "suave and courtly in manner, but adroit and supple as a politician," and university trustee and treasurer William Alves. Opposition to the Cross Creek effort and more broadly to internal improvement projects for the next half century derived from those who feared a monopolization of the public waterways by private entrepreneurs. Smith's committee reported favorably on a charter for the Cross Creek company, though the resulting legislation limited the company to three years to complete its project on pain of losing its privileges. But all the company needed was an entrée. Subsequent legislatures on three occasions granted the company more time, eventually to 1816, to complete its work.[11]

Smith's sincerity in adhering to the principle of internal improvements may be questioned, however, for in the same legislative session he voted in the minority against a statute to cut a canal from the Pasquotank River to the Elizabeth River in Virginia — the Dismal Swamp Canal. Smith's early advocacy of draining Green Swamp lands and supporting the Cross Creek navigation project obviously tended to enhance his interests, directly or indirectly, whereas the Dismal Swamp Canal promised to serve those of the Roanoke Valley and Albemarle Sound regions of North Carolina. Still, Smith may have thought, and, if so, correctly, that the Dismal Swamp Canal would only have cemented the dependence of Carolinians in the Roanoke Valley and the Albemarle upon Virginia.[12]

Smith remained active through the session. He presented memorials by county constituents, including the resignation of a justice of the peace. He found himself in the minority in an effort to instruct the collector of customs in the Brunswick (Wilmington) shipping district to allow debtors more time to pay their charges to the government. The House divided evenly over a resolution to establish the permanent capital, with Smith again digging in his heels against the Wake County site, but the tie-breaking ballot of the speaker in the affirmative carried the measure. The Senate rejected the bill, however, and the question of the capital remained in limbo. As usual, Smith prepared for a hasty retreat, obtaining permission to depart early, if necessary.[13]

During the course of the legislative session Smith met with the board of trustees of the university in its first formal meeting. The trustees decided to hold their annual meeting when the legislature was in session, in part to maintain close ties with the General Assembly upon whose largesse the university depended, and in part in recognition that securing a quorum would be facilitated because many trustees were legislators. While the law failed to penalize trustees for nonattendance at board meetings, it offered no escape to legislators. Thus compelled to attend the General Assembly, legislator-trustees offered a ready bloc by which to achieve a quorum. Smith proved faithful in his attendance of the board during its first decade, aided by his presence in the legislature throughout the 1790s, though it is probable that he would have exerted every effort to attend university board meetings in any case.[14]

The university trustees in their second meeting in 1790 formally accepted Smith's bequest of twenty thousand acres of land that had been promised the previous year. James Hogg presented the deed, which had been signed by Smith on December 18, 1789. Reciprocating, the board unanimously voted a resolution of thanks in which the members "entertained a proper impression of the public spirit and liberality manifested by Colo. Smith in his early and valuable donation," and ordered that the resolution be published in all the state newspapers for four continuous weeks, which must have tickled Smith's vanity.[15]

The trustees then addressed the pressing matter of finances. Knowing that donations by Smith and others would require time to be productive (how much time they could not have imagined) and realizing the difficulty of collecting the grants of arrearages and escheats promised in the building fund act of 1789, the trustees were reduced to the "absolute necessity" of seeking a loan from the legislature. Governor Martin, as president of the board, made the plea. The House of Commons roundly rejected the notion by a vote of 66 to 16. Smith and five other trustees were in the minority. Yet another trustee in the House of Commons agreed to postpone consideration of the proposal until the next legislative session and in the meantime desired to publicize the request in the newspaper. Though the move bordered on apostasy to proponents of the university, newspapers had already proved to be excellent organs of political persuasion.[16]

The following spring witnessed one of the highlights of Smith's life, a visit by George Washington. The president, after taking office in 1789, felt the need to acquaint himself with the southern states of the nation over which he presided. He enjoyed a longstanding relationship with the northern states from his experience in the Revolutionary War, from the temporary location of the nation's first capitals, New York, where he was inaugurated in 1789, and Philadelphia, to which the capital moved in 1790, and from an excursion northward in 1790. Washington was also vaguely familiar with the northeastern area of North Carolina via his involvement in the construction of the Dismal Swamp Canal, a waterway that ultimately connected the Pasquotank River in North Carolina to the Elizabeth River and the Chesapeake Bay in Virginia, though the president was several years in his grave before that canal became a very tenuous reality in 1805.

Thus Washington embarked on his famous Southern Tour early in 1791 to inspect the Carolinas and Georgia, taking a coastal route as he departed but returning by way of the backcountry. After entering North Carolina and staying at "indifferent Houses" (public lodgings or taverns), he and his party in April plodded toward Wilmington along a road that passed "through the most barren country [Washington] ever beheld." Yet the president admitted, "In places ... if the ideas of poverty could be separated from the Land, the appearances of it are agreeable." The Wilmington troop of horse met Washington about twelve miles from town. The gentlemen of the town, no doubt numbering Smith, who owned numerous properties in Wilmington, appeared six miles later at which point the president left his chariot and mounted one of his horses to ride the remaining distance, preceded by four dragoons with a trumpet.[17]

Arriving in Wilmington, Washington received a triple salute, three rounds of fifteen shots each, fired by a battery of four guns, after which the festivities seemed unrelenting. He was escorted to his lodgings "through an astonishing concourse of people of the town and country, whom, as well as the ladies that filled the windows and balconies of the houses, he saluted with his usual affability and condescension." As he alighted, "the acclamations were loud and universal." Ships in the harbor were adorned from stem to stern to topgallant. The following day Washington enjoyed a public dinner with the inhabitants of the town and in the evening attended a ball with "illuminations, Bonfires, &ca.," at which the president "appeared equally surprised and delighted, at the very large and brilliant assembly of ladies"—sixty-two by his count. Despite his obvious devotion to Martha, Washington always appreciated the company of the opposite gender.[18]

The president departed Wilmington the next morning at six o'clock, crossing the river in a United States Revenue barge, with the gentlemen of the town attending in boats in the harbor, cannon booming, and the people huzzaing in the background, to breakfast with Smith at Belvedere. According to tradition, upon landing on the west side of the Northwest Cape Fear River, Washington was met by thirteen young women, dressed in white, who represented the states of the Union. They strew flowers in his path as he made his way from the river through the avenue of umbrageous trees leading to the plantation home of Smith. Alas, for Smith, it must have been a relatively quick repast, for the president traveled another twenty-five miles that day. Indeed, Washington left so quickly, that reputedly he left his easy slippers behind, though why he would have exchanged his riding boots for slippers during a brief breakfast has not been adequately explained. More disconcerting, though Smith claimed to have been an aide-de-camp to Washington during the Revolution, according to a later account, the president and former commander of the Continental Army, seemed not to recognize his host.[19]

Nevertheless, soon after Washington departed, Smith wrote the president, largely to send a packet of letters he had received from persons along the road from Belvedere to Charleston who sought to offer hospitality to the illustrious traveler. Smith also thanked the president for stopping at Belvedere, thereby "softening" a principle that Washington had adopted at the outset of his tour—a determination to eschew private residences, which, according to Smith, "must punish the first Characters of the Country where you travel with great Chagrin." Despite the later misgivings of his detractors, Smith assured Washington of his "attachment" to the president, which had begun at Long Island in 1776, and expressed regret "in having been forced from partaking of your Fortunes, amongst the variety of which I am most pained at by [my] absence ... when you changed the Fate of America at Trenton." In a flourish Smith declared that his disappointment "will end but with my life."[20]

As the fanfare died away and Washington headed toward South Carolina, it is intriguing to note that neither the president nor any contemporary accounts mentioned his traveling from Wilmington to Belvedere by way of Eagles Island, an indication that his barge may have sailed around the southern tip of the island and up the Northwest River to Smith's home. In fact, Wilmington residents in that year complained to the legislature that the causeway had for a long time been "dangerous to travellers" and thus "highly injurious" to the commerce of the town and its environs. For his part, Smith, who had promised to complete the road in timely fashion, had to contend with those who loosed their livestock on the causeway and felled trees across the drainage ditches on the sides of the road. To entice Smith to put his shoulder to the task, the General Assembly in 1791 offered him a five-year extension to finish the project, allowed him to cut canals through the island and charge for their use, raised ferry rates, and reiterated the usual legal penalties for those who damaged the road or ditches.[21]

Like his father-in-law, Smith had made an untenable bargain but really had an advantage. The state and county knew that the usual means of road construction and maintenance of the causeway through Eagles Island would be futile and thus attempted to foist the job on Smith, who had the labor force and incentive to maintain a tolerable road through the island because the traffic redounded to the benefit of his ferries. Still, given the obstacles at hand, Smith was reluctant to use his slaves on such relatively unproductive work. As a result, in 1796, Francis Asbury noted that the ferry from Wilmington to Eagles Island had been discontinued — "the causeway was under improvement" — which forced the famed Methodist circuit rider to detour several miles to the north to take a longer ferry over the river at Point Peter. The Eagles Island causeway remained a work in progress.[22]

After the departure of Washington, the remainder of 1791 must have seemed anticlimactic. Smith persevered, and at the end of the year found himself again in the state House of Commons for a last stint as a representative of Brunswick County in the lower chamber of the legislature. His committee obligations were abbreviated compared to the previous year, but Smith busied himself with county matters — a petition on behalf of an administrator of an estate and the preparation of a bill to change the time for holding elections in Brunswick County for state legislators. Otherwise, his record was spotty. He helped to defeat an amendment to the Dismal Swamp Canal statute of the previous legislature and seconded a successful bill to divide Dobbs County (into Lenoir and Glasgow counties) but fell into the minority in efforts to reform the county courts and to alter the remuneration of legislators.[23]

Smith also lost the ongoing battle against locating the state capital in Wake County. Two close votes in the House of Commons finally paved the way for the implementation of the directive of the Hillsborough Convention in 1788 that gave birth to Raleigh. Nineteen members of the House lodged a formal protest, though Smith, who more gracefully conceded defeat, was not among them. The dissentients could not resist a final venting of their outrage. Claiming that the Hillsborough ordinance had been secured by the efforts of "some artful, assiduous and designing men," the opposition railed against wasting the public's money to build a new capital in a place that never could rise "in reputation above a poor indigent catch penny village," when buildings "comfortable in their construction," and "conveniently situated for the reception for the General Assembly" already existed in Fayetteville.[24]

As customary, during the legislative session the board of trustees of the incipient university, many of whom were members of the General Assembly, met in the evenings. Funding remained a principal concern. And the trustees addressed the complicated situation presented by Smith's donation of 20,000 acres of land which lay within a cession to the Chickasaw nation in 1786 by asking the state legislature for compensation for the ceded lands. The surviving partners of the Richard Henderson Company, whose company had been granted 200,000 acres by North Carolina in 1783, only to find title to their land threatened by subsequent federal treaties with the Chickasaw and Cherokee nations, also petitioned for relief, apparently working with the university. The petitions, presented to the state legislature, were referred to Congress where they languished.[25]

Yet the institution needed funds immediately if it were to become a reality. Unclaimed land warrants and Smith's bountiful gift of land in the west, as Kemp P. Battle, a future university president, so aptly wrote in an oft-quoted phrase, were "for years to the University like the cool waters near the parched lips of Tantalus." In the legislative session of 1791 Davie led a successful charge to secure a loan from the state of $10,000. Archibald D. Murphey, one of the early graduates of the university, wrote some thirty years later that he was present when Davie made his plea for funds, and in the House of Commons "he had no rival and upon all great questions which came before that body[.] [H]is eloquence was irresistible." Later the loan was converted into a gift, "the only appropriation made to the university from tax funds until after the Civil War," according to historian William D. Snider.[26]

When not engaged in state affairs Smith tended to local matters in Brunswick County as justice of the county court. Typically, through the years he showed admirable dedication to his position. Extant minutes of the proceedings of the court in 1792 reveal not only his presence at the quarterly sessions but his input into various decisions made by the justices. In 1792 the court continued to appoint him to return the list of taxable property in the North West District of the county to the sheriff so that poll and property taxes for the county and state might be collected. Customarily, Smith proved tardy in making the returns. In this instance he placed the blame on a constable who had refused to serve in that capacity and thus had not provided the information necessary for Smith to compile the tax list. Otherwise, the justices' concerns ranged from the annual election of a sheriff and probate matters to approving the manumission of slaves, and appointing commissioners to repair the courthouse, clear Town Creek, and build bridges over Town, Allen's, and Orton creeks.[27]

Late in 1792 North Carolina participated in its first presidential election. It was a non-contest in which George Washington reluctantly offered for a second term in office, a decision that he came to regret, given the political recriminations later in the decade that left no man's reputation untouched, even that of the president. Smith, an elector from the Wilmington District, joined fellow electors across the state in a unanimous vote for Washington, whose tour through the state the preceding year had only reinforced confidence in the great man. The vice presidency was another matter. Critical of the elitist ideas of New Englander John Adams, which seemed at odds with republican government, and leery of entrusting leadership of the Senate — by way of the vice president — too long to one individual, particularly one who advocated closed sessions of that body, the North Carolina electoral vote swung unanimously to New Yorker George Clinton.[28]

The presidential election portended another session of the North Carolina General Assembly — frequent elections in the early years of the country being deemed a hallmark of republican government in the sense that representatives were more likely to reflect and respond to the interests of their constituents. Smith, in 1792, reappeared but in the Senate. As in the House of Commons, strict rules governed decorum and the proceedings. All but Quakers removed their hats upon entering the chamber. One spoke after recognition by the speaker of the Senate and then only from his desk. Walking between one who held the floor and the speaker of the Senate was forbidden as were interruptions of anyone declaiming before the upper house. Banned were "personal reflections" and "heats or animosities"; nonetheless, untoward remarks on the floor of the Senate might subject one to the censure of that body. Regulations governed the order of business, the presentation of bills, resolutions, and reports, the submission of motions and seconds, and discussion. Upon adjournment, the speaker of the Senate preceded all from the chamber. Smith came to know well the rules of the day and appreciated them in the years to follow when he served as speaker of the Senate.[29]

Smith, though present on the first day of the legislative session, showed his usual anxiety about lengthy commitments and received permission later to depart before the session ended. While he was present, the legislature replaced United States senator Samuel Johnston with retiring governor Alexander

Martin of Rockingham County in what appeared to be the result of an alliance between the western and Cape Fear sections of the state against the northeast. Lingering resentment over the location of the state capital, perhaps even hopes of reversing that decision, helped to explain the comradeship. The same alliance appeared responsible for a plan to redistrict the state for purposes of congressional elections in a manner that favored the western counties and the Cape Fear region. Meanwhile, during the discussion of a replacement for Martin the Senate added Smith's name to list of gubernatorial nominees. While the action must have pleased Smith, his time had yet to come.[30]

Starting over in the Senate, Smith was less active initially than he had been in the House of Commons. Still, he obtained appointments to committees to consider public bills, the debt of the state, and, importantly, finance. Most significantly, he evidenced a consuming interest in the militia, a hobby horse that he rode for the remainder of his public career. Smith originated legislation to establish and regulate the state militia according to guidelines set by Congress in its Uniform Militia Act of May 1792. While President George Washington mulled over the possibility of a national militia in December 1789, and Secretary of War Henry Knox the following month submitted to Congress a communication of the subject for consideration, the national legislature failed to act until the disastrous defeat suffered by Arthur St. Clair in the Northwest Territory in November 1791. Even then fears of an expanded, standing army led to a watered-down enactment of the original proposals by Knox (and Washington) who envisioned a truly national militia. The Uniform Militia Act of 1792 required all men aged eighteen to forty-five to enroll in militia units, to provide their own arms, and to be trained according to the procedures developed by Baron von Steuben of Prussia during the Revolution. Implementation of the law was left to the states. Significantly, the law permitted the president to call out state militia under specified conditions.[31]

The Uniform Militia Act spurred all the states in the next two years to conform to the federal legislation. In North Carolina, the reprinting of the statute in the newspapers publicized the congressional measure, and Smith, ever attuned to military affairs, goaded the Senate into action by offering a bill to align the state's militia law of 1786 with the national statute. The proposal was exquisitely detailed, reflecting a thorough knowledge of the home guard. In particular, the bill envisioned replacing the county as the basic unit of organization with brigades, regiments, and companies. Smith's bill failed to obtain final approval but was reprinted and annexed to the published laws of the session "for the information of the people at large."[32]

Perhaps Smith took some solace in the legislation that originated the town of Smithville, named for — Benjamin Smith. Near the mouth of the Cape Fear River at the "old Fort" or "Fort," a reference to Fort Johnston, built to protect North Carolina during King George's War and the French and Indian War, and burned by the colonials on the eve of the Revolution, a number of pilots made their homes in anticipation of directing vessels entering and the clearing the river. The legislature in 1784 had incorporated a town called Walkersburg at that location, which was doubtlessly intended as the seat of Brunswick County, and offered plots of land in the environs to the pilots for residential purposes. The county court, however, continued to meet at Lockwoods Folly and Walkersburg became one of many in a long line of paper towns in North Carolina.[33]

Interest continued in the area, largely among Wilmingtonians, who appreciated the invigorating sea breezes that mitigated the miasmatic conditions that prevailed in coastal, southeastern North Carolina. Led by Joshua Potts and John Huske, a group of petitioners who included many residents of New Hanover and Brunswick counties, sought the incorporation of yet another town at the old Fort. The newer version, to be named Nashton in memory of Francis Nash, fallen North Carolina hero in the Battle of Germantown during the Revolution, failed to secure the support of the General Assembly, reputedly due to the opposition of Smith, when a member of the lower house, who may have been miffed that he was not consulted in the matter. After Smith was informed by locals that his legislative services might no longer be needed if he continued to block the incorporation of the town, in 1792, as state senator, he introduced the necessary legislation — for a town named Smithville. While the name may have been intended to satisfy the vanity of Smith, it has been suggested that one of Smith's fellow legislators, noting the failure of so many proposed towns, like Walkersburg, insisted that this one be named for the petitioner, in effect to deride Smith in the case of its failure.[34]

After the incorporation of Smithville in 1792, Smith and Potts, as two of the town's five commissioners, proceeded to lay off the town into one hundred lots with the necessary streets and squares. By law, the commissioners reserved ten lots for the benefit of the town and offered the remainder to the public by lottery, though limiting the number to any one purchaser to six. A lawsuit followed the failure to pay the purchase price of two pounds per lot. Any surplus deriving from the suit beyond the expense of surveying the town went to the state university, a clause perhaps reflecting the input of Smith. The town commissioners held an in open lottery in Wilmington on March 9, 1793, to distribute the lots. Originally self-perpetuating, the board of commissioners, which was entrusted with the governance of the town, became popularly elected by law in 1801.[35]

Meanwhile, the trustees of the university had achieved substantial progress in converting their dream into reality. Convening in December during the legislative session of 1792–1793, the board approved a decision of their designated commissioners to locate the university on New Hope Chapel Hill in Orange County. The location was ideal — about twenty-five miles from the newly approved capital site of Raleigh and twelve miles from Hillsborough, sufficiently close to urban entities but far enough away to shield students from the rowdy influences of town life, court days, and musters. Moreover, the site lay at the intersection of commercial highways from Petersburg, Virginia, to Pittsboro and from New Bern to Salisbury, rendering it for the times easily accessible. And last, it comported with the desires of trustee James Hogg, a "canny Scotsman," expert realtor, and friend of Smith, who lived in Fayetteville and Hillsborough. Before the Revolution Hogg had brought a boatload of 280 Scots to North Carolina, many of whom settled in Orange County, and Hogg proceeded to convince many of his countrymen to donate land and money for the proposed university.[36]

At their meeting the trustees gratefully acknowledged the gifts. However, President Battle later described most of the benefactors as men "possibly more moved to their generosity by the hope of increasing the value of the broad acres retained by them than by love of letters and far-seeing patriotism." The trustees placed Smith on a committee to plan the buildings of the university, though all agreed that the limited funds available restricted their ability to obtain plant and equipment. The board also accepted what apparently was the first book acquired for the future university library, housed ultimately in a building named for Benjamin Smith. The work by Bishop Thomas Wilson, D. D., one of several given to the Congress of the United States in 1785 by Wilson's son for distribution to the states, was destined for North Carolina, "when the wisdom of the Legislature ... shall have caused a college or University to be erected in the State."[37]

CHAPTER 6

GENERAL

Life for Smith was not dulled entirely by musings over the militia, politics, or education. The young planter converted his island, the Cape or Bald Head Island, into a personal refuge as well as a scene for lively social parties for approved guests. Bald Head Island presented to North Carolina a unique subtropical climate that supported flora, including palmettos, largely not found on the coastal mainland above South Carolina. Its varied ecological zones ranged from interior maritime forest of live oak, cedar, and cabbage trees, to sand ridges, ocean beaches, and sandbars that morphed into the perilous Frying Pan Shoals off the coast.[1]

Enjoying the flora and fauna of Bald Head Island before the designs of man so considerably altered its pristine nature was Smith, who as early as 1793 had constructed and occupied a summer retreat on Bald Head. Called Sea Castle, the house was hardly impressive, representing a clapboard structure, the forerunner of the beach cottages that began to dot Nags Head and the Outer Banks by the late nineteenth century. A sketch of the island, drawn after 1817, shows Sea Castle located on the west end of the island. The drawing also shows another house, owned by one S. Springs, who may have enjoyed a grandfathered arrangement with William Dry, a shipyard on Cape Creek (currently Bald Head Creek), and the location of the two lighthouses that eventually were erected on Bald Head Island.[2]

As Smith divided his time among Sea Castle, Belvedere, and Wilmington wherein he owned several lots, buildings, and houses, he also attended the Brunswick County court at Lockwoods Folly during the months of January, April, July, and October in 1793. In addition to the usual responsibilities of the bench, Smith was tapped to serve as a juror at the Wilmington District Court and again to make the list of taxable persons in the North West District of the county. With other justices of the peace, he determined county taxes — in 1793, an imposition of one shilling per taxable and four shillings per one hundred acres of property. Given his property and slave holdings, single-

Coastal scene, Bald Head Island, 1939. Courtesy of State Archives, Office of Archives and History, Raleigh.

handedly he underwrote a goodly portion of the expenses of the county. And public fiscal responsibilities rose in the aftermath of the Revolution. In April the court decided that erecting a bridge over Livingston Creek was too demanding for the local road companies (and perhaps beyond their engineering skills as well), and appointed Smith among others as a committee to contract with workmen to build the bridge at county expense. That practice had become increasingly popular among North Carolina's counties since the mid-eighteenth century.[3]

Halcyon days on Bald Head Island and the prospect of building bridges in Brunswick County, however, gave way to yet another war in Europe that quickly reached across the Atlantic to engage the attention of the United States, the Lower Cape Fear, and Benjamin Smith. As the French Revolution proceeded from the storming of the Bastille, the Gauls beheaded the king and queen in 1793, proclaimed a republic, and declared war on Great Britain in an almost endless exercise of which the two countries seemed never to tire. In the process France sought to align itself with the United States, reminding its former ally of the American Revolution of the Treaty of Alliance of 1778 by which each country had agreed to extend military assistance to the other in time of need. The French government in 1793 dispatched a special minister, Citizen Edmond Genet, to exert pressure on President Washington to fulfill the treaty obligation.

President Washington, fearful of jeopardizing the newly-won American independence (and laying aside memories of the victory of Yorktown in which a French army and navy played indispensable roles), issued a proclamation of neutrality on behalf of the United States. Yet the nation and North Carolina cordially remembered the French intervention during the American Revolution. At the same time, of course, animosities against England lingered. Genet received a warm welcome in the backcountry of North Carolina as he made his way from Charleston, South Carolina, to the nation's capital of Philadelphia in the spring of 1793. Later in the year residents of Edenton sent aid to distressed French in the West Indies, and in 1794 men gathered in Edenton, Halifax, and Warrenton to celebrate French military victories, while the militia in Pasquotank County, "from a just regard for the Rights of Men and the Liberties of the French Republic, wore the National Cockade." And the French cause did not go unappreciated in the Lower Cape Fear.[4]

In North Carolina, Governor Richard Dobbs Spaight, no doubt with some misgivings, dutifully echoed Washington's proclamation of neutrality, but events in North Carolina put the resolve of the president and the governor to the test. While in Charleston in the spring of 1793, the schooner *Hector* of Wilmington was turned over to the French and outfitted as a privateer, the *Bastille*, under the command of Francois Henri Hervieux. The *Bastille* subsequently sailed to the West Indies, captured an English sloop, the *Providence*, and brought the prize to Wilmington. Hervieux dismantled the *Bastille* and converted the more seaworthy *Providence* into a privateer, the *L'Aimee Marguerite*. He then left Wilmington, captured a Spanish brig, the *St. Joseph*, and brought the prize to port in October.[5]

Upon learning of the commissioning of the *Bastille* as a privateer, Secretary of War Knox wrote to Spaight that the matter had engaged President Washington's "serious attention and detestation," and directed the governor as commander-in-chief of the state militia to prevent any repetition of the incident. Spaight reacted quickly, ordering the colonel (actually the lieutenant colonel as the colonel had resigned) of the New Hanover militia to seize the privateer if it appeared in Wilmington. The governor also instructed the collector of customs at the port of Wilmington, who controlled the federal revenue cutter *Diligence*, which was stationed in Wilmington, and Smith, colonel of the Brunswick County militia, to assist the New Hanover militia if necessary.[6]

Although tardy communication militated against immediate action, Spaight expected the New Hanover County militia to intervene when the *L'Amiee Marguerite* brought the *St. Joseph* to Wilmington. To his dismay, the militia failed to respond. After the resignation of the lieutenant colonel of the regiment, command devolved upon Major (later promoted to colonel) Thomas Wright, who could find only four men who were willing to assist in the apprehension of the French ship and her prize. The revenue cutter *Diligence* proved useless, being unarmed and its crew purportedly sick. Nonetheless, upon the rumor that the *Bastille* and its prize were to be seized, pro–French Wilmingtonians notified Hervieux who rushed the *St. Joseph* from port and anchored the *L'Amiee Marguerite* at the mouth of the river beyond the reach of authorities.[7]

Enter Smith. The zeal of the colonel of the Brunswick County regiment was undeniable but circumstances conspired against martial valor. News of the appearance of the privateer and prize in Wilmington reached Smith while he rested at Sea Castle on Bald Head Island. Though facing inclement weather, the "escape of the prize exasperated [Smith] so much" that after three days he hazarded a sail to the privateer, anchored in the river. After three hours, "the river being in one foam with the violent contention between wind and water," not to mention waves that washed "over our heads," he reached Hervieux and ordered the French captain to leave the river. Herveiux refused, claiming the right to take refuge in a neutral port to make emergency repairs to his vessel.[8]

Smith was unable to return home until the following day. Altogether, he declared the experience an "awfal trial," and he was so near disaster that "three (river) pilots in the boat [with him] were perfectly appalled and afterwards declared they had never been in such danger." Smith, though mindful of the peril, was "happy" in the knowledge "that it was in the discharge of my duty." Still, at the time he remembered wishing that his efforts might have been "required upon some service that would have crowned my memory with a more brilliant part than that of being drowned." He perhaps derived some comfort from the eventual apprehension of the *L'Amiee Marguerite* by Colonel Wright and the return of the ship to its English owners.[9]

Recovering at Belvedere from his ordeal, and following the October session of the county court, Smith plodded the familiar road to Fayetteville to join fellow legislators in the Senate for the opening of the state legislature on December 2, 1793. The Senate chose Smith and James Hinton to join representatives of the lower house in presenting the customary address of the legislature to the governor, and then, in quick succession, placed him on joint committees for regulating the militia, finance, and preparing bills presented at the session. Chairing the last, Smith and his committee dealt with varied matters throughout the session. Among its responsibilities was the formulation of a response to Governor Richard Dobbs Spaight's message to the General Assembly in which the governor detailed the proceedings of the affair in Wilmington of the past few months.[10]

Spaight began his address to the legislature by lambasting (as delicately as possible) the New Hanover County militia and Wilmingtonians for thwarting the presidential policy of neutrality and ignoring the governor's directives by allowing the port to be used for privateering. Though the subject of neutrality was highly sensitive and North Carolinians as a whole were doubtless Francophiles, Smith, in speaking for the committee and the Senate, left no doubt about the sentiments of the legislature when he extolled Washington's proclamation as "a new proof of that paternal care and patriotic vigilance which have characterized a life devoted to the welfare of his native country," and lauded the efforts of Spaight, which by some convoluted logic were found "crowned" with "success" in the enforcement of neutrality. While recognizing the treaty of alliance with France, admitting the gratitude due to that nation for its aid during the Revolution, and approving the struggle of the French to establish a republican government, the report declared that threats to "appeal to the public (by Genet)" in an effort to influence decisions by the president "would evince a mistaken estimate of the character of a people who regard order as the essence of civil liberty." The French deserved the wishes of success from the United States but more would require the country "to relinquish its neutrality, its peace, and with them, its growing prosperity," a sacrifice not required by treaty arrangements and "incompatible with the duties which a government owes to its own citizens." In their striking statement of conservatism, the apprehension of Smith and the gentlemen in the legislature over the increasingly volatile situation in France was only too obvious.[11]

Governor Spaight used the contretemps in Wilmington to urge the General Assembly to reform the militia and to consider "the defenseless situation of our ports," given the possibility that "unfortunate circumstances" might place the United States in the midst of the current European conflict. Though the legislature demurred on the latter proposition, at least for a year, it readily enacted legislation to reorganize North Carolina's militia in order to align its citizen force with the requisites of the federal law of 1792. The statute, an abbreviated

Richard Dobbs Spaight. Courtesy of State Archives, Office of Archives and History, Raleigh.

version of the suggested legislation in the previous session, bore the impress of Smith, who labored in committee behind the scenes. It arranged the state's militia into nine brigades corresponding with the judicial districts of the state, which in turn were combined into four divisions. Commanding each division was a major general, selected by joint ballot of the two houses of the General Assembly. An adjutant general, similarly selected, bore the responsibility for implementing the federal and state militia laws.[12]

The chairmanship of the committee to prepare public bills and membership on several joint committees of the Senate and House kept Smith unusually busy but rendered him conversant with various affairs of state. His reports dealt with diverse subjects ranging from the need to protect mountain settlers in Buncombe County from "attacks and depredations of Indian ... savages," and altering quarantine laws to protect against a yellow fever epidemic raging in Philadelphia, to postponing state aid to assist in the establishment of a cotton manufactory and denying a petition by Quakers to repeal laws that prohibited emancipating slaves. Working with committees of the House of Commons, Smith considered proposals to allow wardens of the poor to collect taxes, to find a resolution to the disputed boundary separating North and South Carolina, and to extend jury trials to slaves. Legal protections for bondsmen materialized slowly in North Carolina, but the legislature in 1793 did provide for the trial of slaves accused of capital offenses.[13]

Smith also led his committee in denouncing the recent Supreme Court decision *Chisholm v. Georgia* (1793), which had allowed two citizens of South Carolina to sue the state of Georgia. James Iredell, the eminent North Carolina jurist who had been appointed by Washington to the court, alone dissented from the decision of the court headed by Chief Justice John Jay, arguing that the suit was an infringement upon the sovereign rights of the state. The General Assembly agreed with Iredell, for even proponents of the Constitution in the ratification struggle such as Smith (and Iredell) had promised that the states would be protected from such suits. In referring to that original understanding of the relationship between the states and national government, and adamantly opposing any infringement upon the sovereignty of the states, the General Assembly proposed to its congressmen that they "speedily" work to amend the Constitution. Congress acted with alacrity, sending the eventual Eleventh Amendment on its way to the states in 1794, where surprisingly ratification waited until 1798. The amendment protected states from suits in law or equity by citizens of a different state or foreign entities.[14]

During the course of the legislative session, Smith, as customary, attended meetings of the board of trustees of the university which met simultaneously with the General Assembly. The board tactfully elected Spaight, the governor, to be its presiding officer. On the motion of Smith, it appointed a committee, appropriately including Smith, to report on the means by which land might be conveyed to the university. Previously members of the board, as directed by law, had laid out the university grounds and surveyed a town, Chapel Hill as it became, adjacent to the school. Further, they had contracted for the construction of Old East, the first building, the cornerstone of which was laid on October 12, 1793, by Davie replete in his Masonic regalia as the grand master of North Carolina's Masonic fraternity.[15]

Regardless of ceremony, funding remained paramount for an institution of which the public and many members of the legislature were skeptical at best. On the day of the laying of the cornerstone of Old East, lots were sold in the village of Chapel Hill, at which "all (present) appeared satisfied and content," and, according to the representatives of the trustees, "the amount of Sales furnishes a pleasing and undeniable proof of the high estimation in which this healthful spot is held." Smith reported that the sale of ninety lots in Smithville had produced approximately £150 (or thirty Spanish silver dollars) for the university. The trustees also tabbed Smith among others to represent the board in a meeting in Fayetteville of North Carolinians who owned land in Tennessee affected by the Treaty of Hopewell of 1786. The university hoped to enhance the chances of securing title to its land by joining other claimants, including the Transylvania Company, in what proved to be a legal quagmire that involved the United States, Tennessee, Native Americans, and private individuals and institutions. Last, the board announced its intention to open the university on January 15, 1795.[16]

As the legislative session sped toward adjournment, after more than a month of wearying deliberations, Smith obtained recognition for his faithful support of the government in the French privateering affair along with his intense interest in and promotion of the militia in the state. On January 4, 1794, the two houses of the legislature balloting jointly elected the Brunswick County senator brigadier general of the Wilmington District militia. So elated was Smith that he withdrew from a subsequent contest for major general of the Wilmington or Second Division of the state militia. Thereafter, he was called General, an honorific that he enjoyed immediately.[17]

The General Assembly concluded its deliberations on January 11, 1794, too late for Smith to attend the January session of the Brunswick County Court that began on January 13. True, the legislature met in Fayetteville, but the necessary travel preparations and two-day trip precluded his presence, even discounting the condition of the roads in the winter. Besides, the legislators had to wait for their per diem and travel reimbursements at the conclusion of the sessions. In April, as Smith participated in the usual routine of business of the Brunswick court, the justices decided to "Class Themselves" for the next two sessions, designating six of their number to attend in July and another half dozen to convene the court in October. That singular experiment as it turned out was meant to relieve magistrates of the burden of travel and public business but given its doubtful ethical, if not legal, animus, it was not repeated. The General, excused for July, appeared per arrangement in October, though he contributed little to the court's proceedings.[18]

Well it was that Smith was not needed at Lockwoods Folly for the county court for the July 1794 session, for in that month he hurried to New Bern with other members of the General Assembly, responding to a special, called meeting of the legislature by Governor Spaight, whose seat, Clermont, lay outside New Bern in Craven County. Necessitating the legislative session was the decision of Congress in May to authorize President Washington to require the states to arm, equip, and hold in instant readiness 80,000 militia whose numbers were drawn from the states and territories according to their populations. North Carolina's quota was 7,331. Service was limited to three months after the arrival at the place of rendezvous; federal pay rewarded actual service. Moreover, the law directed the president to order state executives to insure that state militia not included among the requisitioned were armed and equipped according to federal law.[19]

The minatory atmosphere of 1794 that evoked the martial response from the government emanated from several fronts. Two expeditions to the Northwest Territory, one under Anthony Wayne, who commanded the regular army, atoned for the earlier defeats of Arthur St. Clair and Josiah Harmar by chastising the natives in that region at Fallen Timbers. Additionally, President Washington, together with Hamilton and Knox, felt compelled to deal a blow to an increasingly unruly element in western Pennsylvania, the Whiskey Rebels, by using militia from Virginia, Maryland, New Jersey, and eastern Pennsylvania to enforce the laws of the land. Finally, the United States, caught between the warring powers of England and France, found its neutrality (as proclaimed by Washington in 1793) threatened by both belligerents, leading to speculation that war might be in the offing.[20]

Spaight urged the General Assembly to comply with the request of the president by preparing to detach 7,331 men for service and to arm and equip the state's militia. In addition to authorizing the troops requested by Washington, the General Assembly approved an exceptionally detailed militia law similar to the one that had been shelved earlier in 1792. It was probably the handiwork of Smith. In the debate over the militia legislation the General helped to defeat an amendment to the bill to reduce the minimum five hundred-acre estate required of all generals in the state militia but lost an effort to double the fines for those who failed to attend general and private musters.[21]

Despite the success of the militia legislation, the work of the legislature remained unfinished. In his address to the General Assembly the previous

December, Governor Spaight had recommended that the General Assembly consider fortifications along the coast to "remedy the defenceless situation of our ports" by which "the most trifling privateer might interrupt our commerce and insult our harbours." Rather than North Carolina, renowned for its parsimony, Congress had acted. The national legislature, exhorted by Washington, in March 1794 had appropriated moneys for forts to protect sixteen ports along the Atlantic coast. North Carolina merited two installations — Fort Hampton and Fort Johnston to guard Ocracoke Inlet and the Cape Fear River respectively, the two principal ingresses from the Atlantic Ocean into the state. The latter was destined to occupy the site of the original Fort Johnston, which adjoined Smithville, where the old fort lay "in ruins ... shrubs and bushes obscured the view of the broken walls." Happily relieved of any expense, the legislature in July 1794 ceded six acres of land to the national government for the erection of the proposed new structure.[22]

Guided by detailed instructions from Secretary of War Knox, French engineer Nicholas Francis Martinon supervised the painfully slow process of erecting batteries, embrasures, and platforms for twelve cannon together with a magazine and blockhouse or barracks. Though the structure was unfinished in 1797, an undermanned company of artillerists and engineers garrisoned the fort by that time. The following year the Smithville commissioners leased a lot in town to the United States government for use as a hospital for the fort. In the final years of the eighteenth century, desertions eroded the numbers of the small garrison, and during the war with France in 1799, a critical examination of Fort Johnston revealed its woeful inadequacy, resulting in efforts to enlarge and strengthen the fortification.[23]

While work on the fort proceeded in 1794, federal authorities also undertook the completion of the lighthouse on Bald Head Island. The project had originated in the gift of Smith and subsequent efforts of the commissioners of navigation and pilotage of the Cape Fear River. But those efforts, probably rather far along, were superseded by the federal government, specifically the United States Treasury Department headed by Alexander Hamilton, when Congress in 1789 assumed responsibility for lighthouses and similar navigational aids throughout the country. After North Carolina joined the Union, the General Assembly in 1790 transferred title of the land donated by Smith and all funds collected by the state for lighthouse construction to Congress.[24]

The federal authorities, not unexpectedly, moved slowly. Congress made a relatively small appropriation of $4,000 in 1792 to finish the project, an indication that much work had already been accomplished, and President Washington appointed George Hooper, a Wilmington merchant, to oversee the completion of the lighthouse. On the night of December 23, 1794, the Bald Head light first shone forth, and, according to Hooper, burned "very clear." Unfortunately, the original legislative authorization from the North Carolina General Assembly in 1784 required that the lighthouse be located "at the extreme point of Bald-head or some other convenient place" near the Cape Fear bar, and Smith and the early commissioners had taken their instructions so literally that erosion soon threatened the integrity of the lighthouse. The secretary of the treasury attempted countermeasures but in 1813 the collector of customs at the Port of Wilmington announced that "it had become necessary to pull down the lighthouse of Bald Head."[25]

Realizing the indispensability of a lighthouse to Wilmington, which accounted for almost all of North Carolina's foreign trade at the end of the War of 1812, and whose exports were four times greater than the combined total of the remainder of the state's ports, Congress had already appropriated funds to replace the structure. Three years elapsed without any work, necessitating a reiteration of the appropriation in 1816. Work proceeded with unaccustomed dispatch at that point, and a completion date was set for April 1, 1817. That may not have been too much of a fool's errand, for the lighthouse was finished in 1817 or 1818. At 109 feet above water level, built of bricks coated with cement, and located on a bluff about half a mile from the original lighthouse, Old Baldy, as it affectionately became known, withstood the forces of nature and lit the way for mariners until deactivated in 1935.[26]

At the end of 1794, as the first Bald Head light shone forth, the General Assembly and General Smith, again elected senator from Brunswick County, convened finally in the new state capital of Raleigh. Named for Sir Walter Raleigh, the original capital city consisted of four hundred

Bald Head lighthouse. Courtesy of New Hanover Public Library.

acres within an irregularly shaped one thousand acre tract in Wake County purchased from Joel Lane. The state's commissioners apparently had been influenced in their decision by the availability of water, for nine streams crisscrossed the gently rolling hills that sloped toward Crabtree Creek to the north and toward Walnut Creek to the south. One quarter of the tract consisted of an old field that had been farmed. The remainder was untouched forest. The boscage was as compelling for its beauty as it was daunting for the workmen who faced the challenge of clearing the land.[27]

The commissioners platted the city as a square consisting of 254 lots, four public squares, and Union Square on which the statehouse was commenced in 1792. The immediate sale of 212 lots (the remaining lots were offered in 1795 after appreciation had raised their value) helped to finance construction. Though supposedly proceeding "with vigour" in April 1793, the statehouse was still unfinished when occupied by the legislature on December 30 the following year. Measuring 102 feet in length by 56 feet in breadth, and 43 feet from base to cornice, its lower story contained public offices and its upper floor rooms for the two legislative chambers, committee rooms, and clerks' offices. The statehouse was determinedly functional, "a plain, substantial" brick structure "without ornament, inside, or out." Still awaiting completion when Smith and others arrived, local citizens, few as they were, provided temporary furnishings such as tables and supplies which included candles.[28]

Among the original purchasers of the 212 lots in Raleigh was Smith. Never backward when opportunity offered for speculation, he bought lot No. 175, located only a block east of the capitol. According to a plat of the town in 1797, lot No. 175 contained several structures, among the first in Raleigh. Smith sold the lot to William White, who moved from Lenoir County to Raleigh upon becoming secretary of state in 1798. White soon erected an imposing Georgian-Federal style house on the property. Known as the White-Holman House and relocated in 1985 to present 206 New Bern Place, it is one of the two fine homes in Raleigh that date from the turn of the nineteenth century. The other, Haywood Hall, was built by John Haywood, long-time state treasurer and friend of Smith.[29]

Despite the elegance of the two homes, at the time of the meeting of the legislature, Raleigh was a village in the wilderness. Other than axemen and a few artisans, the first residents and businessmen were mostly tavern keepers, a circumstance characteristic of all nascent North Carolina hamlets and towns. By December, "accommodations" in the capital "exceeded all expectations" so much so that "comfortable boarding could [have been] ... furnished for at least one hundred more persons." Laggard legislators, government officers, and those who had business to transact must have rejoiced. But critics

White-Holman House. Courtesy of State Archives, Office of Archives and History, Raleigh.

remained. One, "an English gentleman" writing to a "friend in England," lamented the isolated locale of the capital, along with the "sorry appearance" of its buildings, where the "necessities of the government, and the groveling dissipation of a few, are its whole support." A rejoinder to that critic suggested that the real author was "a disappointed partisan, who had formerly struggled in the interest of that graveyard called Fayetteville."[30]

Unadorned and simplistic, but actually well representative of republican, if not plebian, North Carolina, the capitol building accommodated some of the first characters in the state, including Smith. The General arrived in time to escort governor-elect Richard Dobbs Spaight before a joint session of the legislature to take the oath of office for a third term. Additionally, Smith assumed the chairmanship of several committees, including that to consider and respond to the governor's message to the General Assembly. That committee actually dealt with multifarious issues that ranged from the need for patrols in Buncombe County to protect the southwestern region of the state from the Cherokee Indians to the proposed eleventh amendment of the Constitution that had been received from Congress. Smith also brought forth leg-

Drawing of Old N.C. State House. Andre de Coppet Collection, Manuscripts Division, Department of Rare Books and Special Collections, Princeton University Library.

islation to create a court of chancery in the state, proposed a bill to amend a previous law for the construction of a courthouse in Wilmington to serve the Wilmington judicial district, notified the senate of the arrival of copies of Baron von Steuben's Revolutionary War drill manual which had been ordered by the previous assembly for the state's militia, and, in a change of character, asked that fellow senator Nathan Bryan have leave to depart the service of the house.[31]

Internal improvements, specifically the improvement of the navigability of the upper Northwest Cape Fear River, found favor from another committee chaired by Smith. The Cape Fear, the most promising of the river system in North Carolina other than the Roanoke, early beckoned to promoters. The General Assembly in 1792 had chartered the Cape Fear Company, a private subscription organization that wanted to render "safe and easy" the navigation of the river from Fayetteville to the junction of the Deep and Haw Rivers, the point of origin of the Northwest. The company needed funds for that purpose, quickly, which it "could easily spare was it in their immediate power to command ready cash." Smith and the committee, "deeply impressed with the utility of such a laudable undertaking," which promised to benefit the "commercial and agricultural interests of the state," not to mention individuals such as the General, recommended a non-interest bearing loan from the state to the company to allow it to finish its task. The Senate concurred.[32]

Meanwhile, Smith and the university trustees held forth when the legislature was not in session. They were particularly busy defining the duties of the president of the institution, systematizing the process for acquiring land for the university, and applying to the legislature for a statute to prohibit gaming tables from being located in Chapel Hill or within two miles of the village to which the General Assembly responded by extending the range to five miles from the university. Anticipating the opening of the university and under pressure from the trustees, the General Assembly in 1794 supplemented the Escheats Act of 1789 with the Confiscation Act, which transferred to the university ownership of all unsold lands that had been confiscated by the state. Despite significant limitations in the latter instance, the two statutes effectively released the state government from responsibility to support the new institution. Conversely, the trustees spent an inordinate amount of time and effort trying to secure title to escheated and confiscated lands.[33]

Ultimately Governor Spaight, president of the board, several unnamed trustees, and a few other hardy individuals braved inclement weather to open the university on January 15 — but without a student. The first of "a long line of seekers of knowledge," Hinton James from the Lower Cape Fear, did not arrive until February 9, who then "in his loneliness," according to later university president Kemp P. Battle, constituted the entire student body for two weeks before being joined by additional scholars, who totaled forty-one by the end of the first academic year in 1795. Many, however, were so ill prepared for a higher education that the trustees opened a "grammar school" to accompany the university in order to provide remedial instruction for their benefit. Still, General Smith must have been proud, for he always entertained the highest expectations for the state university, despite its tribulations and later his own.[34]

For their part, Smith and the General Assembly concluded a lengthy session of lawgiving on February 7, 1795. State taxpayers must have heaved a collective sigh of relief, for they footed the bill for per diem, an annual expense that was usually greater than the appropriations made by any one session of the General Assembly. Yet, in parting, the legislators engaged in a laudable act of self-abnegation. On the last day of the session a House resolution, in which the Senate concurred, prohibited the sale of liquor both in the statehouse and on the public square surrounding the capitol. No doubt tavern keepers around Raleigh were delighted as senators and representatives awaited their per diem payments from state treasurer John Haywood and fueled themselves for their journeys home.[35]

CHAPTER 7

SPEAKER

As Smith made his way home in February 1795, a journey of 142 miles from Raleigh to Belvedere according to his claim for travel reimbursement from the state, he perhaps reflected on the emerging political alignment in the state and nation. In North Carolina, the adoption of a constitution in 1776 to confirm independence and erect a state government had produced a division between "conservatives" or "Cosmopolitans" and "radicals" or "Localists." That division in state politics continued into the next decade, reflected in differences over the national government and exacerbated by the Federalist-Anti-Federalist debate over the ratification of the Federal Constitution.[1]

Following North Carolina's reluctant acceptance of the Constitution, the former radicals, Localists, or Anti-Federalists, gradually gained control of the state. Federalist, actually nationalist, ascendance, embodied in the decision to join the Union, proved a brief aberration. Hamilton's program to augment the authority of the general government plus his efforts to stimulate and diversify the economy by promoting manufacturing, commerce, and banking alarmed small, often poor, farmers who composed the bulk of the North Carolina's populace. The Washington administration's heavy-handed reaction to the whiskey rebels in Pennsylvania in 1794 alienated many in North Carolina, where opposition to the excise tax at least equaled, if not exceeded, that of the Keystone State. Abroad, the war in Europe featuring England and France engendered partisanship principally on behalf of France, while the decidedly unsatisfactory Jay Treaty of 1794-1795 alarmed even friends of the administration.[2]

To dignify the political dichotomy in the state and nation in terms of parties in the mid–1790s is slightly premature, but factionalism became ever more evident and voting alignments increasingly polarized in North Carolina and throughout the country.[3] The division in state and nation eventuated in the adoption of the terms (Hamiltonian) Federalists and (Jeffersonian, also Democratic) Republicans. Federalists preferred an orderly, hierarchical society in which the relationship between social classes was one of mutual respect. They sought a talented, educated elite to take control in a political environment where civic virtue trumped raw self-interest, and favored a powerful central government and diversified economy. Abroad, England, a country exhibiting a nice blend of order and liberty, appealed to the Federalists.

Jeffersonian Republicanism proved quite the antithesis. Advocates of a more diverse, open, competitive society, the Jeffersonians preferred a limited national government rationalized by a strict construction of the Constitution that curbed the powers of the executive and Congress. Riding the coattails of French Physiocrats, Jefferson's appreciation for the honest and independent "yeoman farmer" required a dependence on agrarian pursuits and a healthy skepticism of large urban centers. Doubting the ability of the wealthy to govern in the interest of all, Jeffersonians were willing to trust the democratic experiment to the mass of voters, assuming or hoping that a free and spirited press together with Lincoln's later, and purported, adage about "fooling the people" would guard against demagoguism. And France, sans the excesses of the revolution, promised to be a land of liberty, free of aristocratic elites, repressive churches, and feudal encumbrances.

The Jeffersonian understanding of government foundered in the first years of the republic, and, in hindsight, thankfully for a successful start to the new nation. Though the iconic Washington claimed aloofness from party politics, his obvious sympathy for Hamilton readily identified the great man with the Federalists and a vigorous, assertive national government. When Washington, heartily tired of the growing political acerbity, gladly relinquished the reins of government after two terms in office, an avowedly partisan election followed, resulting in narrow electoral victory for Federalist John Adams, who took office in 1797. Thereafter parties quickly coalesced. The elections in 1800 cemented the party system in the nation and state. In the process, the Jeffersonian Republicans decimated the Federalists in what Jefferson, who succeeded Adams as president, later called a revolution, which relegated Federalists forever to the status of a minority party centered mainly in New England.

Smith's political persuasion was hardly in question. His wealth, South Carolina connections, and religious affiliation inclined the General toward the Federalist Party. Though wealth was not a wholly reliable predictor of party orientation, a powerful national government that guaranteed contracts, promoted commercial enterprise, and provided a secure environment for business endeavors appealed to men of substance. South Carolinians with whom Smith retained contact, notably the Rutledges, but Charleston and Low Country families in general, had favored the Constitution and birthed the Federalist Party in that state. And Federalists in North Carolina also evidenced a proclivity to embrace the Episcopal or Presbyterian churches, faiths that valued order and hierarchy, as opposed to the evangelicalism of the burgeoning Baptist and Methodist denominations which celebrated the individual and evidenced a democracy that led to the inclusion of African Americans in their worship services, particularly in Wilmington.[4]

Smith brought the Anglican faith of his family in Charleston, transformed into the Protestant Episcopal Church with the Revolution, with him to North Carolina. His father-in-law, William Dry, also an Anglican communicant, had contributed funds in 1765 to complete St. James Church in Wilmington. Dry owned one pew in the church; his daughter, Sarah, another. Upon his marriage to Sarah and the destruction of St. Philip's Church and Brunswick Town at the time of the Revolution, Benjamin turned to St. James. Yet, St. James had been desecrated by occupation British forces during the Revolution and services did not resume until 1795.[5]

Nonetheless, the Episcopal Church in North Carolina languished for many years after independence. Discredited by its association with England, disestablished by the state constitution of 1776, assaulted by the deistic rationalism of the eighteenth century Enlightenment, and undermined by the evangelical spirit of the Awakening in the early nineteenth century, the church barely survived before exhibiting a modest revival in the second decade of the nineteenth century. Although Sarah Smith may have succumbed to Methodist enthusiasm as did many Episcopal women in the early nineteenth century, Benjamin apparently avoided both the lure of deism and the Awakening. He became a vestryman in St. James, and helped to resuscitate the church by renting out pews, some of which had been vacant for years.[6]

Freemasonry offered an additional explanation for Smith's political inclination. Although avowedly nonpartisan, more open than previously in its membership following the Revolution, and asserting that "real merit and ability" should determine admission and advancement in the order — features that comported well with the growing egalitarian, capitalistic spirit of the nation, the fraternity never replicated society as a whole. Relatively wealthy, cosmopolitan men tended to dominate the rolls. Freemasonry provided a sense of community and offered networks of cooperation for politically active men. In North Carolina, eighteen of the twenty-six governors between 1776 and 1836 were Masons, including Alexander Martin, Richard Dobbs Spaight, and William R. Davie. Smith, a Mason in utero and also future governor of the state, developed working relationships with those men and other members of the order who served in state government, including John Haywood, long-time state treasurer and lifetime friend.[7]

Although Freemasonry in North Carolina may not have contributed to partisan politics, the order appealed to aspiring men such as Smith, whose uncle Benjamin had served as master of Solomon's Lodge in Charles Town and subsequently as provincial Grand Master of the Free and Accepted Masons in South Carolina from 1761 to 1770, well within the memory of an impressionable young nephew. The historical record recognizes the appearance of Freemasonry in North Carolina upon the organization of St. John's Lodge in Wilmington, chartered by the Grand Lodge of England in 1754, and organized probably in the following year. St. John's, a lodge of Free and Ancient York Masons, revived in Wilmington after the Revolution in 1788. In a reconstitution of the state's Masonic societies, the North Carolina Grand Lodge in 1791 recognized St. John's Lodge as the oldest in the state. In 1796, St. Tammany's Lodge appeared when several members of St. John's petitioned to withdraw from the older lodge, occasioned according to legend by the overindulgence of alcohol by members of St. John's.[8]

Regardless of the bibulous habits of the membership of St. John's, Smith became a member in 1798. In late October a disastrous fire that ravaged several blocks of Wilmington counted among its "sufferers" many of the brothers of St. John's and destroyed much of the furniture of the lodge. The next scheduled meeting of St. John's was postponed due the lack of a lodge-room. Not until the construction and occupation of a lodge building on Orange Street in 1804-1805 did the Wilmington Freemasons obtain a permanent home.[9] The structure, now housing the Wilmington Children's Museum, remains the oldest standing Masonic building in North Carolina.

Freemasonry may also have informed and reinforced Smith's support for education, and specifically his loyalty to the fledgling University of North Carolina, an institution given early impetus by many Masons. Virtue and learning were hallmarks of the fraternity. Education fostered a sense of morality, a disinterestedness or selfless dispassion that many founders of the nation, particularly Federalists as it transpired, believed necessary for the advancement of the republican experiment in America. A knowledgeable citizenry both warded off demagogic excesses and elevated the character of the populace. Hence the founders of the university, whose admission was based on learning and merit, meant to open leadership and civic preparation to a wide range of men. Yet, practically, the prerequisite educational preparation plus accompanying expenses skewed matriculation at the university toward the wealthy, in effect, fostering an elitist republicanism.[10]

The university not only reflected the impress of Freemasonry but early became a bastion of the Federalism. As a trustee Smith was surrounded by a phalanx of Federalists, most notably Davie, the "Father" of the university, which influenced, if not reinforced, his political orientation. Beyond the central role of Federalists in pressing for the institution, Davie, as grand master of the Freemasons in North Carolina, laid the cornerstones of Old East and Main (later South) Buildings in 1793 and 1798, respectively, exemplifying the common practice of Freemasons across the country in the days of the early republic of laying cornerstones to consecrate public enterprises. Moreover, the trustees of the university partially adopted Davie's plan for instruction, which called for emphasizing the liberal arts and sciences in the curriculum as opposed to the classics, hallmarks of the Freemasonry attitude toward an education deemed appropriate to prepare young men for leadership roles in society.[11]

Smith, after leaving the increasingly partisan atmosphere of Raleigh after the 1794-1795 session of the legislature, took his place on the bench of the county court in April — a day late. Exemplary of privileges accorded to prominent men of the time, particularly those with slave labor, Smith had earlier obtained permission from the justices to alter the course of a road near the Brick House in the vicinity of Belvedere provided that he — his slaves — do the work. At the April court the General presented a certificate from the local road overseer that the new highway had been put in proper order.[12]

In the July term of court Smith drove another bargain. The justices, finding that the public causeway, including the landing that led from the Northwest Cape Fear to the Brick House on Smith's property, ran through a tidal swamp and could only be maintained with "extraordinary Care and expense," contracted with the General to construct the landing and causeway — "the legal width and one foot above common spring tides at high water mark and sufficiently tight" — on the condition that the whole be deemed a road district for which Smith and his labor force were solely responsible for ten years. Thus Smith enjoyed the privilege of working his slaves in his personal road district under the direction of his overseer and at his convenience — most extraordinary in the annals of highway construction and maintenance in North Carolina.[13]

A bon vivant insofar as it befitted a gentlemen of his station, Smith may have been at Smithville that July when the officers on station at Fort Johnston, gentlemen of the town and neighborhood, and captains of ships lying at anchor in the harbor celebrated Independence Day with "becoming festivity and gratitude." Under a large awning, designed to offer some protection from the broiling summer sun, the group enjoyed a sumptuous meal followed by the requisite toasts, fifteen in number to represent the states of the Union.[14]

At Belvedere the General and Mrs. Smith also gave dinners followed by balls "to close the evening." Attending one of those galas was young Eliza Burgwin, daughter of John Burgwin of Castle Haynes plantation north of Wilmington, and her escort, Dr. George Clitherall. The latter, known to the Smiths via his family's residence in Charleston, stayed at Belvedere when successfully courting Miss Burgwin. After their marriage in 1802, Eliza and George Clitherall became close friends of the Smiths, and cared for the older couple in their later, desperate years.[15]

Young and old enjoyed sailing, oyster roasts, and hunting. From Smithville daily parties organized to visit Bald Head Island, a three-mile sail, roaming the island and taking in the lighthouse. Sometimes the principals used Smith's vacant Sea Castle for dancing. According to Miss Burgwin, those social occasions were "kept up & render'd pleasant to the young folks by the utter disregard of shew, & undue Etiquette."[16] And their elders were not backward in the enjoyment of the good life. Smith once invited his friend and state treasurer John Haywood, who lived in Raleigh, to visit Belvedere after the legislative session, thinking that social life in the capital languished in the winter months. Haywood could spend time among "Friends below — Dancing, Frolicking[,] Hunting[,] Reading[,] Conversing &c. ... [and] pass 2 or 3 months off very agreeably in our fine climate."[17]

In welcoming George Clitherall to their home on his visits to the Cape Fear and permitting sailing parties to Bald Head Island (presumably without firearms unless approved by the General), the Smiths exemplified the reputation of Southerners for hospitality. Upon dining with the General, Methodist circuit rider Francis Asbury wrote in his journal — an "abundance of hospitality." Explained Eliza Burgwin Clitherall, "There is no selfishness in Southerners. [N]o 'I can't, translated I won't' as a reply to a request for the loan of a Boat, & and a hand — or a horse for a day[.] It was always cheerfully complied with. The Southerners carry out the [Christian] principle 'Do as ye wou'd be done by & this surely is the fullest evidence of the term 'a good neighbor.'" Foreigners agreed. From Maryland to South Carolina, people were "hospitable even to generosity" as opposed to those in the northern states.[18]

General Smith returned to Raleigh in November 1795 to represent Brunswick County as senator in the second meeting of the General Assembly that convened in the state's permanent capital. As usual, the election of a speaker was the first order of business. Only two names were placed in nomination: those of Smith and John Williams of Caswell County. The winner was Smith, who became Speaker Smith. A week and half later, the General in conjunction with the speaker of the lower house sent a letter to Samuel Ashe notifying the former speaker of the Senate and present state judge from New Hanover County of his election as governor of the state. Ashe quickly responded, thanking the legislators for their "free and unsolicited" support and declaring that their "good opinion" of the governor-elect imposed an obligation that could only be acquitted by "a faithful discharge of the trust."[19]

Meanwhile, as customary, the trustees of the university convened for a month beginning November 9. Though not recorded in the minutes of the proceedings, the trustees doubtlessly congratulated themselves on the successful opening of the university. Then they proceeded to consider that all important officer of the institution, the steward, the first of whom was a veteran of the Revolutionary War, John Taylor, alias Buck, "a man of strong character and resolute will, of pronounced eccentricity and grim disposition." The trustees ordered the steward to furnish "a sufficiency of Milk" for the breakfast of each student and a "clean" table cloth every day. In addition to compensation from the students the steward enjoyed the privilege of using timber on university property "blown down by the Winds" or lying on the ground for firewood but (anticipating later environmentalists) was forbidden to cut any tree without the express permission of the trustees.[20]

Smith faithfully attended the proceedings of the trustees, at least until the last week when the demands of legislative business became pressing. Ironically, he served on the committee to settle the accounts of the treasurer of the university, little realizing that in the not too distant future the treasurer would scrutinize his accounts with the university. Smith also joined the illustrious Davie on the committee to consider the need for additional buildings and their construction. After Smith turned his attention fully to the legislature, the trustees agreed to purchase several sets of books for the university, whose authors included Burlamaqui, Montesquieu, and Hume, sought a principal professor for the institution, and appointed several of their number to examine the students at the end of the December term.[21]

With the governor in place the General Assembly proceeded with its usual want of alacrity. Among the business at hand was the need to provide jails in every county, designed not only for incarceration of lawbreakers but also for the "humane treatment of persons in confinement," foreshadowing Smith's future advocacy of a state penitentiary. The legislature also addressed the difficulty posed by pesky South Carolinians and Georgians who drove cattle infected with distemper and other diseases into North Carolina. In addition to animals, the General Assembly sought to protect the well being of the state's human population by authorizing the appointment of a "health officer" or physician for the port of Wilmington, The health officer for the port, the first in the state, provided medical expertise for determining the presence of contagions on board ships entering the Cape Fear River and thereby the need to quarantine such vessels, much to the relief of Smith among other residents of the region.[22]

Slavery, in one form or another, usually occasioned discussion during the legislative gatherings, and often resulted in statutory enactments. Toward the end of the legislative session in 1795 Smith may have received a letter from the deputy French agent stationed in Wilmington informing the speaker that a number of French families and their bondsmen had arrived in Wilmington after fleeing the English island of Jamaica, and sought permission to land the slaves. However, in reaction to the successful slave insurrection in Sainte-Domingue in 1791, North Carolina in 1794 had forbidden further importations of slaves and indentured servants, and in the current legislative session prohibited the introduction of slaves over fifteen years of age owned by anyone emigrating from the West Indies, Bahamas, or French, Spanish, and Dutch settlements on the South American coast. The General, who had earlier opposed legislation that restricted slave importations, acquiesced, alarmed by the West Indian uprising and knowing, too, that limitations on the importation of bondsmen might heighten the value of his many slaves.[23]

As a novice speaker, Smith apparently performed his duties satisfactorily. At the end of the legislative session the Senate thanked the speaker "for that particular attention which he has paid to the public business, and for the able, impartial, and satisfactory manner in which he has discharged the duties of the Chair."[24]

Meanwhile the General moved aggressively in the real estate market, rearranging his holdings in the Cape Fear, speculating in western land, and gobbling up plantations and town properties in Wilmington and Smithville. (Among Smith's acquisitions was a tract of land at or near the mouth of Juniper Creek, which rose in Green Swamp in Brunswick County and emptied into the Waccamaw River, land formerly patented by Patrick Henry of Virginia. Brunswick County, Deed Book, C, 260.) Aiding fellow speculator and Washington, North Carolina, merchant John Gray Blount, he sold 60,000 acres of Green Swamp land in Brunswick County through a third party, John Davis, to Blount, participating in a ploy by Blount to delude a prospective buyer in Philadelphia. From his perspective Smith claimed to have sacrificed the land at half its value because he needed ready cash, but was disappointed his receipt of payment by Davis. Smith thus threatened to seek the money "in a manner that will reflect as little on your Credit as it will be disagreeable to me." Interesting, for Smith soon found himself in similarly distressed situations, many times having to face creditors who dunned in like terms for payment.[25]

Confounding Smith for many years were his Transylvania lands, which he inherited from Dry through Sarah and attempted to sell in order to raise funds to extinguish debts and pay for other acquisitions. The company, organized in 1774 as the Louisa Company by Richard Henderson and associates, including Smith's friend James Hogg, and reorganized as the Transylvania Company the next year, owned some thirty million acres in western Virginia (Kentucky) and North Carolina (Tennessee). After interminable wrangling between Transylvania landowners and the states following the Revolution, the imbroglio was settled. In 1797 the company's Virginia lands were surveyed, becoming the town and county of Henderson, Kentucky, and the following year the Tennessee lands were divided among the owners.[26]

The General tirelessly sought buyers for his Transylvania holdings, which included property in both states, and in the interim relied mainly on Hogg to pay the ongoing taxes on the land. All the while he assured Hogg, for whatever "I am liable[,] the cash will be ready at the shortest notice," words repeated ad nauseum to the General's multiple creditors in years to come.[27] Yet, cash was scarce and most Cape Fear planters depended upon the sale of their crops, principally rice, and naval stores and lumber to cover their obligations. But, of course, the cultivation of rice was subject to the hazards of nature, and, if harvested, the vagaries of the market. To assuage his creditors, the General constantly inflated the prospects of his crop—"the best crop ever made in the last fifty years in the Cape Fear"—and wrote to Hogg that sums "may be uncertain as to punctuality. None as to safety."[28]

By the late 1790s, however, Smith had become engaged in a juggling act to remain ahead of his creditors, an art that he honed for years before succumbing to the inevitable. Writing to one creditor, he observed that Hogg had "been so good as voluntarily to offer [a] stay of Execution for a balance ... now in the hands of the sheriff" and hoped that you will not "press me sooner than I can make sale of my present crop which will undoubtedly be the greatest I ever made by a good deal and perhaps than ever made of rice by anyone." A month later, Smith pleaded to one of his creditors, "you will at least give the satisfaction of saying you will not distress or attempt to distress me before the 1st of January next."[29]

In addition to private debts entailed by his land aggrandizements, claims by creditors of the Rowan estate and the university bedeviled the General. William Dry apparently had been the executor of the estate of John Rowan, a Brunswick County planter. Upon the death of his father-in-law, Smith assumed responsibility for one of Rowan's three daughters, Mary, who never married and lived with the Smiths until her death. Throughout the 1790s and as late as 1812, Smith faced suits from creditors of Rowan, leading to the supposition that he had not well managed the affairs of the estate. The General was forced to borrow from Hogg to cover some of the obligations.[30] He also owed money to the university for escheated property in New Hanover County that he bought from the trustees in the mid–1790s.[31]

In addition to the Transylvania lands, Smith also attempted to sell various tracts in Brunswick and Bladen counties as well as acreage in and near New Bern that had belonged to William Dry. In the instance of the New Bern property Smith, ever the entrepreneur, decided to transform the tract, which abutted the town north of Queen Street, into a subdivision called Drysborough. The tract counted 211 residents in 1830. Two decades later New Bern annexed Drysborough, helping to lift the town's population to 5,432 in 1860, second in North Carolina, but distantly, to the 9,552 of Wilmington.[32]

While Smith sought to unload properties in New Bern as well as in Brunswick and Bladen counties, mainly inheritances from Dry, he added to his landed empire, purchasing several plantations along the lower Cape Fear River — Mooresfield, Chatham, Mallory, and the spectacular Orton. Little is known of Mooresfield and Chatham, but Mallory, situated on the west bank of the Cape Fear about four miles below Belvedere, contained some two thousand acres, including four hundred acres of tidal swamp, forty of which were planted in rice. A sawmill and 160 acres of well-timbered pine land augmented the cultivation of rice. Later in the nineteenth century, a substantial, two-story, eight-room house stood in a grove of oaks, accompanied by the usual complement of outbuildings and slave quarters.[33]

Orton, located along the Cape Fear River about halfway between Wilmington and Smithville, first belonged to Maurice Moore, the founder of Brunswick Town, who quickly transferred the property to his brother "King" Roger Moore, Smith's grandfather. Eventually Orton passed to Richard Quince from whom Smith acquired the plantation, probably in an action of debt, in 1796. To Orton the General added the adjacent grounds to the south of Russellborough, the home of former colonial governors Dobbs and Tryon as well as his father-in-law, William Dry, before it burned at the outset of the Revolution, and, beyond Russellborough, the ruins of Brunswick Town.[34]

Orton contained 4,975 acres by the time Smith parted with the plantation, and justly deserved its reputation as a splendid rice plantation with the potential of producing cotton. More than a functional plantation, however, the solid brick house built by Roger Moore looked out over a meadow to the river and offered a beautiful vista of the river and passing vessels. All around yellow jasmines, wild azaleas, and Cherokee roses gave way to primeval forests, creating an atmosphere of solitude and serenity, at least when mosquitoes and yellow flies did not threaten to devour the enraptured onlooker during the summer season.[35]

The General did not neglect town properties in his seemingly boundless quest to enlarge his estate. He acquired a lot on the corner of Dock and Front streets in Wilmington in 1790 and leased another for ten years on Dock Street in 1799 after the fire. The lease required Smith build a brick house similar to the one that burned in 1798 — a two-story structure with garret and cellar — and to erect two additional brick structures on the property. And in newly-developed Smithville, the General purchased no less than ten lots in 1795, one of which was destined to support a magnificent house — for any town in the state. Five years later Smith sold two of the lots located just east of Fort Johnston to the United States, which were incorporated within the fort's boundaries.[36]

Amid the expansion of his lordly domain, Smith remained faithful to his responsibilities as justice of the peace for Brunswick County. He arrived a day late for the January 1796 session of court at which time he obtained permission from the court for his slaves Bob and Tom Gray to hunt on Mooresfield and Chatham plantations respectively. In April, again a day tardy, Smith returned a list of the taxable property in the North West District for 1795, augmented by an addendum in the July session. The magistrates proceeded to impose a tax of one shilling per poll and four pence per one hundred acres of land, the usual regressive levies that favored the rich at the expense of the poor. The court also listened understandingly while David Gamache admitted that he had bitten off a piece of Thomas Ward's ear in a fight, a necessary public admission for Ward, who did not want to be mistaken for a criminal because felons sometimes suffered the cropping of an ear as punishment.[37]

The October session of court found Smith a straggler once more. In the meantime, Alfred Moore, a cousin of the General, presented a commission from the governor as a justice and took his seat on the bench. When Smith appeared the next day, the court excused him for not returning the list of taxable property for the North West District for 1796 as ordered and allowed him another three months to finish the task. Smith also received the indulgence of the court after the county grand jury declared that the bridge over Hood's Creek was in a state of disrepair. As overseer of the bridge, Smith bore responsibility for the neglect. The justices gave Smith time to make the necessary repairs and the state's attorney agreed not to prosecute the General. When the court met on its third day of the session, only Smith and fellow magistrate Abraham Bessent, appeared. After waiting vainly for a third justice to constitute a quorum, Smith and Bessent at 9:30 adjourned the session.[38]

Following the conclusion of the Brunswick court, Smith, senator-elect as usual from the county, traveled to Raleigh for the opening of the state legislative session on November 21, 1796. Without opposition he was reelected speaker of the Senate and no doubt delighted in the rules of decorum established by the body. Among others, when the speaker took the chair, all rose; senators who wished to speak respectfully addressed the chair and only proceeded with the permission of the speaker; no one passed between the speaker and any member holding the floor; the speaker cast a tie-breaking ballot when the Senate evenly divided in voting; and, upon the adjournment of the Senate, the speaker preceded all from the room.[39] Flattering it was to the General.

During the thirty-four day session of the legislature Smith and cohorts considered the usual array of public matters. The perilous times demanded another amendment to the militia act of 1793. Of interest to the General was a petition by Brunswick residents to move the county seat to Smithville, but that proved premature by a dozen years. Similarly, a divorce and alimony bill considered by the legislature awaited approval in 1814 with extensions in 1827, when North Carolina enjoyed its first general divorce law. To that time, rather than a petition the legislature as required by law for a divorce, most unhappy couples simply parted ways.[40]

On a positive note, the legislature provided for an accurate survey of the boundary between Brunswick and Bladen counties, appointing Smith as one of the commissioners to ascertain the dividing line, though his contribution was moot. Several years later, when John Strother, land agent of the Blount brothers and noted cartographer, set out to survey some Green Swamp land in Brunswick County, he wrote that Smith, who had an interest in the survey, proposed to accompany him "constant." It was January, at the time very cold, and Strother foresaw that often he would be wading through water. Still, the presence of Smith, he wrote, "will have a tendency to lessen the Difficulties, for surely I can not think hard of going where the *General* goes." Strother, in fact, surveyed many North Carolina counties and, with Jonathan Price, produced a superlative map of the state in 1808, on which were shown Belvedere and Sea Castle, "Seats" of General Smith.[41]

Most controversial in the legislative session of 1796 were petitions by Quakers in the Albemarle region who sought permission to liberate their slaves. A Senate committee abhorred the "spirit of emancipation, stirred up by the Quaker societies and others," along with the uprising of slaves in the West Indies, which contributed to "an almost common sedition" among the bonded population of North Carolina. For its part the entire Senate emphatically rejected the emancipation proposals of the Friends, claiming that such efforts were "highly dangerous ... and ought by no means to be admitted, as from the state of alarm and just apprehensions which a respectable part of the citizens labour under."[42]

The Senate mirrored the fears of white Carolinians. Grand juries and justices of the peace in the Albemarle had raised alarms, and insurrections had already occurred in the northeastern counties and the Wilmington vicinity. During the previous summer, a number of runaway slaves in the Lower Cape Fear, including Mat[t]hew, who belonged to Speaker Smith, had threatened plantations and murdered a white overseer. The "banditti" had been outlawed. Some were shot; one was captured and hanged. Before adjourning the General Assembly in 1796 authorized the compensation of owners of outlawed and executed slaves in seven counties, including Perquimans in the Albemarle, and reiterated former legislation restricting the emancipation of slaves.[43]

CHAPTER 8

FRANCOPHOBE

As the legislature labored in 1796, interest in politics, at least in Wilmington, shifted to the international scene. In the ongoing conflict in Europe, featuring England and France along the Atlantic main, the latter nation had taken umbrage at the ratification of the Jay Treaty by the United States in 1795. Ironically, the agreement was objectionable to many Americans, including North Carolina's two senators who had voted against its approval. Reacting to the insolence of a second-rate nation, France stepped up its seizures of American ships trading to England. Further, the French government ordered that any American impressed by the British navy and later captured by the French might be executed by hanging. Opinion with respect to the war changed quickly in the port of Wilmington, where only recently Anglophobia had reigned.

In late 1796, when the French privateer *La Bellona* with a prize larded with sugar and rum sailed into Wilmington, the captain and crew received an icy welcome. A brawl ensued, which began in a brothel where some French sailors attacked Americans with swords and pistols, killing one and injuring others. American mariners in port together "with other loose people" responded by attacking and damaging the privateer, throwing the ship's cannon overboard, and trampling the tricolor underfoot. Peace and order were restored in part by the efforts of the captain and officers of the privateer, and a trial later resulted in the acquittal of all parties charged in the affair.[1]

Still, the damage had been done. In Hillsborough, opinion ran strongly against the French, "who are without reserve called a pack of villains," wrote Charles Harris, a member of the faculty at the university. American captains and sailors from the West Indies complained of insults from their Gallic counterparts. And in Wilmington a theater audience in 1797 so "incessantly hissed" French patriot tunes that the musicians ceased their renditions, but "God Save the King," after an initial mild rebuke, received "general and loud applause."[2]

The *La Bellona* incident, in hindsight, may also have marked the beginning of the downfall of Smith and his empire, at least according to contemporary and later accounts of the General's life. James Read, at the time United States collector for the port of Wilmington, apparently took private advantage of the prize's cargo of sugar and rum which resulted in his dismissal and prosecution by the national government. Smith, who stood surety for the Read as collector, shared the responsibility for reimbursing the government. When Smith proved unable to raise the necessary funds, the War Department permitted him to discharge his bond by rebuilding the dilapidated Fort Johnston, a massive project that challenged Smith's financial resources.[3]

Read and Smith, of course, parted ways. Read, as opposed to Smith, represented the self-made man in America, availing himself of the opportunities offered by a fledgling nation, and by choosing the winning side in the Revolution. An Irish immigrant to the colonies, Read "threw himself heartily into the patriot cause," serving admirably under Nathanael Greene at the Battle of Guilford Court House in 1781. In addition to his appointments as a justice of the peace of New Hanover County and collector of the Port of Wilmington, the latter at the hand of President George Washington, Read acquired a rice plantation and some thirty slaves, no doubt by means of a fortunate marriage to the sister of wealthy planter Joseph Eagles, and dabbled in western lands.[4]

The financial repercussions of the *La Bellona* embarrassment forced Read to liquidate his holdings to pay his obligations to the government and Smith, who, of course, sued the former collector. Read, who over the ensuing years suffered from various ailments, including whooping cough, boils, and fevers, compared his lot to that of Job. For a while, he took refuge in a cabin on land contested by Smith, an abode that Read called "Fort Defiance." After selling his estate, largely at fire sale prices due to the lack of adequate circulating media in the Lower Cape Fear, and transferring much of the remainder to Smith, Read hoped to go Louisiana, being "too poor and too proud to remain" in Wilmington, but death intervened in 1804. Eternal departure, however, did not prevent Smith from pursuing the remnants of Read's estate.[5] The General, however, was unable to make the payments due on Read's deficiency, and thus prepared to assume responsibility for the reconstruction of Fort Johnston.

Shipping from North Carolina ports, mainly Wilmington, New Bern, Washington, and Edenton, bore the brunt of heightened French maritime efforts to interdict trade with Great Britain. Picaroons, or small privateers sailing from the French West Indies, ravaged the coast. Yet anger was slow to rise among North Carolinians, who knew that France offered the best market for North Carolina's growing tobacco exports. And since the preponderance of voters in the state lived remote from the sea, and coastal residents were greatly outnumbered by rural voters, Federalists little benefited immediately from the French depredations. Republicans retained a stranglehold on state politics. Despite a stinging rebuff received by Charles C. Pinckney, the American diplomat to France appointed by Federalist president John Adams, Republicans in Congress undermined attempts to prepare the country for hostilities, preferring instead to await the results of further diplomacy.

As trouble brewed in Wilmington, Smith returned home from Raleigh in 1797 to a bitter, frigid January session of the Brunswick County court. Absent as usual on the first day, he appeared on the second, the only justice, at which time he adjourned the court to the tavern of Daniel Bellune on account of the "coldness of the weather and the openness of the [court] house," a telling commentary on the construction of most courthouses in the state. Smith actually returned the tax list for the North West District, though again late, and probably incomplete because the court agreed to accept addenda by March 20. Before the adjournment of the abbreviated, chilly session of court the General presented a commission from the governor that appointed several men as magistrates for Brunswick County.[6]

Later in the year Smith evidenced his growing seniority on the Brunswick court by signing the court minutes at the end of the sessions in April and July to attest to the validity of the proceedings, an action required by law of the ranking justice on the bench at the time. In April, he served with two other justices on a committee to audit the accounts of the treasurer of Smithville. By July Smith's trusted bondsman Bob had moved to Orton, for the court acquiesced in the General's petition to allow the slave to keep a gun on that plantation to preserve stock and kill game for the family. Finally, the long-standing efforts by Smith (and father-in-law William Dry) to construct a causeway across Eagles Island came to fruition. Designated residents from New Hanover and Brunswick counties met on June 15 and certified that the General had complied with the legal requirements for finishing the road.[7]

Returning to the General Assembly at the end of 1797 again as senator from Brunswick County, Smith was unanimously reelected speaker of the upper house of the legislature. The Senate dealt as usual with myriad matters: approving a petition to spare the life of a convicted horse thief, granting Robert Braswell a divorce from his wife, Catty, and offering a retroactive pension to a wounded Revolutionary War veteran who was largely unable to support his "helpless family" then in "very low circumstances."[8] Of interest to Smith was legislation to aid sureties or securities, who like Smith, for Read, waited inordinately long to obtain compensation from their principals. At the conclusion of the session the Senate unanimously presented its thanks to Smith "for his able and distinguished services as Speaker thereof."[9]

Smith continued to double as a legislator and trustee of the university.

The incomplete minutes of the meetings in December 1797 reveal the presence of Smith and include a statement from John Haywood on behalf of the trustees, including Samuel Johnston, Alfred Moore, and Smith, who had been appointed to participate in the semiannual examination of the students at the university in November. Otherwise, the trustees approved the financial report of the trustees to the General Assembly, delivered by Governor Samuel Ashe, in which the governor waxed more than eloquently on the future of the university, which promised to become "the first of national blessings" from which "the seats within your walls will be filled with enlightened statesmen; your judiciary benches, with learned sages in the law; and divine trusts and pure morality promulgated from your pulpits; and citizens of every class fulfilling their several relative duties of life. Pleasing prospect! joyous hope!"[10]

Subsequent months found the country lurching toward war. After the failure of additional diplomatic advances to reach an understanding with the French or to protect American shipping — the so-called XYZ Affair, Federalists nationwide and in North Carolina were rewarded for their long anti–French campaign. The country girded for conflict, though undeclared as it turned out, and a Federalist Congress augmented the armed forces, including the immediate enlistment of an "Additional Army" of ten thousand and the creation of a "Provisional Army" of fifty thousand men, the latter to be raised in the case of war or when the president deemed advisable. Unfortunately for the Federalists, the Quasi-War generated too little enthusiasm and the party undermined its popularity by the ill-considered Alien and Sedition Acts, a clumsy if not unconstitutional effort to diminish the influence of the Jeffersonian Republicans who persistently opposed the war.

Still, anti–French feeling contributed to a revival of the Federalists in North Carolina in 1798, the high-water mark of the party in the state according to historians, though largely the result of the war scare rather than any conformity to principle. The elections in July gave Federalists a majority in the state Senate and increased their numbers in the House of Commons. According to Samuel Johnston, erstwhile governor and proponent of the Constitution, the legislature was "wonderfully federal, I say wonderful because I never conceived it possible there should be so universal a conversion in so short a space." Johnston, who had retired from politics because he objected to sojourning in the backwater hamlet of Raleigh, relented in 1798, perhaps sensing the change in political sentiment. Still, he could not have been too happy given the obloquy heaped upon the capital earlier in the year by an English traveler who cited its crudeness, lack of commercial opportunities, and want of accommodations as arguments against republicanism.[11]

Adding to Johnston's discomfort, the Jeffersonian Republicans were not totally undone. Although the Senate unanimously reelected Smith as speaker and elected Davie governor on the first ballot, a United States Senate seat, occupied by Jeffersonian Alexander Martin, remained. Martin sought reelection, but having recently evidenced more sympathy than usual for the Adams administration, and also characterized by Johnston as "wonderfully federal," the senator was deemed damaged goods by his party. He ran a distant fifth in a field of five, which included General Smith. The contest for senator, which lasted twelve days, eventually narrowed to Smith and Jesse Franklin, a conservative Jeffersonian and rigid proponent of government parsimony, who was sure to try to thwart expenditures for a war. On the ninth ballot Franklin emerged victorious. Despite the Jeffersonian triumph, the General Assembly voted a "very decent address" to President Adams, approved unanimously by the Smith-led Senate, and by 51 to 38 in the House of Commons, a victory for the friends of the government.[12]

Magnifying Johnston's melancholy in Raleigh was the legislature's failure to adopt his proposal to create a court of errors and appeals or semi-supreme court for the state, which failed in the Commons, along "with almost every other useful act of a public nature." The legislature, however, offered some relief to Wilmingtonians whose town was devastated by a fire on October 31. Coming on the heels of a conflagration in April, the flames consumed three-fourths of the remaining structures in the port, including property of St. John's Masonic Lodge, and left only twelve houses standing. Smith's property apparently survived the first, but not the second, fire. The owner of the house wherein the blaze originated ascribed the accident to a defective chimney, though such excuse hardly saved him from the opprobrium of the town. Fortunately, no lives were lost, though two corpses, awaiting interment, were consumed, the victims of double jeopardy.[13]

Governor Samuel Ashe painted the most doleful picture of the calamity for the legislators. Who could not be moved by the "feeble cries of helpless orphans, the uplifted hands and beseeching looks of the forlorn widow, the weeping voice of the distressed mother, and the dejected and sorrowful countenance of the heart-pained father ... supplicating assistance," asked the executive. Ashe proposed that the General Assembly appropriate a moderate sum from the state treasury for relief. But the governor had not reckoned with the habitually tight-fisted General Assembly. The legislature countered by decreeing that no taxes should be collected on the houses or other structures lost in the fires of April and October or on the lots on which they were situated — for one year, no doubt a relief to sufferers seeking shelter and trying to restart businesses.[14]

The fire also prompted the General Assembly to appoint Smith to head a group of five commissioners to pursue funds that had been allocated for the construction of a courthouse and jail in Wilmington to serve the Wilmington judicial district. The courthouse, centered in the square formed by the intersection of Front and Markets Streets, incredibly had survived the flames of '98, but the taxes that previously had been imposed for its construction had not been collected. Tax collectors for such purposes, indeed, almost all purposes, were notoriously lax, often necessitating the appointment of oversight committees. In the aftermath of the Wilmington fires, Smith, as chairman of the committee, and his cohorts decided to slate the roof or somehow protect better the courthouse from future threats.[15]

No doubt at the urging of Smith the General Assembly in 1798 also authorized the establishment of an academy at Smithville. The forerunners of high schools, academies had appeared in North Carolina on the eve of the Revolution. The first, probably in Wilmington about 1760, was followed by academies in New Bern and Edenton, the Rev. David Caldwell's famous Log College in Guilford County, and, upon the unsuccessful effort of Presbyterians to erect a college in Charlotte, Queen's Museum and Liberty Hall Academy in the small town in Mecklenburg County. Those institutions portended the future, for an explosion of academies followed the Revolution, the result in part of the admonition of the state constitution of 1776 that "schools shall be established by the legislature, for the convenient instruction of youth," the same provision that called for the erection of the state university.[16]

The state took the stricture to heart, chartering forty-two academies before 1800, and a legion more in the antebellum era. The legislative rationale for establishing the Smithville Academy reflected the sentiment of many in the state following independence, including Smith and not coincidentally the Freemasons. According to the preamble of the law, "the promotion of learning deserves high encouragement in a Republic, [because] the safety and happiness of the state depend on the knowledge and morality of the people." Smithville seemed an appropriate location. Its proximity to the ocean held out "a prospect of health and plenty." The "abundance of marine provision" might sustain students "at a moderate expence." Among the five trustees named for the academy was Smith, who became the president of the board.[17]

The commissioners of Smithville, also chaired by Smith, no doubt anticipated the request for the academy. In May one Philip Williams had proposed opening a school in Smithville in which he would offer mathematics, navigation, gauging, mensuration, and surveying. A month before the legislature convened Smith advertised that the commissioners had decided to erect "without delay" a frame house, twenty-four by sixteen feet, to serve as a temporary schoolhouse in Smithville. The commissioners intended to impress the legislature with their sincerity and support for a local academy. Smith, in effect, combined his political influence and municipal office to further the cause of education, which always appealed to him, and to heighten interest in a town in which he had a vested economic interest.[18]

In chartering academies, the General Assembly rarely followed its implied constitutional mandate to pay the salaries of the teachers of the institutions or to provide other financial support. Thus the legislature authorized the trustees of the Smithville Academy to hold a lottery to raise $7,000 for the school. Lotteries, a popular means of obtaining funds for education and promoting enterprise in North Carolina and the nation after the Revolution, benefited numerous academies and the university in the state as well as religious societies, fraternal organizations, and individuals such as one Alexander McCall, who wanted to build a nail factory and ironworks. The General Assembly did not overlook municipal and county governments which needed water works. Corruption and increasing religious objections to gambling, however, later doomed lotteries by the 1830s.[19]

Early in 1799 Smith called a meeting of the trustees of the proposed Smithville Academy to formalize plans for executing the lottery, but not until late 1803 were tickets prepared for a first drawing. In trying to sell the tickets the trustees emphasized the healthfulness of Smithville's location, the abundance of seafood in the area which promised to lower boarding costs for the students, and the potential commercial importance of the port. Moreover, they claimed, Smithville had become a "polite and fashionable resort in the summer ... [whereby] the manners of the students would be polished and their understanding refined."[20] However, apathy apparently doomed the Smithville Academy lottery, like so many others in North Carolina.

While Smith and the trustees of the academy considered the prospects of their undertaking, the Quasi-War with France took center stage. The fear of invasion raised by the conflict with France prompted Governor Davie to investigate the defense of Wilmington and the Cape Fear River. After all, the exposed state of the river practically invited "preditory incursions of the Enemy" as exemplified by the Spanish during King George's War and the British during the Revolution.[21]

The governor's concerns were well founded. Fort Johnston, started in 1794, and meant to guard the river and port, appeared altogether inadequate. Two row galleys in the region were too small and drew too much water to navigate in the shallows of the river. Moreover, the U.S. revenue cutter, which appeared sporadically in Wilmington, posed little threat to an enemy. True, the federal government spent considerable sums of money in late 1799 and 1800, no doubt in conjunction with Smith's agreement, to rebuild Fort Johnston. By that time, however, the war had concluded.[22]

The Americans and French fought their quasi-war on the high seas, and North Carolina was never in danger. Really, North Carolinians clung to an exalted opinion of the worth of their state. Although readily open to invasion by foreign enemies, there was little of value to entice foreign belligerents. The

Spanish needed supplies during King George's War. The British and French later found Wilmington, the only port of any consequence, useful for privateering purposes, illegal as it was. Otherwise, North Carolina's coast and ports had little strategic military value. The Franco–American war concluded in 1800, when President Adams courageously (considering his political future) agreed to negotiations with the Napoleonic government that ended the conflict on a satisfactory, though stalemated basis.

Nonetheless, the war offered a glorious opportunity for General Smith to rattle a saber, in the process being mindful of a bit of self-promotion. As several towns, counties, militia companies, and grand juries dispatched addresses to President Adams, professing their support for the president in his stand against France, Smith determined not to be backward. In August 1798, following the congressional action to increase the national army, Smith transmitted to President Adams an adulatory address of the grand jury of Brunswick County, no doubt engineered by the General. Believing the "situation of our country" critical due to "the ambition and rapacity of the French Directory," the grand jury resolved unanimously, "we are determined with one voice and all our force to support the Government of our choice, and the Independence of our own country against ... any government or nation upon earth, who shall be sufficiently rash or base to attempt a violation or invasion thereof."[23]

At the same time the brigadier general of the 3rd Brigade of North Carolina Militia aired his own sentiments in his orders to men, issued from Belvedere in July. Believing that the United States was threatened "with a ferocious and bloody war," the General required the officers of his brigade to set a proper example for the men by arming themselves and preparing for an early review. "Animated with the pure love of liberty & undaunted spirit of the revolutionary war, which alone can ... preserve the Freedom, Happiness and Independence of our Country," Smith felt his men were prepared to defend "their country and her rights" against all comers. In the commitment of his officers and privates to volunteer for service, Smith observed, "I shall ever retain a grateful sense of their zeal and unanimity in offering to serve under me as their General."[24]

While the General prepared the Lower Cape Fear for a possible French onslaught, President Adams, or at least his amanuensis and the secretary of war, busily replied to the bombardment of addresses from North Carolina and the country at large. Unfortunately, the communication from Brunswick County miscarried. Smith pursued the matter, evoking a response from the secretary of war. According to the secretary, the original correspondence somehow had never have reached Adams, because "the justness of the principles it details, the exalted patriotism it breathes throughout, and the determination it evinces of resisting aggression and injury ... would have left an indelible impression on the President." The secretary included a short statement written by the president to the grand jury of Brunswick County in which Adams noted the "correctness" of their political sentiments and thanked them for their "confidence in me" and their "attachment to the general government."[25]

The seemingly self-serving efforts of Smith, abetted by his conceit and an undeniable display of wealth, exemplified by riding about the neighborhood in a London-built coach and a handsome phaeton, produced a tirade of invective against the Brunswick planter by correspondents to the *Wilmington Gazette* in the late spring and summer of 1799. The criticism, reflecting envy, perhaps personal slight, and antipathy toward South Carolina aristocracy, produced one of the most scurrilous personal attacks in North Carolina's eighteenth century newspaper press.[26]

"Whirligig" opened in April with a double-barreled offensive against both Smith and the editor of the *Gazette*, Allmand Hall. After slyly intimating that Smith had altered the letter from the secretary of war by "additions or interlineations being foisted" into the missive, Whirligig took editor Hall to task for perpetually dazzling "the public eye ... with glittering extracts in commendation of that brittle piece of morality, called General Smith ... dressed off in all the gaudy pageantry of South-Carolina pomp and vanity." Had the "field of literature or of politics been so sterile for six months past" that Hall had to resort to airing "romantic exaggerations of General Smith's prowess and patriotism?" Hall, who theretofore had tried to maintain objectivity amid the growing political contentiousness in the Lower Cape Fear, published additional extracts, including remarks by Gen. William Moultrie in Charleston in 1794, praising Smith. That only served to infuriate Smith's detractors.[27]

The General reluctantly responded to Whirligig whose motive, asserted Smith, was not the public good but "private malice, revenge and the blackest malignity." In a coup of sorts, Smith commended the principle freedom of the press but observed that "every good man must lament the frequent abuse of it, and be truly concerned to see this valuable blessing so often perverted to the worst of purposes." When men of the caliber of Washington, Franklin, and Adams suffered defamation, no public character "down to the lowest order" was safe. Smith defended his actions, claiming that in a time of crisis and in an area exposed to danger it was incumbent upon him as brigadier general to rouse a "military spirit" and then share the enthusiastic response of the men under his command with his fellow citizens. Ultimately, Smith wrote, a man who attempted "to exceed a more [than] ordinary and cold performance of his duty in the service of his country, must prepare to run the gauntlet of newspaper remarks."[28]

Well that the General was ready because the invective continued through the summer. "Examiner," investigating Smith's military career, derided the

General's service in the Battle of Long Island — for which there was no tangible evidence of his participation. Why had Washington appointed Smith an aide — if, in fact, he did? When Washington visited Wilmington in 1791, he did not know Smith and "seemed never to have heard of him." As for Long Island and the Battle of Port Royal, "How had Smith so distinguished himself? "What did he plan, how did he execute?" Should we "imitate a man who suffers opportunities to pass away without improvement?" Actually, Smith exhibited "an uninteresting pattern for our imitation," according to Examiner, and thus "vanishes this gaudy vapour, raised by we know not whom, in the city of Charleston, to represent a hero."[29]

Among other charges brought by Smith's adversaries through the vituperative newspaper campaign were those that related to his later Revolutionary experience. Smith had to contend with his infamous surrender letter of 1780 from Charleston during the Revolution, an embarrassment that continued to bedevil him after almost two decades. He could only declare that the revelations of the letter meant nothing because the British through their spies were well aware of conditions in the town. As for charges that he broke his parole after the surrender by leaving his plantation to go to Wilmington and Charleston, Smith claimed in the first instance he sought runaway slaves, by which he was entitled "as a right under the capitulation," and in the second he obtained leave to go to South Carolina to recover from "a very severe indisposition." And responding to doubts cast upon his patriotism, he refuted the claim that he had no interest in serving his country after the fall of Charleston, noting that his corps had not reformed, and that Gen. William Moultrie, to whom he had tendered his service, had received no active command. Nevertheless Smith had returned to South Carolina to offer his services and entered Charleston upon its evacuation by the British.[30]

The newspaper war wound down in August, presaging the elections for the state legislature and reflecting the true intent of Smith's detractors, which was the determination to discredit the General and prevent his reelection to the state Senate from Brunswick County. In a parting shot, Smith may have had the last word, at least given the availability of extant newspapers. He toured a litany of criticisms that reflected the long-standing, deep-seated animus of some of his neighbors. Smith defended his reputation against charges that he had fled the county to avoid sheriffs serving process, had personally arranged to replace the Brunswick County entry taker with an official more subservient to the wishes of the General, had surreptitiously obtained the rights to the causeway and ferries of Eagles Island, had overworked "an orphan boy, small, sickly and friendless," who labored at one of the ferries, had claimed lands in Brunswick County which adversely affected the rights of other county residents, and had failed to pay the state for lands claimed in Tennessee.[31]

Last, Smith contended with the bane of all wealthy people — his affluence, and the envy of it by the less fortunate. The General dismissed such pettiness. By using his resources to advance agriculture and education, by subscribing "liberally to useful publick institutions" in the state, and by assisting charitably those in need "whilst by the haughtiness of others, they are kept at a chilling distance," it could not "be said with justice, that my fortune is not beneficial to the publick, that I am not an active and useful member of society," or, alluding to but mixing Biblical parables, "that I hide my Talent in a Napkin," he asserted. That succinct declaration summed up well the "aristocratical" sense of noblesse oblige inculcated in Smith by the admonition and example of his family and his early South Carolina milieu.[32]

Meanwhile the changing complexion of international politics disappointed any military ambitions of Smith, for President Adams still entertained hopes of a quick settlement of the hostilities with France. In the midst of the war in 1799, the president responded to a possible peace overture by the French secretary of foreign affairs by appointing a commission to treat with the French government. The American ministers included William Vans Murray, Oliver Ellsworth, and, upon the refusal of Patrick Henry, North Carolina governor William R. Davie, much to the regret of Secretary of State Timothy Pickering, who counseled that it was "important to the state and to the Union, that such a man should hold the reins of government." The president persisted and Davie acquiesced, but not without forebodings that his reputation would suffer from such a risky enterprise. The governor left Raleigh in September with the "affectionate and respectful sentiments" of its citizens ringing in his ears as he set out for his home in Halifax, and beyond to Mount Vernon, points north, and overseas.[33]

Yet, the prospects for peace offered some measure of consolation to General Smith. The absence of Davie vaulted Smith temporarily into the governorship of the state, no doubt a source of great satisfaction to the General and, conversely, disappointment to his detractors. The departure of Davie from the state by the end of October left the gubernatorial office vacant. According to the state constitution, in the case of the death or absence of the governor, or his inability to serve the state, executive responsibilities devolved upon the speaker of the Senate, in that case, Benjamin Smith, until the next election for a governor. Thus Davie asked the General to repair to Raleigh to assume his responsibilities as chief executive of the state. Smith complied, but after a brief visit to the capital in October returned to superintend the continued construction of Fort Johnston.[34]

Meanwhile, doubts arose about the legality of Smith's serving as governor. Some felt that his office as speaker of the Senate had expired with the sitting of the legislature in 1798. That, however, proved unconvincing, particularly in light of the short time span, less than two months, between the departure of Davie and the convening of the next General Assembly.[35]

If the surviving records are trustworthy, the executive office burdened Smith but lightly. The letterbook of Davie contains only one missive that required action by Smith, a letter from Governor Edward Rutledge of South Carolina to Davie, dated October 7, asking that a counterfeiter who had escaped from jail in Charleston and since had been imprisoned in Fayetteville for horse stealing be remanded to South Carolina. Doubtlessly he was surprised to received a response from his "aff[e]ct[ionate] friend, B. Smith," who had contacted the appropriate judicial authority, only to learn that the accused had been sent to Salisbury and confined in a new jail from which there "little prospect of his escaping" while he awaited trial the following March. Smith told Rutledge that "compleat Testimony" virtually assured conviction, but if disappointed felt sure that the accused would be returned to South Carolina under federal extradition legislation. Rutledge never learned the outcome. Failing health at the end of the year led to a stroke and subsequent death in January 1800.[36]

Although the General and acting governor had thwarted his newspaper detractors and secured reelection to the state Senate, the opening of the legislature on November 18, 1799, brought new difficulties. When Smith returned to statehouse in Raleigh but before the qualification of the members of the legislature, ardent Jeffersonian Republican Thomas Blount of Edgecombe County announced his reservation about the propriety of Smith's induction as senator inasmuch as the constitution forbade any person from holding more than one "lucrative" office at any one time (justices of the peace and militia officers excepted). Thus Smith should forfeit the office of senator because declining the governorship would occasion "an interregnum in the Executive office," which Blount though unwise.[37]

The General refused, claiming justice to his constituents required him to take his seat as senator. As he observed, at that juncture his service as governor concluded. Yet upon the election of a speaker of the Senate, which was the first order of business of that chamber after the qualifying its members, that individual automatically became the acting governor until the houses jointly elected a new executive. Thus the interregnum promised to be a short one. After "a good deal of conversation" the senate proceeded to swear in its members, including Smith, who then staved off a challenge from Samuel Johnston, former governor and U.S. senator, to win reelection as speaker by a vote of 27 to 21, and continued as acting governor. At it happened Smith entertained notions of the governorship, as did Alexander Martin, but the legislature settled on Benjamin Williams.[38]

After an unexplained absence from the meeting of the university trustees during the legislative session of 1798, Smith reappeared in 1799. The usual committee work engaged his time, but casting a shadow over the proceedings was the consideration of a week-long student riot that had occurred in the spring of the year. The uprising, a culmination of several instances of unrest on the campus during the past two years, centered on strict campus regulations and James S. Gillespie, the principal professor of the university, who had become personally obnoxious to many of the students. After dismissing three of the rebellious students and chastising other offenders, the trustees replaced Gillespie with Joseph Caldwell, a "Man skilled in the Sciences, of polished manners with dignity in his Appearance & established Character — and also an able professor," who enjoyed the additional recommendation of the approval of the students.[39]

In their December meeting the trustees attempted to rehabilitate the reputation of the university. Damage control included the approval of amendments to an already lengthy and authoritarian list of laws for the general governance of the students. Presented by a Smith-led committee, the additions strictly forbade "all striking, and fighting between students" as well playing bandy and other sports within fifty yards of the buildings, given the resultant damages to the windows and structures. An appropriate ceremony by the university community on February 22, 1800, to commemorate Washington and the ideals for which he stood — liberty, morality, dignity — helped to instill confidence in the university. Despite the efforts to restore order and discipline to the university, opposition to the institution flared in the legislature in 1799 and threatened the very existence of the university in the following year.[40]

The Federalist impact on North Carolina politics declined in 1799, though the reelection of Smith as speaker of the Senate and the election of Williams, a lukewarm Federalist, quickened the spirits of party adherents. So, too, did the decision of President John Adams to appoint Alfred Moore of Brunswick County to replace the deceased James Iredell on the United States Supreme Court. The legislature addressed the usual hodgepodge of matters — prohibiting betting on card games in public houses or taverns; incorporating the (first) North Carolina Medical Society; altering the name of Glasgow County to Greene County in order to punish the mastermind of a huge land fraud in Tennessee and recognize the American revolutionary general Nathanael Greene. Disappointing to Smith, the legislature abandoned the custom of requiring the doorkeepers of the Senate and Commons to precede the speakers of the respective houses with "wands, maces or other equipment" upon entering and leaving the capitol building. Still, upon adjournment, all members were required to remain seated until the speaker left the chair.[41]

Importantly for Smith, the legislature in 1799 brought to a close a dispute

8. FRANCOPHOBE

involving the General, John Armstrong, and the state over money that Smith owed from entering claims to 80,000 acres of land in Tennessee in 1784, a matter to which one of Smith's detractors alluded in the newspaper war in 1799. Armstrong had been involved in a massive land fraud orchestrated by James Glasgow, secretary of state of North Carolina. Also involved were some fifty other, often prominent, men, including the Blount brothers, John Gray, Thomas, and William, the first of whom was a sometime business associate of Smith. In addition to his involvement in the land scheme, United States senator William Blount suffered further disgrace by agreeing to aid Great Britain in a preemptive takeover of Florida and Louisiana. That resulted in his impeachment by the House of Representatives and his expulsion by the Senate, the first member so ousted by that body. Subsequently, the Senate refused to try the impeachment charges, citing lack of jurisdiction. Most of those involved in the North Carolina land fraud, including the remaining Blounts, went unpunished.[42]

Although Smith escaped involvement in the Glasgow contretemps, the death of John Armstrong, entry taker for western lands, entangled the General in a costly controversy. Smith had failed to pay Armstrong for 80,000 of the 100,000 acres that he had claimed in 1784. Located in the western territory, later Tennessee, which was ceded by North Carolina to the United States in 1789, Smith's property subsequently fell within the bounds of land assigned by the federal government to Native Americans. Thus the state of North Carolina could not guarantee title or use of the land. The General Assembly could only advise Smith and other aggrieved property owners in 1791, including those who had paid for their land and the University of North Carolina to whom Smith had given the other 20,000 acres, to petition Congress for relief.[43]

After adamantly refusing to pay for the 80,000 acres, Smith succumbed under the pressure of a lawsuit instigated by the administrator of the estate of Armstrong. Still proclaiming innocence, Smith preferred to work with the state with which he thought he could cut a better deal. And the legislature agreed, preferring the state to receive the money owed by Smith as opposed to the Armstrong estate. Still, questions of the terms of the settlement and interest charges remained. Moreover, Smith wanted to be indemnified against any lawsuits by the Armstrong estate. In addition to trumpeting his gift to the university as a reason for indulgence, the General enlisted the aid of state treasurer and friend John Haywood as well as Governor William R. Davie. The former was as solicitous as his office would permit; the latter wrote favorably on behalf of Smith.[44]

The General Assembly had first considered the matter in 1796 but reached a conclusion only three years later. Accordingly, a resolution of the House of Commons in 1799 called for Smith to pay the state treasurer (Haywood) one shilling for every five shillings due with interest from the time the entries were made to 1796. Upon remittance of the principal and interest the state would guarantee Smith indemnification against suits by the Armstrong estate. In the upper chamber, the committee on finance, chaired by Samuel Johnston, who had been bested by Smith in the election for the speakership, rejected the House of Commons' resolution, only to be overruled by the full Senate. Still, the Senate required Smith before the end of the legislative session to guarantee in writing to the state treasurer to abide by the terms of the agreement, to provide appropriate security for the promised payment, and to release the state from the costs and damages of any previous or future lawsuits instituted by the Armstrong estate.[45]

At the end of the legislative session in 1799, the Senate and the speaker exchanged pleasantries as customary. The upper house thanked Smith for his "unwearied attention to the business of the public"; the speaker rejoined with a "grateful sense" of the "flattering terms" in which the senate expressed its approval of his conduct. Yet, Smith wanted more, some additional, symbolic confirmation of his conduct given the controversy that swirled about him. As the last order of business Smith offered his resignation to the Senate, given the contention over his non-payment for the western lands. As Smith expected, the Senate refused, and Smith, feeling vindicated, relented upon the body's "unanimous wish that it might not take place." The Brunswick County speaker proclaimed adjournment, probably never expecting to return the Senate given his financial tribulations and the turn of politics in 1800.[46]

Chapter 9

Planter

As General Smith greeted a new century, he may have felt some uneasiness over his mounting financial obligations. Still, his landed domain remained intact and his 199 bondsmen not only made him the largest slave owner in Brunswick County but provided him with the labor to work rice fields, pine forests, mills, and ferries that in turn enabled Smith to enjoy the life of a North Carolina nabob.[1] Importantly, too, Smith profited from the companionship of an accomplished and supportive wife, whose inheritance had provided the General with the basis of his fortune.

Though young at marriage, Sarah Dry Smith had received the requisite training needed by young women of her social class in the feminine arts — stylish dress, conversational skills, and polite accomplishments such as dancing — as well as a "liberal education," probably by a tutor. Before the Revolution opportunities for girls (and even boys) in the Lower Cape Fear to obtain formal, institutional training were few. Sarah never failed to elicit the highest praise from her acquaintances. Exemplary was James Hogg's request to Benjamin following a visit by Sarah with the Hogg family in Hillsborough. Tell Sarah, he implored, that "I respect and esteem her highly."[2]

The Smiths had no progeny of their own, no doubt a disappointment to the General at least, who not only appreciated the company of his brothers and sisters but must have hoped for a direct lineal descendant. Nevertheless, Sarah and he assumed responsibility for a number of children. They adopted two orphans of John Rowan for whom Smith acted as executor of estate, sent two boys to the university, and upon the death of a close family friend, Dr. John L. Griffin, in 1805 assumed responsibility for his daughter, educating the child until her "early death."[3]

As the distaff head of her household, Sarah exhibited the maternal instincts so often attributed to plantation mistresses. She had cared for Griffin, the physician attached to Fort Johnston, and Joseph Gardner Swift, commander of the fort, "as if she had been our parent," claimed Swift. On his deathbed, when not reciting the death scene of Shakespeare's "Julius Caesar," Griffin in his more lucid moments bequeathed his portrait to Sarah and asked to be interred in the flower garden of the Smiths' residence in Smithville. There he was buried, joined later by his daughter.[4]

In the process of ministering to her surrogate family, Sarah, like so many women of the time, formed close ties with others of her class, including Eliza Burgwin Clitherall, a generation younger, and Elizabeth Lord. The bonds among such women were profound and affectionate, more especially because opportunities for travel limited their experiences to a narrow world. Just the thought of a visitor could bring tears to the eyes of an isolated plantation mistress. Thus the chance to reach beyond the home to the outside world, in the case of Sarah, the sojourn with the Hoggs for several months in early 1798, must have been exhilarating, if not liberating. Upon her departure the General and she, of course, did not forget the courtesy of leaving suitable presents for Mrs. Hogg and her daughter.[5]

Beyond the social graces and amenities, Sarah was remembered as a Christian woman, one who treated others with grace and who endured the tribulations of life and ultimately death with Christian forbearance. Although raised in the Anglican, subsequently Protestant Episcopal, Church, she may well have succumbed to the influence of Methodism. At the turn of the nineteenth century, Methodist evangelicals, in the vanguard of the Second Awakening, took their message from the countryside to towns like Fayetteville and Wilmington. They found receptive audiences among less affluent whites and especially slaves. The white elite objected initially to the potential challenge posed to the existing social order and possibility of unrest among the bonded population, but their opposition abated once they understood the pacific influence of religious conversion on restive slaves.[6]

Upper class males for the most part successfully resisted the Methodist appeal, deeming the emotionalism and anti-intellectualism of the evangelicals to be unmanly, evidence of weakness associated with inferior beings such as poor whites and slaves. But women of the elite social strata often found Methodism attractive. They had more leisure time and fewer emotional and social outlets than the men. Perhaps they were bored and sought a fulfilling religious experience. Too, like lower class whites and blacks, they were accustomed to deference — to fathers and husbands — and found submission to the church and demands of evangelical Christianity easier to accept than males.[7]

Like many women of the region, Sarah may have found Methodism more satisfying than the staid, sedate Episcopal Church, though her husband remained attached to the church of his boyhood. The Methodists were active in the Lower Cape Fear at the turn of the century. Circuit rider Francis Asbury preached several times in Wilmington, occasionally at Town Creek in Brunswick County, and once in Smithville. He also dined with the Smiths at Belvedere.⁸

Rather than the famed Bishop Asbury, however, Smith turned to Jeremiah Norman, another Methodist itinerant who exhibited increasing interest in North Carolina at the turn of the nineteenth century and eventually preached regularly in the Bladen District or the southeastern part of the state. At the invitation of the General, in July 1800, Norman visited Belvedere after delivering a sermon in Wilmington "to a large assembly of Blacks and 3 or 4 whites." Smith urged Norman to preach regularly in Smithville, promising the minister suitable living quarters while in town, offering to attend religious assemblages with his family, and pledging to maintain proper decorum during those services "by his authority," if necessary — the last a telling commentary on Methodist gatherings, Smith, or both.⁹

Yet behind the parties, visitations, and possibly evangelical fervor lay as aspiring businesswomen. Perhaps caught up in the speculative frenzy of her husband, Sarah ventured into the real estate market. On two occasions, she purchased a combined, though modest, 220 acres of land on Town Creek in Brunswick County. Thereafter, unfortunately, Sarah's involvement in legal affairs consisted principally of acquiescing in the sale of the General's lands to satisfy debts. Still, she clung adamantly to her property, and in her will insisted upon her rightful claim to inherited land of disputed ownership along New River in Onslow County, an area just to the north of New Hanover County that was rich in soil, pine forests, and oyster beds.¹⁰

Wealth failed to protect the Smiths from the afflictions occasioned by the hot, humid, malarial conditions of the Lower Cape Fear. More than once Benjamin complained of febrile discomfort. Writing in August from Belvedere to John Haywood, who with his wife was visiting in Wilmington, Smith claimed that frequent visits to the town had left him with a "violent fever" and apologized for "blunders" in his missive because "my head is much confused." Sarah, seemingly of delicate constitution, was confined to the plantation at the time, unable to go to Wilmington to see her good friend, the wife of Haywood. According to the General, Sarah was "easily overcome by the heat and had not stirred abroad" for some time except to assist one "supposed to be dyeing."¹¹

All recognized that Southern summers and early autumns were "proverbially sickly," particularly in the coastal regions where malaria and other fevers prevailed. A major contributing factor was the cultivation of rice, which not only rendered the air putrid but provided a hospitable breeding ground for mosquitoes. A traveler who made his way through the Southern states and Brunswick County in 1816 concluded that the months of August, September, and October were "remarkable for fevers: influenza, catarrhal and rheumatic afflictions, [which] sometimes occur in November and December." Also threatening the commonweal were the epidemic contagions of smallpox and yellow fever, all too common in the Lower Cape Fear given that Wilmington was the principal shipping center of North Carolina and nicely opened the region to the importation of hitchhiking bacteria and mosquitoes on board incoming vessels. All welcomed eagerly the "generally healthy" winter months.[12]

In the forbidding summer and fall months planters and their families fled to the interior, including Hillsborough and vicinity, where Judge Alfred Moore had purchased a residence, or to the Sound as Wrightsville and Masonboro were called, or to Smithville, which had originated as a summer refuge. Dr. George C. Clitherall practically destroyed his family when he chose to remain on his plantation along the Northeast Cape Fear River throughout the summer of 1809. Thereafter he prudently parked his loved ones in Smithville, and after an unsuccessful venture in rice planting, moved permanently to the town. Lower Cape Fear families erected summer residences in Smithville; others took rooms in a boarding house. They luxuriated on oysters and fish among other marine life, and enjoyed the fine ocean breezes and pleasant society. Frost was the signal to leave the confines of Smithville and return to winter quarters.[13]

Smithville's friendly environs encompassed a population of three hundred permanent residents, a figure that doubled with the seasonal influx of visitors. Beginning in 1801 permanent residents gained a measure of self government by electing their town commissioners. In 1804 the legislature required the popularly elected commissioners to purchase a fire engine and other firefighting equipment and to upgrade the appearance of Smithville by ordering residents to clean their lots, trim all but fruit-bearing trees, and clear brush and weeds. Later, to protect the health of the town, the legislature empowered the commissioners to appoint a health officer to inspect any vessel anchored within six (later two) miles of the town to determine if communicable diseases were on board and to impose, if necessary, quarantine.[14]

While most of the early houses in Smithville were modest, exemplified by the nineteen by fourteen foot structure advertised for sale in 1804, others reflected the opulence of genteel culture and refinement. Skillful artisans built in a simple vernacular style. Yet the houses evidenced an esthetic taste which ranged from elaborate mantels, staircases with carved balusters, and mahogany Chippendale tables and chairs to an occasional piano in the parlor, "manufactured by Broadwood of London, [and] inlaid in the most beautiful manner with brass ornaments." Even the bricks used for foundations and chimneys were imported from England.[15]

The Smiths' residence, as might be expected, stood as the piece de resistance among those early dwellings in Smithville. Though Smith downplayed the house with a "humble Roof & suitable Furniture" in the "little Village" of Smithville, a later resident remembered a "large and perhaps at the time a palatial residence which might have been called the Governor's palace" that occupied "the most beautiful spot that then existed or does now exist on the Cape Fear River." Fronting the water on the corner of Bay and Potts Streets and offering a magnificent vista of the entrance to the river, the imposing two-story white house served as a beacon for mariners who took their bearings by the structure as they entered the Cape Fear from the Atlantic Ocean.[16]

Smith's town house left no doubt about the pretensions of its owner. A grand entrance opened to a hallway that was flanked on the one side by a dining hall thirty to forty feet long and on the other by drawing rooms. A "spacious and highly ornamental" staircase led to rooms above. A large flower garden graced the yard and served for the interment of Dr. Griffin and his daughter. Entertaining distinguished guests from both the Carolinas, the Smiths' reputation for "lavish hospitality and generosity" was remembered many years later.[17]

Life was not always idyllic about Smith's house and the town however. The General, residents, and visitors periodically contended with disorderly slaves and sailors, who in fact proved the bane of all the state's port towns. Wilmington particularly suffered from waterfront brawls as well as boisterous gatherings of slaves in the streets and houses. But even small towns like Smithville were not immune. In 1803, the commissioners of Smithville turned for relief to the commandant of Fort Johnston, whose garrison at the time numbered twenty-seven men, including two musicians and a physician, and asked that he authorize a military patrol to "pass through the streets" and take whatever action might be necessary to repress the noisy and unruly.[18]

Smithville — familiarly known as "the Fort" because it arose about Fort Johnston — also marked the site of the General's halfhearted effort to fulfill his obligation to the United States government by rebuilding the fort. Little headway had been made by 1800, when a visitor commented that the "paltry" structure "would [not] stand many fires of the cannon." Yet, work soon resumed. All the while a small garrison of soldiers continuously manned the fort, much to the delight of the young ladies of Smithville and vicinity. Festivities at the fort included an appropriate memorial service early in 1800 to observe the death of Washington and the annual celebrations of the Fourth of July. Recognition of the Fourth was marked by the discharge of cannon, with rejoinders from the revenue cutter in the bay, a dinner capped by appropriate toasts on the grounds of the fort or at a home in the town, and sometimes more bursts of artillery and a dance in the evening.[19]

In 1804, Lt. Joseph G. Swift, U.S. Corps of Engineers, assumed command

of Fort Johnston. He worked closely with Smith, of course, and quickly became part of the Wilmington-Smithville community, which encompassed the General and "his lady," Joshua Potts, one of the town's founders, John and Elizabeth Lord, and Dr. John Lightfoot Griffin, post surgeon and scion of the Lightfoot family in Virginia. Their congeniality extended to politics, for most were Federalists except for the apostate Smith, and all were "sensibly impressed" by the death of Hamilton in his duel with Burr in 1804. In little more than a year after moving to the Fort, Swift married a local woman and began to dabble in rice planting along

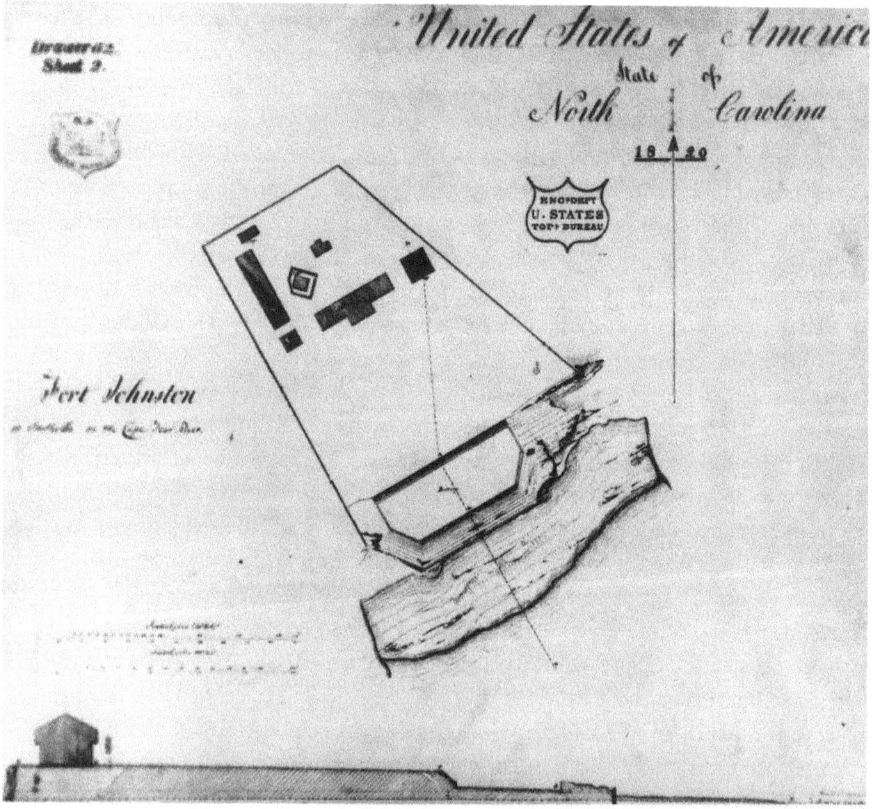

Top: Joseph Gardner Swift. Courtesy of New Hanover Public Library. *Bottom:* Fort Johnston. Courtesy of State Archives, Office of Archives and History, Raleigh.

Rice Culture on the Cape Fear River. Courtesy of New Hanover Public Library.

the river, the latter proving not only disappointing but detrimental to his health.[20]

Upon reporting to the War Department about the defenses of the region, Swift was ordered to finish the work begun on Fort Johnston, namely the construction of a tapia battery. Smith, awaiting instructions, put his slaves to work making the tapia, a mixture of sand, oyster shells, and lime produced by burning oyster shells. The resultant smoke and noisome odor of burning shellfish considerably annoyed the neighborhood. After a trip to Washington, D.C., Smith secured the approval of the War Department of an alteration to his contract for the "more convenient discharge" of his obligation. The protracted negotiations between the War Department and Smith effectively brought work on the fort, little that it was, to a standstill, which was no doubt the intention of the General, who preferred that his slaves work for him as opposed to the national government.[21]

After all, Smith's extravagant lifestyle rested on his bondsmen who provided the labor for his plantation operations and ancillary activities which centered on the cultivation of rice, the money crop of Brunswick County. Planters grew the seed in the tidal marsh along the lower Cape Fear River and its tributary creeks and streams. The rice-growing area was limited to marshlands far enough upstream to avoid salt water and yet sufficiently close to the ocean to take advantage of the tidal flow needed to cultivate the seed and kill intruding plants. The expense entailed by tidal cultivation, which required extensive irrigation, and threshing, either by hand or mechanized, confined that approach to the cultivation of rice to the wealthy, who in turn benefited from the economies of large scale production.[22]

Smith planted rice on both sides of the Northwest Cape Fear River at Belvedere Plantation and later cultivated the seed at Orton, which contained a rice machine and threshing mill. He marketed his crop in New York and Philadelphia. In the latter he had correspondents, "two honest Quakers who never deceive me." Nonetheless, from an always undependable slave labor to the insatiable appetites of the rice birds or bob-o-links, which "toothsome little pests" might devour a quarter of a crop, to the vagaries of the weather and the market, Smith and fellow rice barons found themselves subject to forces beyond their control. "Precarious" and "indebted" described the financial situation of most Cape Fear planters.[23]

Cotton, a potentially appealing crop, was early grown in the Lower Cape Fear, but in limited quantity meant mostly for home use. According to an observer on the eve of the Revolution, "under proper management" cotton "would be an Article of great consequence." A quarter century later, though dubious, Smith was "very much inclined to try Cotton," no doubt impressed by the vigor and profit with which South Carolinians pursued the crop. In fact, those neighbors to the south may have contributed to the "rage" to grow cotton in the Lower Cape Fear at the turn of the nineteenth century. Tidal swamp was unsuitable for the crop, but the General owned "a great deal of cleared high River Swamp" that offered possibilities. Indicative of Smith's interest and perhaps cultivation of cotton was his advertisement in 1801 of a "cotton mill" of the saw-tooth variety at Orton, where cotton could be separated from the fiber "for the customary Toll," an indication that at least some fiber was grown on an ongoing basis in the region.[24]

The presence of Smith's cotton mill or "gin" and others at the same time in Fayetteville and the vicinity of Topsail Sound north of Wilmington, not to mention many in South Carolina, reflected the growing popularity of Eli Whitney's design which had a profound impact upon the cultivation of cotton in the South. Whitney patented his famous his famous "wire tooth" gin in 1794, which replaced the longstanding roller gin, and with his inestimably astute business partner, Phineas Miller, fought off challenges to the new design and secured the rights to an improved "saw tooth" gin. In 1802, the North Carolina legislature purchased the patent rights of Whitney and Miller for the benefit of the state, justifying the outlay by claiming that cotton was "likely to become a valuable staple article of exportation."[25]

Still, there is little indication that many Cape Fear planters vigorously pursued cotton in the early years of the nineteenth century despite the demand of the British textile industry and the increasing presence of gins. A visitor to Brunswick County in 1816 observed that "cotton has been attempted [only] in a small way." Nevertheless, in the advertised sale of Orton eight years later, forfeited by Smith for debt, the Bank of Cape Fear claimed, no doubt hyperbolically, that on the plantation some 400–500 acres might produce one thousand pounds of the fiber. And at the same time a plantation for sale on the Northeast Cape Fear River contained about two hundred acres of land, devoted equally to cultivating corn and cotton.[26]

Other than rice, and the outside possibility of cotton, commercial agriculture languished as planters and farmers relied mainly upon subsistence crops of corn, sweet potatoes, peas, and beans. Corn was a favorite, indeed of all farmers, everywhere, in America. It grew, and usually well, on any soil in any climate, and admitted of many uses. The grain fed humans and animals, and converted to liquor. Corn shucks, if needed, stuffed mattresses, though feathers from barnyard fowl were preferred. Corncobs also proved utilitarian.

For their own convenience and to augment their income, planters erected grist mills to grind the grain, charging their neighbors a toll for the work. The grist mills, fairly simple operations that only demanded sufficient running water to turn a mill wheel, were common throughout the state but required the approval of the county court if used for public milling or if erected on a stream abutting another's property. The General's home plantation, Belvedere, contained a mill, and upon the acquisition of Orton, Smith sought permission of the Brunswick Court to repair the mill on that property where there was a "never failing mill stream." In 1801, his request to the court to put a mill on Judah's Creek in vicinity of Smithville met a favorable reception, because "no grist mill within ten miles [of the town] ... can be depended upon in a dry season," according to local residents. A year later, however, Smith had only one mill in operation, but "4 more very fine Seats on three of which the Dams are already made," However, without a millwright, "*which I want very much*," his efforts were stymied.[27]

Not only was Smith willing to "try cotton," he expressed an interest in experimenting with other crops. Such activity depended upon wealthy planters who not only had the requisite time, land, and labor but who assumed like Smith that such efforts were expected of men of their standing. The General reflected the urge to improve agricultural techniques in the post–Revolutionary era, motivated particularly by his South Carolina contemporaries. Through his service in the legislature and in his capacity as trustee of the university, Smith made the acquaintance of fellow Federalist Henry William Harrington, deemed by the General, "without compliment ... the first farmer in the State." In fact, Harrington had spent the years after his military service in the Revolution in the pursuit of agriculture on his Richmond County plantation and property in South Carolina, in the process earning the appellations "The First Farmer in North Carolina" and the "Father of Export Cotton in North Carolina."[28]

Smith was adventuresome. In his correspondence with Harrington, the General evidenced a desire to plant wheat and barley to ascertain whether those grains might be grown safely or if they took the "rust." He sought to obtain winter oats, vetch, and spelt, the last a variety of wheat grown in Europe for livestock feed at the time. Smith also proposed an exchange of black-eyed peas with Harrington.[29]

Additionally, the General contributed, albeit inadvertently, to the viniculture of the United States and overseas. Huguenots in colonial South Carolina apparently had crossed the Burgundy grape of France with the native fox variety to produce a large, juicy, deep purple, hardy grape that needed no protection during the winter months—the Isabella. The General, on a trip to the state in 1808, obtained cuttings of a vine from Dorchester, South Carolina, which he cultivated in his garden in Smithville. In 1817, Isabella Gibbs, for whom the grape was named, transplanted a vine from Smithville to her home in Brooklyn, New York. That property was soon purchased by Joseph G. Swift, Smith's friend and former commander of Fort Johnston in Smithville, who doubtlessly was acquainted with the grape in North Carolina.[30] Swift proceeded to distribute cuttings and roots of the Isabella to acquaintances in New York from which it spread quickly to Europe and eventually around the world.[31]

Rather than wine, the principal exports of the Lower Cape Fear other than rice were naval stores and wood products. The former industry, based on the extensive longleaf pine forests that blanketed the region, resulted in an outpouring of vast quantities of tar, pitch, distilled turpentine, and rosin whose export contributed to Wilmington's reputation as the world's foremost naval stores port in the nineteenth century. Of the wood products, pine timber and boards, cypress shingles of "inferior quality," millions of which were shipped annually to the West Indies, and to a lesser degree barrel staves, were paramount. But Smith, given his South Carolina background, felt most comfortable with rice. He worked his slaves in the forests, mainly for tar, and secondarily for timber, mainly for plantation needs, but he emphasized the grain for which there was a ready, though always unpredictable, market.[32]

Early in the nineteenth century the General also toyed with the idea of constructing one or more ships in Smithville. Shipbuilding, modestly conducted in Brunswick County along the river before the Revolution, had not revived after the war, probably because it had depended upon timber taken from Bald Head Island, which thereafter belonged to Smith, who was loath to part with that resource. Now, the General, who leased five waterfront lots in Smithville in 1801, thought that his proposed enterprise "might assist others, benefit our little town at the mouth of the River[,] and employ my Resources of Timber[,] plank[,] Jobbing[,] Carpenters[,] & Blacksmiths to advantage." Smith simultaneously hoped to serve public ends and private by increasing employment and heightening property values in Smithville while utilizing his bountiful timber and skilled slaves for profit and watching the appreciation of his investments in the town.[33]

As in agriculture, and even under financial pressure, Smith prepared to dare new enterprises. Diversification, after all, marked the enterprises of ambitious Southern planters. Seeking advice from his fellow land speculator, Washington, North Carolina, merchant John Gray Blount, the General admitted that he had "Irons enough in the Fire & Ship building is a new business altogether to me." Nonetheless, he hoped that Blount, with experience in all facets of maritime commerce, including shipbuilding, might provide the necessary guidance for Smith's leap into the unknown. In the process Smith also considered the construction of a cargo wharf in Smithville, in part to provide a docking facility for his proposed 200-ton schooner and in part to gain experience for a similar, though more ambitious project he planned for Charleston, South Carolina.[34]

Although the shipbuilding project failed to materialize, in the process of making inquiries for workmen in England, Smith became embroiled in a familial contretemps. Some years prior to his planned project, he had contacted a shipwright in England also named Benjamin Smith, who claimed to be a long lost brother of the General. The Brunswick County Smith attempted to disabuse the Englishman of the notion, but gave him some encouragement of assistance and employment if he desired to come to America to work for Smith. In advance of the Englishman, his daughter, or presumed niece of Smith, with her husband and their child sailed to Baltimore and then to Washington, and expressed her hope that Smith would meet and care for them. That forced Smith to respond to his "affectionate Niece" to correct her misunderstanding of their genealogy, but he did send money for their welfare to Blount in Washington, and asked his friend to dispatch the family to Belvedere. The outcome of the tale, unfortunately, is not known.[35]

Toiling in the fields and forests for Smith and caring for the family at Belvedere were the General's slaves, whose numbers comprised 12 percent of the bonded population in the county in 1800. Ditching, harvesting, and threshing rice was particularly abominable work, given the mephitic atmosphere and pestilential conditions of the labor, though working in the pine forests was hardly an improvement. Somewhat mitigating the drudgery and threat to health was task system which was used in the cultivation of rice in

South Carolina and in the turpentine forests in the Lower Cape Fear. As a result of informal accord reached over time between masters and slaves, masters assigned bondsmen a task or specified amount of labor per day. Upon finishing, the slaves might use their free time to personal advantage, whether relaxing, socializing, or tending to gardens, crops, and livestock, which in turn led to a thriving underground economy.[36]

Still, no amount of limited autonomy could compensate for the regimen of forced labor, and more especially the deprivation of personal freedom. Advertisements for runaway slaves peppered the newspapers of the time. Although there is no indication that Smith treated his slaves more harshly than did other slave owners in the region, given his large number of bondsmen, the General predictably sought runaways on many occasions. Particularly troublesome was Mercury, Smith's personal servant, who was "handy and expert" about the house, kitchen, and garden as well as a fine carpenter. Though "very civil and mannerly when sober," Mercury was "insolent and quarrelsome when intoxicated," which was "nearly as often as he can get at liquor." One can imagine constant tension between a haughty master and a resentful subordinate. After two unsuccessful attempts to abscond, Mercury's elopement in 1803 elicited a third advertisement for his apprehension. His quest for freedom remains moot.[37]

Smith's advertisements for runaways reflected the opportunities available to runaways to obtain their freedom. The General offered a graduated scale of compensation for the return of his slaves; in the case of Toney (a frequent delinquent) in 1797, $15 if harbored by a slave, $20 if by a free person, and $50 if taken on board a vessel with the intent to leave the state. Rather than complete freedom, some runaways, perhaps Margaret, "an old wench" whom Smith had hired in Wilmington, and Nanny, "young and small," simply wanted a respite from their life of bondage before returning to work. Larry, on the other hand, may have sought permanent freedom, having departed after he allowed a valuable flat loaded with ballast stones to sink "by his extreme carelessness." Mercury, posing as a free man and a cook, sought to escape on board a vessel leaving the Cape Fear.[38]

CHAPTER 10

REPUBLICAN

While Smith contended with refractory slaves and corresponded with Harrington in 1800 about the prospects of cotton and vetch, he no doubt remained abreast of politics. The revival of Jeffersonian Republicanism in the state threatened to overwhelm the Federalists, whose brief resurgence, occasioned by the Quasi-War with France, had been undermined by their own president's effort to arrive at a peaceful solution to the differences separating the countries. Throughout the United States the approaching congressional and presidential elections found the Federalists weakened by the division between the Hamilton and Adams wings of the party, by conflict between Northern and Southern party leaders, and in the South by the deaths of George Washington and South Carolina Federalist leader Edward Rutledge within a month of each other at the turn of the nineteenth century. As the party system came of age in the elections of 1800, the Jeffersonian Republicans appeared to enjoy the momentum and exhibited a greater willingness to engage in the necessary organization and politicking needed to carry a close election.

Not that the Federalists conceded the outcome, for the party members often forswore gentlemanly independence to attack Jefferson in the lowest and meanest terms, rendering the presidential campaign in 1800 one of the most sordid in the history of the country. In North Carolina party leaders pursued a grassroots campaign, "exerting their best talents and using their most zealous endeavours to save our sinking Country," by appealing to yeoman farmers misguided by an infatuation with Jeffersonian Republicanism. Federalists in the state resorted to the distribution of propaganda—advertisements, circulars, and pamphlets to preserve the "independence of our Country"—and made good use of their newspapers in Halifax, Raleigh, and Wilmington.[1]

Nonetheless, the tide turned. The elections in 1800, as Jefferson later observed, marked a political revolution in the nation. His party carried the presidency, both houses of Congress, and most state governorships and legislatures, in effect relegating the Federalist Party forever to minority status until the organization disappeared after the War of 1812. In the August elections in North Carolina the Federalists lost control of both houses of the General Assembly to the Republicans, and though the party polled a respectable 43 percent of the congressional vote, it captured only four congressional seats, down from seven in 1798. In the presidential contest later in the year the Federalists won some 44 percent of the popular vote and four electoral votes for Adams, as opposed to one in 1796, all in a losing effort. The heyday of the Feds had been meteoric.[2]

All the while Benjamin Smith had considered his speakership in the 1799 legislature to be his political swan song after which he intended to focus on his agricultural improvements and multitudinous properties. Yet he remained popular in Brunswick County, one suspects especially among the members of the militia whose virtues he lauded while extolling his own. In 1800, without overt campaigning and after explaining to the public that his attendance at the fall session of the superior court in Brunswick County would delay his arrival in Raleigh, he was reelected to the state Senate without opposition.[3]

The General was concerned, however, about a debt to the state, hoping that it would not disqualify from him from the senatorship. He complained to John Haywood that a public notice of the obligation was "very unexpected and most disagreeable," and he had hoped that his name would not have appeared on that "hideous list ... altho' there is no more disgrace in owing the Public money than an Individual," and he intended to pay the obligation from funds due from the secretary of war for the construction of Fort Johnston. Still the embarrassment was "galling." Moreover, he asked Haywood if he had "the smallest Idea that my Seat [in the Senate] can be disputed with any Propriety."[4] Haywood's response, if any, remains unknown, but Smith encountered no opposition.

As promised, the General arrived unusually late for the legislation session of 1800 in Raleigh, appearing for duty on December 6, after the session was more than half completed. As a result, he wrote, he "thus escaped the mortification of witnessing much political violence and passion." According to one observer, the political atmosphere was so highly charged "between Federalists & Antifederals (Republicans), that even the door keepers are elected upon these principles."[5] Federalist William Polk denigrated the collective ignorance of the General Assembly which was marked "with a higher tone of Jacobinism than has ever heretofore appeared," and John Haywood complained that he had never seen a legislature "in which there were so few men of talents or of business." Nonetheless, the Republicans controlled the proceedings.[6]

Prior to the arrival of the General the legislators contended with the business of the day. First, after many years of dealing with dirt and grime, they decided to cover the tables of the clerks and speakers with cloth in order to prevent the soiling of papers. Moving to more substantive issues, the lawmakers required all bets on horse racing to be in writing in order to be legally valid. Although the Senate rejected a bill to amend the penal laws of the state, which included the construction of a state penitentiary, a favorite subject of Smith, a copy of the proposed bill appeared with the statutes of the session, indicating the importance that the legislature attached to the matter.[7] On the final day of the session, the always stingy, Republican-controlled legislature surprisingly approved a resolution instructing the governor to purchase two portraits of George Washington for placement over the chairs of the speakers of the respective houses.[8]

After taking his seat in the Senate, Smith contributed modestly to the proceedings. On behalf of one of his constituents, he presented a petition for a duplicate warrant for land purchased during the Revolution. Following yet another revision of the state's militia law, Smith proposed that the public printer reproduce sufficient copies for all militia officers of the rank of captain and above. And on another subject with which he had considerable personal experience, the General suggested a means by which members of the General Assembly might be reimbursed properly for their per diems if they left before the conclusion of a legislative session.[9]

The session of 1800 found the Republicans prepared to follow up their initiative of 1799, when the General Assembly suspended the escheats and confiscations acts of 1789 and 1794 respectively, which offered essential funding to the state university. From the outset critics of the university had complained that it was intended to perpetuate an aristocracy, mainly Federalist. Indeed a motivating factor in the founding of the institution had been the desire to perpetuate the existing social order. One critic of the university, "Ignoramus," avowed in 1793 that the college would serve the needs of the few, while eschewing the majority. By forcing students of modest means to try to keep "pace in appearance and extravagance" with the sons of plutocrats, the university would doom the American experiment in republicanism.[10]

In addition to politics, other factors worked against continued state support of the university. The principle of self-perpetuation governing the replacement of trustees bred conservatism within the ranks and distrust from the outside. Constant litigation by the trustees or their agents to secure title to escheated or confiscated land evoked ire. The misbehavior of students brought denunciation. Claimed Ignoramus, confining young men in close company promoted "vicious habits" that would spread like an epidemic among them. Later one student admitted that "cursing & swearing ... [have] become very fashionable here[.] [T]here can be hardly a sentence spoken without some of those highflown words which sailors commonly use to divert each other."[11] But ultimately, according to an early historian of the university, "the suspicion of being aristocratic, a suspicion fatal to its popularity in the days where there existed among the people a real fear of the introduction of English class distinctions and of a government monarchical in nature, though not in name," undermined the attempt to fund the university at the expense of the public.[12]

While the General Assembly prepared to eliminate permanently the funding for the university, Smith joined a board of trustees not yet resigned to their fate. The trustees drafted two reports — an account of the income and disbursements of the university since its inception, by which they hoped to impress the legislators with the penury of the institution, though at the same time flaunting the progress made with so little money, and a statement espousing the merits of the institution. Both documents were entrusted to Smith to present to the General Assembly. The trustees also offered to negotiate, surrendering claims to escheated lands in return for the interest on the funded debt of the state. But the legislature remained adamant.[13]

Drawing of UNC's first building, Old East, by John Pettigrew, a student in 1797. From the North Carolina Collection, Wilson Library, University of North Carolina at Chapel Hill, copy courtesy of State Archives, Office of Archives and History, Raleigh.

The General met regularly with the trustees, though with little fanfare. He served on the board's committee of appointments, heard a report by Archibald D. Murphey, class of '99 and university librarian, and approved a resolution to draft a list of donations to the school, whether land, books, "Philosophical Apparatus," or other articles. The trustees decided to print one hundred and twenty copies of the list which were intended for their own edification, though no doubt the legislature was a targeted audience as well. Recognizing their gravely restricted revenue base, the trustees also crafted an address to the Tennessee legislature requesting an exemption from taxation on land owned by the university in that state, knowing that such property must "for the time to come, form its principal fund and support."[14]

The trustees were correct. Despite its short history, the university had graduated three classes, beginning in 1798, and conducted an eminent preparatory school on campus, but an antagonistic legislature, depressed economy, and apathetic public combined to undermine the funding of the institution. The General Assembly in 1800 repealed the Escheats Act and Confiscation Act. Although Smith opposed the attack on the university's funding, a number of Federalists in the legislature joined Republicans to overturn the funding statutes, all deeming the university a nursery of elitism, if not Federalism. Although the opposition apparently could not muster enough votes to close the institution, in the words of historian Darryl Peterkin, they probably assumed that the university, deprived of escheats and confiscated lands, would "collapse into a misshapen pile of bricks."[15]

In the aftermath of the legislative session of 1800, Smith found his creditors pressing hard. In apologizing to university treasurer Gavin Alves for not having money that he owed the university, Smith explained that recently he had paid claims owed by the Rowan estate, and had been disappointed in not receiving money from the secretary of war after "a strong representation I sent forward early in April." The General mentioned other sources of funds, and weakly claimed that he proposed to write "soon on the Transylvania business." In any case, he hoped to avoid "the disagreeable interference of the Sheriff."[16]

The General then wrote to James Hogg, his friend in Hillsborough, hoping Hogg might put pressure on Alves, who in fact was Hogg's son, having adopted his mother's name. Regretting that Alves intended to bring his name before the trustees or involve the sheriff, Smith again mentioned "the little consideration and indulgence shewn to me[,] one of the earliest and largest donors" to the university. Though he expected "little indulgence," Smith remained loyal to the university, harboring the "most ardent wishes for the prosperity of the institution which I believe essential to the happiness and honors of the State." However, whether embarrassed or in a state of pique, the General informed Hogg that he would not attend the next meeting of the university trustees.[17]

Smith continued to hope to realize some relief from his speculation in the Transylvania lands as they were still termed. He beseeched Hogg, a fellow speculator and one of the founders of the Transylvania Company, for assistance in paying taxes on his property, promising that he would be ready with cash "at the shortest Notice." Compounding Smith's difficulties were numerous claimants in South Carolina to the same Transylvania lands. A trip to Charleston in 1802 and the most threatening advertisements failed to bring satisfaction. In 1803 Smith admitted that he had "so neglected the business ... that it is difficult for me to recover a train of thinking respecting [it]."[18]

Smith actually had time to contemplate the increasingly intricate web of his financial affairs after his appearance in the state Senate in 1800, which he must have considered his political farewell. The General took a respite from politics, a decision largely dictated by the sweeping tide of Republicanism in the state. In the estimation of the Federalists, demagogic Republicans had used the gullibility of the lower classes to create a popular hostility toward the well-to-do. Politically, the opposition had substituted an unmixed democratic polity for a deferential society and balanced government in America. Although Federalists sought to educate the benighted citizenry through a newspaper campaign early in the nineteenth century, the attempt never moved beyond the planning stage, and a declining Federalist press throughout the Southern states handicapped any political revival.[19]

Nonetheless, the Federalists in North Carolina had evidenced considerable strength in the elections in 1800, and thereafter to the War of 1812 fielded the strongest state party in the Union outside New England. In the process, Republicans, knowing they controlled the governmental apparatus and leveraging their legislative majorities with great party cohesiveness, generously allowed Federalists a substantial number of state political and judicial offices. And the Federalists seemed content to remain a minority party. They lacked organization, having no central committee or state caucus. More importantly, they refused to play politics. As historian James H. Broussard has noted, "The most serious handicap to Federalist success ... was a self-imposed failure to make political capital from promising state issues" such as taxation, funding the university, court reform, a constitutional convention, and legislative malapportionment. The Federalists might have been a more effective minority, but ultimately North Carolina had reverted to its original principles, those of the Revolution and its aftermath, that reflected the importance of individual and states rights, rigid adherence to the Constitution, and fiscal economy.[20]

As the Federalists struggled to adjust to their minority status, Smith sensed a futility in running for office and opted for "retirement," permanently he said, from politics. The General declared publicly that he would not seek reelection to the state Senate in 1801, though did hold out the promise that if elected, he would serve, rendering his retirement somewhat suspect. Although Federalists in Brunswick felt deserted, Smith remained politically active. The following year the General was appointed "president" of the "numerous company" of Federalists who met in Wilmington to observe the Fourth of July (on July 5 since the Fourth fell on Sunday).[21]

After finishing a repast at a table "richly spread with the choicest viands," Smith and his fellow Federalists moved on to the highly anticipated toasts, sixteen in all or one for each state in the Union. After obligatory obeisance to the "The Day," with attendant enjoyment of "social order and happiness," the memory of Washington, the state of North Carolina, and the ladies of North Carolina, the party left no doubt about their political inclinations. The group recognized John Adams; the Constitution; the national judiciary — "May it ever shield [the people] from legislative usurpation and executive violence," a bald statement of the fledgling principle of judicial review; the national credit; the "virtuous and enlightened [Federalist] minority" in both houses of Congress; and freedom of elections, uncontrolled by "demagogues" and uninfluenced by "intrigue." Not forgotten was the University of North Carolina, which deserved the generous support of the state legislature.[22]

Nevertheless, the General may soon have had second thoughts about his political affiliation. As President Jefferson remarked about the Federalists a few years later at a private dinner, "There are many men of high talent and integrity in that party, but it is not the rising power." In March 1803, when Federalists in Wilmington and vicinity hosted a dinner for William H. Hill, retiring congressman from the Wilmington District, Smith was absent. Moreover, the General, who had long evidenced aspirations for congressional office, failed to take advantage of the opening. Rather Alexander Duncan Moore offered for the seat on behalf of the Federalist Party, only to be defeated by Republican James Gillespie.[23]

Smith's return to politics was predicated on his desertion of the Federalists in favor of the Republicans. Writing to Jefferson in 1802, Timothy Bloodworth, the embodiment of the Republican Party in the Lower Cape Fear and flatterer par excellence, avowed "from the sincerity of my Heart" how "Dear" Jefferson was to Bloodworth "as an Individual ... but to your Country eminently so, when I reflect on the precipice to which we were exposed, & observe the Change that has already taken place by the Measures of your Administration." The "Blinded multitude[,] bewildered in the dark error of delution, & ready to subscribe to their own destruction, appear to have discovered a ray of light, to direct their wandering steps from the Gloomy regions of Aristocracy, to the bright sunshine of Republican Government," opined Bloodworth.[24]

Among the blinded who saw the light was Smith, traveling to the nation's capital in January 1804 to rework his contract with the War Department to build Fort Johnston. At that juncture, Bloodworth wrote to Jefferson, proclaimed his "constant, & Unremitted endeavours, to reconcile Youre inviterate Enemies to Your Administration," alerted the president to Smith's visit, and counseled that appropriate adulation might confirm the General's "attachment to Youre Person, & Administration," which in turn would have a "powerfull Influence on all his Adherents" and add "no small number" to the "Republican Interest in this District." Not that "a thousand Enemies" could shake Jefferson's popularity, but the more numerous the friends of government, wrote Bloodworth, the less arduous the conflict in North Carolina, and the more complete the conquest. The record is silent, but Smith returned to Belvedere with a favorable agreement from the War Department, and he soon reenlisted in politics — as a Republican or, initially at least, a non-party man.[25]

Smith moved quickly into the political arena. He sought election to Congress from North Carolina's Fifth or Wilmington District, contesting incumbent Republican James Gillespie and Federalist Alexander Duncan Moore. Claiming no party allegiance, but offering as "a friend to our common county," Smith hoped to solicit votes from both parties. Yet the popular Gillespie was more than a match for his opponents, winning 53 percent of the vote as opposed to 40 percent for Smith and 7 percent for Moore.[26] The General perforce contented himself with another run for the state Senate from Brunswick County.

After Smith's claque in Brunswick carried him to victory in his quest to represent the county in the General Assembly, the General arrived in timely fashion after an absence of four years, appearing on the first day of the session. The Senate responded by appointing him to assist in escorting the governor to deliver his address to a joint session of the legislature, to chair the committee to respond to the governor's message, to serve on the finance committee, and to chair the committee on rules of decorum. Smith and his colleagues addressed numerous concerns of the governor that ranged from surveying the South Carolina and Georgia boundaries with North Carolina and the distribution of the revisal of the public laws of North Carolina to a challenge of the state's monopoly of the Miller and Whitney cotton gin. Smith readily became reacquainted with the affairs of state.[27]

Smith remained active on behalf of his county, his district, and himself. He presented a bill for the regulation of Smithville that called for overhauling the means of electing town commissioners and adding to their responsibilities.[28] Also finding favor with the legislature was his bill to replace the jail and refurbish the courthouse in Wilmington, both of which served the judicial district of the southeastern North Carolina that included Brunswick County.[29] On his own behalf Smith successfully sought title to a tract of one hundred acres of land in Brunswick County which had been surveyed and purchased earlier but for which he had not received title.[30]

All occurred in the course of a relatively uninspiring session. According to one senator, "The business ... has ... been so unimportant that it accords scarcely anything worth relating." Nothing seemed to excite partisanship, and "I think a disposition to conciliate prevails except with a few who are ready to give the *war hoop*." The election of a United States senator failed to stir the legislators. After incumbent Jesse Franklin decided to vacate the office, several offered, including again Smith, Thomas Blount, an old antagonist of the General, and Montfort Stokes. The cloakroom machinations were played to the hilt, but within the Republican Party and without rancor. Stokes prevailed, and Smith remained the bridesmaid in his search for a national office.[31]

Among its other business the legislature, as was frequently its wont, addressed the militia laws of the state, following emendations in 1801 and 1803. General Smith, all the while, was ever mindful of his responsibility in that regard. In April 1801 and again in September 1803, the brigadier general issued orders to the lieutenant colonels of the Third Brigade to prepare for a general muster. Just prior to the meeting of the General Assembly in 1804, general and brigade musters were held at Long Creek in upper New Hanover County, in Wilmington, and at Lockwoods Folly in Brunswick County. In 1804, no doubt at the suggestion of General Smith, the legislature permitted the Brunswick militia to hold general musters at two places in the county, finding it "very inconvenient and expensive" for all to meet at the courthouse at Lockwoods Folly.[32]

Also affecting the General was the institution of banking in North Carolina. The state became the last of the original thirteen to embrace commercial banking when the legislature in 1804 erected two private institutions, the Bank of Cape Fear at Wilmington with a branch in Fayetteville and Bank of Newbern, to serve the principal commercial centers in the state. Agrarians were suspicious of financial institutions, but the need for investment capital and the scarcity of circulating media, which rested on "worn, torn, and suspect" paper money from the Confederation days, rendered banking inevitable. At the outset the banks were poorly managed and flooded the state with paper emissions that promptly depreciated, though that practice failed to distinguish them greatly from most banking facilities in the country with the notable exception of the Bank of the United States.[33]

Upon his appearance in Raleigh, Smith once again attended meetings of the university board of trustees. The General had shown little interest in the university after 1801, perhaps due to his perceived shabby treatment by the trustees. Still, in the interim he had sent two young men to the institution and had participated in the lottery, authorized by the legislature in 1801, to allow the university to raise $4,000 to complete Main Building, the cornerstone of which had been laid in 1798. Not only were lotteries popular in the state, helping to support numerous academies, the members of the General Assembly may have seen gaming as a form of voluntary taxation that relieved the government of imposing unpleasant and unnecessary levies, or, in the instance of the university, a means of avoiding the unpleasant repercussions of the decision to eliminate state funding.[34] The university held two drawings of its lottery, realizing over $5,000. Smith bought sixteen tickets. Wanting "to know their Fate," he asked his friend John Haywood, one of the managers of the second drawing, to balance his accounts, not knowing if he won enough money, if any, to cover the expense of his purchase of the tickets. Despite the success of the lottery, the university needed more funds, and the hapless Main Building remained unfinished.[35]

Though Smith participated desultorily in the proceedings of the trustees in November-December 1804, to his credit he was one of only seven members of the trustees to appear at the outset in an evident show of despair. The last three legislative sessions had considered the repeal of the acts depriving the university of escheats and confiscated lands but to no avail. The current session proved no different. Even a proposed carriage tax, the proceeds of which would be used to fund the university, failed. Observers contrasted North Carolina starkly to South Carolina and Georgia where "munificent support" was given to their public institutions of higher education.[36]

But the trustees, few as they were in 1804, made a critical decision for the future of the university when they elevated Joseph Caldwell from presiding professor to president (and increased his salary to $1,000 a year). Though slightly built, Caldwell exhibited a "sinewy physique," and thought it "not undignified to engage in a wrestle or race with midnight [student] disturbers." Whether by his discipline, classical curriculum, or his fundraising efforts, Caldwell proved to be the salvation of the university. Due largely to his personal solicitations, which evoked generous contributions by Smith and others in a fundraising campaign between 1809 and 1811, sufficient money was raised to finish the construction of Main Building in 1814, relieving the pressure on East Building where fifty-six students were "huddled together with their trunks, beds, tables, chairs, books and clothes into 14 little rooms which by the excessive heat of summer are enough to stifle them and in the winter scarcely admit them to sit around the fireplace."[37]

As usual, Smith sought and obtained permission to leave the legislative session early, but in a shift of endurance the General managed to stay to the end. Thus he had the opportunity to offer a successful joint resolution of the General Assembly to instruct North Carolina's congressional representatives to seek an amendment to the Constitution to prohibit the further importation of slaves or "people of color" into the United States, a proposal that failed to gain traction in the national government for another three years.[38] And in the last order of business in the legislative session, Smith voted with a decided majority in the Senate to approve another joint resolution that expressed "the highest confidence in the integrity, abilities and republicanism" of the Jefferson administration — an indication of Smith's conversion to Republicanism — and lauded the president for his "wise, pacific and honourable measures" to acquire the Louisiana Territory, which not only thwarted British ambitions in the West but also doubled the size of the American experiment in democracy.[39]

CHAPTER 11

DUELIST

Smith returned to Belvedere at the conclusion of the 1804 session of the General Assembly to enjoy his customary respite between his responsibilities as a legislator and a justice of the Brunswick County court. When the county justices met in Lockwoods Folly in January 1805, he delivered copies of the public laws to the court according to a directive by the legislature. He also assumed responsibility as usual for compiling the tax list for the Northwest District of the county. Otherwise, both in January and again in April he participated marginally in the business of the court, which included serving on a commission with fellow magistrate Maurice Moore to divide the estate of a deceased county resident in order that the property might be distributed among the heirs.[1]

At the conclusion of the April court the General prepared to weather the heat and humidity of the summer in his town houses in Wilmington and Smithville. The furnishings of the former marked the abode on the corner of Dock and Second streets as large and luxurious. Seven paintings, four etchings, a set of satinwood furniture consisting of two sofas, twelve chairs with cushions and covers, a tea table, and two card tables, along with two large matching carpets, six small carpets, and nineteen window curtains, graced the lower floor; three busts adorned the entry of the second floor; complete furniture (bedsteads, mattresses, bolsters, pillows, bed curtains, sheets, blankets, quilts, and coverlets) for five bedchambers, six bedside carpets, five dressing tables, six basins with mugs, and eight dressing glasses highlighted the living quarters above stairs; thirty-six wine glasses, twelve tumblers, thirty-six knives and forks, twelve tablecloths and napkins, eighteen towels, a set of gilt and white tea china, a set of table china, and the usual kitchen utensils acknowledged the need for food and drink.[2]

At that residence in Wilmington in June, Sarah and the General gave a party to recognize the recent marriage of their friend Lt. Joseph G. Swift, commander of Fort Johnston. According to Swift, the "hilarity" of the occasion was "temporarily intercepted" by a note from Capt. Jack Grange on behalf of Capt. Maurice Moore, the Brunswick magistrate and son of Judge Alfred Moore, to Benjamin Smith, in which the younger Moore challenged the General to a duel. Smith took Swift aside to ask the newly-married lieutenant to serve as his second and make the necessary arrangements with his counterpart who represented Moore. Swift agreed without hesitation, and the festivities resumed as if the interruption were but another of the mundane events of the day.[3]

Dueling, relatively rare in the colonies, and certainly in North Carolina, before the Revolution, became almost fashionable among the elite during the war for independence, popularized as it was by visiting French, German, and English army officers. Affairs of honor were so prevalent in the Continental Army that a Frenchman declared, "The rage for dueling here has reached an incredible and scandalous point." Toward the end of the century another Frenchman visiting America described in some detail boxing and cockfighting, and concluded, "I shall not speak of duels with pistols except to say that this English sport becomes daily more popular with Americans."[4]

Of course Americans, certainly in the South, built upon a heritage of gentlemanly confrontation. Duels became increasingly common in South Carolina after 1760, abetted by such prominent natives as Edward Rutledge, under whom Smith studied briefly for the bar, and his brother John Rutledge, an acknowledged friend of the General. Even those opposed in principle to dueling, such as merchant and patriot Henry Laurens, found themselves drawn inexorably into affairs of honor. And in 1778, Brigadier General Robert Howe, North Carolina's highest ranking officer in the Continental Army, confronted Christopher Gadsden, the counterpart of Samuel Adams in Charleston, South Carolina, in a bloodless affair, after Gadsden had questioned Howe's military talents.[5]

Yet, it was the Revolution that gave impetus to dueling. Affairs of honor were common among the officer corps of the Continental Army, perhaps as Joseph Ellis has suggested, because that was the source of a burgeoning aristocracy in American, home-made as it was, and honor was defended at all costs. Moreover, men in leadership positions feared that avoiding such confrontations might brand them as cowards, thus impairing their ability to command. Subsequently, the rough-and-tumble democratic age of egalitarianism that followed independence accentuated the need for the elite to validate their courage and authority. According to Clement Eaton, the Southern proclivity for dueling reflected an obsession with martial hubris. After all, the land below the Mason and Dixon Line teemed with generals, colonels, and captains. Note Smith, Grange, and Moore.[6]

Duels were elaborate rituals designed to resolve conflicts of honor among peers. Writing of Anglicans in the Lower Cape Fear, of whom Smith was one, historian Richard Rankin believes that "men of honor" shared a primitive ethical system "that recognized personal valor, hospitality, and risk taking among the most respected male attributes." Offense might be given or taken at a moment's notice. Any perceived slight was taken seriously, for honor at all times was prized. It was the core of a man's identity, his self, his manliness. But it could not be imposed or asserted. Honor was other-directed, bestowed by the recognition of others, both peers and subordinates. Thus, according to Rankin, "men sought public approval and esteem through demonstrations of manliness which included the prescribed use of violence."[7]

Although dueling had its detractors, among them John Adams and Thomas Jefferson, and in North Carolina eminent Republican newspaper publisher Joseph Gales of the *Raleigh Register* (who also denounced slavery), defenders abounded. In debating the question, "Is dueling consistent with the laws of honor and justice?" student societies at the University of North Carolina decided in the affirmative. According to a later apologist, "At its worst ... dueling was not so bad as those shocking unregulated encounters which occur ... when the passions of men are beyond control, and which cost more lives than were ever sacrificed to the old code duello." Chimed another, "It must ... be acknowledged that this ... custom ... renders the social intercourse of life far more decent and agreeable than among the most civilized nations of antiquity." The cult of honor, in effect, was a source of political and social stability, a ritualized means of settling affairs in the barely controlled chaos of early national politics and society in the United States.[8]

Smith came to manhood in a age that straddled two worlds, a modern world of constitutional law and a feudal world based on social order and dignity. In the latter dueling became almost de rigueur among gentlemen, particularly in the coastal regions of the South, and, it has been noted, among Anglicans in North Carolina. And the practice was not unfashionable in New York, where historian Joanne Freeman counted sixteen duels between 1795 and 1807, including the most famous confrontation of all, that between Aaron Burr and Alexander Hamilton in 1804. From his boyhood in Charleston and his association with the Rutledges, Smith encountered the spirit, if not the actuality, of the code duello. His service in the Continental Army, however extensive or restricted it may have been, valorized his appreciation of the practice.[9]

Closer to home dueling periodically enlivened the often dull routine of life among the Lower Cape Fear populace. In 1787, a fatal confrontation occurred in Wilmington from a dispute over the theft of some rings. Wilmington merchant John Bradley accused an English officer staying with John Swann of the robbery. Swann, described as "a highstrung gentleman of fortune" and expert marksman, sprang to the defense of his guest by issuing a challenge to Bradley. In the ensuing encounter Bradley was wounded in the hip, but as he fell he fired a shot that killed Swann instantly. Following a charge of manslaughter, Bradley sought and received a gubernatorial pardon. Almost a decade later, another duel occurred in the vicinity of Wilmington, which left one of the combatants wounded.[10]

Smith was more than an acquaintance of the victim of North Carolina's most famous affair of honor, which featured Richard Dobbs Spaight and John Stanly of New Bern in 1802. Spaight, former governor, congressman, and recent convert to Republicanism, took umbrage at remarks by Stanly that questioned Spaight's newfound attachment to Republican principles. According to one, "some good-natured friends carrying tales from one to the other," exacerbated the differences between the men. Stanly, much the younger of the two, sought to avoid the ultimate trial by pistol, but Spaight would not be placated At a meeting on the outskirts of New Bern on September 5, three exchanges failed to produce satisfaction, though one ball pierced Stanly's coat. On the fourth round Spaight received a mortal wound, dying the following day.[11]

Public reaction to the Spaight-Stanly duel, more particularly to the death of the popular ex-governor, led the General Assembly within three months to enact an anti-dueling law. According to the statute, all persons sending, receiving, or transmitting challenges were barred from public office and subject to fine, and if death occurred, the survivor and all attending parties faced prosecution. Nonetheless, Stanly obtained a pardon the next year from Gov. Benjamin Williams after appealing "to the feelings of every gentleman" and "to that dignified sense of honor which adorns your own character." After all, Stanly wrote, he had been provoked and could not have rejected the challenge without becoming "the object of scorn, contempt, and derision of mankind."[12]

The legislation of 1802 hardly dampened the enthusiasm for dueling, but only drove North Carolinians to Virginia and South Carolina to protect their honor on legal grounds. A younger brother of John Stanly was killed in a duel in 1813. At a party he had playfully tossed a piece of cake that fell into a cup of tea, spattering the dress of a young lady. She turned to her escort and asked, "Do you stand for that?" A challenge followed, and the parties went to the Virginia to settle the matter, to the misfortune of Stanly. Two decades after the death of Richard Dobbs Spaight, a duel between his son and namesake and the same John Stanly was barely averted after a heated political encounter between the two.[13]

As for Smith, the General exhibited a haughty demeanor that led to trouble. In 1804, Smith avoided a duel with the same Jack Grange who delivered the note from Maurice Moore in 1805. Grange had taken offense at a remark by Smith that seemed to impugn Grange's veracity, whereupon the two men submitted the dispute to a committee of four, including, ironically, Moore, for binding mediation. Smith blinked. He denied any malicious intent. The adjudicators decided that Smith's explanation was sufficient to absolve Grange of the need to pursue a challenge to the General.[14]

In June 1805, Smith was not so fortunate after Grange unceremoniously intruded upon the party in Wilmington. According to Lt. Swift, "Family rancour ... was the cause of the duel." And, in fact, a misunderstanding over the ownership of property had been festering between Smith and his cousins the Moores for almost a year, occasioned by an "infamous" entry by the General with the secretary of state for a tract of land that was claimed by Judge Moore. Most immediately, however, at least according to Moore family tradition, a tongue loosened by alcohol, combined perhaps with the intent to impress a group of political toadies, led the newly-minted Republican Smith to speak "with underserved abusiveness" about Judge Alfred Moore, a staunch Federalist.[15]

The judge, born in New Hanover County in 1755, educated in Boston, and admitted to the bar in North Carolina in 1775, served in the Continental Army in the Revolution. He owned Buchoi plantation to the south of Belvedere on the Cape Fear River, which was ravaged by the British during their occupation of Wilmington in 1781. Moore recovered to become one of the leading planters and slave owners in Brunswick County. Following the Revolution a distinguished career of public service began with a stint in the state legislature, then the attorney generalship, and last a seat on the United States Supreme Court at the appointment of President John Adams, who sought to fill the vacancy caused by the death of North Carolinian James Iredell in 1799. Poor health forced the resignation of Moore from the court in 1804 but did not detract from the esteem in which he was universally held.[16]

Judge Alfred Moore. Courtesy of New Hanover Public Library.

Judge Moore, whether from

failing health or tolerant character, had seemed willing to overlook the General's indiscretion. Not the judge's older son, Maurice, who was "very popular because of his fine social qualities, but was known to be a very high-spirited and recklessly courageous man." One of the first students of the university, a planter, and with Smith a justice of the peace in Brunswick County, Capt. Moore stepped up for his dishonored parent and undertook to vindicate the family name. After Maurice issued the challenge, the judge tried to assume responsibility, asserting that it was he who had taken the initiative, but his sons would have none of that.[17]

Smith was also an impetuous man, proud and imperious. He has been implicated in three other duels, but the confrontation with Maurice Moore is the only one for which there is credible support. Many disputes, of course, were settled long before they reached the field of honor. Smith's contemporary, Alexander Hamilton, was a master at avoiding opponents and at the same time saving face — until his meeting with Burr in 1804. Smith quickly realized his mistake. As in the case of Grange the previous year, the General tried to secure mediation of the affair through mutual friends. Maurice Moore refused to be satisfied by anything less than an apology in writing which he would dictate. Smith balked, and the affair proceeded.[18]

Duels were elaborately contrived forms of conflict resolution, details of which were left to seconds — Swift and Maj. Duncan Moore for Maurice Moore — subject to input and approval by the principals. Rulebooks from England offered guidance but left room for interpretation and extenuating circumstances. Under the articles of agreement reached by seconds Swift and Moore, the combatants agreed to meet on June 28, the anniversary of the Battle of Sullivan's Island of which Smith was so proud, between seven and ten o'clock in the morning on the South Carolina side of the Boundary House, a longstanding, local landmark straddling the border of North Carolina and South Carolina.[19]

By 1805 the Boundary House had assumed almost iconic status. Located on the highway leading from Wilmington to Georgetown, South Carolina, the only road of consequence in the east that connected the Carolinas, the structure derived its name from the fact that the line dividing the two states ran "thro' the middle of it, one half of the hall in one Province and the other half in another." The Boundary House was a way station for the postal service, a place for itinerant ministers to address the people of the neighborhood, and a point of refreshment for travelers. As Methodist circuit rider Francis Asbury wrote, other than at the Boundary House, "Cross where you will between the [Carolinas], and it is a miserable pass for one hundred miles west," because the "country abounds with bays, swamps, and drains."[20]

The agreement for the duel was explicit. Upon taking their stand on the field of honor, the combatants would not leave until one was "shot dead or so disabled as to be incapable of firing." The words of command, "Gentlemen[,] are you ready[?]" opened the proceedings. Following concurrence from both quarters, the duelists were ordered to prepare their pistols after which they had two minutes in which to fire. Following the first round, the parties might advance two paces (a stipulation inserted at the demand of Smith) before resuming fire.[21]

Moore enjoyed the advantage from the outset, for Smith and he used a brace of dueling pistols belonging to his father, the judge. Moreover, the day before the duel, Moore spent some time target practicing in the woods with one of the pistols. At that juncture Moore's fortune inadvertently changed. The night before the duel Grange and a companion prepared the pistols for the next day's work. In the process they installed hair trigger mechanisms in the firearms but forgot to tell Moore of the alteration. That oversight almost cost Moore a foot, if not his life.[22]

At dawn on June 28, Moore and his party appeared at the Boundary House, followed closely by Smith and his assemblage. Dr. Andrew Scott stood ready to serve both men, though Dr. John L. Griffin, the physician attached to Fort Johnston, also attended. North Carolina law officers had pursued the combatants, but could not cross the imaginary line to the south of the house, where "the duellists and their friends, triumphant under the jurisdiction of South Carolina, were laughing over their fruitless chase." The ground was marked off and the weapons mutually examined.[23]

Then Duncan Moore, Maurice's second, observed that the combatants should be clothed in ordinary dress, whereas Smith appeared in his usual finery. The General was affronted, thinking that Moore insinuated that he was wearing some protective article or, more likely, that loose layers of clothes made it more difficult for his opponent to distinguish his body from his garments. Thus the General furiously stripped off his coat, vest, shirt, and finally undershirt, defiantly baring himself to the waist. A large man in the rising sun of the June morning, Smith made an outstanding target.[24]

Grange took charge. After asking if the duelists were ready, and receiving affirmatives, all waited. Moore, moving quickly, raised his pistol, but unaware of its hair trigger, discharged its load into the ground near his foot. Smith then had two minutes to fire. His slightly errant bullet removed a button from Moore's coat, leaving threads dangling. The pistols were reloaded, and again given to the men. After Smith failed to advance, oddly, since he had insisted on that option, Moore took two steps forward and "shot him down." Believing that it was only a flesh wound, Moore wanted to "take another crack at him," but Smith was finished for the day.[25]

The General slumped to the ground, blood oozing onto the grass, as

Drs. Scott and Griffin rushed to his aid. Swift claimed that Smith was wounded in the side, which he later amended to "near the left shoulder blade." Interestingly, all subsequent accounts placed the wound in the side, but the "right" side. Wherever the injury, the damage looked serious. The physicians prepared to take the General to Smithville. Swift, meanwhile, rushed to Belvedere to inform Sarah Smith of the outcome. From Belvedere they tore through the night in a two-wheeled riding chair, braving a raging summer thunderstorm. At one point lightning simultaneously destroyed two trees on opposite sides of the road, "for a moment blinding us," according to Swift, "but the anxiety of the wife was superior to the alarm." When they reached Smithville, anticlimactically, they found the General alive and "quite cheerful."[26]

The group moved the next day by water to Wilmington where Smith recovered after several weeks of convalescence.[27] Little significance attached to the event beyond that given by the immediate participants. Swift proceeded to renew his hand at fishing and other sports of the season. Six days after the affair, the Fourth of July was observed in Smithville with the usual fanfare. Smith's popularity in the county remained undiminished, attested by two of the toasts following the banquet dinner: "The recovery of General Smith, and the population of Smithville," followed by the supplication, "May the wounds received in a virtuous cause be speedily healed."[28] Heal the wound did, though the bullet was not removed. The missile became a badge of honor and eventually identification that the General carried to the grave.

Chapter 12

Adjutant General

While Smith recuperated, he reentered politics, or, at least, in the fashion of the day, permitted his name to be put forth for consideration for political office. Gentlemen did not want to appear solicitous. Rather than woo the voters, they assumed, or hoped, that their merits were obvious to all. After the unexpected death of Congressman James Gillespie, Smith tried his luck again in an election in 1805 to select a replacement for the deceased. Thomas Kenan, plantation owner in Duplin County, provided the opposition. The General was soundly trounced by a two to one margin in the six-county electoral district, though the vote in Duplin, 854 to 8 in favor of Kenan, effectively decided the outcome.[1]

Nonetheless, the General's loyal cadre in Brunswick County, which Smith had carried in the contest against Kenan, 330 to 17, reelected him to the state Senate. During the electioneering, Smith, of course, skipped the July session of the Brunswick County court but had recovered sufficiently by October to take his seat on the bench with his fellow magistrates, where no doubt the duel was the subject of some conversation. Inured by the journey to Lockwoods Folly, the General prepared for the trip to Raleigh.[2]

Although the 1805 session of the legislature began on November 18, another fifteen days elapsed before Smith appeared on the scene to present his credentials to represent Brunswick County in the Senate. Immediately, Sen. John Binford of Northampton County countered with a petition from John G. Scull that claimed Smith had been fraudulently elected and that his seat ought to be vacated. Scull, planter, magistrate, and former member of the House of Commons from New Hanover and Brunswick counties, may well have been encouraged by the Moores in an effort to frustrate Smith. As customary, the petition was referred to the committee on privileges and elections. Two days later that committee reported that the evidence presented in support of the petition was "unfounded and insufficient," and recommended that the petition be rejected. Smith, not without friends in high places, retained his seat.[3]

After Governor Nathaniel Alexander greeted the legislators with "felicitation[s]" on the "treaty with the Bashaw of Tripoli," which ended the four-year war with that Barbary state on a high note for the United States, the Senate and Commons grappled with a longstanding, contentious issue — the university. Critics of the institution continued their relentless assault, referring to the institution as a bastion of aristocracy and the proposed Main Building as a "Temple of Folly." Students did not help the cause by engaging in another uprising in the spring of 1805. And William R. Davie, the "Father of the University," despaired as he left the state permanently to reside in South Carolina. In his estimation, "friends of science in other states regard the people of North Carolina as a sort of Semi-Barbarians, among whom neither learning, virtue nor men of Science possess any Estimation. The conduct of the Legislature for several years past has stamped this character on the State."[4] On the bright side, North Carolina's Court of Conference, forerunner of the state Supreme Court, declared by split decision that the Gothic Law of 1800 was unconstitutional.[5]

The legislature responded to the crisis by acknowledging the decision of the court but at the same time politicizing and assuming control of the university. Escheats were restored, and well they were, because they provided 69 percent of the university's revenue during the coming half-century. However, the governor of the state, elected by the General Assembly, was made president of the board of trustees. And, building upon an enactment in 1804 that authorized the legislature to augment the number of trustees and thereafter appoint all new trustees, the General Assembly in 1805 assumed the discretion to fill the seats of trustees who failed to attend meetings of the board for two consecutive years.[6] At the same time both houses rejected committee reports that would have appropriated money to finish Main Building.[7]

For his part, Smith, who had always been interested in promoting internal improvements, not only for the benefit of the state but also for his own interests, introduced a bill to construct a canal in Brunswick County to connect Lockwoods Folly River and Elizabeth River which emptied into the Cape Fear River. The waterway would have offered residents of the Lockwoods Folly area a safer and quicker passage to market in Wilmington, obviating the need for them to exit into the Atlantic Ocean and enter the mouth of the Cape Fear River to reach the port. The statute incorporated the Smithville Canal Company to underwrite the project through private subscriptions and a lottery. Ultimately, like most proposed canals of the day, large and small, that one failed to materialize.[8]

As the Senate closed its session, one of the last orders of business was to enter a protest by Smith. Earlier in the session the General had presented petitions and depositions by ship captains from Massachusetts and New York who complained about the "improper and tyrannical conduct" of Robert Potter, one of the justices of the peace in Brunswick County, and sought his removal. Potter apparently without legal process had taken a sailor from one of the vessels on suspicion of committing a felony, "subjected him to the disgrace of being escorted through the streets [of Smithville] as a criminal," and "confined him in a loathsome apartment." Potter rebutted with affidavits of his good character, including a letter signed by a Baptist minister who Smith decried as "a principal instigator of ... [recent] disorganizing and turbulent proceedings" in Dobbs County and an "unworthy preacher of the gospel and profaner of the true christian religion." After both houses failed to take action against Potter, Smith transferred his outrage to the pages of the Senate Journal.[9]

That battle fought and lost, the General returned to Belvedere but failed to join the January session of the Brunswick County court in what may have been a silent protest against Potter. But Smith dutifully appeared in April, on the first day, and took his seat on the bench along with his dueling partner, Maurice Moore. The justices directed the general to take the tax list as usual for the Northwest District of the county which Smith returned to the October court. Otherwise, the General's presence in the sessions of the court in 1806 was manifested principally by his acknowledgment of several deeds and a bill of sale for the disposition of property, an ominous indication of his growing need for cash to meet dunning creditors.[10]

Land and slaves, too, constituted primal assets that were jealously guarded. But the multiplicity of land transactions along with the infamous haphazard boundaries of Southern real estate produced endless controversy. When Smith sought to sell a tract of tidal swamp between Mallory Creek and Old Town Plantation, another contested his claim to the land in the Wilmington newspaper. The General rebutted with an extensive genealogy of the ownership of the acreage in question, a quotation from a relevant deed, and a description of the boundaries as distinctly as they could be ascertained. Smith was never backward in defending his property, though his legal entanglements eventually became so tortured as often to leave everyone at sea.[11]

When the General was not protecting his property rights, exacting a few more grains of rice from his tidal swamp, or issuing brigade orders to the militia under his command, he subtly engineered his reelection to the state Senate. In 1806, Maurice Moore decided to challenge Smith rather than hide behind John G. Scull. But the General was equal to the task, defeating Moore by 151 to 91, evidencing again the minimal impact of the duel and the popularity of the General.[12]

Sallying into the Senate in 1806 eight days late, in the company of three other laggards, Smith and his cohorts presented their excuses to the appropriate

Senate committee, which readily accepted their explanations for tardiness. Once more he offered for election to the United States Senate. Unfortunately for the General, his competition included the ever popular Jesse Franklin, who had bested Smith (and others) in 1798 for the Senate seat. Having served one term and retired for two years, Franklin was returned by the General Assembly to Washington to the despair of Smith and another challenger and longtime adversary, Thomas Blount of Edgecombe County.[13]

After an absence in 1805, Smith rejoined the university board of trustees, which sat concurrently with the legislature, not wanting to risk expulsion for absenteeism. Business was lackadaisical, centering mainly on pursuing escheated lands. The board divided the state into nine geographic districts and named an attorney in each to represent the university. Coincidentally, one of the lawyers was Matthew Troy, upon whom the trustees conferred a master of arts degree immediately before his appointment. Otherwise, the board launched an investigation into an allegation by Moravians in Wilkes County that they were deprived of lands erroneously deemed escheated.[14]

Smith was more active than usual in the General Assembly in 1806, evidencing his presence by the introduction of a number of bills. His affirmative vote also helped to carry a proposal in the Senate to prevent free blacks from leaving the county in which they were reared without a certificate of their freedom, seemingly a gross affront to their liberty but in effect an attempt to protect them from enslavement or re-enslavement.[15] The General also felt repercussions from his protest against Robert Potter in the previous legislative session. Abraham Baker, the Baptist minister maligned by Smith, and various Baptist associations presented petitions of counterprotest, asserting that Baker was "a religious and worthy man" against whose character Smith had cast "improper reflections," and sought redress from the Senate. Instead, that body "*Resolved unanimously*" to table the petitions "without further notice."[16] Again, Smith showed that he merited the esteem of fellow senators, though appreciation for ranting Baptists was hardly widespread among the legislators.

Two months into the following year, after his usual tardy presence at Lockwoods Folly at the quarterly session of the Brunswick County court in January, Smith reached the pinnacle of military career when Governor Nathaniel Alexander in February 1807 appointed him adjutant general of the North Carolina militia. Smith retained his brigadier generalcy. By law the governor was required to select an adjutant general from the brigadier and major generals of the state. Thus doubly a general, Smith marched more erectly into the Brunswick courthouse in May where he showed a gentlemanly magnanimity in helping to reelect John G. Scull, his political rival in 1805, sheriff of the county.[17]

Beyond the pedestrian affairs of the county, the first order of business for Adjutant General Smith was to locate some military stores loaned by the United States government in 1806 to the state. The matter became something of a farce. The governor, who had been requested by Secretary of War Henry Dearborn to find the materiel, knew nothing. Apparently the bulk of the items resided in private hands in Fayetteville. The remainder, more or less, found their way to Wilmington where some gun carriages had burned in a fire, gunpowder lodged in a store or warehouse along the Cape Fear River had been destroyed by an unusually high tide, and muskets, defective upon receipt but repaired at private expense, were in the lands of a local volunteer company of infantry.[18] All in all, the episode well exemplified North Carolina's preparation for military security.

Soon after satisfying the query of the secretary of war, the international scene played to Smith's sense of military grandeur. In June 1807, a British man-of-war, the *Leopard*, attacked an American naval frigate, the *Chesapeake*, off the coast of Virginia, killing several United States seamen and impressing four putative British deserters. The opening years of the nineteenth century proved to be an almost instant replay of the 1790s, when the British and French vied for supremacy in Europe. Napoleon Bonaparte began his grand adventure in 1803, provoking another world war in which the United States attempted fruitlessly to remain above the fray as a neutral. There was no way to avoid the aggressors, who harassed American shipping. The worse culprit was Great Britain with her powerful navy. As evidenced by the *Chesapeake* affair, the British navy sought forcibly to remove deserters not only from United States merchant vessels but even from ships of the navy.

The news of the attack on the *Chesapeake*, which upstaged the ongoing trial of Aaron Burr for treason that was taking place in Richmond, Virginia, strained relations with England to the breaking point. Had Jefferson wanted war, it was his for the asking after the aggression by the *Leopard*. Instead, the president temporized, closing American ports to the Royal Navy, seeking an apology from the British government, scapegoating Commodore James Barron, commander of the *Chesapeake*, with a court-martial, and calling for a special session of Congress to meet in October. By that time war fever had dissipated. Jefferson successfully deflected a confrontation with England, but he only postponed the inevitable.

Naturally the observation of the Fourth of July reflected the concern over the *Chesapeake* incident. After waking Wilmington's citizens at 5:00 A.M. with a seventeen-round salute, a local volunteer company repeated the effort at noon, after which a suitable repast at the courthouse at 3:00 in the afternoon was slaked by seventeen toasts, marking the number of states in the Union, and another twelve volunteers, including that of Gen. Smith — "the glorious spirit of '76." Many of the toasts referred to the topic of the day, including that of John Mitchell: "the enemies of our country — may they be blessed with ... Sails rent, Grog spent, Wormy bread, Wind a-head, Cloudy noon, At night no moon, Compass lost, Tempest tost, A winter's coast."[19]

In the meantime, outrage spread from Virginia, north and south. Federalists even vied for a time with Republicans to prove their patriotism. Reactions to the attack found their way to North Carolina newssheets. Expectedly, town and county meetings from the coast to the interior of the state expressed their indignation at the British. A Wilmington gathering on July 8 denounced the attack, which was deemed tantamount to a declaration of war, praised the Virginians for their manly opposition, declared as enemies those who rendered aid to British warships, and sought to dissuade pilots on the Cape Fear River from assisting British warships and privateers. Smith headed a committee of seven who were directed to implement the resolutions and to correspond with the president and governor about the need to defend the port of Wilmington, which at the time enjoyed the aegis of a single federal gunboat.[20]

Pursuant to the meeting, Smith and company found a sympathetic ear in Washington, where the secretary of the navy assured Wilmingtonians that he would do all in his power to protect Wilmington. He authorized an immediate contract for materials with which to build three gunboats for the port under terms that could be obtained from Smith. The gunboats, more properly galleys similar to those used in the earlier Franco–American conflict, were part of a more general naval program consisting of mobile land and naval floating batteries by which Jefferson proposed to protect the coastal regions of the country. Federalists derisively referred to the gunboats as Jefferson's "mosquito fleet." As noted by historian Marshall Smelser, the tactics of the administration "were not those of the American eagle, but of the terrapin."[21]

Although seeking a peaceful solution to the problem of British aggression, Jefferson felt compelled to pursue congressional legislation in 1806 and 1807 that permitted the president, if he deemed necessary, to call forth one hundred thousand militia troops from the states. Secretary of War Dearborn thus notified Governor Alexander to "arm and equip" North Carolina's quota of 7,003 militia within the shortest period circumstances will permit" and hold them ready for action. The governor, acting upon precedent established during the crisis with France in the late 1790s, ordered Adjutant General Smith to prepare to meet the federal mandate. Smith, summering at Smithville, responded enthusiastically, hoping that the "militia of N. C. will evince the same glorious ardour in the cause of their country that distinguished true Americans in Seventy Six and that should it become necessary they will give George the third an-other proof that the U.S. will be truly free, sovereign and independent."[22]

Within a week Smith prepared orders for the major generals of the state's militia. However, defective militia returns from around the state made it a time consuming and difficult task to ascertain the number of men in the militia, identify the officer corps, and determine seniority within the ranks, information that he needed in order to apportion the 7,003 among the five militia divisions and to divide that number along a quota of infantry, artillery, and cavalry suggested by Dearborn. After informing the major generals of their expectations, Smith closed effusively, "The breast of every patriotic American must swell with indignation at the late degrading and cruel insult offered to his Country.... We must be ... prepared to curb [England's] injustice by a glorious resort to arms ... [and] press forward to vindicate the rights of our Country and place them beyond control of the proud and lordly tyrants of the ocean."[23]

At the same time Smith began to draft general orders to the militia on behalf of the governor. By mid–August the adjutant general sent those orders along with the allocation of infantry, artillery, and cavalry, all to be "properly armed & equipped for service," to the governor for his approval and publication. According to the General, volunteers would be particularly distinguished from draftees, but he expected liberal enlistments, given the "strong indignation and military ardour universally displayed throughout the union, at the late cruel outrage and intolerable insult to the national honour." Moreover, he was certain that "party prejudices" and "personal animosities" would be overshadowed by the need to punish the perpetrators of "foreign aggression" and "cause the United States to be respected and ranked amongst the most honoured & powerful nations of the Universe."[24]

Without a doubt Adjutant General Smith toiled mightily to fulfill the demands of the secretary of war and Governor Alexander. But he suffered — from the "indisposition" of his aide-de-camp, which forced the General "to double my exertions," from illness in August that beset Smith and his entire family, both white and "coloured," and from efforts to secure printed forms on which to obtain militia returns. His labors on one occasion forced him to work "so hard that I feel too much indisposed to write as fully as I could wish," a circumstance that he did not hesitate to share with Alexander. Yet, as Smith later wrote the governor, though the office of adjutant general has "reengaged much of my attention & incessantly employ[ed] me for some weeks," he was determined to justify the confidence of Alexander in his appointment.[25]

No doubt that conscientiousness contributed to Smith's umbrage when questions were raised by the *Raleigh Register*, the unofficial mouthpiece of the government, about the propriety of his serving both as brigadier general of troops in the service of the United States and adjutant general of the state of North Carolina. Governor Alexander had appointed Major General Thomas

Brown and Brigadiers Smith, John Hamilton, and Samuel Benton to command the 7,003-strong militia force — if needed. According to the *Raleigh Register*, if Smith accepted the appointment, he would "of course" vacate the office of adjutant general, to which Smith asserted he had no intention of resigning unless he took actual command of troops beyond the state of North Carolina.[26]

Smith was never required to make a decision because Jefferson found a more pacific means to assuage America's anger over the attack on the *Chesapeake*. The president was no more prepared to fight the British than Commodore Barron was ready to take on the *Leopard*. Military preparations were made by Jefferson, which included recalling American naval vessels abroad, constructing gunboats, and readying a hundred thousand militia troops, but for Jefferson, the head of a third-rate nation, foreign trade was the trump card. After Congress convened, he convinced that body in late December to adopt a wide-ranging embargo on United States foreign trade in hopes of bringing the British and French to their senses.

Before the North Carolina General Assembly convened in November, Adjutant General Smith was surprised to learn from Governor Alexander that the War Department had never received the expected militia returns from North Carolina, requested by Dearborn in July. Perhaps the post miscarried. Perhaps the returns were lost in the maw of the operations of the War Department. In any case, Smith was put to the time, trouble, and expense of sending another copy of the list of 7,003 North Carolina militia to Washington, which left the General in a foul mood as he approached Raleigh.[27]

Nonetheless, Smith clocked into the Senate on the first day of the session, thereby obtaining the dubious honor of chairing the committees to respond to the governor's message and finance, which as Smith knew from experience were two of the most onerous assignments of the house. The former committee addressed the sundry subjects raised by Governor Alexander that ranged from an adjustment of the North Carolina border with Georgia to the promotion of education, a bill for which was introduced by Smith but lost. From the finance committee came the usual action to raise an annual revenue for the state and the opinion that the painting of the statehouse, including the choice of colors, should be left to the "taste and care" of the state treasurer.[28]

In his spare moments in Raleigh, few that they were, the General attended the meetings of the university's trustees. Among the usual train of business, the board evidenced a ongoing concern for rabble-rousers among the student body, and approved a resolution banning the admission of any applicant to the university who had been expelled from another college in the nation. In fact, the board felt that some general agreement to that effect among all institutions of higher education in the country would be worthwhile. To Smith and a fellow trustee fell the responsibility of preparing an ordinance to implement the resolution of the board.[29]

But for Smith, at least, the militia was the focal item of interest in Raleigh. As required by a statute of the previous year, the adjutant general presented a report to the legislature, albeit a summary of what he had conveyed earlier to the governor in response to Jefferson's demand for 7,003 troops. After devising appropriate forms for returns of militia by the officers, and threatening to cashier those who failed to respond, Smith found that the North Carolina militia had suddenly swelled to 52,777, including infantry, artillery, and cavalry, 8,521 more than he had previously indicated to the War Office, and a force 30 percent greater than that reported by his predecessor in 1806. Smith also discovered a number of cannon in Edenton that belonged to the state which were lying about under no particular authority and suggested a rescue mission.[30]

Smith also reminded the legislators of the expense and difficulty occasioned by the demands on the adjutant general, particularly in light of the current crisis. The General politely but firmly told his fellows that the office of adjutant general carried no compensation, and he did not seek "*any pecuniary reward whatever.*" Yet the costs were great — stationery, postage, and clerical assistance necessary to obtain and copy muster rolls of 7,003 names (at least twice), not to mention travel. The General admitted that with "considerable diffidence" he had drawn on the state treasury for $99, but suggested that an annual allocation of a precise sum might be "more consonant to Republican principles" than leaving the decision to the discretion of the adjutant general and treasurer.[31]

Smith's report brought several bills to the floors of the Senate and House of Commons. The General Assembly eventually accepted a proposal by the General that sought to ensure more complete returns from the militia companies. Another statute, finding a large number of men in the districts of the first and second militia divisions, expanded the two to three, thereby creating six divisions in the state. A third reorganized the fourth and fifth divisions, in the process adding a brigade. The legislation reflected the successful efforts of Smith to secure a more accurate compilation of the militia in the state.[32]

But the General was disappointed. His bill to establish arsenals and to authorize the governor to purchase arms for the troops, particularly from E. T. Dupont de Nemours & Co., arms manufacturers of Wilmington, Delaware, which had written Governor Alexander (and other state governors) to offer its services, failed to gain traction. The legislature assumed that properly arming and equipping the militia was the responsibility of the federal government. Also lost was a bill to amend previous militia statutes to secure their conformity with federal legislation. And the always tight-fisted General Assembly refused to offer any assistance to the adjutant general to underwrite the expenses of the office.[33]

Thus Smith chose to abandon his position as adjutant general. He claimed that the present militia law "places the Adjutant General in such a responsible situation and imposes such incessant Labour in case of requisition from the General Government, without allowing any assistance to work through the drudgery of the office, that I feel myself compelled to resign the appointment." No matter. Earlier in the session the General Assembly had promoted him from brigadier to major general, one of two in the state, and a position attended by less work and more glamour.[34]

In the time of mini-crisis the legislature also considered the unfinished state of Fort Johnston. Smith had resumed work on the post in 1805 upon renegotiating his contract with the federal government. After expending $27,826 on the project from 1794 through 1804, Washington hoped that Smith would pursue his responsibility with vigor, but the General preferred all deliberate speed. So at the end of 1806 the secretary of war only reported "further progress" had been made. Lt. Joseph Swift, supervising the operation, had been distracted by marriage and then poor health, which occasioned a leave of absence and subsequent reassignment. In December 1807, the secretary of war observed that additional money had been lavished on Fort Johnston and a battery erected across the bay from Smithville at the mouth of the river, the inception of Fort Caswell, which subsequently superseded Fort Johnston.[35]

In the aftermath of the *Chesapeake* incident the United States upgraded its coastal defense program, spending more than three million dollars on seacoast fortifications between 1807 and the outbreak of war with Great Britain in 1812. The North Carolina legislature in 1807 again extended the time allotted to the federal government to finish Fort Johnston, noting that while "not perfectly completed it was so far done as to be ready for the mounting of cannon." Ready it may have been, but two years later cannon had not been placed and barracks had not been built. A further extension was needed and granted in 1809, at which time the United States took full command of the fort, presumably discharging Smith of his contractual obligation to the government. Joseph Swift returned to take command of all fortifications along the North Carolina coast.[36]

Finally, in 1807, the Republican-controlled legislature spent three weeks debating an endorsement of Jefferson and his policy regarding the *Chesapeake* affair. Expectedly, it delivered an enthusiastic encomium which originally took a swipe at the Federalists before the deleting a reference to "a party which seeks to subvert because they cannot direct." Nonetheless, the resolution strongly endorsed Jefferson's "measures which have been pursued for the defence and interests of the country" and encouraged the president to seek a third term in 1808. Smith voted in the minority, apparently preferring a more militaristic address that omitted reference to the third term.[37]

Following the conclusion of the session of the General Assembly, defense and the militia were never far from Smith's mind. From Belvedere in late December he wrote Governor Benjamin Williams that he had heard, "as [if] it were a passing dream," that the secretary of war had yet to receive the militia returns from North Carolina. The General offered to forward another copy to the governor and, despite his retirement as adjutant general, agreed to assist Williams if he could.[38]

Uncharacteristically, the General failed to attend to the February session of the Brunswick County court. Speculatively, he may have gone to South Carolina to assist his brother James, whom Smith had been cultivating for as many as two years for North Carolina residency, in permanently relocating to the state. James had divided his time between Charleston and Brunswick since 1805, when the Brunswick court apprenticed a young man to the South Carolinian. At least by 1807, he was living part time on Kendal plantation, and at the July 1808 session, Benjamin acknowledged a deed of gift of Kendal

Kendal. Courtesy of New Hanover Public Library.

and Benvenuto plantations to James, no doubt evidence of brotherly love, though the elder brother might have wanted to protect the properties from the potential creditors.[39]

As the Smiths reunited in the Lower Cape Fear, another presidential election year, 1808, found North Carolina Federalists upbeat. In 1804, Jefferson had handily won reelection and carried the party to crushing victories throughout the country and the state. The embargo, the Republicans' attempt to avoid war by economic coercion, traumatized Americans more than the British or French, sending the United States economy into a funk and converting citizens into lawbreakers. Among the latter was the "unprincipled wretch" of a captain who sailed a schooner reportedly bound from Wilmington to the West Indies with a cargo of rice and flour.[40] Under pressure from a flood of petitions and grand jury presentments which sought relief from the embargo, Governor David Stone twice convened his advisors, the council of state, but on both occasions decided against calling a special session of the General Assembly.[41]

Smith, at least, saw that Brunswick County remained faithful to the Jeffersonian cause. The grand jury of the county castigated efforts "to alienate the minds of the good citizens of their country from a confidence in the General Government." After Congressman Thomas Kenan had purportedly received some instructions by residents of the county to try to secure a repeal of the embargo, the grand jury, no doubt activated by the General, asked Smith to relay a number of resolutions to Jefferson that strongly endorsed the administration's policy. Reminiscent of 1798, the president, or his amanuensis, responded in kind, lamenting the opposition to the maritime restrictions, particularly in New England, but optimistically observing that the country appeared "heartily to approve & support the embargo."[42]

The Federalists in 1808 tilted at windmills. The Republicans won eleven of the fourteen electoral votes in North Carolina (and mounted a good claim to a twelfth), as James Madison, the Jeffersonian presidential nominee, handily won the right to succeed Jefferson. The Jeffersonians, however, had overreached with the embargo and punitive enforcement legislation. Threats of disunion rained from the north. Consequently Congress cravenly but realistically retreated from that stringent ban on foreign trade. Still, restrictions on trade through the War of 1812 had the effect of stimulating American manufacturing, particularly in the northeast, ironically bestowing on Jefferson, who had reservations about non-agrarian pursuits, the distinction of fostering industrialization in the country.

An unusually conscientious Smith again appeared for the opening of the legislature in Raleigh in November 1808. His timeliness was rewarded by appointments to committees to examine engrossed bills, to respond to the governor's message, and to oversee finance.[43] Once more the subject of the militia proved contentious for the legislature and Smith. The secretary of war had earlier informed the governor that congressional legislation required North Carolina to provide, if needed, 8,071 militia, "completely armed and equipped." Reacting to the governor's report, Smith's committee proposed a resolution by which the state would "chearfully" furnish its quota of men, but insisted that arming them fell within the province of the national government. After dutifully representing his committee, Smith offered a substitute resolution that authorized the governor to purchase six thousand stands of arms and ten brass cannon, or, at least, to obtain a loan of such materiel from the United States. The Senate divided, but stingy legislators doomed Smith to defeat, and the original resolution was approved, 31 to 20.[44]

Before Smith left Raleigh, early per his request to the Senate, the General Assembly approved his bill to move the seat of Brunswick County from Lockwoods Folly to Smithville in 1808. When incorporating Smithville the General Assembly failed to locate the seat of county government in the new town, the usual modus operandi for counties in which there was an incorporated community. Initially, Smithville's survival was moot, and even though it slowly grew as a minor port and resort, the town was not centrally located in the county. Thus from 1804, when Smith first introduced a bill to relocate the county seat, there was opposition to the estrangement from Lockwoods Folly.[45]

The legislation in 1808, though based on the claim that a majority of the county residents favored the relocation of the county seat, nonetheless reflected the ongoing opposition. The law was studded with restrictions. Removal was predicated on the erection of a courthouse, jail, and stocks in Smithville at least equal to those in Lockwoods Folly, and the structures were to be built at private expense rather than being funded by taxes, a highly unusual, and probably unique, set of prerequisites for the relocation of a county seat in North Carolina. Moreover, jurors who attended the county court were entitled to an extra allowance if they had to travel farther to Smithville than they would have traveled to Lockwoods Folly. Finally, during the same session the General Assembly created a new county, Columbus, from parts of Brunswick and Bladen, largely to accommodate those who lived distant in western Brunswick.[46]

The battle was not over. Opponents of the move petitioned the General Assembly in 1812 to return the county seat to Lockwoods Folly. They complained of the remoteness of Smithville, which was also a place of "extravagance and want," where public accommodations were so scarce that some were forced to "camp in the woods in the worst of weather." A counterpetition by advocates of Smithville successfully bested the challenge and the issue remained mostly dormant for over a century and a half. Proponents of removal persevered, however, and in 1975, emerged victorious when the General Assembly agreed to move the county seat from Smithville, which had been renamed Southport in 1887, to the "general vicinity of Supply and Bolivia." There, the complex of county buildings moved in 1977, residing today under the address of Bolivia.⁴⁷

While Smith and the other commissioners responsible by law for constructing the county buildings in Smithville deliberated, and in June 1809, offered the job to the lowest bidder at public auction, the General appeared at the April session of the Brunswick court. He took his seat with his brother James, who had been named a justice of the peace by the governor. Later in the year, the General, who had enjoyed the privilege of operating a toll bridge over Livingston's Creek, agreed to build a free bridge over the watercourse in order to facilitate the passage of the stage to Fayetteville and to absolve travelers of the need to pay ferriage. Given the General's longstanding interest in the improvement of internal transportation, surely in principle he had little reason to complain.⁴⁸

Although the war fever had abated and a limited maritime commerce resumed after the modification of the Embargo of 1807, at the time that James Madison assumed the presidential office in March 1809, tensions between Great Britain and the United States remained high. Moreover, North Carolinians read with alarm, as Jefferson earlier had indicated to Smith, of the discontent in the New England states. So great was the disaffection in that region that some feared rebellion and civil war. Preparing for the worst, Major General Smith solemnly but no doubt delightedly issued orders to the divisions under his command for raising the quota of the militia required by the national government.⁴⁹

Another opening day presence in the state Senate in 1809, which marked his sixth consecutive term after a quasi-retirement, found Smith's stature soaring. Not only was he appointed again to chair the committees on finance and the governor's message, he also chaired the select committee on the militia and the select joint committee (with the House of Commons) to consider resolutions on foreign relations, and served on three additional committees. All the while the General participated in the concurrent meetings of the university board of trustees, though his role was that of a passive actor, and in the annual meeting of the Grand Lodge of North Carolina and Tennessee Free Masons in a far more prominent capacity.⁵⁰

The General, in fact, had been elected grand master of the Grand Lodge of North Carolina and Tennessee in 1808, effective in 1809, and thus presided over the annual meeting of the grand lodge of the two states which coincided as customary with the session of the General Assembly in 1809. Long a member of St. John's Lodge No. 1 in Wilmington, Smith had been speaker of the

Senate in 1797, when the grand lodge was incorporated by the General Assembly. He rose rapidly in the ranks of Masonry, representing St. John's in the Grand Lodge in 1805, where he was elected junior grand deacon for 1806, senior grand deacon for 1807, and senior grand warden for 1808. During the course of those years the Grand Lodge named the General one of two North Carolina representatives to attend a meeting in Washington, D.C., to frame a constitution to form a grand lodge for the United States.[51]

Grand Master Smith appeared to ably and conscientiously fulfill the demands of the Brotherhood. Indicative of his activity were his visits during the year to local lodges in New Bern, Beaufort, Washington, and Pitt County, where he found some "expert" in their knowledge of the craft, and others "tolerable." He also presented a book (title unknown) on the subject of Masonry that was well received by the grand lodge. Altogether, he merited a resolution of thanks by the grand lodge for "his able and faithful discharge of the several and many duties" in his first year, and was reelected grand master for 1810.[52]

Back home, in Brunswick County, the Moore family had not finished with the General. Though Maurice had failed to dispatch him permanently, and John G. Scull had unsuccessfully challenged Smith's seat in the Senate in 1805, Smith's former dueling partner tried to embarrass the General by claiming that his election to the Senate in 1809 was fraudulent. The accusation arrived late in the legislative session, which rather clearly indicated a provenance of pique rather than substance. The Senate committee on privileges and elections concluded unanimously that the allegations by Moore were not sufficiently substantiated and that Smith was entitled to his seat, a decision in which the entire Senate concurred.[53]

The distraction was innocuous, and thankfully, for the General was deeply engrossed in the business of state. In the course of his committee responsibilities, Smith brought forth bills to promote manufacturing and internal improvements, to assist debtors, and to increase the funding of the university, and a resolution to permit the governor to appoint a commission to consider revising the militia laws. All met varying degrees of success.[54] The General also successfully negotiated a real estate swap. Bald Head Island, his island, in New Hanover County, was transferred to the jurisdiction of Brunswick County where the General via his magistracy might better control the island. By way of compensation, a portion of Eagles Island in Brunswick County, which faced Wilmington across the river and served the maritime needs of the port, was granted to New Hanover.[55]

After a month-long stint in Raleigh, the legislators gladly prepared to shed their public mantle and late December temperatures for some home cooking and the warmth of domestic fires. As a last order of business, the two houses heard from the Smithian-led joint select committee on foreign relations. In language obeisant to republicanism and fit for a president, the General Assembly approved an adulatory address to President James Madison, in which the lawmakers praised his "firmness, wisdom and patriotism," and pledged "individually and as representatives of the free-men of North Carolina, to support with energy, and at the risk of our lives and fortunes, such measures as the General Government shall think proper to pursue to protect from insult and aggression our common and happy Country." The "Spirit of '76" did not appear but the language was clearly influenced by Smith.[56]

Chapter 13

Governor

The second decade of the nineteenth century opened amid continuing frosty relations with England and the belligerency of Republicans toward John Bull, both well exemplified by Benjamin Smith. Yet the General was focused on more immediate matters, such as his ongoing battle with rice swamps and responsibilities as a public official. And despite occasional executions by creditors, the General maintained his accustomed perch atop the economic hierarchy in Brunswick County. His 204 bondsmen in 1810 marked him still as one of the principal slave owners in the state and the largest in Brunswick County. Brother James, master of 102 slaves, ranked a distant second in the county.[1]

Although two hundred and more slaves might appear advantageous, liabilities accompany assets. Those bonded men and women, who yearned for recognition as human beings rather than chattel, took their toll on Smith. Runaways continued to bedevil the General. Among them was Frank, who, wrote Smith, left "from no other cause but a consciousness of deserving punishment." And pilfering, the bane of all slave owners, but magnified by the large number of Smith's bondsmen, threatened the masters constantly. When slaves did not use or consume stolen property, they always found a ready market for their ill-gotten goods among unscrupulous whites despite manifold laws to the contrary.[2]

In 1806, an exasperated General Smith "determined to establish an income independent of the cares, anxieties and disappointments attending expectations from Negro Labour." The General became "daily more & more disgusted with Tide Swamp & Slave property." He probably reflected upon his father and namesake uncle, who had enjoyed the comforts of Charleston as rentiers. Land and slaves, however, failed to find a ready market in the Lower Cape Fear. By 1810 Smith had discontinued advertisements in the Wilmington newspaper and sought a market for his bondsmen in Charleston. At the same time the General notified John Steele in Salisbury in the western part of North Carolina that he was willing to part with fifty to eighty slaves, "well used to work — orderly & country born," and some of the "best Tide Swamp" in the Carolinas. Finding few takers for his slaves, the General continued to struggle with recalcitrant laborers and unhealthy rice land.[3]

Resigned to his fate as a planter, Smith had returned to Belvedere after the December 1809 session of the General Assembly to find his old acquaintance, Joseph G. Swift, now a major, in Smithville. Swift had been ordered to North Carolina to take charge of the state's coastal fortifications, and, of course, he felt most comfortable in the Lower Cape Fear. Swift, admitted to the Masonic fraternity in 1802 while at West Point, accompanied Grand Master Smith to annual meeting of St. John's Lodge in Wilmington late in December. However, the major declined membership in any lodge, having once observed "an abuse of the test for admission, and considering the objects of the society, as a secret society, not agreeable to the spirit of our political institutions." His reservations were shared by many, but not by Smith.[4]

Swift's opinion of Masonry failed to dampen his friendship with Smith. Together with the General, Joshua Potts, John Lord, and commandant of Fort Johnston, Lt. Robert Roberts, Swift examined the recently completed installation and found the works dilapidated. Moreover, the barracks of the post lay beyond its bounds in the middle of Moore Street in Smithville. Thus the town commissioners ordered Smith, who at the time was the intendant or principal executive officer of the town, to "apply to the Secretary of War to have ... new barracks erected as soon as possible" within the fort and to "use his utmost endeavour to obtain such arrangements as will leave the streets clear of public buildings."[5]

Swift received orders from the War Department in April personally to take charge of Fort Johnston, construct brick barracks within the post, and make occasional repairs. The barracks were finished before the end of the year, at which time Swift moved the troops to their new quarters. Through the early years of the twenty-first century the barracks, or Garrison House, a brick, two-story structure, remained in the heart of Southport (formerly Smithville), a remnant and reminder of Fort Johnston. In 2006, after declaring the property surplus, the United States government transferred ownership of the 5.75 acre site to the town of Southport.[6]

The refurbishing of Fort Johnston, Smith's longstanding interest in protecting the Lower Cape Fear against foreign incursion, and the lingering impact of his effusive address of support for President Madison in the previous legislative session inspired the General to pursue the orphaned cannon in Edenton that he had discovered in 1807 as adjutant general. The joint committee of which he had been a member in 1809 had recommended that the governor try to exchange the iron cannon at Edenton for brass field pieces

Fort Johnston Garrison House. Courtesy of New Hanover Public Library.

belonging to the United States. Smith took a personal interest in the project. The procurement of artillery, he wrote to Gov. David Stone, had "long been a favorite object with me," to which the governor responded in kind, "effecting the heavy cannon for Field Pieces is ... vastly important.... I have lost not one moment in my exertions to render that endeavour effectual."[7]

In fact Smith had begun to make arrangements to travel to Washington, D.C., probably in an attempt to revise his contract with the United States for the completion of Fort Johnston. That presented the perfect opportunity to broker an exchange of cannon. Thus the General offered his services to Stone to negotiate with William Eustis, the secretary of war, while in the capital, affirming to the governor his "ardent desire to serve with the utmost cheerfulness & fidelity our common beloved Country." All Smith required, he wrote, were a list of the cannon and accoutrements in Edenton and authority from Stone to represent the state. The governor readily complied with Smith's request.[8]

Before leaving Belvedere for Washington, the General made the customary short journey to Lockwoods Folly to attend the January session of the Brunswick County court. Other than acknowledging the sale of property, which became increasingly necessary to satisfy his creditors, and losing two lawsuits, which also became more frequent occurrences, Smith agreed to accept responsibility for two apprentices, sons of one Temperance Chavis, though exactly to what trade the boys would be put was unclear, given the General's occupation of gentleman planter. Smith signed the minutes at the end of the session as senior justice and looked forward to his northward excursion.[9]

By March, Smith had arrived in Washington, where he spent perhaps a month enjoying the society of the nation's capital. Upon enquiring at the War Department about an exchange of cannon, Smith encountered the usual bureaucratic bumbledom. After gentle prodding by Smith, Secretary Eustis declared that he lacked the authority to conclude such an arrangement. However, on the General's recognizance, Eustis agreed to loan Smith two brass field pieces which were housed in Charleston, South Carolina.[10]

David Stone. Courtesy of State Archives, Office of Archives and History, Raleigh.

Upon leaving Washington, Smith returned to Raleigh and then to Belvedere. During his layover at Belvedere, Smith met with Brunswick County magistrates on April 30, 1810, in the new county seat of Smithville, which had been designated for the honor by the legislature in 1808 once the public buildings had been erected. The General appreciated the shorter trip from Belvedere to his namesake town, not to mention the impressive courthouse whose construction he had helped to direct. The single-story brick building, supported by seven arches that rose eleven feet in height, was described as commodious and "finished off very neatly, being plastered and glazed with ten by twelve window lights." Business at court proceeded as usual, with the General detailing once again why he was late in submitting the tax list for the Northwest District. By that time his excuses must have been reduced to rote explanation.[11]

The General then proceeded to Charleston where he sought the cannon offered by the secretary of war. On his own initiative Smith decided to send the cannon to New Bern and Wilmington at his "*own expense*" (italics added). When Stone at long last inquired about Smith's mission, the General informed him of the fait accompli. Smith justified his action with the observation that obtaining field pieces was so critical that he would have ridden "throughout

Brunswick County Courthouse. Courtesy of New Hanover Public Library.

the United States" to have acquired them, though he supposed that the General Assembly would not have underwritten the expense. Nevertheless, Smith magnanimously added, "No charge will be made for what I have done."[12]

Following his return from Charleston the General prepared to spend the summer months at his town homes in Wilmington and Smithville. If in the latter on July 4, he was awakened in the morning by the discharge of thirteen cannon at Fort Johnston. At one o'clock in the afternoon officers of the garrison, residents of Smithville, and visitors gathered in Samuel Potter's hotel to enjoy a meal prepared for the occasion, offer sixteen toasts accompanied by booming cannon, and listen to an oration by Maj. Swift, the speaker of the day.[13]

At the end of the month, on July 30, Smith took his place on the bench at the quarterly session of the Brunswick county court which met in Smithville. His brother James also made an appearance, rare in fact, for James divided his time between the two Carolinas. The three-day session reflected the humdrum of business except for the annual election of a sheriff—John G. Scull, unanimously—and the determination of a polling place for elections in the Lockwoods Folly District since the county court no longer convened there. The General again signed the minutes as senior magistrate.[14]

Two days after the conclusion of the three-day July-August session of the county court, Smith and Major Swift, in the company of Robert Cochrane, collector of the Port of Wilmington, sailed to Bald Head Island to meet lighthouse keeper Sedgwick Springs. The General rarely visited his island refuge in his later years. But Swift, apprehensive of the ocean waters encroaching on the lighthouse and anticipating the construction of another, wanted to mark off more accurately the ten acres of land given by Smith to North Carolina and transferred to the United States some two decades earlier.[15]

By that time Bald Head may have supported a small population in addition to Springs, as indicated by Smith in 1809, when he told the state senate that "certain inhabitants ... residing" on the island wanted to be annexed to New Hanover County. In any case Bald Head was well known by that time for harboring "a fine brand" of wild sheep, resembling the Merino just recently brought into the United States from Spain. Apparently Smith did not, or could not, object to residents or mainlanders who rounded up the animals and sheared them twice a year. Accompanying the sheep on Bald Head in January and February were prodigious numbers of pigeons. Again Smith seemed powerless to prevent sportsmen from bringing down "many thousands of these birds," according to Swift.[16]

When Swift and Smith returned from their excursion to Bald Head, elections loomed on August 9 for members of the state legislature. The major gave the men of Fort Johnston the day off, ostensibly for a fishing excursion across the river to Oak Island but actually in order to obviate any question of "interference of troops at the polls," because questions had been raised about officers' abuse of their subordinates' right of the franchise.[17] Whether the soldiers fished or voted, in the latter instance expecting to be swilled at the polls, General Smith again was elected to the state Senate to represent Brunswick County.

After the uneventful two-day session of the Brunswick County court in late October, Smith was on the road again, this time to Raleigh for the meeting of the General Assembly, scheduled to convene on November 19, 1810, and for the convention of the Grand Lodge of Freemasons. Presiding over the grand lodge, Smith shared communications from lodges across the country and from Nova Scotia. He continued to visit local lodges in North Carolina, finding some "deficient in symbolic masonry," but most "expert." Smith particularly praised the charitableness and "brotherly love" exhibited by those in the local lodges, not only toward members of the craft but their communities as well, which, he said, "characterizes the Mason from other individuals." The General was in turn reelected and installed as grand master for 1811.[18]

As for the General Assembly, Smith, along with all but two of the senators and six of the commoners, answered the roll on the opening day at which time the houses chose their respective speakers, clerks, and doorkeepers. The General for a last time sought a United States Senate seat from the state. However, resigned to another negative decision after a second ballot, he withdrew from the contest, and the legislators elected former governor James Turner over incumbent governor David Stone.[19]

Smith sought solace in his committee endeavors. He again chaired the committee on rules of decorum for the Senate and served on the committee to respond to the governor's message. In addition, evidencing due republican concern for the people's money, he proposed that all committee reports and resolutions requiring appropriations from the state treasury be read three times in both houses before their passage. He also presented a petition from residents of Crusoe Island, a remote section of Green Swamp in Brunswick County, so named because of its isolation, to be annexed to Columbus County.[20]

About two weeks into the session the lawmakers turned to the heady business of choosing a governor, who was elected jointly by the two houses of the General Assembly. Smith, current governor David Stone, longtime, active Orange County legislator James Mebane, and current speaker of the Senate Joseph Riddick vied for the honor. Smith and Stone were the frontrunners from the outset. After the second ballot Riddick, who had little support, withdrew, and after the third Mebane followed suit. Smith, who trailed Stone by seven votes on the first ballot, took the lead on the second, held it by a narrow margin on the third, and picked up a number of Mebane's supporters to win on the fourth, 97 to 85, on November 29. The General appeared before the two houses in the Commons Hall of the capitol on December 5, and took the oath of office, which was administered by Henry Seawell, justice of the peace of Wake County.[21]

The governorship was the product of Smith's carefully cultivated relationships, a demonstrated record of service in the General Assembly, and a genuine concern for the welfare of his adopted state. It was a fitting capstone for one who embraced the ethos of noblesse oblige and a life of public service, and marked the pinnacle of Smith's political career. At the same time the gubernatorial office must have afforded Smith great satisfaction when he compared his record of public service with those of his father and namesake uncle, who, as colonials, never had the opportunity to achieve the highest public office in South Carolina.

From the inception of the state many prominent men served as governor of North Carolina, including Caswell, Johnston, Martin, Spaight, Davie, and Stone, but the gubernatorial office was largely honorific, accompanied by little authority and some real expense that was not adequately compensated by the salary of the executive.[22] The state constitution of 1776 had purposely subordinated the executive to the legislature, and not surprisingly, given the fear of Americans at the time of their former royal masters, governors and king. Thus the representatives of the people in assembly elected the governor, who, deprived of a veto, was unable to exert any real pressure on the legislature.

Governors thus served at the pleasure of the General Assembly, executing various directives issued to them by the legislature. For Smith the tasks included procuring seals for Montgomery County and for the state Supreme Court,[23] and salvaging the twenty-seven iron cannon at Edenton, which retiring Governor Stone reported were slipping in the water of the bay fronting the town. In the instance of the cannon, whatever course of action may have been taken by Governor Smith, the twenty-seven, unmounted and without ammunition, still graced Edenton's waterfront at the beginning of the War of 1812. Late in the war, they were dispersed to Wilmington, New Bern, and Beacon Island, which guarded Ocracoke Inlet.[24]

Additionally, according to legislation in 1805 by which the General Assembly assumed control of the university, the legislatively-elected governor automatically served as the president of the board of trustees for the institution. In the ensuing years partisan rancor subsided, and the Republican-dominated board accepted Federalist president Joseph Caldwell, whose merits were beyond reproach. But the financial woes of the university continued. In April 1809, treasurer Gavin Alves wrote to trustee Archibald D. Murphey that the "situation of the University Coffers is truly deplorable.... [T]here is not one cent on hand." And he worried that salaries would go unpaid.[25]

Circumstances proved not quite so dire, though had little improved the following year. Before the adjournment of the legislature Governor Smith, as president of the university trustees, presented the financial report of the board to the legislature as required by law. Alves had managed his moneys well, for income exceeded expenditures by the princely sum of approximately $10 (though President Caldwell had to pay for a tutor for the preparatory school out of his own pocket). Nonetheless, the trustees were clearly concerned about the state of the university's finances during the session of the board that coincided with the meeting of the General Assembly in 1810.[26]

As the newly-minted governor, Smith assumed command of the board at its third meeting on December 7, and presided over five subsequent sessions. The quest for funding was paramount, and collections depended principally upon the attorneys appointed by the board to retrieve escheated properties in the name of the university. Unfortunately, those "Gentleman" had failed to attend to their responsibility "with all that Industry and zeal which might be wished." But that was understandable, given the unpopular nature of their job and their meager pecuniary reward. After all, according to a committee report, "in times of difficulty and danger the Republic has an undoubted right to command the active services of all its Citizens; but that in the sunshine of peace it will very rarely be found that any are disposed to labour for the common weal without adequate reward." Thus the trustees tripled the commission of the attorneys for taking possession and selling land and doubled their allowance for forwarding the sums to the university treasurer.[27]

Sundry other matters occupied the attention of the board. At virtually every meeting the trustees fielded protests of those whose land was threatened or had been confiscated by the university. In addition, the trustees agreed to continue work on the chapel and to purchase a commemorative marble slab to recognize Thomas Person, who had donated a sizable sum of money to underwrite the chapel's construction. Of course additional solicitations were needed to finish Main Building. Smith was appointed to a committee to find "suitable" men, "fully instructed, but likewise carefully & sufficiently warned of the delicacy & importance of their mission," to canvass the state for such donations. At the suggestion of President Caldwell the trustees voted to replace the single vacation for university students with two (May-June, November-December). As had become customary, the trustees agreed to a mid-year, July meeting in Raleigh in 1811.[28]

Not only had Benjamin Smith assumed the governorship and presidency of the university trustees, but, in effect, he had inherited the nominal command of the capital town of the state in which he was expected to reside. Raleigh numbered 976 permanent residents in 1810—342 free white males, 266 free white females, 43 free blacks, and 325 slaves.[29] Though small in numbers, as the capital and seat of Wake County, the town was a hotbed of activity, hosting sessions of the federal Circuit Court, state Supreme Court, and county superior and inferior courts.

To accommodate visitors and transients, including judicial figures and members of the General Assembly, Raleigh offered excellent facilities. The most famous by 1810 were William Scott's Indian Queen Tavern, Mrs. (Margaret) Casso's Tavern, and Josiah Dillard's Boarding-House, all of which were advertised extensively before the General Assembly met in 1810. The Indian Queen had recently added a 44-foot long dining room, and offered spacious stables, a variety of forage for horses, and a carriage house. Casso's boasted a three-story, 34- by 28-foot structure plus annexes, two kitchens, and a paved "horse yard" and "stable, equal to any on the Continent." Dillard, whose boarding house was only seventy-five yards from the State House, had rented a house that allowed him to accept an additional thirty to thirty-five patrons.[30]

However, separate quarters were available for the governor. Initially, the General Assembly demanded that only the treasurer, secretary of state, and comptroller reside permanently in Raleigh. The chief executive remained a part-timer, required by law in 1794 to stay in the town at least half the year exclusive of the time in which the legislature sat. Two years later the state provided lodging for the governor when it purchased a two-story residence on the southwest corner of Fayetteville and Hargett streets, which included a garden, stables, and other outbuildings. However, according to a correspondent to a New Bern newspaper the following year, "the house in which the governor resides, and the stile in which he lives, are no way suited to the dignity of the first magistrates of a state."[31]

Nonetheless, after purchasing a domicile for the governor, the General Assembly in 1797 mandated that the executive reside in Raleigh throughout his tenure, pointedly adding "permanently" to the charge in 1802. Yet, so distasteful was the prospect of residing in the Governor's Palace, the derisive appellation of the gubernatorial residence, that executives initially resorted to renting properties in the capital for themselves and their families. And despite the frequent criticism of the governor's quarters, penny-pinching legislatures in 1805, 1807, and 1810 refused to take action, or for that matter raise the governor's salary to enable him to afford more suitable housing.[32]

Regardless of the law, Smith spent most of his gubernatorial tenure at Belvedere, often incurring criticism for his frequent absences from the capital. At the end of the legislative session in December 1810, he left Raleigh to spend two months in Brunswick County before reappearing in the capital on February 24. After a two-week sojourn he departed on March 8, not to return until May 12. Hardly unpacking his trunk, five days proved sufficient for Smith to dispatch gubernatorial business. He again took flight, reappeared in July for a sojourn, and returned to the capital on November 15 in time for the opening of the General Assembly.[33]

Smith's tenure in absentia rankled. Although giving notice of his departures and leaving his secretary in the capital as required by law, Smith certainly appeared to violate the statute that required the permanent residence of the governor in Raleigh. A Rowan County man became a cause celebre in January 1811, when he traveled one hundred and twenty miles to see the executive, only to be disappointed upon reaching the capital. Yet, on the whole, governors found themselves in little demand. Smith inconvenienced few, and the General Assembly in 1811 considered relaxing the stringent gubernatorial resident requirements.[34]

In fact, Smith was unaware of his impending election and had no time to prepare for an extensive absence from home. He faced pressing business at the superior courts of New Hanover and Brunswick counties — and business (or creditors) became increasingly pressing on the General. Moreover, the governor's house in Raleigh was hardly habitable and the social amenities of the capital, compared to Wilmington and the resort of Smithville in the summer, left much to be desired. But the General's most serious concern, and one that necessarily remained private, was the unstable mental condition of his wife, Sarah.

The governor had been warned about the deteriorated state of the palace in Raleigh, and was forced to agree "with all who view it" that it was not "fit for the family of a decent Tradesman and certainly none could be satisfied if ever safe in it." A recent storm had damaged the chimneys, plaster frequently fell, and the roof was so leaky that during a rain "a wetting [was] experienced" in walking from the bedchambers to the sitting room. In a wilder moment he even considered bringing some of his own workmen to make repairs. Though Smith was "not apt to stand on trifle," he wrote, still he could not keep his family in the house "with any degree of comfort," particularly, Sarah whom he hoped to bring to the capital in July.[35]

Apparently a woman of delicate health, whom Smith tried to protect from the "baleful effects of our sickly Climate," Sarah escaped the ague and rheumatic fevers only to fall prey to an "incomprehensible" mental disorder. Restless and nervous, without any apparently physical disorder, she suffered from a sort of paranoia about her husband's well being. Her bouts worsened, of course, during his absences, when "nothing could persuade her at times but what I was dead," the governor confided to John Haywood.[36]

Smith had left Sarah at Belvedere when he journeyed to Raleigh in July for meetings with the council of state and university trustees but expected his wife to join him soon. Each evening he rode to the edge of town in hopes of meeting her, but after a week received notice that she was ill at home. The news so upset Smith that he decided to return to Belvedere the next day. During the following months Smith once tried to return to Raleigh, but found on the day of the planned departure that "it would have been impossible to ... [leave Sarah] without the utmost cruelty." Late in October 1811, however, the impending session of the legislature forced Smith to make the inevitable journey. He hoped to take Sarah, but she was worse than ever, "I may say horribly so," wrote the governor. Sarah apparently did not accompany Smith to Raleigh in November.[37]

More troubling, perhaps, than Smith's absence from the capital, was his penchant for ostentation. As he had throughout his life, Smith reveled in attention and display. On his return to the Lower Cape Fear in January after his election, the governor entered Wilmington in full uniform where he was given a military escort to his residence on Dock Street. At that point the town commissioners, magistrates, officers of the United States government, and several "very respectable" citizens who failed to occupy any of those positions together with the two attending military companies partook of appropriate refreshment.[38] At his arrival in Raleigh in March the scene was repeated — an escort by a troop of cavalry, a salute with the discharge of cannon at the governor's house, and a dinner for dignitaries and the military at the Indian Queen Tavern.[39]

While Smith and others may have argued that the insignificance of the governor's office in North Carolina demanded the display in order to elevate the importance of the position, the pomp and circumstance aroused the objections of those who felt that needless ostentation did not comport well with republican institutions. The *Minerva* printed a rousing caricature of Smith's entrée into Wilmington by a correspondent who concluded his piece, "Sic transit gloria mundi."[40] Upon Smith's return to Wilmington and Belvedere early in 1811, he received an invitation from Major Swift to inspect a refurbished Fort Johnston. The governor, of course, was "received with military honors."[41] Indeed, Smith was hoisted on his own petard, given his frequent espousal of republican principles over the years.

Smith was not idle like European monarchy. He had already proved to be a conscientious public servant. In the course of the year of his gubernatorial tenure Smith fielded the correspondence that attended his office, though sometimes from Belvedere. The governor's papers of Smith's administration, though not voluminous, reveal the nature of the business that crossed the desk of the chief executive of North Carolina. Broadly, the eighty-seven items in his executive correspondence fell into nine categories: criminal matters, principally extraditions of criminals from neighboring states but also requests for clemency and proclamations for the apprehension of escaped prisoners (24); resignations of public officials (15); receipt of copies of the journals of Congress and laws of the United States and other states (13); notices of elections of public officials by the General Assembly (8); approval of a proposed constitutional amendment by five states (5); matters relating to the survey of the state's borders with South Carolina and Georgia (3); acknowledgment of payments for services to the state government (3); banks (3); and miscellaneous, including perfecting the titles of North Carolinians to land in Tennessee and fortifying North Carolina's coast (13).[42]

Most of the correspondence treated pedestrian matters, but some was anything but trivial. The border disputes with the South Carolina and Georgia were sources of ongoing controversy, and the land claims of North Carolinians in Tennessee, including Smith's bequest to the university, remained unsettled for decades to come. Governor Smith also hoped to impress the General Assembly with the necessity of protecting the coastal region, particularly the Lower Cape Fear, from invasion, and enlisted the aid of Major Swift to draft a lengthy disquisition to that end. The death of Wilmington acquaintance Judge Joshua G. Wright required the governor to fill a vacancy on the state superior court of law and equity (forerunner of the state supreme court, 1819). Earlier Wright had submitted a contingent resignation to Smith, citing ill health. He died on June 10 in time for the governor to appoint his replacement on his visit to Raleigh in July.[43]

Though nominally subservient to the legislature, governors could not be dismissed offhandedly. Among their patronage they appointed notaries public, adjutants general, and directors to represent the state on the boards of the

Bank of Newbern and the Bank of Cape Fear. Governors made interim appointments to the Council of State, an executive advisory body of seven elected by the General Assembly, and the state superior court. The executives also granted pardons and reprieves. Breaking with precedent, Smith, who realized that he likely would know very little about the circumstances surrounding a proposed pardon, announced that he required a favorable statement from the judge or justices, or a recommendation of mercy from the jury that brought a guilty verdict, strengthened by a statement of support from "numerous and respectable Inhabitants of the County" in which the condemned criminal resided or was found guilty, to justify executive clemency.[44]

In the course of his restricted forays to Raleigh, Governor Smith spent a week in the capital in early July, necessitated by the previously arranged meeting of the trustees of the university, but which opportunistically permitted a called meeting of the council of state to select a successor to Judge Wright, and coincided with the Fourth of July. After the usual military displays and orations to celebrate the Fourth, dignitaries led by Governor Smith sat down in the statehouse to a dinner prepared by Mrs. Casso. The governor presided. Appropriate toasts followed the meal, the last of which recognized "His Excellency the Governor of North Carolina." A ball in the evening rewarded the presence of the ladies.[45]

Members of the Council of State arrived on the anniversary of independence, and Smith convened the group the next day. Regarding a successor to Judge Wright, Smith acknowledged that no applications for his vacant position had been made. Although the constitution invested the governor with the power to appoint judges to the state superior court on an interim basis, Smith felt the responsibility was not an *"indispensable duty."* Thus he sought a recommendation from the Council of State. Unable to agree on a candidate, the council retired, returned the next day, and suggested Henry Seawell, lawyer, state attorney general, and Wake County magistrate who had administered the gubernatorial oath of office to Smith. The governor approved, and appointed Seawell, who took his place on the bench of the court that currently sat in Raleigh.[46]

Smith also informed the Council of State of correspondence from the governor of Georgia, who had rejected an earlier agreement defining the boundary between Georgia and North Carolina. Smith claimed that the matter had been settled, at least from the perspective of North Carolina, and that he had no "power or disposition" to take further action. Moreover, to accede to the wishes of the governor of Georgia would directly contravene decisions already made by the North Carolina General Assembly. The Council of State agreed, and the longstanding border controversy awaited another day for resolution.[47]

13. Governor

Following the meeting of the Council of State, Smith convened the university trustees on July 6 for a brief and uneventful gathering that had been planned the previous December. A respectable turnout of fourteen members, including Smith, on a hot July day in Raleigh dealt with such mundane matters as compensating the treasurer of the board for several expenditures, paying the tutor employed by the university, replacing one of the university's attorneys, and suspending the collection of moneys from a debtor of the university pending further consideration by the trustees.[48]

Among other responsibilities of the governor, Smith reviewed the state's troops when possible, an exercise at which he had become proficient as brigadier and major general. It was mostly a ceremonial occasion, which Smith certainly appreciated, but it also offered the men the opportunity for much needed drill. Yet, Smith was disappointed in his intention to inspect the militia in the western part of the state, in part because of "the unprecedented scarcity of corn," fodder needed to support the horses of the governor's considerable entourage, and in part because of Smith's failure to receive opportune responses to inquiries about times and places of reviews from his general officers. Consoling the governor, however, was his review of the militia of Wake County in November, with an all-star cast that included two major generals, three brigadier generals, and the governor's military staff.[49]

The governor and legislators gathered in Raleigh for the opening of the General Assembly on November 18. Five days later Smith convened the university trustees, chairing four meetings as governor until his successor was elected. The business confronting the board consisted principally of electing a steward and a superintendent of buildings for the university, paying the tutor of the preparatory school, hiring a tutor for the university, confirming the authority of the president and professor to confer degrees with distinction, subject to the approval of the trustees, and settling a dispute over land in which the university had an interest. The final item of business on Smith's watch was the decision to limit the number of students residing within the halls of the college to thirty, a response to the difficulties engendered by intense overcrowding in the dorm. Once replaced as governor, Smith took flight to the low country, never again to attend meetings of the board.[50]

Meanwhile, as customary, upon the sitting of the legislature and before he bade farewell to his office (unless reelected), the governor by his private secretary dispatched his annual address to the General Assembly. Ritually, the governor tried to impress the legislators with their weighty responsibility as representatives of the people in a republic whose governance rested upon the consent of the governed, alluded to matters that had come to his attention during the previous year, suggested matters worthy of the attention of the legislature, and reflected on the affairs of the times. In effect, the gubernatorial speech was the bully pulpit for executives of North Carolina, an opportunity, limited as it was, to air their views and prod the General Assembly to action.

In a rambling address to the legislature in 1811 Smith broached several topics for special consideration, all of which had been the subjects of previous gubernatorial communications — a penitentiary, education, domestic manufacturing, and, of course, the militia. He also shared with the General Assembly a missive from the secretary of state of the United States which conveyed a proposed amendment to the Constitution that would strip any American of his citizenship and bar him from public office if he received a title of honor, office, or preferment from a foreign country without the consent of Congress; the exchange of statutes with other states; a letter from DeWitt Clinton, mayor of New York City, about the suppression of counterfeiting in that state; a request from the state of New York seeking assistance for a proposed canal — the Erie Canal (which Smith lauded); correspondence relative to the ongoing boundary differences between North Carolina and its southern neighbors; a proposal to establish an independent chancery court for the state; and the suggestion that the legislature fill vacancies occasioned by the deaths of Judge Wright and Secretary of State William White.[51]

The reform of North Carolina's penal system had long been a concern of Smith and, too, the General Assembly, which had often considered but rejected several bills to revise the penal code and establish a penitentiary, including one the previous session, which was lost to the tie-breaking vote of the speaker of the Senate. During his tenure as governor Smith gathered information about penal systems, principally from Virginia, intending to use the example of that state's penitentiary to buttress his proposal to establish a prison in North Carolina. Smith clearly hoped that a penitentiary would lead to reform in the penal code by offering the possibility of incarcerating rather than executing convicted lawbreakers. Moreover, Virginia's system indicated that such an institution, utilizing the labor of the prisoners, might actually turn a profit if managed properly. In an obvious appeal to the pecuniary instincts of the legislature, the governor suggested that a small tax, a "trifling" sum divided among the thousands of taxpayers, might be imposed until the system became self-supporting. And, added Smith, a penitentiary would offer the means to reform "the too sanguinary Criminal Code derived from Great Britain whilst under her government."[52]

Smith also importuned the legislature in the cause of education in which he had an abiding interest, not only higher education, which seemed firmly rooted in the state in the form of the university, but elementary learning. "Too much attention cannot be paid to that all-important subject," claimed the governor. From "earliest infancy" the advantages of a free republic should be inculcated into every citizen, he thought, in order "to produce an enthusiastic attachment to their own country, and ensure a jealous support of their own constitution, laws and government, to the total exclusion of all foreign influence or partiality." Education, based on "the true principles of Christian religion," would uplift morality and prevent the criminal activities "now too frequently perpetrated in the country." Hence, Smith claimed, a "certain degree of education should be placed within the reach of every child in the State," including "the poorest of every neighborhood."[53]

The governor briefly adverted to the need to promote domestic manufactures, a patriotic reflection of anti–British sentiment that had been aroused by the embargo of 1807. North Carolinians embraced the Jeffersonian effort to punish the British. Soon after the imposition of the Embargo a society to encourage the manufacture of local cloth appeared in Caswell County, and the legislators of that county appeared in Raleigh in clothing that "at once did honour to *their* patriotism, and the taste and industry of *the Ladies*." In 1809, the General Assembly with Smith voting in the affirmative approved a resolution urging all members of the legislature to appear in Raleigh in 1810 clad in clothing "entirely either the manufactures of this State, or of the United States." Smith obliged, standing proudly before the General Assembly "dressed in a suit of American cloth" to take the oath of office as governor.[54]

Smith unsurprisingly devoted a substantial part of his message to the subject of the militia and the increasing threat of war. As captain general and commander-in-chief of the military forces in North Carolina (though as governor he had to relinquish the major generalship of the sixth division), Smith took charge of a reported 51,727 militia (50,251 infantry, 1,474 cavalry, and 2 artillery). About two-thirds of the infantry was armed, mainly with shotguns. However, with the exception of rifles, the firearms generally were defective. Less than half of the cavalrymen claimed sabers or cutlasses.[55]

Well that Governor Smith did not have to call on the militia to defend the state, given the caustic criticism of William Croom, brigadier general of the twelfth brigade. According to that officer, the firearms of the men under his command were fit only for training exercises. He complained about the absence of uniformity of modes of training and bemoaned the lack of discipline among the men. Croom attributed the last in part to the "prevailing practice of candidates for Congress and the Assembly attending company musters for the purpose of electioneering." As a result musters degenerated into drinking bouts and fights. The brigadier general recommended more frequent gatherings of militia officers and the establishment of military schools to elevate the status of militia personnel.[56]

Smith declared that Carolinians could not enjoy their many blessings in peace and security if they were not willing "to defend [their] rights ... punish insults and avenge wrongs.... To be prepared for war, frequently ensures peace." While the burden of defense fell to the national government, the states should take the responsibility for providing a well trained, well equipped, and properly led militia which could accomplish "the most brilliant victories" as at King's Mountain during the Revolution. Although the governor had been unable to review the militia in the western part of the state as he had planned, he promised to communicate further with the legislature "on this [actually his] favorite object of *improving the Militia*."[57]

Last, the governor reminded the legislators of the current crisis in foreign affairs, the "portentous & threatening clouds [that] darken our political horizon, [and] which must soon be dispelled, or they will generate a storm that will burst on our heads with redoubled fury." According to Smith, after years of suffering the European belligerents to ignore American rights, imprison its citizens, plunder its property, and degrade the United States with "insults not to be endured by a nation having any pretensions to honor or independence," it was "full time to make a determined stand." He counseled a cessation of party hostilities, support for President Madison, and opposition to any efforts that threatened the division of the union. Above all, he concluded, reflecting his Christian principles and command of the Scripture (and, of course, the assumption that his audience was of like mind), the legislators should regard "the one thing needful" which would ensure "peace, liberty, and happiness to our common and beloved country."[58]

Later in the session the governor fulfilled his pledge to elaborate on the subject of the militia, though the past reluctance of the General Assembly to reform and arm the troops and to provide for coastal defense rendered the governor's effort to rouse a martial ardor problematic at best. Yet Smith persevered, proposing in this instance to create elite, volunteer companies of infantry, and then cavalry, in each county which would serve to "raise a military spirit and emulation." The governor also suggested that the state arm the companies at the expense of the public, which, as he pointed out, would have the doubly desired effect of stimulating domestic manufacturing. Anticipating the crisis of 1812, Smith pointed out the vulnerability of North Carolina's extensive coast and offered guidelines for protecting Edenton, Ocracoke Inlet, and particularly the Cape Fear, which required "very considerable works" in addition to Fort Johnston. He urged the legislature to instruct the state's members of Congress to call Washington's attention to the need to defend better North Carolina's coast. Since President Madison had recently informed Congress that defensive works for major Atlantic ports had been finished, surely the southern states merited more attention.[59]

With the insignificant exceptions of adopting a resolution to instruct North Carolina's congressional delegates to seek funds for coastal defense, approving the proposed constitutional amendment (which was never ratified by a sufficient number of states to add to the Constitution), and electing replacements for Wright and White, the legislature responded to the governor's message with a resounding negative.[60] The Senate and House felt that support for the laudable Erie Canal project was best left to the "general Government" and stood firm on the commitments already made to South Carolina on the boundary question. As for the crux of Smith's proposals, the legislators deemed any consideration of education "inexpedient," refused to recommend steps to arm the militia or the alter the militia laws, failed to pursue a Senate bill to establish courts of equity (a measure that had been introduced before Smith's gubernatorial message), and remained silent on the subject of the penitentiary.[61]

Perhaps the governor should not have been too disappointed, for the legislative session of 1811 was hardly productive. Only twenty-two public laws emerged from the General Assembly, and half of those were additions or amendments to existing legislation. Of the remainder, four dealt with state or county tax collections. Otherwise, the legislators ratified the proposed amendment to the federal Constitution, deemed thefts of bank notes, public securities, corn, rice, and cotton to be felonies, and decided that stills were personal rather than real estate.

The highlight of the session was a controversial measure designed by the Republicans to deprive the Federalists of electoral votes by vesting the choice of presidential electors in the General Assembly rather than voting by congressional district (which usually permitted the Federalists three or four votes). The law evoked formal protests in both houses of the legislature. Eventually the public outcry forced the Republicans to repeal the law in 1815, though not until after the presidential election in 1812 in which Madison received all fifteen of North Carolina's electoral ballots.[62]

Where the General Assembly made its mark in 1811, as had become increasingly common, was in the realm of private acts, 112 in total, which treated singular subjects rather then the body politic. Leading the way were laws relating to individual county courts (28), followed by internal improvements (navigability of rivers, roads, turnpikes, bridges, canals) (17), towns (14), militia (13), elections (9), fisheries (6), demographic considerations (15 — divorce, altering names, restoring citizenship, emancipation), and miscellanea. However, as recognized by a joint resolution that was designed to limit the introduction of private bills, such legislation became increasingly burdensome and, by extension, expensive, because it prolonged legislative sessions and elevated per diem compensation.[63]

While the legislators digested and rejected most of Governor Smith's proposals, they began the quest for an executive for the ensuing year. William Hawkins of Granville County, the current speaker of the House of Commons,

Smith, and the unsuccessful contenders in 1810, Joseph Riddick and James Mebane, were the nominees. Hawkins led on the first ballot, closely followed by Smith, but the General then opted out, claiming that he had been nominated "without his desire or knowledge." As he explained to the General Assembly in his promised address on the militia, "Circumstances of too delicate a nature, and too uninteresting for public detail, but wholly uncontroulable by me, confirmed an opinion long before entertained, that my present and future happiness would be promoted by retirement and tranquility." As some members of the legislature might have realized, Smith could not cope with Sarah, travel, and the prospect of residency in Raleigh for another year. Riddick withdrew as well. On the second ballot, Hawkins easily outdistanced Mebane to win the governorship, which he assumed on December 9, 1811, bringing to an end Smith's one-term tenure as governor.[64]

Smith used his speech on the militia and defense as the medium not only to forswear future gubernatorial aspirations but also as a means of self-adulation in which he reminded the legislators of his "never-failing attendance" at the Brunswick County Court to the time of his gubernatorial election and of his "never being absent" from his seat in the legislature "but for a very few minutes" when he was able to attend.[65] And he had not finished. Five days after Hawkins became governor, Smith sent an addendum to his gubernatorial message to the House of Commons. He reviewed his service as speaker of the Senate and closed with a tour of his military offices — brigadier general, adjutant general which at the time required "much beyond the common Routine of Service & knowledge," and major general, when he was rewarded by the creation of "a new Division for my especial Command" that included the maritime section of the state which was most exposed to attack, and "assuredly the Post of Danger & of course the Post of Honor."[66] On that note, the former governor departed Raleigh for a decade and a half of increasing disappointments and indignities that ended only with his death.

CHAPTER 14

DENOUEMENT AND DEATH

A certain irony attached to Benjamin Smith's decision to renounce the governorship in 1811 and return to private life. Understandable and necessary though it was, another term or two, if permitted by the legislature, would have placed Smith in command of the state during a war, a full-fledged, protracted conflict with his old nemesis, Great Britain. How the General must have regretted his self-imposed exile to Belvedere. Moreover, not only was he bereft of political influence, he had lost his militia command when elevated to the governorship. He could engage the British only by imagination and conversation.

As indicated by his gubernatorial address, Smith anticipated the conflict variously termed the War of 1812 and Mr. Madison's War. From the onset of the Napoleonic wars in 1803, the old antagonists, England and France, played havoc with Americans and their putative neutral rights. But what began as an instant replay of the 1790s played out to a different conclusion, a war with the British rather than the French. Tippecanoe in November 1811 may have been the tipping point, though President Madison did not tip his hand until June 1, 1812, when he sought a declaration of war against Great Britain from Congress.

Reflecting sentiment across the country, a badly divided Congress responded half-heartedly by voting for war but offering little in the way of monetary support for the conflict, an unfunded mandate of sorts. Western and southern states plus Pennsylvania carried the day; New York and New England opposed. North Carolina, always suspicious of the national government, evidenced less enthusiasm than other southern states, though Congressman William R. King, who represented the Fifth Congressional District, including the Lower Cape Fear region, cast an affirmative ballot for war.

The War of 1812 touched North Carolina lightly. Luckily, North Carolina had no need for General Smith's leadership or exhortations, or even the minimal defenses erected in the Lower Cape Fear to confound an enemy invasion.

Attempts to fortify Clark Island in the Cape Fear River below Wilmington would have seemed risible to the British. Gunboats that had been constructed in Wilmington in the wake of the *Chesapeake* crisis in 1807 were retired in 1813, but following Napoleon's defeat in 1814 and fearing a British invasion of the Lower Cape Fear, President Madison authorized another flotilla of little boats to protect the region, but they were too late for service and too short on firepower had the vessels been needed.[1]

Actually the British appeared in the area on several occasions in 1814. Mildly threatening were three enemy vessels that stood off the main bar of the Cape Fear River for several days in June. Three local pilots were captured but released. The following month the *Peacock* approached Federal Point but departed upon espying local militia. Not so fortunate were sailors sent ashore south of Wilmington by the *Lacedemonian* to find cattle. Leaving their barge laxly guarded, the entire British party was captured by local militia.[2]

Had the British chosen to invade the Lower Cape Fear, they would have found Fort Johnston "a mere apology" for a defense work, as so many had attested since the mid–1790s. General Smith's construction efforts had accomplished little. Barracks were insufficient, necessitating the construction of crude log houses. The battery was located so near the water that it suffered damage from high tides, and a bluff of oyster shells stood thirty feet behind the fort, promising to scatter like shrapnel if hit. Yet, an enemy assault was unnecessary because the British could send light-draft vessels through New Inlet upriver and bypass Fort Johnston altogether.[3]

The war concluded on a happy note for President Madison and the United States. Americans confirmed their independence, patriotic feeling ran high, and Madison enjoyed an esteem scarcely imaginable at the beginning of the conflict. Gov. William Miller congratulated members of the General Assembly in November 1815 on the "brilliant termination" of the contest with Great Britain. The following year he later reported to the satisfaction, if not astonishment, of most in the legislature that the national government had reimbursed North Carolina for its wartime expenditures to the sum of $30,000.[4]

The end of the war returned North Carolina to a sense of normalcy. Overwhelmingly a state of small, scattered, and ergo individualistic agriculturalists, North Carolina maintained its devotion to the democracy of the Jeffersonian party. Not only did agriculture reign supreme, but axiomatically, it seemed, commerce and manufacturing would never flourish in a state whose roads were impassable, whose rivers were clogged, and whose coast was blocked by sand islands punctuated by shifting and shallow inlets. Lacking commercial centers, adequate banking facilities, and staple exports, the state's economy stagnated.

14. Denouement and Death

Given its penchant for a strict construction of the Constitution, an ongoing distrust of the national government, and a perceived need to economize in public affairs, all reinforced by the dominance of the Jeffersonian Republican party, North Carolina lacked an impetus or agency for change. Despite gubernatorial hints or even remonstrances to the General Assembly, the state paid little more than lip service to the need for public education and internal improvements for many years, preferring instead to rely upon the problematic endeavors of its citizens in a private capacity to institute academies, build turnpikes, and improve the navigability of the rivers and streams. The result was an exodus of the more ambitious and industrious North Carolinians, who left their Rip Van Winkle state to seek their fortunes elsewhere.

The Lower Cape Fear region constituted something of an exception to the rule, benefiting as it did from its extensive system of navigable rivers and streams and staple exports of rice and naval stores. Yet, even Wilmington, North Carolina's only deepwater port of consequence, languished for decades after the War of 1812. Recessionary conditions reigned for a quarter century. Along the Cape Fear River valleys the wealth and extravagance of pre–Revolutionary days waned. By definition the planter elite were always few in North Carolina, and their scant number was reduced by one with the decline and fall of Benjamin Smith.

Frustrated as the General must have been by his political and military separation from the war, at least he could resume his position of eminence and responsibility as justice of the peace, or so he thought. As governor he had eschewed the quarterly sessions of the Brunswick County court. But in January 1812, upon relinquishing the executive department, he returned to the bench, only to encounter doubts about his eligibility to serve as a justice after the governorship. However, at the opening of the session of the county court the seven other magistrates agreed that the General might take his seat. Nonetheless, the court harbored reservations. Two years later the justices asked the county attorney for a formal investigation into the matter. Apparently counsel found no impropriety or illegality, and the General continued to attend and preside at court.[5]

In 1812, Smith, joined occasionally by his brother James, maintained a high profile as the senior justice and thus chairman of the court. Yet the chairmanship was honorific. Smith was actually primus inter pares. When seventeen justices met in July to elect a new sheriff, John Gause, Jr., son of one of the magistrates, the General objected, claiming that the younger Gause had not reached his legal majority and thus was ineligible for the office. Six other magistrates agreed, but the seven were outvoted. Smith accepted defeat with good grace, and later joined in a unanimous decision to reelect Gause sheriff.[6]

Ever observant of opportunities to turn a dollar, though North Carolina continued to use the British monetary standard until 1809, and informally for many years beyond that time, the General obtained permission from the Brunswick justices to convert his toll ferry over Livingston Creek to a toll bridge. The creek, a tributary of the Northwest Cape Fear River, crossed the main road that led from Wilmington past Belvedere and Blue Banks to Elizabeth Town, seat of Bladen County, and beyond to Fayetteville. It was a well-traveled, hence rewarding, route. Not only would a bridge eliminate the labor required for maintaining the ferry, but the magistrates agreed to raise the toll charges by 25 percent to compensate Smith for the cost of erecting the structure. The General completed construction in 1814, but a year later relinquished his right to the bridge to David Lloyd of neighboring Bladen County, no doubt to satisfy one of many creditors.[7]

Responsibilities of the county justices encompassed more than attendance at the quarterly sessions of court at which they endured a litany of registering of deeds, settling suits at law (in which the General was often a party), caring for orphans (of whom two more were placed in Smith's custody), emancipating slaves, naturalizing citizens, ordering overseers to mark and post roads, and granting licenses to sell alcoholic beverages. As chairman of the court, Smith initially served on the committee to mark off the prison bounds of the county for the benefit of debtors, six acres in Smithville that included as many boarding houses as possible so that debtors, though confined, might not have to spend time in jail waiting for the disposition of their cases. The General also served as a tax assessor for Smithville. And constables and patrollers appointed by the court stopped at his house or plantation to be sworn into office.[8]

All the while Smith found himself in a vortex of debt which increasingly threatened, and eventually required, the alienation of assets, including, most importantly, his slaves, whose labor was critical to Smith's rice plantations and his ancillary activities. The Bank of Cape Fear offered a temporary reprieve. The state legislature in 1804 had chartered the Bank of Cape Fear in Wilmington (with a branch in Fayetteville) and the Bank of Newbern, largely to provide credit to merchants in the two principal ports of North Carolina. The General, always sensing investment opportunities, became a stockholder in the Bank of Cape Fear. At the same time he envisioned the bank as a cash cow to advance his speculations, only to find himself quickly overextended and a debtor to the institution.[9]

In 1805, Smith supported the establishment of a rival state bank. It was largely a Republican-driven initiative to counter the Federalist-controlled banks along the coast. At the same time it was a necessary venture due to the need to provide credit in the central and western portions of North Carolina, the depreciation of over-issued notes by the New Bern and Wilmington institutions, and the desire by many to retire outstanding state paper that dated from the days of the Confederation in the 1780s. Six years elapsed before the emergence of the State Bank of North Carolina, whose opening in 1811 was announced by Smith in a gubernatorial proclamation.[10]

Reflecting the efforts of the General to repay loans to the Bank of Cape Fear and to satisfy other creditors, the county records after 1810 are replete with mortgages and sales of Smith's slaves and real estate. Exacerbating the General's financial travails in 1812 was an obligation of $50,000 to the university, incurred by his improbable decision to stand security for one Carleton Walker, who was indebted to the institution. Smith later defended his action by claiming that he merely wanted to insure that the university received the money due from Walker. Incredibly, after the Read surety, the General failed to realize that he might actually have to assume responsibility himself. Smith later claimed that Walker had the money but the General eventually paid most of the debt himself.[11]

Smith poured out his troubles to his friend and creditor John Haywood. After learning of Walker's default, the General wrote apologetically, I am "mortified at the impossibility of my paying the Note given you for the present without the most complete Sacrifice of property." However, the Walker affair had "knocked up" his credit at the Bank of Cape Fear and "occasioned every body to be pressing upon me." Those demands quickly exhausted the proceeds of a disappointing rice crop. And, adding to his "anxiety & weariness," Sarah again was ill.[12]

Smith's prospects had not improved a year later, when once again he wrote to seek a reprieve from Haywood, an always obliging friend. The General had endured another crop failure which rendered him unable to pay Haywood "without selling property to sacrifice." He had been confined to bed by sickness for six weeks at harvest time when his supervision was desperately needed, more especially considering the alleged incompetence of his overseer. Yet, even had the General been well, he could not have forestalled the predatory rice birds that feasted on his crop or the storm that sank two of his boats loaded with rice as they were headed to his mill. Smith expended the proceeds from the rice that remained on clothes, taxes, and the repurchase of slaves who had been sold to satisfy debts.[13]

The General and his family were driven to the brink. Desperation was evident. Sarah and he "suffered privations never to be expected & [were] practicing an economy beyond ... Conception." In late March they had less than a week's provisions left. A pathetic though unsubstantiated story described of the plight and pride of Benjamin and Sarah. A lady in Wilmington, who lived next to the couple, saw a servant carrying a larger silver waiter at mealtimes from the kitchen to the main house, as if serving dinner. Knowing the distressed condition of the Smiths, the lady one day asked the servant what she carried in the elegant salver. The reply, it was empty, but "De Genal make me carry it. Miss — he don want people to tink he aint got nutting to eat."[14]

Smith confided to Haywood that he wished he could sell all his property and live "retired & happy." Yet, an ongoing recession pushed real estate prices to the bottom. So he considered another year's planting. If that failed, he contemplated "another Coarse" or "perhaps I might be happily relieved from this Scene of troubles & Vale of Sorrows." For the nonce the General asked Haywood to grant a stay of execution on his personal debt and to intercede with the trustees of the university to buy more time on their suit.[15]

All the while the Carleton Walker debacle in conjunction with other executions forced Smith to alienate valuable property. In 1812 he mortgaged his fine house on the corner of Dock and Second streets in Wilmington and conveyed a deed of trust for Belvedere and Orton Plantations to the Bank of Cape Fear. Three years later the Bank of Cape Fear proposed to auction Belvedere and Orton together with seven additional tracts of land containing approximately 5,300 acres to satisfy unpaid loans by the General. Though Smith lost the Wilmington town house and Belvedere, he retained possession of Orton until 1824, when the bank again advertised the property for sale.[16]

Meanwhile the Haywoods did their best to assist the Smiths. In 1814, John continued to accede to pleas for dispensation on the debts owed to him. His wife sent the Smiths some cuttings for their nursery and muskmelon seeds for their garden. Briefly, fortune smiled upon Smith. Haywood had been too slow in advising the Brunswick County sheriff to stay the execution on the General's property, but an attack of the measles felled the officer and forced a postponement of proceedings by which time Haywood's instructions arrived. Still the crushing debt took its toll, physically and mentally. In September, when Smith asked Haywood about the university trustees' position on the Walker debt, he was "very weak & but slowly recovering from Sickness partly owing to an uneasy mind."[17]

The following year Smith's prospects grew ever dimmer. The "clouds are surrounding me thicker & thicker," he wrote to Haywood early in 1815, particularly the executions by the university. The trustees had secured the able legal services of attorney William Watts Jones, resident of Wilmington, brigadier general of the militia, and several times member of the General Assembly from Wilmington and New Hanover County, to pursue the Walker obligation. Jones proceeded to attack Smith with the tenacity of a pit bull, attaching even the household furniture at Belvedere which included personal possessions of Sarah. Among them were a watch that belonged to her mother and a bureau that contained her clothes and library.[18]

Smith appealed to Haywood, a university trustee who in turn might intercede for the General. "Is not my case different from all others?" asked Smith. He had not received one cent from the property for which Walker had contracted the debt. That property had been sold without the consent of Walker or Smith for a pittance of its value when pledged to the university for Walker's obligation. Last, had not Smith given twenty thousand acres of land to the university when the institution was in its infancy? The General apologized to Haywood for the trouble, but noted that "to your good heart the consciousness of doing well is a rich reward" and yet another testimony of honor "bestowed on you by others...."[19]

By mid–1816, Smith's financial house of cards came crashing down. Plaintively, on July 1, he wrote to his friend John Haywood, "Of all the days of my life this is the most distressing." He enumerated his many creditors, public—the United States for the remainder of the Read surety, and private, including Haywood and the university. The General was beset by the United States district attorney and marshal and the Brunswick County sheriff, all of whom sought to attach his slaves. Many of the bondsmen had already been mortgaged and even sold, to the detriment of "honest Creditors." Suffering with the General, and adding to his distress, was his "excellent wife," Sarah. "She was a heroine & every thing that is good," according to Smith, "but the distress of those both with & under her" naturally affected Sarah, "notwithstanding all her fortitude."[20]

For unknown reasons Jones seemed to delight in persecuting Smith despite his protestations to the contrary. Reciprocating, the General came to think of Jones as his declared enemy. Rather than schadenfreude, Jones was conscientious and assiduous, determined not to let the General off the hook. But given Smith's haughty demeanor, Jones may well have taken umbrage at some slight or perceived slight at the hands of the General. Jones wrote in a chastising manner to the board in 1816, if the trustees had sent the necessary authorizations in a timely fashion, Jones "cou'd have caught him [Smith] and got the money, because ... he has been off his guard."[21]

Thereafter Jones pursued Smith unrelentingly. The General, entangled in a mesh of obligations, sought relief from the university trustees. Ill health, well known to all, he claimed, had prevented him previously from taking his seat on the board "of which I feel proud of being a Member & having frequently united with in their patriotic labors." He admitted that he had named March 1, 1816, as the date for which he would give security for his debt, because on that day he intended to make a "large payment" to the Bank of Cape Fear. That in turn, he thought, would release property that he could use to secure the university encumbrance. The General appealed to the "liberality" of the trustees.[22]

Astonishingly, in the midst of those troubles, and about a month after his sad letter to John Haywood in 1816, the General was elected to represent Brunswick County once more in the state Senate. The circumstances of his reelection remain obscure. Why would Smith have chosen to be a candidate, or allowed himself to be drafted, after a gap of six years and an apparent disregard for politics? The record is silent. What was obvious, however, was the popularity of the old warrior in Brunswick.

Once the General arrived in Raleigh in November, on the second day of the session, he threw himself into the legislative fray with gusto. Immediately, the Senate tapped his experience by appointing Smith to the committee on finance.[23] For his part the General quickly pursued a favorite topic, the penitentiary. He proposed that Governor Miller transmit all information in the executive office regarding penitentiaries in other states to the legislature. Smith had allies in the House of Commons, where a committee had been appointed to collect information on penitentiaries, including the one in Virginia, and had recommended that a "penitentiary in some form ... calls aloud for Legislative sanction."[24] That report eventuated in a bill to erect a penitentiary, but like previous efforts it failed to secure approval.[25] Smith's call for a revision of the penal laws of the state suffered a similar fate.[26]

The Senate honored Smith by nominating him for a seat on the Council of State, but the General demurred, preferring to continue in his active legislative capacity, where he turned to another subject of longstanding interest.[27] Smith chaired the committee to revise the militia laws of the state, a perennial subject in the legislature but one made manifestly more important by the experience of North Carolina troops in the War of 1812. Like the penitentiary, a bill that addressed the militia laws suffered rejection. Smith then temporized. Given the magnitude of the effort and the press of time during a legislative session, he proposed that a five-man committee, named jointly by the Senate and House, be authorized to revise the militia laws, meet during the recess of the General Assembly, and report to the following legislature. The Senate concurred.[28]

Beyond his abiding interest in a penitentiary, penal laws, and the militia, Smith sought particularly to further the interests of his county. He presented bills to alter the responsibilities of Brunswick officials (clerk, register, and entry taker), and for changing times for holding superior courts in the county's judicial district. Neither was successful, though the General Assembly enacted legislation to regulate the activities of officers of the county courts throughout the state, perhaps an expansion of the proposed bill for Brunswick County.[29] Smith, however, was able to secure legislation to emancipate the children of Brunswick resident Balaam Howe, a man of color. Although the children at least were free, they faced a life of manifold legal encumbrances as white North Carolinians became increasingly apprehensive of the growing free black population in the state.[30]

14. Denouement and Death

And Smith's eponymous town also enjoyed the attention of the General. Though his proposals to provide for a health officer and commissioners of navigation and pilotage for the port of Smithville failed to gather sufficient support during the current legislative session, the General Assembly in 1817 created the position of health officer, similar to that in Wilmington and other ports, whose duty was to guard against contagions that might arrive in incoming vessels.[31] Smith also attempted to revive the Smithville Academy, which apparently had failed to attract sufficient students to justify its opening early in the century. Yet the future remained moot, and all the more so after the General Assembly rejected a bill in 1817 to allow the trustees of the academy to hold a lottery to raise needed operating funds.[32]

Although the session was not a rewarding one for Smith, no one could question his effort. As always, he remained busy. Remembering his circumstances in Raleigh during his gubernatorial tenure, the General voted to raise the governor's salary by 25 percent, to two thousand dollars annually, but that was another bill that awaited 1817 for fruition. And, with the majority of his fellows, he tried to protect the state capitol by voting to ban all dances and shows, "natural or artificial," in the legislative building, a commentary, of course, on past activities that had boded ill for the integrity of the structure.[33]

Once Smith left Raleigh to return to Orton, he faced a legion of creditors. The university trustees had granted the indulgence he sought, giving him an extension of a year, to March 1, 1817. But when that day arrived, the General, as always, had excuses prepared. "Perpetual ill health" and inclement weather prevented him from offering the necessary security for his indebtedness to the university. He admitted he could have sent the necessary paperwork to Jones, but Smith, careless as usual, and trusting that a few days would make no difference, found Jones, "whose rancor & spleen against me will never end but with life," disagreed. Jones had placed executions in the hands of the New Hanover County sheriff, who was prepared to put Smith in jail. With difficulty the sheriff was persuaded to grant Smith and Sarah, who "would not be separated from me," the liberty of the prison bounds in Wilmington.[34]

While Sarah and the General passed time in confinement, Jones importuned the trustees. Did they want "the business pushed and the money paid," or was "it is their wish to indulge him," for Jones had "no sort of wish to press Smith ... unless it is the desire of the Trustees." The trustees, embarrassed that one of their number and a major benefactor had been consigned to debtor's prison, directed Smith's release. However, they authorized Jones to continue to seek assets sufficient to pay the General's obligation to the university. The property mainly took the form of slaves. In many cases the bondsmen were already legally encumbered. Furthermore, Smith apparently tried to hide the slaves to prevent their attachment.[35]

Jones would not be denied. By March 1818, "after much difficulty and trouble," he had caught some of the slaves mortgaged by Smith to the university, but extra deputies had to be engaged by the sheriff to ferret out and secure the bondsmen. Jones felt that he was close to success and warned against further indulgence for Smith because "the debt must be got now or never." At the same time, in exasperation, Jones declared that he would never pursue the same course in the future, "even if I cou'd succeed." Three months later, when he sent a check to the trustees to satisfy the execution and costs, Jones breathed a sigh of relief that he was "nearly done collecting from Smith for I never had harder chases after foxes and wildcats than I have had after him and his negroes."[36]

Throughout the ordeal the General remained faithful to the university. In 1819, following the settlement of the suit, he wrote to one of the trustees about the "wound ... inflicted by the Representatives of an Institution I had fondly cherished from its Infancy." Still, Smith reiterated his support for the institution, "for how many bright ornaments has the university produced? How many more will it produce & secure to North Carolina the high Standing & Rank She deserves in the American Constellation." However, after failing to attend the meetings of the trustees following his tenure as governor, the General finally retired from the board in 1824. Of the original trustees of the University, only John Haywood served longer (to his death in 1827).[37]

Though relieved of his debt to the university, the General still contended with his obligation to the United States, dating from his surety for Read, which dogged the General to the end of his days. A trip to Washington, D.C., in 1817 proved unavailing. At the time Smith visited his friend Joseph G. Swift, who was recovering from an illness. Swift wrote a letter to the secretary of the navy proposing that Smith might erase the obligation by transferring title of Bald Head Island to the government. Bald Head contained extensive stands of live oak and cedar which would be useful for shipbuilding. The matter remained unsolved until 1820, when Swift, as an agent of the United States Treasury Department, accepted a deed of trust for Bald Head, Mallory Plantation, and Blue Banks Plantation along with additional lands by which Smith hoped to absolve his responsibility to the national government.[38]

Swift returned to North Carolina in 1818, and late in February spent a day at Orton with Smith and Sarah, writing, "The pleasure of our reminiscences of that spot, and of Belvidere, were clouded by the aspect of the failing fortunes of the General." Yet, "Mrs. Smith presented us with a bottle of the nearly consumed stock of old sherry, with which, and blue perch from the adjacent pond, we were used to regale in more prosperous days." Sarah had rebounded from her earlier bouts with paranoia, quite possibly through the solace of the Methodist Church, because Swift found "Mrs. Smith evincing

14. Denouement and Death

Orton. Courtesy of New Hanover Public Library.

a well-balanced serenity, to cheer her husband." The next day Swift returned to Wilmington in "a fruitless essay to liquidate the large claims of the general's creditors."[39]

Sarah may have recovered, but the General's health faltered. Mental anguish and physical deprivation occasioned by his financial reverses took their toll. Fevers constantly assailed him, leaving him abed for weeks at a time and requiring Sarah, a frail reed on which to depend, to act as his amanuensis. On one occasion the General exacerbated an inflammation of his eyes by "riding up against the wind through a very smoky atmosphere."[40]

While writing with a bandage to protect his eyes, the General solicited legal advice from his nephew in Charleston, attorney Thomas S. Grimke, to whom he increasingly turned for assistance. Thomas, son of Smith's sister Mary, who had married John Faucheraud Grimke, studied law with Langdon Cheves and practiced with Robert Y. Hayne. The young man seemed genuinely solicitous of his uncle's welfare, and responded at great length to many queries posed by Smith. But Thomas could scarcely help with tangled affairs that had been decades in the making and still included former Transylvania Company land in distant Tennessee and Kentucky that was subject to various claims.[41]

Nonetheless, in Thomas Grimke the General tapped a fine resource. The nephew achieved eminence at the bar and later in politics, where he vehemently opposed South Carolina's stand in the nullification controversy. In the turbulent age of reform in antebellum America, Grimke championed various social causes ranging from temperance to world peace, and was deeply committed to education, wherein he emphasized science, modern literature and history, manual training in schools, and higher education for women, all grounded firmly on a proper understanding of the Bible. Yet, in the pens of historians he has been overshadowed by his siblings — Sarah and Angelina — the Grimke sisters.[42]

The correspondence with Grimke also revealed Smith's depression. He wrote with affection for his sister and his birthplace, and longed for the comforts and serenity of the life he had known is his childhood. "I most heartily wish I lived near her & hope once more to live in my native City," mused Smith. He urged his nephew to try to protect his houses in Charleston from creditors because they were all that were left of his paternity and their loss "would almost if not entirely prevent" his return to South Carolina.[43] Although relocation to Charleston may have been improbable, the General seriously considered the prospect. According to his will, written in late 1825, Smith wanted to be buried near Sarah if he died in North Carolina, but if in South Carolina, in the family vault in St. Philip's Church "with his venerated parents & much loved brothers & sisters."[44]

Fate, however, determined that Benjamin and Sarah live out their days at Orton and in Smithville. Despite occasional visitations of yellow fever which certainly justified the appointment of a health officer for the port, Smithville remained a tranquil river resort abutting Fort Johnston. Local governance seemed lax. Elections for town commissioners were held so infrequently that the General Assembly intervened to force the issue. Waxing poetically, a soldier in the Civil War who passed through Smithville declared, "The houses generally are pretty old and have an ancient appearance; but the live oaks make it a pretty place. But little imagination is necessary to picture the pleasure that was enjoyed beneath the cool shade of those stately oaks in the spring days of 'Auld Lang Syne.'"[45]

After the War of 1812, Smithville numbered some three hundred permanent residents, a population that swelled to five hundred or more during the summer season. Many in fact were pilots waiting to be hailed by vessels entering the river or who offered assistance to ships crossing the always treacherous bar upon leaving the Cape Fear River. In 1820 the town enjoyed a post office, much to the delight of Smith, who made frequent use of the service, a girls boarding school operated by Eliza Clitherall, and a Methodist church, the last no doubt the result of the efforts of the Smiths.[46]

14. DENOUEMENT AND DEATH

Punctuating the serenity of the village on April 17, 1819, was the visit of President James Monroe, who traveled from Wilmington to Smithville on board the steamboat *Prometheus* as he made his way to Charleston. Steam vessels, a novelty in the country before the war, appeared in North Carolina in 1818, when a Virginia-built steamboat sputtered into New Bern, and two, including the *Prometheus*, began to churn the waters of the Cape Fear River. The *Prometheus* had been built in Swansboro, North Carolina, by Otway Burns, famed privateer in the War of 1812, and towed to Wilmington to be outfitted with her engine. The little vessel rendered that April day memorable for Smithville.[47]

Two and a half years later Smithville marked the end of a difficult journey through life for Sarah, an heiress who had long suffered physically, psychologically, and financially. Buoyed by her Christian faith and close friends, Elizabeth Lord and Eliza Clitherall, Sarah maintained a "sweetness of temper[,] kind feeling, and hearty welcome" to the last, even to a well intentioned husband who was on the verge of losing all. In November 1821, after an illness of a week, Sarah sensed the inevitable. She asked Eliza Clitherall, who stayed with her in a rundown house in Smithville, to send for Elizabeth Lord. The

Steamboat on the Cape Fear River. Courtesy of State Archives, Office of Archives and History, Raleigh.

two women, long the closest of friends, had agreed to call upon the other if one suspected an imminent demise.⁴⁸

Upon receiving the request late in the morning of November 20, without hesitation Lord left her home in Wilmington for the thirty-mile trip to Smithville. Her horses hitched to the riding chair on that very cold fall day, she and her servant reached Orton, about halfway to Smithville, by sundown. There the horses stopped, then reared and ran with breakneck speed toward Smithville until worn out. At that very time Sarah suffered a stroke from which she did not recover. Lord always thought the action of the animals gave credence to the belief that horses (and dogs) somehow were able to fathom spiritual presences. Lord remained overnight at Orton. When she arrived in Smithville the next morning about eleven o'clock, frightened and almost frozen, she was too late.⁴⁹

The night had been a trying one for Eliza, Mary Rowan, Benjamin Smith's former ward, and a "faithful servant," probably Lucetta, who stayed by the side of Sarah. Neither Dr. Clitherall nor the General seemed to have been present. The women endured a gusty wind which rattled blinds and sent a "hollow moaning" through the creaky house. Temporary bed hangings (for one who could no longer afford the luxury of permanent fixtures) flapped horribly. A raging fire failed to intimidate the intense cold of the drafty building. And therein Sarah died amidst a scene of poverty so uncharacteristic of her former years.⁵⁰

Sarah Dry Smith had voiced the hope of resting beside her parents. Dr. Clitherall, post surgeon at Fort Johnston, took charge of the funeral. He secured the garrison barge from Fort Johnston and with the General and servants took the body up the Cape Fear River to Brunswick Town for interment in the churchyard of St. Philip's. Eliza Clitherall and Mary Rowan went by land. Though doubtlessly cold, the scene was placid. The ruins of the mostly deserted town had fallen into greater decay during the four decades following the Revolution. The wind whistled through the trees around the large bricks walls, which were all that remained of the once imposing church edifice. Sarah joined her parents who rested peacefully near oaks and small ponds in close proximity to the onrushing waters of the river.⁵¹

The will of Sarah Dry Smith was brief, for she left all to her "dear husband" except sums of money bequeathed to Mary Rowan, who had lived with the couple from childhood, and to a friend. Her only specific request was that Benjamin "use every possible means" to emancipate Lucetta, the daughter of the Smiths' "faithful servant" Sam, who had been purchased as an infant by Sarah from Mary Rowan with the intention of freeing her. Otherwise she left her estate to Benjamin until in his appointed time they should meet again "where the wicked cease from troubling & where the weary are at rest," an appropriate adaptation from the Book of Job.⁵²

The loss of Sarah, compounded by the death of his brother Peter in Charleston in August 1821, shook the General. He had returned the affection shown to him by his wife in a marriage shaken by financial tragedy but marked by love. Six months after the death of Sarah, Smith wrote to his nephew Thomas Grimke, apologizing for his failure to reply after receiving the notice of the death of his brother Peter, "friend, playfellow of my childhood & my very near relation." Soon thereafter, Smith explained, he had lost Sarah, "whom my Soul loved, who was upward of 44 years my bosom friend, the kind partner of all my joys and sorrows. The loss is irreparable & I shall never cease to deplore it." My greatest consolation, he wrote, is that "she is now enjoying the smiles of her blessed Redeemer, & that bliss which hath not entered into the heart of Man to conceive."[53]

Though obviously despondent and bereft of close family, Smith continued philosophically, "Yet it is our duty to submit with patience and resignation" to our fate. Death came so often and so suddenly in the Lower Cape Fear that the living could not linger too long over the departed. So, at that juncture, Smith returned to business in his missive to Thomas, taking two pages to detail the need to sell a slave and asking for Grimke's legal advice in the matter.[54]

Adding to Smith's woes at the time was an estrangement from his brother James. Like the General, James had fallen upon hard times due to unwise speculations. He lost his property in North Carolina, including plantations Kendal and Benevenuto, and as late as 1824 the Brunswick County sheriff auctioned additional property and slaves to satisfy unpaid taxes. Worse, after a quarrel between the brothers, James left permanently to live in South Carolina. Two years after his death in 1835, his six sons assumed the maternal surname Rhett in order to revive and perpetuate the family name "held dear ... and consecrated by natural regard and affection."[55] Among those sons of James and nephews of Benjamin Smith was Robert Barnwell Rhett, the famed Southern fire-eater.

With the departure of James, the General may well have looked toward his ultimate end, but his duties as a justice of the peace and his legal troubles served as distractions to the last. Smith maintained a fairly constant presence on the Brunswick County bench. Of course, living in Smithville was advantageous because he had only to walk a block or two to reach the courthouse. Illness interfered with a formerly robust lifestyle, but the General usually managed to attend two or more of the quarterly sessions of court each year, including that in October 1825, the last time the court convened before his death.

During his forty-year tenure on the Brunswick County court Smith witnessed many changes in policy and procedure. Among them was the requirement that the sheriff ring the courthouse bell or a vendue bell when he auctioned property for taxes and other debts. It became an agonizing clang heard all too often by Smith who saw thousands of acres, numerous lots in Smithville, and many slaves fall to the hammer. Yet despite his precarious finances, the court astonishingly allowed the General to stand security for newly-elected county clerk Alexus Forster in 1821. For his part, it seemed that Smith never learned, though he suffered no ill consequences from the Forster surety. In fact, the court must have entertained the utmost confidence in Forster, for all knew the financial disability of the General.[56]

A year before his death Smith still sought to recompense the United States for the Read surety obligation, which had yet to be extinguished by the construction work at Fort Johnston and the transfer of property to the government. Optimistically, the General, through the offices of Joseph Swift, hoped to sell timber on Bald Head Island to raise needed funds. At the same time he sought to order his affairs with John Haywood, writing his friend, "You have been very good & both of us have been too easy in case Death ... overtakes either." Actually, as the General recognized, Haywood had been the generous partner in the relationship, and thus Smith considered him "entitled to the amount of your debt in the *past* instant & previous to one Cent going to pay the U States Debt."[57]

Yet, the General was tilting at windmills. At that juncture he was virtually a pauper and dependent upon the Clitheralls. Eventually George Clitherall abandoned his futile (and for his children sometimes fatal) efforts to pursue rice planting and moved with his family to Smithville upon securing an appointment as post surgeon to Fort Johnston.[58] George's inability to pay the bills led him reluctantly to accept Eliza's decision to open a boarding school for young ladies in Smithville, locally called The Convent. Opportunities for obtaining instruction in the area were few and usually limited to itinerants like Monsieur de Chanla, a refugee of the French Revolution who claimed to have been educated at the University in Paris, and who briefly taught at Orton in 1804 under the aegis of Smith. Eliza, who had received an excellent education in England, was well qualified to teach English, French, arithmetic, drawing, and needlework.[59]

The Clitheralls cared for Smith to the end, an almost merciful death for the General. He had lost a vast fortune to the spirit of speculation and the folly of unwise sureties. Orton, the last of his fine plantations, had been lost, put up for auction by the Bank of Cape Fear in 1824. His once vast slaveholdings, over two hundred bondsmen at one time, had been scattered by auction and sale. There remained only an "old pitiful dwelling" in Brunswick Town and a partially finished house in Smithville along the bay where Smith lived. Penury was his lot. He looked to Eliza and George Clitherall even for the necessities of life.[60]

14. Denouement and Death

Still, fate reserved a last indignity for Smith. While the General lay ill in Smithville in January 1826, Eliza and a friend, escorted by two officers from Fort Johnston, took the fort's barge to Wilmington. As the river's tide turned against them, they stopped at nearly deserted Brunswick Town and prepared to have lunch at Smith's house. During the meal flames erupted from the roof of the building. Sparks from a nearby chimney, transported by a brisk wind, were responsible for the fire. Almost all was lost, including lunch, which was "fried finely," in part due to the apathy of onlookers. According the Eliza, the General was "hated all around."[61]

Smith bore the loss stoically, perhaps realizing that his end was also near. His health had been declining for several months, and an attack of typhus fever, or putrid fever, hastened the inevitable. He asked Dr. Clitherall to sit with him daily. Mary Rowan and Eliza Clitherall also kept vigil. While George held Smith's hand, the General called for his slaves and ordered his flat loaded. There were also moments of lucidity in which Smith quoted Scripture, "Set thy House in order for surely thou shalt die." Sensing the inevitable, the doctor called for an officer of the fort and Robert Howe, a longtime friend of Smith, to join him.[62]

The weather was stormy, rendering the night of Sarah's death almost calm by comparison. Rain pounded the wood-shingled roof of Smith's house loudly and relentlessly. The wind blew open the front door with such force that one man could not close it. Loose fitting window casings banged with every gust. And spray of the waves of the nearby bay beat against the panes. A quilt that substituted for bed hangings flapped violently, even in the house. From the shrunken body with half-closed eyes came a heavy breathing and slurred sounds. Finally, in the evening of January 27, "*'Doctor Doctor! oh Doctor!'* — and a convulsive struggled closed the scene."[63]

The wicked finally ceased troubling and the weary were at rest.

CHAPTER 15

REMEMBRANCE AND REHABILITATION

General Smith died a lonely and bitter man. Friends were few other than those who kept vigil at his death. Persecuted by his creditors, unappreciated by the university, and forgotten by those who had benefited from his generosity and hospitality, Smith had reason to be resentful. Of course through the years he appeared to be vain and pompous, bearing an aristocratic mien that alienated lesser men. Flaunting his riches, or so it seemed, the General together with his South Carolina pedigree invited envy and contempt. Quick-tempered, perhaps sharp-tongued, he made enemies. Increasingly he became antiquated, not only in years but in weltanschauung. The egalitarian, aggressive, commercial, acquisitive America that he had helped to sire by the Revolution had little patience with a domineering, aristocratic country squire overseeing his lordly domain. Even founders John Adams and Thomas Jefferson, who also died in 1826, felt somewhat estranged from the handiwork of their creation.

Still, throughout his life the General unquestionably worked to further the interests of his country and his adopted state, even if, on occasion, he benefited personally as well. But public and private interests often intertwined at that time. Certainly no one doubted Smith's desire to protect the United States against foreign threats, though some deemed it self-serving. His support for the university was unwavering despite his tribulations and embarrassments. Moreover, regardless of criticism, the General enjoyed the favor of the electorate in Brunswick County. Multiple times voters sent him to the state legislature where he was held in high esteem by his colleagues as evidenced by his weighty committee assignments and election as governor. Smith had dedicated his life to public service.

Privately, the General appeared to live an exemplary life. A fondness for the bottle of which there is only the barest hint may have constituted a possible exception, but alcoholic drinks were the order of the day, and for all members of a family. From the little information that exists about his personal character,

15. REMEMBRANCE AND REHABILITATION

Smith appeared to be a devoted husband and surrogate father. Without children of his own, he cared for a ward throughout her life, adopted two youngsters, and sent others to the university. The General also lived by one of the abiding tenets of Masonry — charity — in both private and public affairs, and seemed to embody fully the tradition of Southern hospitality.

Indeed, Smith reflected the attributes of Southern male gentility after the Revolution, which included an appreciation of family and a charitable spirit. Additionally, a fortunate marriage, a sense of pride and self-esteem, and a determination to achieve a reputation, also indicative of elitist masculinity, led to a life of public service. Independence, both national to ensure newly-won freedom from England and personal to protect reputation, helped to explain his martial ardor and manly pride that led to the field of honor. Ironically, Smith's independence, like that of so many Southern men, rested upon bonded labor about which he seemingly had no moral reservations, though he rued its practical encumbrances and unsuccessfully sought to escape its clutches.

Though Smith may have had few friends at the time of his death, the posthumous rehabilitation of his reputation soon began, largely aided by the sale of the twenty thousand acres of land that he had donated to the university. The proceeds from that gift reminded all anew that he was the first and most significant benefactor of the institution and, by extension, an advocate of education in general. The General's faults, attributed to those of the elite class from which he emerged, were downplayed, and excused when necessary, by his reputed magnanimous and chivalrous character. Financial difficulties were ascribed to his generosity, standing surety for acquaintances who betrayed him.

Shifting trends in North Carolina politics and the state's economy contributed to Smith's rehabilitation. Local historians in the Lower Cape Fear, finding their region marginalized in the late nineteenth and early twentieth centuries when political and economic influence in North Carolina gravitated to the Piedmont region of the state, compensated in part by eulogizing past luminaries of their area. None surpassed Smith, a man of immense wealth and governor of the state. In fact, some North Carolinians even claimed that he was a native son of Brunswick County. Phoenix-like, the General rose from the ashes of debt and despair to become a folk hero in the Lower Cape Fear.

Although Smith had hoped for a final resting place by Sarah in Brunswick Town or, if in Charleston at the time of his decease, interment in the family plot at St. Philip's Church in the South Carolina port, his travails continued even in death. Following his demise on that stormy night in January, the barge of Fort Johnston was unavailable and heavy fog on the river prevented the hire of other craft to sail upriver to Brunswick Town. Thus the corpse was taken a short distance to the old burying ground in Smithville.[1]

After an initial fruitless search, George Clitherall found the General's will, dated November 21, 1825, apparently written in anticipation of his impending death. Smith bequeathed small sums of money to family friends and desired that his executors manumit six slaves, particularly Laura who had cared for Sarah in her final days. He left the remainder of the estate to his sister, Mary Grimke in Charleston. In a codicil, the General variously apportioned furniture, a gold-headed cane, a sword, and family pictures, including that of "our illustrious ancestor Wm. Rhett," to the Clitheralls, Mary Rowan, a niece, and two nephews.[2]

There is no evidence that any of the South Carolina executors named in Smith's will rushed to Smithville to help settle the muddled estate as they were urged to do by George Clitherall. Still Smith's relatives in South Carolina, principally Thomas S. Grimke, acting on behalf of his mother, Mary Grimke, sought information about the estate. Grimke was especially interested in Smith's claims to potentially valuable lands in Kentucky and Tennessee.[3] The ultimate disposition of the General's property is moot, but given the debts of Smith, little of the estate remained for the family.

Not only were the Charleston relatives disappointed, but the General's apparent intention to assist Archibald D. Murphey in writing a history of North Carolina failed of fruition. In the codicil of his will the General left all his maps of North Carolina and histories of the colony, including those of John Lawson and John Brickell, to Murphey for his proposed study. At the direction of Smith's executors, Junius A. Moore of Smithville sent the books to Hillsborough, the residence of Murphey. The maps, more valuable, awaited instructions from Murphey for their transmission.[4] Apparently neither books nor maps reached Murphey, but no matter. The history never materialized.[5]

For his part Murphey remembered Smith as one of a handful of men to whom the university was "principally indebted for its existence and progress," a recognition of the General's unwavering support and his gift of twenty thousand acres of land. After interminable wrangling with Native Americans, the United States, and Tennessee, the university finally obtained title to its benefaction. Unfortunately Smith's donation lay in Obion County in northwestern Tennessee, perfectly positioned to be rocked by the New Madrid earthquakes of 1811–1812. As a result of earthquakes, much of Smith's donation was practically "unsalable." Nevertheless, the university trustees finally sold the land to a Boston company in the mid–1830s for seventy cents an acre, or $14,000.[6]

The university honored its first donor a decade and a half later when the trustees named an elegant structure on the campus Smith Hall. Designed by distinguished New York architect Andrew Jackson Davis, it was recognized as one of the most beautiful buildings on the campus. Initially intended as a library, Smith Hall was transferred in the twentieth century by the university trustees to the Carolina Playmakers for conversion into the Playmakers' Theater. The theater was recognized as a National Historic Landmark in 1974 and depicted on a U.S. postal card issued 1993 as part of the University of North Carolina's bicentennial observance.[7]

By the time that Smith Hall had been dedicated in 1851, General Smith apparently had been relocated to his final resting place, near Sarah, in the churchyard of St. Philip's in Brunswick Town. Initially the move entailed the identification of the remains in the Smithville cemetery, a daunting task after a decade and a half. According to tradition, Mary Elizabeth Bensel Stuart came to the rescue. An independent spirit who operated an inn on Bay Street in Smithville, Stuart knew the approximate location of Smith's grave in the cemetery and remembered that the bullet had never been removed from Smith's body after the duel with Maurice Moore. Thus she proceeded to sift the ashes "with a display of nerve and resolution, which might even test the courage of a man ," according to local historian Louis T. Moore. Upon finding a lead projectile, Stuart announced to the satisfaction of all that the remains were indeed those of Smith. The date and party responsible for the putative reinterment are moot.[8]

At mid-nineteenth century and coinciding with the dedication of Smith Hall at Chapel Hill, Benjamin Smith came to the attention of North Carolina historians. The first was John H. Wheeler, in *Historical Sketches of North Carolina*, who cursorily mentioned the General, characterizing him as "by nature ardent," and "sudden and quick in quarrel." Smith's life was "checkered by difficulties" in which he conducted himself "with great firmness and magnanimity," observed Wheeler. His generous gift of twenty thousand acres to the university overshadowed "many greater defects."[9]

Considerable improvement in the narrative presentation of North Carolina's past flowed from the pen of Wheeler's namesake, John Wheeler Moore, in his *History of North Carolina*, published in 1880. Lamenting Smith's penury after giving the university twenty thousand acres of land, Moore characterized the governor as "impulsive and generous," a man "genial and kindly but quick in his resentments," who was thus prone to dueling "in which he was both chivalrous and magnanimous." Wheeler and Moore set the stage for a basic remembrance of Smith's character and life: impulsive, magnanimous, good-natured, benefactor of the university.[10]

Hard on the heels of Moore's history appeared a sketch of Smith in *Appleton's Cyclopedia of American Biography* (1888) that destroyed the factual integrity of the General's biography. Smith possibly served with Washington, no doubt was present in South Carolina during the British invasion, and definitely gave 20,000 acres to the university which named a building for him. Yet Smith was not born in Brunswick County, or in 1750, did not raise his own regiment of volunteers when war threatened with France in 1796, was not governor from 1810 to 1812, did not have an island named for him, and did not die in 1829, as claimed by the *Cyclopedia*.[11]

On the eve of the publication of *Appleton's Cyclopedia* major changes were in store for the town named for Benjamin Smith. The General Assembly, in 1887, reincorporated Smithville as Southport, anticipating the development of the "Port of the South" that would rival, if not eclipse, Wilmington.[12] Disappointment followed. Wilmington remained the maritime shipping center of North Carolina.

For those who championed the cause of history and the memory of Benjamin Smith, the change from Smithville to Southport transgressed the heritage of southeastern North Carolina and represented a melancholy example of public amnesia. The president of the University of North Carolina wrote disparagingly of forgetting the "old hero."[13] In concluding a series of articles about the General, published in the *Southport Leader* in 1896, W. B. McKoy also lamented the passing of the name.

> *Smithville* was distinguished in history, loved and cherished by many who could recall romantic stories of the past concerning its former inhabitants. Mothers told stories to their children at their knees of former happy days in the old town. Fathers recalled their younger days spent there. Soldiers remembered the idleness and gaiety of the garrison life, and ... relat[ed] anecdotes of the people of *Smithville*. But who knows this upstart and parvenu *Southport*, that enjoys the right to brag of the advantages built to commemorate one of North Carolina's heroes. I can imagine that should they ask General Smith's opinion, he might answer in the words of Hamlet:
>
> "Here (Hear) you Sir; what is the reason that you use me thus?
> I loved you ever. But it is no matter;
> Let Hercules himself do what he may,
> The cat will mew, the dog will have his day."[14]

McKoy, in those newspaper pieces, offered the first full account of the life of Benjamin Smith. It was exquisitely written, romantic, filiopietistic, and replete with errors, adding to the misconceptions already foisted on the public by *Appleton's Cyclopedia*. According to McKoy, Smith was born in North Carolina, accompanied Washington at Long Island, and subsequently engaged in many battles in South Carolina during the Revolution. When the British invaded the Lower Cape Fear, Smith abandoned Belvedere which the enemy then used as an important military post. Following the war, the university seemed a hopeless enterprise until Smith donated a tract of land to the institution which he had received "in remuneration for his service in the Continental army of this State."[15]

15. REMEMBRANCE AND REHABILITATION

Most shocking, however, was the account of Smith's hasty burial. According to local lore and McKoy, upon the death of Smith, one or more of Smith's creditors decided to take advantage of a common law custom that allowed creditors to retain possession of the body of a deceased debtor until family or friends in effect ransomed the corpse by paying the obligations. In the case of Smith, the sheriff of Brunswick County was informed of the impending demise of the General by one or several creditors, and that official waited for death, the "sure deliverer."[16] At that juncture the story, as later told, diverged slightly. The sheriff and his minions may have secured the body, after which friends of Smith tricked the officers and stole the corpse, or friends of the General stealthily and secretly buried the body at midnight before the law could intervene. The latter version generally prevails.

Embellishing the story was the belief that Smith had died in a debtor's prison. Confusing the fact that he earlier had spent time in a debtor's prison and the belief that creditors awaited the body upon his death, some assumed that the General spent his last days in incarceration in Smithville. Louis T. Moore particularly helped to propagate the tragedy of death in the debtor's prison together with the midnight burial of Smith. Popular writers, fascinated by Smith's demise, continued to regale the public with the yarn throughout the twentieth century.[17]

The tale no doubt originated with Mary Elizabeth Bensel Stuart and was perpetuated by her daughter Kate Stuart, renowned and respected resident of Southport, and perpetuated by area historians. Kate claimed that she had been told by her mother that the commander of Fort Johnston had gone to her mother's house "early in the evening [of Smith's death] and asked her to prepare a midnight lunch with plenty of hot coffee as they were to bury Governor Smith that night." Given the esteem enjoyed by Stuart, few questioned her version of the dispatch of Smith. In the words of Louis T. Moore, since the details of the "real story" of Smith's death had been given to "an estimable lady" by her mother, "There can be no question as to the authenticity of the surrounding circumstance." Thus within five hours of his death Smith was furtively buried a few miles beyond Smithville by the light of flickering pine torches, one of which was held by Mary Elizabeth Bensel Stuart.[18]

All was untrue. Smith died on the evening of January 27, a stormy night that precluded any midnight caper, and he was interred the following day in the Smithville cemetery according to Eliza Clitherall, an eyewitness. Burial was quick, but no doubt occasioned by the rapid decomposition of the body. The General had been ill for some time during the winter months and personal hygiene posed an obstacle to those who cared for him. Then, a week before his death, he contracted typhus fever, or putrid fever, so named from the offensive discharges and decomposition of the body, which in extreme cases begin to occur even before death. It was imperative to lay Smith to rest, and posthaste.[19]

The tale of death in a debtor's prison is patently false. No evidence exists to support that contention. In extensive correspondence with his family and heirs, Smith's executors never mentioned his confinement, which would have affected the disposition of his property. As the years passed, locals apparently confused Smith's earlier incarceration in 1817 with the common knowledge that he died in debt.

Indeed, they may have conflated the memory of his indebtedness and quick burial, and have drawn the conclusion that creditors sought the body. Yet, substantive proof again is missing. The practice of creditors attaching a corpse to force payment by heirs existed in Rome, in Europe during the Middle Ages, and in the American colonies, but it found little favor after the Revolution.[20] And on a practical note, given the danger posed by a typhus-ridden corpse, it is doubtful that the sheriff or anyone would have wanted to take possession of the body.

Adding to the heightened interest in Smith at the beginning of the twentieth century and the continuing the effort to rehabilitate his reputation was the presentation in 1911 of a portrait of the General by the North Carolina Society of the Sons of the American Revolution to Gov. Claude Kitchen, who accepted the gift on behalf of the state of North Carolina. The public address on the occasion, delivered by a professor of geology of the University of North Carolina, Collier Cobb, was a tour de force of the virtues of Benjamin Smith and his contributions to the commonweal of North Carolina. The publication of Cobb's address in the *North Carolina Booklet* followed by seven years the appearance of a brief but flattering biographical essay of Smith by respected state historian Samuel A. Ashe.[21]

Together Ashe and Cobb announced the arrival of Smith as a major player on the historical landscape of North Carolina. Discounting the dissenting voice of university president Kemp P. Battle, who noted that towards the end of his life Smith was "assailed by misfortunes mainly the result of ill temper and recklessness caused by too frequent indulgence in ardent spirits," the General's reputation was on the upswing. Wilmington historian Louis T. Moore led the charge, building on Cobb's panegyric of Smith as a "patriot, legislator, soldier, statesman, and philanthropist; builder of highways and of fortifications, conservationist and drainer of swamps; opener of waterways; believer in education for every child within the State, and the first benefactor of the University; Grand Master of Masons; Governor of North Carolina ... and dreamer of dreams."[22]

For Moore, Smith stamped himself as "a leader possessed of constructive and far-reaching policies for State development and expansion." A "patriot and builder," the General "reflected honor and glory" upon North Carolina. According to Moore, writers of "modern history seemed in thorough agreement that Smith left an impress upon the commonwealth which reflects itself today in our modern and splendid university, and in our common school [system]." From Moore to the end of the twentieth historians played constantly on the themes of military service — fighting valiantly in the Revolution; legislative accomplishments; and gubernatorial recommendations — industrial development, penitentiary reform, and public education, which were interpreted by some as having been effected even in the early nineteenth century.[23]

Dismissing Battle, local historians found Smith's character unblemished. They agreed with McKoy, who had written, "The same noble spirit which had wrought such wonders for the welfare of the State and for the individual advancement of many of its citizens, remained untainted." A man of deep religious conviction, Smith evidenced a magnanimous disposition and keen sense of gratitude. He exhibited "rare personal charm," "high character," and "openhearted and openhanded hospitality," and was "always willing to forgive and forget." Toward the end the old hero "suffered undeserved buffetings at the hand of an unkind world." Smith's "generosity and informal business methods got him into financial trouble."[24]

In the 1920s Smith benefited not only from the effusive praise of Louis T. Moore but also by an effort of Moore and the New Hanover Historical Commission to advertise and promote the history of Wilmington and vicinity with strategically-placed granite markers. Numbering at least sixteen, the approximately four-hundred pound memorials included a marker on Dock Street between Front and Second streets to designate the location of Benjamin Smith's fine Wilmington home, and another on or near Eagles Island to denote the construction of the causeway by William Dry and Smith. The former still stands.[25]

Moore was also the driving force behind the decision of the Grand Lodge of the North Carolina Freemasons to mark the grave, or supposed grave, of Smith, their past Grand Master from 1809 through 1811, at St. Philip's in Brunswick Town. The Grand Lodge passed a resolution and set aside funds for that purpose in 1917, but twelve years elapsed before a stone was laid in a solemn ceremony on July 12, 1929. Past Grand Master Francis D. Winston gave a stirring address for the occasion, relying upon some dubious history to regale more than two hundred people, including Masons and members of the Colonial Dames and Daughters of the American Revolution, who gathered at St. Philips.[26]

Little more than a decade later World War II brought further if fleeting acclaim to Smith when his name was attached to a Liberty Ship, one of the merchant class vessels designated EC2-S-C1 by the Maritime Commission that was destined to help defeat the Axis powers. The North Carolina Shipbuilding Company, located about three miles south of Wilmington on the east bank of the Cape Fear River, turned out 126 of the "ugly ducklings" as they were termed by President Franklin D. Roosevelt between 1941 and 1943. The Wilmington yard laid the hull of No. 25, the SS *Benjamin Smith*, on September 11, 1942, and launched and delivered the vessel on October 28 and November 11, respectively. The *Benjamin Smith* served briefly in the war, succumbing to three German torpedoes off the coast of Africa in 1943.[27]

Benjamin Smith received his most recent, though much belated, recognition in the form of a North Carolina Highway Historical Marker that was erected in 1987, approximately five miles south of Wilmington on U.S. 17, and in a resolution by the North Carolina General Assembly in 1992.[28] Smith was the last eligible governor at that time to be recognized by a marker, whose inscription not only noted his gubernatorial service but also his contributions as "legislator, soldier, and benefactor of UNC." The legislative resolution memorialized the bicentennial of the founding of Southport (Smithville) and recognized the General for his role, reluctant though it had been, in the establishment of the town.

If Smith rests at Brunswick Town, on property he once owned and which now serves a North Carolina State Historic Site, he reposes with the quiet assurance that he left his impress on the state of North Carolina. A true representative of southern elite men in the post–Revolutionary era, he exuded boundless energy, daring, and courage that led to the accumulation of an immense fortune and a life dedicated to public service. Unwise decisions and arrogance of character left him penniless and almost friendless in the end. Yet the life of Benjamin Smith, today remembered as governor rather than general, ultimately is the story of the Lower Cape Fear of North Carolina in the days of the early American republic.

NOTES

Chapter 1

1. Fred Anderson, *Crucible of War: The Seven Years War and the Fate of Empire in British North America, 1754–1766* (New York: Knopf, 2000); William N. Fowler, Jr., *Empires at War: The French and Indian War and the Struggle for North America, 1754–1763* (New York: Walker, 2005).
2. *South-Carolina Gazette* (Charles Town), January 13, April 28, May 12, August 18, 1757.
3. *South-Carolina Gazette*, January 20, 27, May 12, 1757.
4. *South-Carolina Gazette*, June 12, 1757.
5. D. E. Huger Smith and A. S. Salley, Jr., eds., *Register of St. Philip's Parish, Charles Town, or Charleston, S.C., 1754–1810* (Columbia: University of South Carolina Press, 1971), [5], 35; Robert Barnwell Rhett, "The Descendants of Col. William Rhett, of South Carolina," *South Carolina Historical and Genealogical Magazine* 4 (January 1903): 41; George C. Rogers, Jr., *Evolution of a Federalist: William Loughton Smith of Charleston (1758–1812)* (Columbia: University of South Carolina Press, 1962), 403. Smith's date of birth, like so many of that time, has been subject to disagreement. Traditionally, historians have used January 10, 1756, a date that became popular in local Lower Cape Fear lore (though *Appletons' Cyclopedia of American Biography* [New York: D. Appleton, 1888], 5: 557], listed 1750), was inscribed on his tomb when placed in 1929 in Brunswick Town and which continues to be used today. See Robert Sobel and John Raimo, eds., *Biographical Directory of the Governors of the United States, 1789–1978*, 4 vols. in 1, reprint (Westport, CT: Merkler, 1988), 3: 1118; Michael Hill, ed., *The Governors of North Carolina* (Raleigh: Office of Archives and History, North Carolina Department of Cultural Resources, 2007), 130. However, given the church register, the early genealogical record, and careful scholarship of Professor Rogers, January 10, 1757, seems more appropriate.
6. David Ramsay, *History of South Carolina, From Its First Settlement in 1670 to the Year 1808*, 2 vols. (Newberry, SC: Duffie, 1858), 2: 251.
7. Walter B. Edgar and N. Louise Bailey, eds., *Biographical Directory of the South Carolina House of Representatives*, 5 vols. (Columbia: University of South Carolina Press, 1974–1992), 2: 637; Mattie Erma Edwards Parker, ed., *North Carolina Charters and Constitutions, 1578–1698* (Raleigh: Carolina Charter Tercentenary Commission, 1963), 128–164; Robert M. Weir, "'The Harmony We Were Famous For': An Interpretation of Pre-Revolutionary South Carolina Politics," *William and Mary Quarterly*, 3rd Series, 26 (October 1969): 479.
8. Edgar and Bailey, *Biographical Directory of the South Carolina House of Representatives*, 2: 637–639; M. Eugene Sirmans, *Colonial South Carolina: A Political History, 1663–1763* (Chapel Hill: University of North Carolina Press, 1966), 80–81, 93–95, 146, 151, 156, 158, 162,
9. Edgar and Bailey, *Biographical Directory of the South Carolina House of Representatives*, 2: 639–640.
10. Agnes Leland Baldwin, *First Settlers of South Carolina, 1670–1680* (Columbia, University of South Carolina Press, 1969), unpaginated; Edgar and Bailey, *Biographical Directory of the South Carolina House of Representatives*, 2: 466–468; *Dictionary of American Biography*, s.v. "Moore, James"; Mabel L. Webber, comp., "The First Governor Moore and His Children," *South Carolina Historical and Genealogical Magazine* 37 (January 1936): 1–5.
11. Edgar and Bailey, *Biographical Directory of the South Carolina House of Representatives*, 2: 472–473; *Dictionary of North Carolina Biography*, s.v. "Moore, Roger"; Webber, "First Governor Moore and His Children," 12–14; *A New Voyage to Georgia. By a Young Gentleman. Giving an Account of His Travels to North Carolina, and a Part of South Carolina*, 2nd ed. (London: Printed for J. Wilford, 1737), 55.
12. Sirmans, *Colonial South Carolina*, 105 (first quotation), 127–128, 130–131; Edgar and Bailey,

Biographical Directory of the South Carolina House of Representatives, 2: 554–556 (second and third quotations).

13. Edgar and Bailey, *Biographical Directory of the South Carolina House of Representatives*, 2: 641–643; Rogers, *Evolution of a Federalist*, 22 n. 68, 27; Richard Hofstadter, *America at 1750: A Social Portrait* (New York: Knopf, 1971), 131–179.

14. Thomas Smith to Isaac Smith, April 17, 1762; January 31, 1763, Smith-Carter Family Papers, Massachusetts Historical Society, Boston.

15. Rogers, *Evolution of a Federalist*, 29–30; A. S. Salley, ed., "Diary of William Dillwyn During a Visit to Charles Town in 1772–1773," *South Carolina Historical and Genealogical Magazine* 36 (October 1935): 109; Thomas Smith to the Reverend William Smith, February 20, 1766, Smith-Carter Family Papers.

16. George C. Rogers, Jr., *Charleston in the Age of the Pinckneys* (Norman: University of Oklahoma Press, 1969), passim; Newton D. Mereness, ed., "Journal of an Officer Who Travelled in America and the West Indies in 1764 and 1765," *Travels in the American Colonies* (New York: Antiquarian Press, 1961), 397–398; H. Roy Merrens, ed., *The Colonial South Carolina Scene: Contemporary Views, 1697–1774* (Columbia: University of South Carolina Press, 1977), 285.

17. Suzanne Krebsbach, "The Great Charlestown Smallpox Epidemic of 1760," *South Carolina Historical Magazine*, 97 (January 1996): 37; Mark A. DeWolfe Howe, ed., "Journal of Josiah Quincy, Junior, 1773," Massachusetts Historical Society Proceedings (June 1916): 444. Benjamin Smith, young Benjamin's uncle, lost his wife and young daughter in the epidemic of 1760, not to smallpox but to the effects of inoculation. Nonetheless, he still subscribed to the efficacy of inoculation. Benjamin Smith to Isaac Smith, May 24, 1764, Smith-Carter Family Papers.

18. Mereness, "Journal of an Officer Who Travelled in America and the West Indies," *Travels in the American Colonies*, 397–398 (quotations); Merrens, *Colonial South Carolina Scene*, 280–283. In inviting his cousin in Boston to a visit, Thomas Smith wrote, "I will not recommend your coming here in the Summer as our Climate is then rather too warm for those who are Used to Colder Climates." Thomas Smith to Isaac Smith, January 31, 1763, Smith-Carter Family Papers.

19. "Journal of Josiah Quincy, Junior, 1773," 448, 451.

20. Thomas Smith to Isaac Smith, May 17, 1764, Smith-Carter Family Papers; Walter Edgar, *South Carolina: A History* (Columbia: University of South Carolina Press, 1998), 208–211.

21. Rogers, *Evolution of a Federalist*, 43–45; Benjamin Smith to the Reverend William Smith, May 16, 1766, Smith-Carter Family Papers.

22. Oliver M. Dickerson, *The Navigation Acts and the American Revolution* (Philadelphia: University of Pennsylvania Press, 1951), 211–212; Benjamin Smith to Isaac Smith, December 12, 1769, Smith-Carter Family Papers. For a useful corrective to Dickerson's evaluation of the customs establishment in the colonies see Thomas C. Barrow, *Trade and Empire: The British Customs Service in Colonial America, 1660–1775* (Cambridge, MA: Harvard University Press, 1967).

23. Thomas Smith to Isaac Smith, May 17, 1764, Smith-Carter Family Papers; *South-Carolina Gazette*, August 24, 1769; Philip Hamer, et al., *The Papers of Henry Laurens*, 16 vols. (Columbia: University of South Carolina Press, 1968–2003), 7: 128; Thomas Harrison Montgomery, *A History of the University of Pennsylvania* (Philadelphia: 1900), 530–554.

24. *South-Carolina Gazette*, August 24, 1769; J. H. Easterby, *A History of the College of Charleston, Founded in 1770* (Charleston, SC: n.p., 1935), 1–20; Martin R. Zahniser, *Charles Cotesworth Pinckney: Founding Father* (Chapel Hill: University of North Carolina Press, 1967), 26.

25. Thomas Smith to Isaac Smith, January 31, 1763; Thomas Smith to the Reverend William Smith, February 20, 1766, Smith-Carter Family Papers.

26. Carl Bridenbaugh and Jessica Bridenbaugh, *Rebels and Gentlemen: Philadelphia in the Age of Franklin* (New York: Oxford University Press, 1962), passim; Carl Bridenbaugh, *Cities in Revolt: Urban Life in America, 1743–1776* (New York: Capricorn Books, 1964), passim.

27. Henry M. Tinkcom, "The Revolutionary City, 1765–1783," in *Philadelphia: A 300-Year History*, Russell F. Weigley, ed. (New York: Norton, 1982), 114–117; Joseph E. Illick, *Colonial Pennsylvania: A History* (New York: Charles Scribner's Sons, 1976), 262–265, quotation on 264; Gary B. Nash, "The Transformation of Urban Politics," *Journal of American History* 60 (December 1973): 605–632.

28. *American National Biography*, s.v. "Duche, Jacob"; James C. Spalding, "Loyalist as Royalist, Patriot as Puritan: The American Revolution as a Repetition of the English Civil War," *Church History* 45 (September 1976): 335, 340; www.archives.upenn.edu/people/1700s/duche_jacob.html.

29. Hamer, *Papers of Henry Laurens*, 8: 133.

30. J. G. de Roulhac Hamilton, "Southern Members of the Inns of Court," *North Carolina Historical Review* 10 (October 1933): 273–277, 279–280; James Haw, *John & Edward Rutledge of South Carolina* (Athens: University of Georgia Press, 1997), 8–9; Zahniser, *Charles Cotesworth Pinckney*, 17–18; Rogers, *Evolution of a Federalist*, 403.

31. Haw, *John & Edward Rutledge*, 8, 10 (quotation).

32. Thomas Smith to Isaac Smith Junior, April 11, 1772, Smith-Carter Family Papers; Rogers, *Evolution of a Federalist*, 63–70.

33. John Pringle to William Tilghman, July 30, 1774, Preston Davie Collection, Southern Historical Collection; Haw, *John & Edward Rutledge*, 19–20.

34. Haw, *John & Edward Rutledge*, 8; Merrens, *Colonial South Carolina Scene*, 283.

35. *South-Carolina Gazette*, December 6, 1773. Smith's remarks were followed by "repeated thanks, and loud shouts of applause." It might be observed that Smith's was one of two companies to which the initial East India Company tea had been consigned, and that his patriotic gesture came in response to a well-attended meeting of Charles Town residents who drafted an agreement that read, "receiving the ... tea, subject to a duty which they apprehended to be UNCONSTITUTIONALLY laid, would be exceedingly disagreeable to their fellow-citizens, and the body of inhabitants of this province." *Ibid.*

36. John W. Gordon, *South Carolina and the American Revolution: A Battlefield History* (Columbia: University of South Carolina Press, 2003), 34–44; Dan L. Morrill, *Southern Campaigns of the American Revolution* (Mount Pleasant, SC: The Nautical & Aviation Publishing Company of America, 1993), 15–27; Zahniser, *Charles Cotesworth Pinckney*, 42–45.

37. Barnet Schechter, *Battle for New York: The City at the Heart of the American Revolution* (New York: Walker, 2002), chapters 7–10; David Hackett Fischer, *Washington's Crossing* (New York: Oxford University Press, 2004), 88–102.

38. Donald Jackson and Dorothy Twohig, eds., *The Diaries of George Washington*, 6 vols. (Charlottesville: University Press of Virginia, 1976–1979), 6: 118–121; *Wilmington Gazette*, June 13, August 8, 1799.

39. Merrens, *Colonial South Carolina Scene*, 284; *South-Carolina American and General Gazette* (Charles Town), November 20, 1777; Brent H. Holcomb, *South Carolina Marriages, 1688–1799* (Baltimore: Genealogical, 1980), 230.

40. Baldwin, *First Settlers of South Carolina, 1670–1680*; Edgar and Bailey, *Biographical Directory of the South Carolina House of Representatives*, 2: 210–211; Alan D. Watson, "William Dry: Passive Patriot," Lower Cape Fear Historical Society *Bulletin*, 17 (October 1973), unpaginated. Roger and Rebecca Moore, children of Gov. James Moore, were twins according to family lore. Webber, "First Governor Moore and His Children," 21.

41. William L. Saunders, ed., *The Colonial Records of North Carolina*, 10 vols. (Raleigh: State of North Carolina, 1886–1890), 6: 600 (quotation), 1077; New Hanover County, Deed Books, D, 497, microfilm, Office of Archives and History, Raleigh, NC; Watson, "William Dry."

42. Janet Schaw, *Journal of a Lady of Quality; Being the Narrative of a Journey from Scotland to the West Indies, North Carolina, and Portugal, in the Years 1774 to 1776*, Evangeline W. Andrews and Charles M. Andrews, eds. (New Haven, CT: Yale University Press, 1921), 145; Saunders, *Colonial Records*, 10: 100–101; Watson, "William Dry."

43. Charles S. Lesser, *South Carolina Begins: The Records of a Proprietary Colony, 1663–1721* (Columbia: South Carolina State Archives, 1995), 238–245; Edgar and Bailey, *Biographical Directory of the South Carolina House of Representatives*, 2: 681–684; *South Carolina Gazette*, February 24, 1746.

44. New Hanover County, Deed Book, H, 48–49.

45. William Moultrie, *Memoirs of the American Revolution*, 2 vols. (New York: New York Times and Arno Press, 1968); 1: 283–284, 290; Lawrence S. Rowland, Alexander Moore, and George C. Rogers, Jr., *The History of Beaufort County, South Carolina*, Volume 1, *1514–1861* (Columbia: University of South Carolina Press, 1996), 215–217.

46. Moultrie, *Memoirs of the American Revolution*, 1: 291–195, *South-Carolina and American General Gazette*, February 4, 18, 1779; Rowland, Moore, and Rogers, *History of Beaufort County*, 217–219, quotation on 218.

47. Moultrie, *Memoirs of the American Revolution*, 1: 303–304; Haw, *John & Edward Rutledge*, 118; Rowland, Moore, and Rogers, *History of Beaufort County*, 219.

48. Elmer O. Parker, *Roster: Fort Sullivan (later Fort Moultrie), 1776–1780* (n.p.: n.d.), 281; Carl P. Borick, *A Gallant Defense: The Siege of Charleston, 1780* (Columbia: University of South Carolina Press, 2003); Henry Lumpkin, *From Savannah to Yorktown: The American Revolution in the South* (Columbia: University of South Carolina Press, 1981), 41–50; Haw, *John & Edward Rutledge*, 130–134.

49. Edward McCrady, *The History of South Carolina in the Revolution, 1775–1780* (New York: Macmillan, 1901), 490–491 n. 1.

50. McCrady, *History of South Carolina in the Revolution*, 489; Gordon, *South Carolina and the American Revolution*, 71–86; Haw, *John & Edward Rutledge*, 135; *Wilmington Gazette*, August 8, 1799.

51. Thomas Bee to Isaac Smith, July 10, 1780; Thomas Smith to Isaac Smith, August 19, 1783, Smith-Carter Family Papers; "Correspondence of Hon. Arthur Middleton," *South Carolina Historical and Genealogical Magazine* 27 (January 1926): 8.

52. McCrady, *History of South Carolina in the Revolution*, 712–719; John S. Pancake, *This Destructive War: The British Campaign in the Carolinas, 1780–1782* (University: University of Alabama Press, 1985), 66; Thomas Smith to Isaac Smith, August 19, 1783, Smith-Carter Family Papers; Rogers, *Evolution of a Federalist*, 87.

53. Thomas Bee to Isaac Smith, July 10, 1789, Smith-Carter Family Papers; *Wilmington Gazette*, August 8, 1799; Smith to ?, May 19, 1783, Grimke Family Papers, Rare Book, Manuscript, and Special Collections Library, Duke University, Durham, NC.

Chapter 2

1. See Lawrence Lee, *The Lower Cape Fear in Colonial Days* (Chapel Hill: University of North Carolina Press, 1965); Bradford J. Wood, *This Remote Part of the World: Regional Formation in Lower Cape Fear, North Carolina, 1725–1775* (Columbia: University of South Carolina Press, 2004). For purposes of simplicity, the Lower Cape Fear might be deemed that area within a fifty-mile radius of Wilmington. See Janet K. Seapker, ed., *Time, Talent, Tradition: Five Essays on the Cultural History of the Lower Cape Fear Region, North Carolina* (Wilmington: N.p., 1995), 11.

2. The nomenclature has changed over the years. The term Thoroughfare disappeared. The Cape Fear River continued east by the southern tip of Eagles Island or the forks past Wilmington and split into the Northwest or Cape Fear and Northeast branches at the northeast corner of Eagles Island above Wilmington. In effect, the designation Thoroughfare was replaced by the Northwest Cape Fear. The watercourse extending from the southern tip of Eagles Island west of the island to the junction of the Northwest Cape Fear became the Brunswick River. Eagles Island, early called Great Island. New Hanover County, Deed Book, C, 30, 124; D, 89, microfilm, Office of Archives and History, Raleigh, NC.

3. M. Eugene Sirmans, *Colonial South Carolina: A Political History, 1663–1763* (Chapel Hill: University of North Carolina Press, 1966), 159.

4. Wood, *This Remote Part of the World*, 21.

5. Lee, *Lower Cape Fear in Colonial Days*, 123–140; Alan D. Watson, *Wilmington, North Carolina, to 1861* (Jefferson, NC: McFarland, 2003), 8–27.

6. Marvin L. Michael Kay and Lorin Lee Cary, *Slavery in North Carolina, 1748–1775* (Chapel Hill: University of North Carolina Press, 1995), 221, 226–229; Kay and Cary, "A Demographic Analysis of Colonial North Carolina with Special Emphasis on the Slave and Black Populations," in *Black Americans in North Carolina and the South*, Jeffrey J. Crow and Flora J. Hatley, eds. (Chapel Hill: University of North Carolina Press, 1984), 73–84; Wood, *This Remote Part of the World*, 34–38; William S. Powell, ed., *The Correspondence of William Tryon and Other Selected Papers*, 2 vols. (Raleigh: Division of Archives and History, Department of Cultural Resources, 1980, 1981), 1: 139.

7. Donald R. Lennon and Ida B. Kellam, eds., *The Wilmington Town Book, 1743–1778* (Raleigh: Division of Archives and History, Department of Cultural Resources, 1973), 148, 165–167, 204–235 passim; *Cape-Fear Mercury* (Wilmington), September 22, 1773; Watson, *Wilmington, North Carolina*, 30–31, 33–35.

8. Walter Clark, ed., *The State Records of North Carolina*, 16 vols. (11–26) (Raleigh, NC: State of North Carolina, 1895–1906), 23: 622–623, 662–667; Lee, *Lower Cape Fear in Colonial Days*, 139–140.

9. Hugh Meredith, *An Account of the Cape Fear Country*, Earl Gregg Swem, ed. (Perth Amboy, NJ: Charles F. Heartman, 1912), 14–15; Janet Schaw, *Journal of a Lady of Quality; Being the Narrative of a Journey from Scotland to the West Indies, North Carolina, and Portugal, in the Years 1774 to 1776*, Evangeline Walker Andrews and Charles McLean Andrews, eds. (New Haven, CT: Yale University Press, 1921), 145; Lawrence Lee, *The History of Brunswick County, North Carolina* (Charlotte, NC: Heritage Press, 1980), 73–75.

10. Jerry Cross, "St. Philip's Church, Brunswick County, North Carolina," Research Report, Office of Archives and History, Raleigh, NC, 1975, 11–14.

11. Clark, *State Records*, 24: 248–249; Lee, *History of Brunswick County*, 86. In 1825, the sheriff of Brunswick County announced the sale of ten lots in Brunswick Town valued at $100 to satisfy unpaid taxes amounting to $.45. Minutes of the Brunswick County Court of Pleas and Quarter Sessions, July 1825, microfilm, Office of Archives and History.

12. Alfred Moore Waddell, *A History of New Hanover County and the Lower Cape Fear Region, 1723–1800* (Wilmington; N.p., 1909), 42–48; Wilson Angley, "A Brief History of the Eagles Plantation," Research Report, 1989, Research Branch, Office of Archives and History, 1–5.

13. Edward D. Seeber, trans., *On the Threshold of Liberty: Journal of a Frenchman's Tour of the American Colonies in 1777* (Bloomington: Indiana University Press, 1959), 16–17; Hugh Finlay, *Journal kept by Hugh Finlay, Surveyor of the Post Roads on the Continent of North America* (Brooklyn: Norton, 1867), 65; John Collet, "A Compleat Map of North-Carolina from an Actual Survey (1770)," Office of Archives and History; Henry Mouzon and Others, "An Accurate Map of North and South Carolina (1775)," Office of Archives and History; Lee, *Lower Cape Fear in Colonial Days*, 275.

14. Finlay, *Journal*, 65–66; Johann David Schoepf, *Travels in the Confederation [1783–1784]*, 2 vols., trans. and ed. by Alfred J. Morrison (Philadelphia: Campbell, 1911), 2: 153; Hugh Buckner Johnston, ed., "The Journal of Ebenezer Hazard in North Carolina, 1777 and 1778," *North Carolina Historical Review* 36 (July 1959): 380; Winslow C. Watson, ed., *Men and Times of the Revolution; or Memoirs of Elkanah Watson* (New York: Dana, 1856), 57. Causeways were constructed by laying logs in the direction of the road and covering those with small trees, brush, and dirt. Ideally, causeways were elevated in the middle and tapered to the edges. See Craven County Court Minutes of Pleas and Quarter Sessions, April 1765, microfilm, Office of Archives and History, Raleigh, NC; Schaw, *Journal of a Lady of Quality*, 280.

15. Finlay, *Journal*, 67.
16. Brunswick County, Deed Book, B, 162–165, microfilm, Office of Archives and History.
17. "Inscriptions of Tablets over Graves in St. Philips Churchyard, Brunswick," communication from Millie Hart, Brunswick Town/Fort Anderson State Historic Site, North Carolina, August 1, 2006. The inscription was a reworking of a phrase found on Roman boundary stones (Terminus stones): Quisquis hoc sustulerit aut laeserit, ultimus suorum moriatur (Whosoever removes or injures this [stone], may he die the last of his race), an ancient curse meant to protect the boundary. The author is indebted to Scott King-Owen, communication dated August 29, 2006, for the translation and explication.
18. John Brickell, *The Natural History of North Carolina* (Murfreesboro, NC: Johnson, 1968), 31; James M. Gallman, "Determinants of Age at Marriage in Colonial Perquimans County, North Carolina," *William and Mary Quarterly*, 3rd Series, 39 (January 1982): 176–191; James Matthew Gallman, "Relative Ages of Colonial Marriages," *Journal of Interdisciplinary History*, 14 (Winter 1984): 609–617. In a study of planter elites in antebellum North Carolina, Jane Censer found that daughters of the wealthy married on the average at age 20.5 years, though almost 17 percent were younger than eighteen. Jane Turner Censer, *North Carolina Planters and Their Children, 1800–1860* (Baton Rouge: Louisiana State University Press, 1984), 91–92.
19. William L. Saunders, ed., *The Colonial Records of North Carolina*, 10 vols. (Raleigh: State of North Carolina, 1886–1890), 6: 737–738; *Dictionary of North Carolina Biography*, s.v. "Davis, Justina."
20. John L. Cheney, Jr., ed. and comp., *North Carolina Government, 1585–1979: A Narrative and Statistical History* (Raleigh: North Carolina Department of the Secretary of State, 1981), 20, 22, 49, 58; *Dictionary of North Carolina Biography*, s.v. "McGuire (or McGwire), Thomas." During the revolution the governor of North Carolina offered McGuire the state attorney generalship, but he refused.
21. *A New Voyage to Georgia, by a young Gentleman*, 2nd ed. (London: Printed for J. Wilford, 1737), 55; Brunswick County, Deed Book B, 157–159; New Hanover County, Deed Book, AB, 134; C, 169.
22. *The Wilmington Centinel, and General Advertiser*, July 2, 1788.
23. Clark, *State Records*, 15: 155; Brunswick County, Deed Book, D, 85; New Hanover County, Deed Book D, 340; Mark A. DeWolfe Howe, ed., "Journal of Josiah Quincy, Junior, 1773," Massachusetts Historical Society *Proceedings* (June 1916): 459; Alan D. Watson, "William Dry: Passive Patriot," Lower Cape Fear Historical Society *Bulletin*, 17 (October 1973), unpaginated.
24. "Inscriptions of Tablets over Graves in St. Philips Churchyard, Brunswick," Brunswick Town/Fort Anderson State Historic Site, North Carolina.
25. For Harnett see R. D. W. Connor, *Cornelius Harnett. An Essay in North Carolina History* (Raleigh: Edwards & Broughton, 1909); Alan D. Watson, "Cornelius Harnett," in Watson, Dennis R. Lawson, and Donald R. Lennon, *Harnett, Hooper & Howe: Revolutionary Leaders of the Lower Cape Fear* (Wilmington: Wilmington, 1979), 3–31.

Chapter 3

1. Benjamin Smith to ?, May 19, 1783, Grimke Family Papers, Rare Book, Manuscript, and Special Collections Library, Duke University, Durham, NC.
2. Benjamin Smith to ?, May 19, 1783, Grimke Family Papers.
3. Brunswick County, Deed Book, B, 162–165, microfilm, Office of Archives and History, Raleigh, NC.
4. Alan D. Watson, "Cornelius Harnett," in Watson, Donald R. Lennon, and Dennis R. Lawson, *Harnett, Hooper & Howe: Revolutionary Leaders of the Lower Cape Fear* (Wilmington, NC: Wilmington, 1979), 19.
5. Brunswick County, Deed Book, B, 157–161, 206–216; Minutes of the Brunswick County Court of Pleas and Quarter Sessions, December 1784, microfilm, Office of Archives and History; *North Carolina Gazette or Impartial Intelligencer, and Weekly General Advertiser* (New Bern), July 28, 1784.
6. Walter Clark, ed., *The State Records of North Carolina*, 16 vols. (11–26) (Raleigh: State of North Carolina, 1895–1906), 23: 662–663; 25: 487–489.
7. Clark, *State Records*, 25: 487–489; Hugh Finlay, *Journal kept by Hugh Finlay, Surveyor of the Post Roads on the Continent of North America* (Brooklyn: Frank H. Norton, 1867), 74.
8. Brunswick County, Deed Book, B, 125, 127, 129–130; C, 47, 49, 55–56; New Hanover County, Deed Book, H, 68, microfilm, Office of Archives and History; Clark, *State Records*, 16: 985; John C. Cavanagh, *Decision at Fayetteville: The North Carolina Ratification Convention and General Assembly of 1789* (Raleigh: Division of Archives and History, Department of Cultural Resources, 1989), 11. For James Hogg, friend and fellow land speculator with Smith, see Bernard Bailyn, *Voyagers to the West: A Passage in the Peopling of America on the Eve of the Revolution* (New York: Knopf, 1986), 499–534.
9. *Cape-Fear Recorder* (Wilmington), May 23, 1832; R. V. Asbury, "Belevedere Plantation," Brunswick County Historical Society *Newsletter* (February 6, 1966), no pagination. The records render the name of the plantation "Belvedere" and

"Belvidere." For consistency, "Belvedere," the more popular spelling, will be used.

10. *Wilmington Centinel and General Advertiser*, July 2, 1788; January 29, 1789; New Hanover County, Deed Book H, 376; Don Higginbotham, Donna Kelly, and Lang Baradell, eds., *The Papers of James Iredell*, 3 vols. (Raleigh: Office of Archives and History, North Carolina Department of Cultural Resources, 1976, 2003), 3: 183 n. 8.

11. Brunswick County Court Minutes, September 1782; March, September, December 1783.

12. Brunswick County Court Minutes, September 1783.

13. Mark A. DeWolf Howe, ed., "Journal of Josiah Quincy, Junior, 1773," Massachusetts Historical Society *Proceedings*, 49 (June 1916): 463; Janet Schaw, *Journal of a Lady of Quality; Being the Narrative of a Journey from Scotland to the West Indies, North Carolina, and Portugal in the Years 1774 and 1775*, Evangeline W. Andrews and Charles W. Andrews, eds. (New Haven, CT: Yale University Press, 1921), 154; Winthrop D. Jordan, *White over Black: American Attitudes Toward the Negro, 1550–1812* (Baltimore: Penguin Books, 1969), 145; Brunswick County, Deed Book, B, 162–165.

14. Brunswick County, Deed Book B, 294.

15. Brunswick County Court Minutes, September 1782; December 1783; June 1785.

16. Clark, *State Records*, 21: 1028; Brunswick County Court Minutes, October 1794.

17. Francisco de Miranda, *The New Democracy in America: Travels of Francisco de Miranda in the United States, 1783–1784*, John S. Ezell, ed. (Norman: University of Oklahoma Press, 1963), 5.

18. Jedidiah Morse, *The American Geography* (London: John Stockdale, 1792), 418. For boxing, see Johann David Schoepf, *Travels in the Confederation [1783–1784]*, 2 vols., Alfred J. Morrison, trans. and ed. (Philadelphia: William J. Campbell, 1911), 2: 123–124.

19. Higginbotham, Kelly, and Baradell, *Papers of James Iredell*, 3: 76; H. G. Jones, *For History's Sake: The Preservation and Publication of North Carolina History, 1663–1903* (Chapel Hill: University of North Carolina Press, 1966), 57–76.

20. Higginbotham, Kelly, and Baradell, Papers of James Iredell, 3: 78, 157; *Elkanah Watson, Men and Times of the Revolution; or, Memoirs of Elkanah Watson*, Winslow C. Watson, ed. (New York: Dana, 1856), 253; Alan D. Watson, ed., *An Index to North Carolina Newspapers, 1784–1789* (Raleigh; Division of Archives and History, Department of Cultural Resources, 1992), xii.

21. "An Estimate of the allowances made to Members Clarks and other officers of the Senate June 1784," Estimates of Members Pay, Joint Papers, General Assembly Session Records, April–June 1784, Office of Archives and History.

22. Journal of the Senate of North Carolina, April–June 1784, 4, microfilm, Office of Archives and History; Higginbotham, Kelly, and Baradell, *Papers of James Iredell*, 3: 47.

23. *Dictionary of North Carolina Biography*, s.v. "Caswell, Richard," "Johnston, Samuel," "Jones, Willie," "Williams, Benjamin," "Rutherford, Griffith," "Haywood, John"; *Dictionary of American Biography*, s.v., "Robertson, James"; Cavanagh, *Decision at Fayetteville*, 15.

24. Senate Journal, April–June 1784, 4, 6; Memorial of Robert Rowan and others to the General Assembly, April 24, 1784, Joint Select Committee Reports, General Assembly Session Records, April–June 1784, *Dictionary of North Carolina Biography*, s.v. "Strudwick, Samuel."

25. Senate Journal, April–June 1784, 12, 16; Clark, *State Records*, 24: 543–546, 580–586;

26. *Dictionary of American Biography*, s.v. "Blount, William"; *Dictionary of North Carolina Biography*, s.v. "Blount, John Gray"; s.v. "Blount, Reading"; s.v. "Blount, Thomas"; William H. Masterson, *William Blount* (Baton Rouge: Louisiana State University Press, 1954), esp. 348–349.

27. Senate Journal, April–June 1784, 29; Journal of the House of Commons of North Carolina, April–June 1784, 9, microfilm, Office of Archives and History; Gov. Alexander Martin to the General Assembly, April 24, 1784, Joint Select Committee Report, General Assembly Session Records, April–June 1784; James R. Morrill, *The Practice and Politics of Fiat Finance: North Carolina in the Confederation, 1783–1789* (Chapel Hill: University of North Carolina Press, 1969), 100–124; B. U. Ratchford, "An International Debt Settlement: The North Carolina Debt to France," *American Historical Review*," 40 (October 1934): 63–69.

28. Senate Journal, April–June 1784, 9; Clark, *State Records*, 24: 631–632.

29. Grady L. E. Carroll, ed., *Francis Asbury in North Carolina: The North Carolina Portions of the Journal of Francis Asbury* (Nashville, TN: Parthenon Press, 1964), 110; Brunswick County Court Minutes, June 1786; Lee, *History of Brunswick County*, 87–88. William S. Powell, ed., *The North Carolina Gazetteer* (Chapel Hill: University of North Carolina Press, 1968), 294; Brunswick County Court Minutes, June 1786.

30. Clark, *State Records*, 19: 611, 612, 615, 678; 24: 636–637; Brunswick County Court Minutes, September 1783.

31. Clark, *State Records*, 24: 590.

32. Higginbotham, Kelly, and Baradell, *Papers of James Iredell*, 3: 205; New Hanover County, Deed Book C, 77, microfilm, Office of Archives and History; David Stick, *Bald Head: A History of Smith Island and Cape Fear* (Wendell, NC: Broadfoot, 1985), 8–13, 30. The conveyance of Bald Head or Smith Island by the Lords Proprietors to Landgrave Thomas Smith on May 8, 1713, has been deemed the oldest land grant in southeastern North Carolina, but see a reference to a grant dated May 13, 1691, from the proprietors to Landgrave Smith that included land along the Northwest Cape Fear River. New Hanover County, Deed Book, E, 35.

33. Senate Journal, April–June 1784, 34, 52; Clark, *State Records*, 24: 561–563; *Dictionary of North Carolina Biography*, s.v. "Rutherford, Griffith"; Bailyn, *Voyagers to the West*, 536–542.

34. Louise I. Trenholme, *The Ratification of the Federal Constitution in North Carolina* (New York: AMS Press, 1967), 32–33, 54–57; Carl Driver in the introduction to Samuel C. Williams, *History of the Lost State of Franklin* (Johnson City, TN: Watauga Press, 1924), xvii. See also Carl Driver, *John Sevier: Pioneer of the Old Southwest* (Chapel Hill: University of North Carolina Press, 1932).

35. Walter F. Cannon, "Four Interpretations of the History of the State of Franklin," East Tennessee Historical Society *Publications*, 22 (1930): 3–18; Thomas P. Abernethy, *From Frontier to Plantation in Tennessee: A Study in Frontier Democracy* (Chapel Hill: University of North Carolina Press, 1932), 89; Higginbotham, Kelly, and Baradell, *Papers of James Iredell*, 3: 552; Trenholme, *Ratification of the Federal Constitution*, 54–57.

36. Statement of Benjamin Smith, c. 1798, Benjamin Smith Papers, Southern Historical Collection, University of North Carolina, Chapel Hill, NC; Masterson, *William Blount*, 105–107; www.tngenweb.org/tnfirst/chicksaw/treaties.htm; Kemp P. Battle, *History of the University of North Carolina*, 2 vols. (Raleigh: Edwards & Broughton, 1907, 1912), 1: 119; Irene M. Griffey, *John Armstrong's Entry Book, October 21, 1783–May 25, 1784*, Vol. II (Clarksville, TN: the author, 1993), 86, 126, 127, 136, 137; A. B. Pruitt, "Land Grants in Tennessee by North Carolina," 1998, http://www.tngenweb.org/tnland/pruitt2.htm. Smith's speculation was part of the "great land grab." Since Armstrong's land office was open only from October 1783 through May 1784, the claimants perforce grabbed their land, or, in effect, recorded their claims quickly.

37. Clark, *State Records*, 24: 547; Brunswick County Court Minutes, December 1784.

Chapter 4

1. Smith to ?, May 19, 1783, Grimke Family Papers, Rare Book, Manuscript, and Special Collections Library, Duke University, Durham, NC.

2. Delbert H. Gilpatrick, *Jeffersonian Democracy in North Carolina, 1789–1816* (New York: Columbia University Press, 1931), 24–26.

3. Mark A. DeWolfe Howe, ed., "Journal of Josiah Quincy, Junior, 1773," Massachusetts Historical Society *Proceedings*, 49 (June 1916): 458.

4. Ron Chernow, *Alexander Hamilton* (New York: Penguin Press, 2004), 157.

5. Smith to ?, May 19, 1783, Grimke Family Papers.

6. Spaight quoted in Alan D. Watson, "The Constitution and North Carolina: Rebellion, Rights, and Ratification, 1776–1789," in *The Constitution and the States: The Role of the Original Thirteen in the Framing and Adoption of the Federal Constitution*, Patrick T. Conley and John P. Kaminski, eds. (Madison, WI: Madison House, 1988), 255.

7. Alan D. Watson, "Timothy Bloodworth," Lower Cape Fear Historical Society *Bulletin*, 29 (February 1986): 1–[6]

8. Walter Clark, ed., *The State Records of North Carolina*, 16 vols. (11–26) (Raleigh: State of North Carolina, 1895–1906),18: 718; 20: 901–902; Edmund C. Burnett, *The Continental Congress* (New York: Norton, 1964), 658–659.

9. Benjamin Smith to "Gentlemen," December 27, 1786, Miscellaneous Correspondence, General Assembly Session Records, November 1786–January 1787, Office of Archives and History, Raleigh, NC; Paul H. Smith, ed., *Letters of Delegates to Congress, 1774–1789*, 26 vols. (Washington, DC: Library of Congress, 1976–2000), 21: xxiii; 22: xxiv; 23: 230–231; Clark, *State Records*, 17: 79,143; 18: 165; 24: 578.

10. Benjamin Smith to "Gentlemen," December 27, 1786 and enclosure, General Assembly Session Records, November 1786–January 1787, Office of Archives and History. Smith, however, did not mean to tarry in Fayetteville after his explanation. Although he was prepared to meet legislators individually or collectively, he noted in his letter that he intended to depart the town early the following morning.

11. Don Higginbotham, Donna Kelly, and Lang Baradell, *The Papers of James Iredell*, 3 vols. (Raleigh: Office of Archives and History, North Carolina Department of Cultural Resources, 1976, 2003), 3: 326.

12. Higginbotham, Kelly, and Baradell, *Papers of James Iredell*, 3: 314; Clark, *State Records*, 17, 168; Brunswick County, Deed Book, B, 271–273, 274, 275, microfilm, Office of Archives and History; Brunswick County Court Minutes of Pleas and Quarter Sessions, June 1785, microfilm, Office of Archives and History.

13. Brunswick County Court Minutes, June, September, December 1785; June 1786.

14. Walter Edgar, *South Carolina: A History* (Columbia: University of South Carolina Press, 1998), 251–252.

15. Clark, *State Records*, 22: 1–26, 31–33. For the debates in the convention see Jonathan Elliot, ed., *The Debates of the Several State Conventions on the Adoption of the Federal Constitution as Recommended By the General Convention at Philadelphia in 1787*, 5 vols. (New York: Franklin, 1968), 4: 1–252.

16. Clark, *State Records*, 22: 26–28.

17. Ibid., 22: 28–31.

18. Donald Jackson and Dorothy Twohig, eds., *The Diaries of George Washington*, 6 vols. (Charlottesville: University of Virginia Press, 1976–1979, 6: 119; Higginbotham, Kelly, and Baradell, *Papers of James Iredell*, 3: 453–454; John

Cavanagh, *Decision at Fayetteville: The North Carolina Ratification Convention and General Assembly of 1789* (Raleigh: Division of Archives and History, Department of Cultural Resources, 1989), 1; Roy Parker, Jr., *Cumberland County: A Brief History* (Raleigh: Division of Archives and History, North Carolina Department of Cultural Resources, 1990), 10–26; H. Roy Merrens, *Colonial North Carolina in the Eighteenth Century: A Historical Geography* (Chapel Hill: University of North Carolina Press, 1964), 157–169.

19. *Wilmington Centinel, and General Advertiser*, July 23, 1788; Cavanagh, *Decision at Fayetteville*, 4.

20. *Wilmington Centinel, and General Advertiser*, July 2, 23, 1788.

21. Clark, *State Records*, 22: 33–35.

22. *State Gazette of North-Carolina* (Edenton), July 9, 1789; Cavanagh, *Decision at Fayetteville*, 17; Lenoir quoted in Watson, "The Constitution and North Carolina: Rebellion, Rights, and Ratification, 1776–1789," 265.

23. Clark, *State Records*, 22: 36–40; Higginbotham, Kelly, and Baradell, *Papers of James Iredell*, 3: xliii–xliv; Cavanagh, *Decision at Fayetteville*, 24.

24. Clark, *State Records*, 22: 48–49; Higginbotham, Kelly, and Baradell, *Papers of James Iredell*, 3: 540, 541, 544.

25. Clark, *State Records*, 22: 49–52; Louise I. Trenholme, *The Ratification of the Federal Constitution in North Carolina* (New York: AMS Press, 1967), 239; Bruce Frohnen, ed., *The American Republic: Primary Sources* (Indianapolis: Liberty Fund, 2002), 457.

26. Clark, *State Records*, 22: 52–53; Mary Phlegar Smith, "Borough Representation in North Carolina," *North Carolina Historical Review* 7 (April 1930): 177–191. Borough representation for all towns was eliminated by an amendment to the state constitution in 1835.

27. Cavanagh, *Decision at Fayetteville*, 19.

28. Clark, *State Records*, 21: 387–388; Higginbotham, Kelly, and Baradell, *Papers of James Iredell*, 3: 536, 537–538; Cavanagh, *Decision at Fayetteville*, 21–22.

29. Clark, *State Records*, 21: 357–358; Higginbotham, Kelly, and Baradell, *Papers of James Iredell*, 3: 542.

30. Clark, *State Records*, 21: 249, 253–254, 264.

31. Clark, *State Records*, 25: 7; New Hanover County, Deed Book, I, 262 [325], microfilm, Office of Archives and History.

32. Clark, *State Records*, 25: 6–7; 22: 618–620.

33. Clark, *State Records*, 21: 383, 385, 693–694.

34. Clark, *State Records*, 21: 233–234, 294.

35. Clark, *State Records*, 25: 21–24, 24–25; R. D. W. Connor, ed., *A Documentary History of the University of North Carolina, 1776–1799*, 2 vols. (Chapel Hill: University of North Carolina Press, 1953), 1: 39, 46; John L. Cheney, Jr., ed., *North Carolina Government: A Narrative and Statistical History* (Raleigh: Department of the Secretary of State, 1981), 815. For escheats see Blackwell P. Robinson, *The History of Escheats* (Chapel Hill: University of North Carolina Press, 1955).

36. Clark, *State Records*, 25: 21–24; Connor, *Documentary History of the University of North Carolina*, 1: 47–54.

37. Clark, *State Records*, 21: 417–418, 720; Alan D. Watson, ed., *An Index to North Carolina Newspapers, 1784–1789* (Raleigh: Division of Archives and History, North Carolina Department of Cultural Resources, 1992), xi–xii.

38. Alexander Martin to the honourable General Assembly, December 23, 1789, Governor's Letter Books, Alexander Martin, microfilm, Office of Archives and History.

Chapter 5

1. Don Higginbotham, Donna Kelly, and Lang Baradell, eds., *The Papers of James Iredell*, 3 vols. (Raleigh: Office of Archives and History, North Carolina Department of Cultural Resources, 1976, 2003), 3: 552.

2. "Belvidere," undated manuscript, Benjamin Smith Papers, Office of Archives and History, Raleigh, NC.

3. *Heads of Families at the First Census of the United States Taken in the Year 1790. North Carolina* (Baltimore: Genealogical, 1966), 19, 188–190; Guion Griffis Johnson, *Ante-Bellum North Carolina: A Social History* (Chapel Hill: University of North Carolina Press, 1937), 55–56.

4. Brunswick County, Deed Book, C, 180, 316, microfilm, Office of Archives and History, Raleigh, NC; *North-Carolina Chronicle; or, Fayetteville Gazette*, April 30, 1793; Walter Clark, ed., *The State Records of North Carolina*, 16 vols. (11–26) (Raleigh: State of North Carolina, 1895–1906), 24: 792–793; 25: 80; Journal of the Senate of North Carolina, 1793–1794, 34, microfilm, Office of Archives and History; *Laws and Resolutions of the State of North Carolina, 1793–1794*, ch. 2.

5. Will of Thomas Smith, Charleston County Wills, Vol. 23: 689, South Carolina Department of Archives and History, Columbia, SC; *North-Carolina Chronicle; or, Fayetteville Gazette*, December 27, 1790; H. M. Wagstaff, ed., *The Papers of John Steele*, 2 vols. (Raleigh: Edwards & Broughton, 1924), 1: 76; Delbert H. Gilpatrick, *Jeffersonian Democracy in North Carolina, 1789–1816* (New York: Columbia University Press, 1931), 42–46; Jeffrey J. Crow, "The Whiskey Rebellion in North Carolina," *North Carolina Historical Review* 66 (January 1989): 1–28.

6. Clark, *State Records*, 21: 865–866, 867, 877, 1021, 1055; Gilpatrick, *Jeffersonian Democracy in North Carolina*, 48–49, 51. Martin's biogra-

pher, however, goes to great lengths to try to demonstrate Martin's early and continued attachment to the Constitution. Charles D. Rodenbough, *Governor Alexander Martin: Biography of a North Carolina Revolutionary War Statesman* (Jefferson, NC: McFarland, 2004), passim.

7. *North-Carolina Chronicle; or, Fayetteville Gazette*, February 7, 1791; Gilpatrick, *Jeffersonian Democracy in North Carolina*, 53–54.

8. Clark, *State Records*, 21: 871, 876, 882, 883, 897–898, 901, 909, 916, 929, 939, 940, 950, 953–954, 970.

9. Alan D. Watson, *Internal Improvements in Antebellum North Carolina* (Raleigh: Office of Archives and History, North Carolina Department of Cultural Resources, 2002), 1–4.

10. Clark, *State Records*, 19: 498.

11. *Ibid.*, 21: 936; 25: 98–99; *Laws, 1791*, ch. 36; *1793–1794*, ch. 35; *1806*, ch. 25; J. H. Myrover, *Short History of Cumberland County and the Cape Fear Section* (Fayetteville, NC: North Carolina Baptist, 1905), 21.

12. Clark, *State Records*, 21; 929–930; 25: 83–95.

13. *Ibid.*, 21: 965; 947, 1031–1032.

14. R. D. W. Connor, ed., *A Documentary History of the University of North Carolina, 1776–1799*, 2 vols. (Chapel Hill: University of North Carolina Press, 1953), 1: 65–66 n. 14.

15. Connor, *Documentary History of the University of North Carolina*, 1: 73; *North Carolina Chronicle; or, Fayetteville Gazette*, December 6, 13, 20, 1790; January 1, 1791.

16. Connor, *Documentary History of the University of North Carolina*, 1: 83–84; Clark, *State Records*, 21: 999.

17. Donald Jackson and Dorothy Twohig, eds., *The Diaries of George Washington*, 6 vols. (Charlottesville: University Press of Virginia, 1976–1979), 6: 119–120; Archibald Henderson, *Washington's Southern Tour, 1791* (Boston: Houghton Mifflin, 1923), 105–107.

18. Jackson and Twohig, *Diaries of George Washington*, 6:120; Henderson, *Washington's Southern Tour*, 108–114.

19. Jackson and Twohig, *Diaries of George Washington*, 6:121; Henderson, *Washington's Southern Tour*, 118–120; 1799; *Wilmington Gazette*, June 13, 1799.

20. Benjamin Smith to George Washington, May 1, 1791, entry 113 (Miscellaneous Letters received, 1789–1906), microfilm 179: Roll 5, National Archives, College Park, MD.

21. *Laws, 1791*, ch. 28.

22. Grady L. E. Carroll, ed., *Francis Asbury in North Carolina: The North Carolina Portions of the Journal of Francis Asbury* (Nashville, TN: Parthenon Press, 1964), 146.

23. Journal of the House of Commons of North Carolina, 1791–1792, 20, 42, 44, 53, microfilm, Office of Archives and History; *Laws, 1791–1792*, chs. 47, 67.

24. House of Commons Journal, 1791–1792, 35, 38, 63–64.

25. Connor, *Documentary History of the University of North Carolina*, 1: 131–135.

26. *Ibid.*, 1: 141–143; Kemp P. Battle, *History of the University of North Carolina*, 2 vols. (Raleigh: Edwards & Broughton, 1907), 1: 11; William D. Snider, *Light on the Hill: A History of the University of North Carolina at Chapel Hill* (Chapel Hill: University of North Carolina Press, 1982), 12–14.

27. Minutes of the Brunswick County Court of Pleas and Quarter Sessions, April, July, October 1792, microfilm, Office of Archives and History.

28. *North-Carolina Chronicle; or, Fayetteville Gazette*, December 11, 1792; *North Carolina Journal* (Halifax, NC), December 19, 1792.

29. Journal of the Senate of North Carolina, 1792–1793, 2, microfilm, Office of Archives and History.

30. Senate Journal, 1792–1793, 20, 46; Gilpatrick, *Jeffersonian Democracy in North Carolina*, 55–59.

31. John K. Mahon, *The American Militia: Decade of Decision, 1789–1800* (Jacksonville, Fla.: Miller Press, 1960), 14–21; Lawrence Delbert Cress, *Citizens in Arms: The Army and the Militia in American Society to the War of 1812* (Chapel Hill: University of North Carolina Press, 1982), 116–120.

32. Senate Journal, 1792–1793, 28; *Laws, 1792–1793*, Militia Bill, pp. 33–36.

33. Clark, *State Records*, 24: 586–592, 611–613.

34. Joshua Potts, "The Location of Smithville," *Letters and Documents, Relating to the Early History of the Lower Cape Fear*, James Sprunt Historical Monograph No. 4 (Chapel Hill: University of North Carolina Press, 1903), 86–89.

35. *Laws, 1792–1793*, ch. 62; *1801*, ch. 63; Brunswick County, Deed Book, C, 335–336.

36. Snider, *Light on the Hill*, 4.

37. *North Carolina Journal*, November 14, 1792; Connor, *Documentary History of the University of North Carolina*, 1: 177–184; Snider, *Light on the Hill*, 14.

Chapter 6

1. David Stick, *Bald Head: A History of Smith Island and the Cape Fear* (Wendell, NC: Broadfoot, 1985), 1–5, 79; "Topographical and Historical Description of the County of Brunswick, in North Carolina," *National Register* 1 (July 1816): 341.

2. Alice Barnwell Keith, William H. Masterson, and David T. Morgan, eds., *The John Gray Blount Papers*, 4 vols. (Raleigh: North Carolina Department of Cultural Resources, Division of Archives and History, 1952–1982), 2: 316; Michael Hill, "Historical Overview of Smith Island (Bald

Head Island) Brunswick County, North Carolina," 4–5, Research report, 1984, Office of Archives and History, Raleigh, NC; Catherine W. Bishir, "The 'Unpainted Aristocracy': The Beach Cottages of Old Nags Head," *North Carolina Historical Review*, 54 (October 1977): 367–392.

3. Brunswick County Court Minutes of Pleas and Quarter Sessions, January, April, July, October 1793, microfilm, Office of Archives and History.

4. *State-Gazette of North Carolina* (Edenton), January 31; Delbert H. Gilpatrick, *Jeffersonian Democracy in North Carolina, 1789–1816* (New York: Columbia University Press, 1931), 62–63.

5. Gilpatrick, *Jeffersonian Democracy in North Carolina*, 63.

6. Henry Knox to Richard Dobbs Spaight, May 24, 1793; Spaight to John A. Campbell, James Read, Benjamin Smith, June 22, 1793, Governor's Letter Books, Richard Dobbs Spaight, microfilm, Office of Archives and History.

7. Richard Dobbs Spaight to George Washington, October ?, 1793; Spaight to Thomas Wright, October 24, 1793, Governor's Letter Books, Richard Dobbs Spaight.

8. Benjamin Smith to Richard Dobbs Spaight, October 11, 1793, and enclosures, Governor's Letter Books, Richard Dobbs Spaight.

9. Benjamin Smith to Richard Dobbs Spaight, October 11, 1793, Governor's Letter Books, Richard Dobbs Spaight; Alan D. Watson, *Wilmington: Port of North Carolina* (Columbia: University of South Carolina Press, 1992), 40–41.

10. Journal of the Senate of North Carolina, 1793–1794, 1, 2, 3, 6–7, microfilm, Office of Archives and History.

11. Richard Dobbs Spaight to The Honourable the General Assembly of the State of North Carolina, December 4, 1793, Governor's Letter Books, Richard Dobbs Spaight; Senate Journal, 1793–1794, 7.

12. Senate Journal, 1793–1794, 2, 6, 18; *Laws and Resolutions of the State of North Carolina, 1792*, pp. 33–36; *1793–1794*, ch. 1.

13. Senate Journal, 1793–1794, 8–9, 16, 17, 24; *Laws, 1793–1794*, ch. 5.

14. Senate Journal, 1793–1794, 35–36; Willis P. Whichard, *Justice James Iredell* (Durham, NC: Carolina Academic Press, 2000), 157–171.

15. William D. Snider, *Light on the Hill: A History of the University of North Carolina at Chapel Hill* (Chapel Hill: University of North Carolina Press, 1982),19–20, 22–23; Blackwell P. Robinson, *William R. Davie* (Chapel Hill: University of North Carolina Press, 1957), 233–242. The previous month, on September 18, 1793, President George Washington, dressed in Masonic apron, dedicated the United States Capitol in a stirringly impressive ceremony. Steven C. Bullock, *Revolutionary Brotherhood: Freemasonry and the Transformation of the American Social Order, 1730–1840* (Chapel Hill: University of North Carolina Press, 1996), 137.

16. R. D. W. Connor, ed., *A Documentary History of the University of North Carolina, 1776–1799*, 2 vols. (Chapel Hill: University of North Carolina Press, 1953), 1: 253–259, 268, 271.

17. Senate Journal, 1793–1794, 37–38, 40.

18. Brunswick County Court Minutes, January, April, July, October 1794.

19. John K. Mahon. *The American Militia: Decade of Decision, 1789–1800* (Jacksonville, FL: Miller Press, 1960), 26.

20. Lawrence Delbert Cress, *Citizens in Arms: The Army and the Militia in American Society to the War of 1812* (Chapel Hill: University of North Carolina Press, 1982), 121–124.

21. Senate Journal, July 1794, 1–9; *Laws, July 1794*, chs. 2, 3.

22. Richard Dobbs Spaight to The Honourable the General Assembly of the State of North Carolina, December 4, 1793, Governor's Letter Books, Richard Dobbs Spaight; Walter Clark, ed., *The State Records of North Carolina*, 16 vols. (11–26) (Raleigh: State of North Carolina, 1895–1906), 23: 505–506; *Laws, July 1794*, ch. 1; Wilson Angley, *A History of Fort Johnston on the Lower Cape Fear* (Southport, NC: Southport Historical Society, 1996), 36–37.

23. Angley, *History of Fort Johnston*, 37–42.

24. Stick, *Bald Head*, 32.

25. *The Wilmington Chronicle and North-Carolina Weekly Advertiser*, August 7, 1795; Stick, *Bald Head*, 32–34.

26. Stick, *Bald Head*, 34–38.

27. Elizabeth Reid Murray, *Wake: Capital County of North Carolina*, Vol. 1 (Raleigh: Capital County, 1983), 80–81.

28. *North Carolina Journal* (Halifax), April 10, 1793; Murray, *Wake: Capital County of North Carolina*, 86–93.

29. Murray, *Wake: Capital County of North Carolina*, 118 and n. 55; Catherine W. Bishir and Michael T. Southern, *A Guide to the Historic Architecture of Piedmont North Carolina* (Chapel Hill: University of North Carolina Press, 2003), 111–112.

30. *North Carolina Journal*, January 12, 1795; Murray, *Wake Capital County of North: Carolina*, 90–91, 104.

31. Senate Journal, 1794–1795, 7, 10, 22, 29, 32, 33, 37, 38, 43–44, 47; *Laws, 1794–1795*, ch. 88. See Baron von Steuben, *Regulations for the Order and Discipline of the Troops of the United States: To Which is Added an appendix containing the United States Militia Act, Passed by Congress, May 1792* (Boston: Thomas and Andrews, 1794). Actually, 1,190 copies of the manual were acquired by the state, far more than necessary. Unneeded copies were lodged with the secretary of state. Resolution of the House of Commons relative to Baron [von] Steuben ['s] Military Guide, January 26, 1795, concurrence by the Senate, January 26, 1795, Senate Resolutions, General Assembly Session Records, 1794–1795, Office of Archives and History.

32. Senate Journal, 1794–1795, 39; Alan D. Watson, *Internal Improvements in Antebellum North Carolina* (Raleigh: Office of Archives and History, North Carolina Department of Cultural Resources, 2002), 64.
33. *Laws, 1794–795*, chs. 3, 33; *North Carolina Journal*, February 23, 1795; Darryl Lynn Peterkin, "'Lux, Libertas, and Learning': The First State University and the Transformation of North Carolina, 1789–1816," unpubl. Ph.D. diss., Princeton University, 1995, 19–22.
34. Connor, *Documentary History of the University*, 1: 351–357; Kemp P. Battle, *History of the University of North Carolina*, 2 vols. (Raleigh: Edwards & Broughton, 1907, 1912); 1: 61–65; Snider, *Light on the Hill*, 26, 29–30.
35. Resolution of the House of Commons relative to the sale of liquor, February 7, 1795, concurrency by the Senate, House of Commons Resolutions, General Assembly Session Records, 1794–1795.

Chapter 7

1. Journal of the Senate of North Carolina, 1796, 47, microfilm, Office of Archives and History, Raleigh, NC. For the political divisions in the state see Alan D. Watson, "States' Rights and Agrarianism Ascendant," in *The Constitution and the States: the Role of the Original Thirteen in the Framing and Adoption of the Federal Constitution*, Patrick T. Conley and John P. Kaminski, eds. (Madison, WI: Madison House, 1988), 251–252; Robert L. Ganyard, "Radicals and Conservatives in Revolutionary North Carolina: A Point at Issue, the October Election, 1776," *William and Mary Quarterly*, 3rd Series, 24 (October 1967): 568–587; Louis I. Trenholme, *The Ratification of the Federal Constitution in North Carolina* (New York: Columbia University Press, 1932), chs. 3–4; Jackson T. Main, *Political Parties before the Constitution* (Chapel Hill: University of North Carolina Press, 1973), 32–33, 311–317. See, also, Norman K. Risjord, *Chesapeake Politics, 1781–1800* (New York: Columbia University Press, 1978), 591 n 32, for reservations about the terms "conservative" and "radical."
2. Jeffrey J. Crow, "The Whiskey Rebellion in North Carolina," *North Carolina Historical Review*, 66 (January 1989): 1–28; Griffith J. McRee, ed., *Life and Correspondence of James Iredell, One of the Associate Justices of the Supreme Court of the United States*, 2 vols. in 1 (New York: Smith, 1949), 2: 450.
3. Risjord, *Chesapeake Politics*, 523–524.
4. Richard Rankin, *Ambivalent Churchmen and Evangelical Churchwomen: The Religion of the Episcopal Elite in North Carolina, 1800–1860* (Columbia: University of South Carolina Press, 1993), 3–5; 28–29; Alan D. Watson, *Wilmington, North Carolina, to 1861* (Jefferson, NC: McFarland, 2003), 140–141.
5. Ida Brooks Kellam and Elizabeth Francenia McKoy, *St. James Church, Wilmington, North Carolina, Historical Records, 1737–1852* (Privately printed, 1965), 3, 27; *Laws and Resolutions of the State of North Carolina, 1797*, ch. 42. Smith later gave communion silver, one flagon, two chalices, one paten, and an altar spoon, to St. James. Susan Taylor Block, *Temple of Our Fathers: St. James Church* (Wilmington, NC: Artspeaks, 2004), 38.
6. *Wilmington Gazette*, June 19, 1804; May 7, 1805; Grady L. E. Carroll, ed., *Francis Asbury in North Carolina* (Nashville, TN: Parthenon Press, 1964), 183; Rankin, *Ambivalent Churchmen and Evangelical Churchwomen*, 11–20, 27–33.
7. Stephen C. Bullock, *Revolutionary Brotherhood: Freemasonry and the Transformation of the American Social Order, 1730–1840* (Chapel Hill: University of North Carolina Press, 1996), 152, 224–225, 228, 235; Earley Winfred Bridges, *The Masonic Governors of North Carolina. Their Masonic Records and Orations; Newspaper Articles of Events Pertaining to Their Craft, and Other Information of Interest to Masonry About the Governors of North Carolina* (Greensboro, NC: n.p., 1937).
8. *Wilmington Centinel and General Advertiser*, January 8, 1789; George C. Rogers, Jr. *Evolution of a Federalist: William Loughton Smith of Charleston (1758–1812)* (Columbia: University of South Carolina Press, 1962), 31; Watson, *Wilmington, North Carolina*, 44; Thomas C. Parramore, *Launching the Craft: The First Half-Century of Freemasonry in North Carolina* (Raleigh: Litho, 1975), 143.
9. Parramore, *Launching the Craft*, 173, 174–175, 214; Janet K. Seapker, "St. John's Masonic Lodge, Part 1," Lower Cape Fear Historical Society *Bulletin* 50 (January 2006): 2, 7.
10. Bullock, *Revolutionary Brotherhood*, 139–143, 148–150, 237–238.
11. *Ibid.*, 137,147–148,150, 228; R. D. W. Connor, ed., *A Documentary History of the University of North Carolina*, 2 vols. (Chapel Hill: University of North Carolina Press, 1953), 2: 310–313; William D. Snider, *Light on the Hill: A History of the University of North Carolina at Chapel Hill* (Chapel Hill: University of North Carolina Press, 1992), 19–21, 25–26. See more fully, Darryl Lynn Peterkin, "'Lux, Libertas, and Learning': The First State University and the Transformation of North Carolina, 1789–1816," Ph. D. diss., Princeton University, 1995, 39–49.
12. Minutes of the Brunswick County Court of Pleas and Quarter Sessions, April 1795, microfilm, Office of Archives and History, Raleigh, NC.
13. Brunswick County Court Minutes, July 1795.
14. *Wilmington Chronicle; and North-Carolina Weekly Advertiser*, July 17, 1795.
15. Eliza Carolina (Burgwin) Clitherall, "Au-

tobiography and Diary of Mrs. Eliza Clitherall," 17 vols., typescript, Clitherall Books, Southern Historical Collection, Chapel Hill, NC, 4: 34.

16. Clitherall, "Autobiography and Diary," 5: 34; 6: 44.

17. Smith to Dear Sir [John Haywood], August 30, 1798, Ernest Haywood Collection of Haywood Family Papers, Southern Historical Collection.

18. Carroll, *Francis Asbury in North Carolina,* 183; Clitherall, "Autobiography and Diary," 5: 33; Kenneth Roberts and Anna M. Roberts, trans. and eds., *Moreau de St. Mery's American Journal [1793–1798]* (Garden City, NY: Doubleday, 1947), 335.

19. Senate Journal, 1795, 1, 14, 17.

20. Connor, *Documentary History of the University of North Carolina,* 1: 441–442; Snider, *Light on the Hill,* 27.

21. Connor, *Documentary History of the University of North Carolina,* 1: 440–448, 453–460.

22. *Laws and Resolutions of North Carolina, 1795,* chs. 4, 10, 19, 20.

23. Letter from the deputy agent for the French Republic, resident in Wilmington, to Benjamin Smith, December 2, 1795, Slave Collection, Office of Archives and History; *Laws, 1794,* ch. 2; *1795,* ch. 16.

24. Senate Journal, 1795, 46.

25. Alice Barnwell Keith, William H. Masterson, and David T. Morgan, eds., *The John Gray Blount Papers,* 4 vols. (Raleigh: State Department of Archives and History, 1952–1982), 3: 26–27 n. 61, 80–81.

26. Bernard Bailyn, *Voyages to the West: A Passage in the Peopling of America on the Eve of the Revolution* (New York: Knopf, 1986), 536–540, 544; William Stewart Lester, *The Transylvania Company* (Spencer, IN: Guard, 1935).

27. Benjamin Smith to "Sir" [James Hogg], January 26, July 26, 1798; July 12, 17; December 19, 1799; October 5, 1800 (quotation), Benjamin Smith Papers, Office of Archives and History.

28. Benjamin Smith to "Sir" [James Hogg], January 26, 1798, Benjamin Smith Papers, Office of Archives and History.

29. Benjamin Smith to "Sir," August 10, 14, Benjamin Smith Papers, Office of Archives and History.

30. New Hanover County, Deed Book, L, 21, 307; O, 442, 443, microfilm, Office of Archives and History; Minutes of the New Hanover County Court of Pleas and Quarter Sessions, May-June 1793, microfilm, Office of Archives and History; Benjamin Smith to "Sir" [James Hogg], September 14, December 20, 1797; April 22, 1798, Benjamin Smith Papers, Office of Archives and History.

31. New Hanover County, Deed Book, L, 23, 150, 426.

32. Walter Clark, ed., *The State Records of North Carolina,* 16 vols. (11–26) (Raleigh: State of North Carolina, 1895–1906), 25: 491–492; *Laws,*

1806, ch. 40; *Newbern Spectator* (New Bern, NC), August 28, 1830.

33. *Hall's Wilmington Gazette,* February 22, 1798; Brunswick County Court Minutes, January 1796; *Cape-Fear Recorder* (Wilmington), June 29, 1831; Claude V. Jackson, III, *A Maritime History of the Cape Fear and Northeast Cape Fear Rivers, Wilmington Harbor, N.C.* Vol. I. Edited by Jack E. Fryar, Jr., as *The Big Book of the Cape Fear River* (Wilmington: Dram Tree Books, 2008), 113.

34. Brunswick County Court Minutes, July 1796; New Hanover County, Deed Book L, 518; Jackson, *The Cape Fear—Northeast Cape Fear Rivers,* 117–121; Stanley A. South, "'Russellborough': Two Royal Governors' Mansion at Brunswick Town," *North Carolina Historical Review* 44 (October 1967): 360–372. The author wishes to thank Joseph Sheppard, New Hanover County Public Library, Wilmington, North Carolina, for obtaining the information about the transfer of Orton to Benjamin Smith.

35. *Cape-Fear Recorder,* October 16, 1824; James Laurence Sprunt, *The Story of Orton Plantation* (Wilmington, n.p., 1958).

36. Ida B. Kellam, "Kellam's Block Files of Wilmington, North Carolina," 15 vols. and index (N.p., n.d.), 15: 169, 171, New Hanover County Public Library, Wilmington, NC; New Hanover County, Deed Book, L, 617; Brunswick County, Deed Book, C, 352–355, microfilm, Office of Archives and History; Wilson Angley, *A History of Fort Johnston on the Lower Cape Fear* (Wilmington: Broadfoot, 1996), 42–43.

37. Brunswick County Court Minutes, January, April, July 1796.

38. Brunswick County Court Minutes, October 1796.

39. Senate Journal, 1796, 1, 2.

40. Senate Journal, 1796, 3; *Laws, 1796,* ch. 8; p. 61; Guion G. Johnson, *Ante-Bellum North Carolina: A Social History* (Chapel Hill: University of North Carolina, 1937), 216–223.

41. *Laws, 1796,* ch. 35; Keith, Masterson, and Morgan, *John Gray Blount Papers,* 3: 331; *Dictionary of North Carolina Biography,* s.v. "Strother, John"; Mary Lindsay Thornton, "The Price and Strother *First Actual Survey of State of North Carolina," North Carolina Historical Review,* 41 (October 1964): 477–483.

42. Senate Journal, 1796, 14, 22.

43. *State-Gazette of North Carolina* (Edenton), July 23, 30, 1795; *Laws, 1796,* chs. 5, 27.

Chapter 8

1. *North Carolina Journal* (Halifax), January 9, 1797; Journal of the House of Commons, 1796, 25; 1797, 4, microfilm, Office of Archives and History, Raleigh, NC; H. G. Wagstaff, ed., "The Harris Letters," *James Sprunt Historical Publica-*

tions, Vol. 14 (Durham, NC: Seeman Printery, 1916), 43.

2. Delbert H. Gilpatrick, *Jeffersonian Democracy in North Carolina, 1789–1816* (New York: Columbia University Press, 1931), 84; Wagstaff, "Harris Letters," 43.

3. Deposition by William Campbell and others, August 24, 1798, Ernest Haywood Collection of Haywood Family Papers, Southern Historical Collection, Chapel Hill, NC; *North Carolina Journal* (Halifax), September 3, 1798; Joseph Gardner Swift, *The Memoirs of Gen. Joseph Gardner Swift* (Boston: Privately printed, 1890), 57; Wilson Angley, *A History of Fort Johnston on the Lower Cape Fear* (Wilmington: Broadfoot, 1996), 44.

4. Archibald Henderson, *Washington's Southern Tour, 1791* (Boston and New York: Houghton and Mifflin, 1923), 112 n; Don Higginbotham, Donna Kelly, and Lang Baradell, eds., *The Papers of James Iredell*, 3 vols. (Raleigh: Office of Archives and History, North Carolina Department of Cultural Resources, 1976, 2003), 3: 140 n. 1; Wilson Angley, "A Brief History of the Eagles Plantation and Mill Facility in Brunswick County," Report, Research Branch, 1989, Office of Archives and History, Raleigh, NC, 6–7.

5. James Read to "Dear Sir," May 2, 1799; April 6, 1801; December 6, 1803, Ernest Haywood Collection of Haywood Family Papers, Southern Historical Collection, University of North Carolina, Chapel Hill, NC; New Hanover County, Deed Book, M, 310, microfilm, Office of Archives and History, Raleigh, NC; *Raleigh Register*, October 29, 1804; *Wilmington Gazette*, January 7, 1806.

6. Minutes of the Brunswick County Court of Pleas and Quarter Sessions, January 1797, microfilm, Office of Archives and History.

7. Brunswick County Court Minutes, April, July 1797.

8. Journal of the Senate of North Carolina, 1797, 1, 5, 21, 27, microfilm, Office of Archives and History.

9. *Laws and Resolutions of the State of North Carolina, 1797*, chs. 22, 24; Senate Journal, 1797, 44.

10. R. D. W. Connor, ed., *A Documentary History of the University of North Carolina*, 2 vols. (Chapel Hill: University of North Carolina Press, 1953), 2: 209, 226–227, 245–246.

11. Griffith J. McRee, ed., *Life and Correspondence of James Iredell, One of the Associate Justices of the Supreme Court of the United States*, 2 vols. in 1 (New York: Peter Smith, 1949), 2: 538, 540; *North Carolina Journal*, March 12, 1798; Gilpatrick, *Jeffersonian Democracy in North Carolina*, 99–100, 105; Charles D. Rodenbough, *Governor Alexander Martin: Biography of a North Carolina Revolutionary War Statesman* (Jefferson, NC: McFarland, 2004), 182.

12. Senate Journal, 1798, 2, 77, Gilpatrick, *Jeffersonian Democracy in North Carolina*, 101–102;

Lisle A. Rose, *Prologue to Democracy: The Federalists in the South, 1789–1800* (Lexington: University of Kentucky Press, 1968), 176; McRee, ed., *Life and Correspondence of James Iredell*, 2: 541–542; Rodenbough, *Governor Alexander Martin*, 183–184.

13. Benjamin Smith to "Dear Sir" [James Hogg], April 22, 1798, Benjamin Smith Papers, Office of Archives and History; *North Carolina Journal*, November 19, 1798; Kenneth Roberts and Anna M. Roberts, trans. and eds., *Moreau de St. Mery's American Journal [1793–1798]* (Garden City, NY: Doubleday, 1947), 333. Smith's South Carolina connections proved useful after the disaster. The Ancient York Masons of that state offered $234.62 to help those "in the greatest distress" from the fires in Wilmington, the money to be distributed by Smith, Griffith McRee, and George Hooper. *Wilmington Gazette*, March 7, 1799.

14. Journal of the House of Commons of North Carolina, 1798, 8, microfilm, Office of Archives and History; *Laws, 1798*, ch. 64.

15. *Laws, 1798*, ch. 59; *Wilmington Gazette*, March 7, 1799.

16. *Laws, 1798*, ch. 55; Alan D. Watson, *Society in Colonial North Carolina*, rev. ed. (Raleigh: Office of Archives and History, State Department of Cultural Resources, 1996), 75–76; John L. Cheney, Jr., ed., *North Carolina Government: A Narrative and Statistical History, 1585–1979* (Raleigh: North Carolina Department of the Secretary of State, 1981), 815.

17. *Laws, 1798*, ch. 55; William S. Powell, *North Carolina Through Four Centuries* (Chapel Hill: University of North Carolina Press, 1989), 216.

18. *Hall's Wilmington Gazette*, May 31, November 19, 1798.

19. *Laws, 1798*, ch. 56; Alan D. Watson, "The Lottery in Early North Carolina," *North Carolina Historical Review*, 69 (October 1992): 373–387.

20. *Wilmington Gazette*, March 7, 1799; October 11, 1803.

21. William R. Davie to Gen. McRee, May 1, 1799, Governor's Letter Book, William R. Davie, microfilm, Office of Archives and History.

22. Thomas Brown to Gen. Davie, May 29, 1799, Governor's Letter Book, William R. Davie; Angley, *History of Fort Johnston*, 44.

23. *North Carolina Journal*, September 3, 1798 (quotation); Gilpatrick, *Jeffersonian Democracy in North Carolina*, 99–100; Rose, *Prologue to Democracy*, 169–170.

24. *North Carolina Journal*, September 3, 1798; *Wilmington Gazette*, April 4, 1799.

25. *Wilmington Gazette*, April 4, 1799.

26. *Ibid.*, June 26, 1810.

27. *Ibid.*, April 18, 1799; Gilpatrick, *Jeffersonian Democracy in North Carolina*, 88–90.

28. *Wilmington Gazette*, April 18, 1799.

29. *Ibid.*, June 13, 1799.

30. *Ibid.*, August 8, 1799.
31. *Ibid.*
32. *Ibid.* Matthew 25:14-30 contains the parable of the talents; Luke 19:11-27, the parable of the pounds with the reference to the napkin in 19:20.
33. Blackwell P. Robinson, *William R. Davie* (Chapel Hill: University of North Carolina Press, 1957), 319-325; McRee, *Life and Correspondence of James Iredell*, 2: 584; *North Carolina Minerva* (Raleigh), September 17, 1799; *Wilmington Gazette*, October 3, 1799.
34. Cheney, *North Carolina Government*, 813; *Wilmington Gazette*, October 3, 1799.
35. *Raleigh Register*, October 22, 1799.
36. Edward Rutledge to [William R. Davie], October 7, 1799; Ed. Jones to Governor Smith, November 1, 1799; B. Smith to Edward Rutledge, November 16, 1799, Governor's Letter Books, William R. Davie; James Haw, *John & Edward Rutledge of South Carolina* (Athens: University of Georgia Press, 1997), 273-274.
37. Cheney, *North Carolina Government*, 815; *Raleigh Register*, November 19, 1799.
38. *Raleigh Register*, November 19, 1799; Keith, Masterson, and Morgan, *John Gray Blount Papers*, 3: 323.
39. Snider, *Light on the Hill*, 79-80; Peterkin, "Lux, Libertas, and Learning," 146-155; Connor, *Documentary History of the University of North Carolina*, 2: 442-443, 445-446, 455, 458.
40. Connor, *Documentary History of the University of North Carolina*, 2: 451-453, 457, 459-460, 482-484, 499-501; Peterkin, "Lux, Libertas, and Learning," 167-168.
41. *Laws, 1799*, chs. 10, 18, 38, 39; Senate Journal, 1799, 4; Gilpatrick, *Jeffersonian Democracy in North Carolina*, 107-108.
42. *Wilmington Gazette*, August 8, 1799; William H. Masterson, *William Blount* (Baton Rouge: Louisiana State University Press, 1954), 298-342; Rodenbough, *Governor Alexander Martin*, 176-182; *Dictionary of North Carolina Biography*, s.v. "Glasgow, James"; Russell Scott Koonts, "'An Angel Has Fallen!: The Glasgow Land Frauds and the Establishment of the North Carolina Supreme Court," master's thesis, North Carolina State University, 1995.
43. "Statement of Benjamin Smith," c. 1798, Benjamin Smith Papers, Southern Historical Collection; Connor, *Documentary History of the University of North Carolina, 2: 320-323*; Masterson, *William Blount*, 105-107; Journal of the House of Commons, 1791, 49.
44. "Gen[era]l Davie[']s opinion respect[in]g the mode of settling the debt due to Armstrong Entry Taker of Western Lands," June 2, 1798; Benjamin Smith to "Dear Sir" [John Haywood], January 25, April 9, June 3, 1798, University Papers, Southern Historical Collection.
45. Connor, *Documentary History of the University of North Carolina*, 2: 322; House of Commons Journal, 1799, 41-42; Senate Journal, 1799, 44, 57-58.
46. Senate Journal, 1799, 60.

Chapter 9

1. William Perry Johnson and Dorothy Williams Potter, *1800 North Carolina Census. Brunswick County* (N.p.: privately printed, 1975), 6.
2. Eliza Carolina (Burgwin) Clitherall, "Autobiography and Diary of Mrs. Eliza Clitherall," 17 vols., typescript, Clitherall Books, 6: 54, Southern Historical Collection, University of North Carolina, Chapel Hill, NC; Benjamin Smith to James Hogg, December 20, 1797; April 22, 1798; Hogg to Smith, May 7, 1798, Benjamin Smith Papers, Office of Archives and History, Raleigh, NC; Joseph Gardner Swift, *The Memoirs of Gen. Joseph Gardner Swift* (Boston: privately printed, 1890), 52.
3. Benjamin Smith to "Dear Sir" [John Haywood], January 25, 1798, University Papers, Southern Historical Collection; Benjamin Smith to "Sir" [Gavin Alves], October 29, 1802, Benjamin Smith Papers, Office of Archives and History; Clitherall, "Autobiography and Diary," 6: 54; 7: 4; *Raleigh Register*, July 29, 1805; Swift, *Memoirs of Gen. Joseph Gardner Swift*, 59.
4. Swift, *Memoirs of Gen. Joseph Gardner Swift*, 59.
5. Alice E. Matthews, *Society in Revolutionary North Carolina* (Raleigh: North Carolina Department of Cultural Resources, Division of Archives and History, 1976), 61; James Hogg to Benjamin Smith, May 7, 1798, Benjamin Smith Papers, Office of Archives and History.
6. Clitherall, "Autobiography and Diary," 6: 54; Richard Rankin, *Ambivalent Churchmen and Evangelical Churchwomen: The Religion of the Episcopal Elite in North Carolina, 1800-1860* (Columbia: University of South Carolina Press, 1993), 27-29.
7. Rankin, *Ambivalent Churchmen and Evangelical Churchwomen*, 30-33.
8. Grady L. E. Carroll, ed., *Francis Asbury in North Carolina* (Nashville, TN: Parthenon Press, 1964), 68, 155, 183, 184, 195, 211, 221, 226, 231-232, 240, 246, 250, 268, 211.
9. Diary of Jeremiah Norman, 18 vols., quotation on 17: 923; 17-18 passim, Stephen Beauregard Weeks Collection, Southern Historical Collection, University of North Carolina, Chapel Hill, NC; C. Franklin Grill, *Methodism in the Upper Cape Fear Valley* (Nashville, TN: Parthenon Press, 1966), 18, 92.
10. Brunswick County, Deed Book, D, 81, 82, 127 (Will of Sarah Smith, January 17, 1818), microfilm, Office of Archives and History; Benjamin Smith to "Sir," [James Hogg], July 5, 1798; Oc-

tober 5, 1800, Benjamin Smith Papers, Office of Archives and History.

11. Smith to "Dear Sir," April 18, 1799, Benjamin Smith Papers, State Archives; Smith to "Dear Sir" [John Haywood], August 30, 1798, Ernest Haywood Collection of Haywood Family Papers, Southern Historical Collection.

12. "Topographical and Historical. Description of the County of Brunswick, in North Carolina," *National Register*, 1 (July 1816): 341.

13. Clitherall, "Autobiography and Diary," 5: 28; 6: 17, 18; Alfred Moore Waddell, *Some Memories of My Life* (Raleigh: Edwards & Broughton, 1908), 43–44.

14. *Laws and Resolutions of North Carolina, 1801*, ch. 63; *1804*, ch. 44; *1817*, ch. 68; *1823*, ch. 61.

15. *Wilmington Gazette*, January 10, 1804; Walter G. Curtis, *Reminiscences, 1848–1900*, 2nd ed. (Southport, NC: Southport Historical Society, 1999), 58–59.

16. Benjamin Smith to John Haywood, November 5, 1800, Ernest Haywood Collection of Haywood Family Papers; Curtis, *Reminiscences*, 59.

17. Benjamin Smith to John Haywood, November 5, 1800, Ernest Haywood Collection of Haywood Family Papers; Curtis, *Reminiscences*, 59–60; *Wilmington Gazette*, January 13, 1816.

18. A. D. Schenck, "The History of Fort Johnston, North Carolina, 1745–1879," 36–37, A. D. Schenck Paper, original in the New York Historical Society, typescript copy, Office of State Archives.

19. Jeremiah Norman Diary, 18: 959, Stephen Beauregard Weeks Collecton; Swift, *Memoirs of Gen. Joseph Gardner Swift*, 51–52; Bill Reaves, *Southport (Smithville): A Chronology*, 4 vols., *1520–1970* (N.p.: Southport Historical Society, 1978–1999), 1: 11.

20. Swift, *Memoirs of Gen. Joseph Gardner Swift*, 52, 61–62.

21. *Ibid.*, 51, 54, 57, 61. The state perforce extended legislation of 1794 and 1798 to allow the national government an additional two years to finish the construction of the fort. *Laws, 1804*, ch. 7.

22. For the cultivation of rice in the Lower Cape Fear see Lawrence Lee, *The History of Brunswick County, North Carolina* (Charlotte, NC: Heritage Press, 1980), 100–102; James M. Clifton, "Golden Grains of White: Rice Planting on the Lower Cape Fear," *North Carolina Historical Review*, 50 (October 1973): 365–393; Joyce E. Chaplin, *An Anxious Pursuit: Agricultural Innovation and Modernity in the Lower South, 1730–1815* (Chapel Hill: University of North Carolina Press, 1993), 138–148, 251–259.

23. Clifton, "Golden Grains of White," 383; *Cape-Fear Recorder* (Wilmington), October 16, 1824; Benjamin Smith to [James Hogg], January 29, August 10, 1797, Benjamin Smith Papers,

Office of State Archives; Sarah McCulloh Lemmon, ed., *The Pettigrew Papers*, 2 vols. (Raleigh: North Carolina Department of Cultural Resources, Division of Archives and History, 1971, 1988, 1: 304. If any consolation could have been derived from the avian invaders, according to a local historian of the late nineteenth century, "For a dainty supper, a fat rice bird is perhaps the most delicious morsel that ever tickled the palate of the epicure." James Sprunt, *Tales and Traditions of the Lower Cape Fear, 1661–1896* (Wilmington, NC: LeGwin Brothers, 1896), 39–40.

24. Janet Schaw, *Journal of a Lady of Quality; Being the Narrative of a Journey from Scotland to the West Indies, North Carolina, and Portugal, in the Years 1774–1776*, Evangeline Walker Andrews and Charles McLean Andrews, eds. (New Haven, CT: Yale University Press, 1921), 195 (quotation), 203; H. M. Wagstaff, ed., *The Harrington Letters*, James Sprunt Historical Monographs, vol. 13, no. 2 (Chapel Hill: Published by the University, 1914), 18–19; *Wilmington Gazette*, December 10, 1801.

25. *Laws, 1802*, ch. 1; *Raleigh Register*, October 7, 1800; *Wilmington Gazette*, December 10, 1801; Chaplin, *Anxious Pursuit*, 224, 310–319.

26. "Topographical and Historical. Description of the County of Brunswick, in North Carolina," 341; *Cape-Fear Gazette*, October 16, 1824.

27. Minutes of the Brunswick County Court of Pleas and Quarter Sessions, July 1797; October 1801, microfilm, Office of Archives and History; Alice Barnwell Keith, William H. Masterson, and David T. Morgan, eds., *The John Gray Blount Papers*, 4 vols. (Raleigh: North Carolina Department of Cultural Resources, Division of Archives and History, 1952–1982), 3: 538; *Cape-Fear Gazette* (Wilmington), October 16, 1824. For controversy over the construction of dams which impeded waterways, see Chaplin, *Anxious Pursuit*, 331, and, in North Carolina, "Petition of a number of Inhabitants of the county of Northampton," n.d. [1804], Petitions to the General Assembly, General Assembly Session Records, 1804, Office of Archives and History. The General Assembly in 1809 enacted legislation that attempted to protect persons adversely affected by the erection of mills. *Laws, 1809*, ch. 15.

28. Wagstaff, *Harrington Letters*, 19; *Dictionary of North Carolina Biography*, s.v. "Harrington, Henry William."

29. Wagstaff, *Harrington Letters*, 18–19.

30. *American Agriculturist*, 4 (June 1845): 179; William Robert Prince and William Prince, *A Treatise on the Vine* (New York: Swords, Carvill, Bliss, Collins, 1830), 165–167.

31. Clarence C. Gohdes, *Scuppernong: North Carolina's Grape and Its Wine* (Durham, NC: Duke University Press, 1982); Prince and Prince, *Treatise on the Vine*, 167–169.

32. "Topographical and Historical. Description of the County of Brunswick, in North Carolina," 340; H. Roy Merrens, *Colonial North Car-*

olina in the Eighteenth Century: A Study in Historical Geography (Chapel Hill: University of North Carolina Press, 1965), 85–106; Benjamin Smith to "Sir" [Gavin Alves], May 23, 1801, Benjamin Smith Papers, Office of Archives and History.

33. "Topographical and Historical Description of the County of Brunswick, in North Carolina," 341; Keith, Masterson, Morgan, *John Gray Blount Papers*, 3: 520–521, 522–523, 538–539; Brunswick County Court Minutes, October 1801.

34. Keith, Masterson, and Morgan, *John Gray Blount Papers*, 3: 538–539.

35. Ibid., 3: 538–539, 551–553.

36. Robert B. Outland III, "Slavery, Work, and the Geography of the North Carolina Naval Stores Industry, 1835–1860," *Journal of Southern History*, 62 (February 1996): 27–56; Chaplin, *Anxious Pursuit*, 265–275; Philip D. Morgan, "Work and Culture: The Task System and the World of Lowcountry Blacks, 1700–1880," *William and Mary Quarterly*, 3rd Series, 39 (October 1982): 563–599.

37. *Wilmington Gazette*, June 3, 1802; May 26, 1803.

38. *Hall's Wilmington Gazette*, April 29, 1797; *Wilmington Gazette*, October 15, 1801; May 5, 1803.

Chapter 10

1. Charles O. Lerche, Jr., "Jefferson and the Election of 1800: A Case Study in the Political Smear," *William and Mary Quarterly*, 3rd Series, 5 (October 1948): 467–491; Lisle A. Rose, *Prologue to Democracy: The Federalists in the South, 1789–1800* (Lexington: University of Kentucky Press, 1968), 247, 257–259.

2. Rose, *Prologue to Democracy*, 259–260; James H. Broussard, *The Southern Federalists, 1800–1816* (Baton Rouge: Louisiana State University Press, 1978), 29–30.

3. *Wilmington Gazette*, August 21, 1800; Benjamin Smith to John Haywood, November 5, 1800, Ernest Haywood Collection of Haywood Family Papers, Southern Historical Collection, University of North Carolina, Chapel Hill, NC.

4. Benjamin Smith to John Haywood, November 5, 1800, Ernest Haywood Collection of Haywood Family Papers.

5. H. M. Wagstaff, ed., *The Harrington Letters*, James Sprunt Historical Monographs, Vol. 13, No. 2 (Chapel Hill: Published by the University, 1914), 20; Alice Barnwell Keith, William H. Masterson, and David T. Morgan, eds., *The John Gray Blount Papers*, 4 vols. (Raleigh: North Carolina Department of Cultural Resources, Division of Archives and History, 1952–1982), 3: 453.

6. H. M. Wagstaff, ed., *The Papers of John Steele*, 2 vols. (Raleigh: Edwards & Broughton, 1924), 1: 190–192, 195.

7. Journal of the Senate of North Carolina, 1800, 3, 4, microfilm, Office of Archives and History, Raleigh, NC; *Laws and Resolutions of North Carolina, 1800*, ch. 21; pp. 46–48.

8. Senate Journal, 1800, 56. The unanticipated expense of the purchase necessitated the postponement of the acquisition of the portraits however. Delbert H. Gilpatrick, *Jeffersonian Democracy in North Carolina, 1789–1816* (New York: Columbia University Press, 1931), 130.

9. Senate Journal, 1800, 35, 41, 55; *Laws, 1800*, ch. 28.

10. *Laws, 1799*, ch. 2; *North Carolina Journal* (Halifax), January 16, February 6, 20, 1793; R. D. W. Connor, ed., *A Documentary History of the University of North Carolina, 1776–1799*, 2 vols. (Chapel Hill: University of North Carolina Press, 1953) 1: 206–207, 208, 211–214.

11. Sarah McCulloh Lemmon, ed., *The Pettigrew Papers*, 2 vols. (Raleigh: State Department of Archives and History, 1971, 1988), 1: 121.

12. Kemp P. Battle, *History of the University of North Carolina*, 2 vols. (Raleigh: Edwards & Broughton, 1907, 1912), 1: 9, 141.

13. Minutes of the Trustees of the University of North Carolina, December 11, 17, 1800, Vol. 2, typescript, North Carolina Collection, University of North Carolina, Chapel Hill, NC; Senate Journal, 1800, 34, 37, 42; *Laws, 1800*, ch. 5; *Raleigh Register*, January 20, 1801.

14. Minutes of the Trustees, December 13, 17, 19, 1800.

15. Darryl Lynn Peterkin, "'Lux, Libertas, and Learing': The First State University and the Transformation of North Carolina, 1789–1816," Ph. D. diss., Princeton University, 1995, 57, 62 quotation, 180; James H. Broussard, "The North Carolina Federalists, 1800–1816," *North Carolina Historical Review*, 55 (Winter 1978): 36–38.

16. Benjamin Smith to Gavin Alves, May 23, 1801, Benjamin Smith Papers, Office of Archives and History.

17. Smith to "Sir" [James Hogg], June 10, 1801, Benjamin Smith Papers, Office of Archives and History; Battle, *History of the University of North Carolina*, 1: 128.

18. Smith to "D[ear] Sir" [James Hogg], October 5, 1800; Benjamin Smith to Sir [Gavin Alves], October 29, 1802; Smith to "Sir," June 13, 1803, Benjamin Smith Papers, Office of Archives and History.

19. Broussard, *Southern Federalists*, 309–310; Scott King-Owen, "North Carolina Federalists in an Evolving Public Sphere, 1790–1810," master's thesis, University of North Carolina Wilmington, 2006.

20. Broussard, *Southern Federalists*, 226, 295, 301.

21. Benjamin Smith to John Haywood, October 28, 1801, Ernest Haywood Collection of Haywood Family Papers; *Raleigh Register*, July 20, 1803.

22. *Raleigh Register*, July 20, 1803.
23. Joseph G. Swift, *The Memoirs of Gen. Joseph Gardner Swift* (Boston: Privately printed, 1890), 59, quotation; *North-Carolina Minerva* (Raleigh), March 7, April 11, 1802; Gilpatrick, *Jeffersonian Democracy in North Carolina*, 242.
24. Timothy Bloodworth to Thomas Jefferson, December 14, 1802, Thomas Jefferson Papers. Series 1. General Correspondence, 1651–1827, Library of Congress, Washington, DC; http://memory.loc.gov/cgi-bin/query/P?mtj:4:./temp/-ammem_HQjy::. Accessed August 6, 2008.
25. Timothy Bloodworth to Thomas Jefferson, January 17, 1804, Thomas Jefferson Papers. Series 1. General Correspondence, 1651–1827. http://memory.loc.gov/cgi-bin/query/P?mtj:2:./temp/-ammem_E5Cz::. Accessed August 8, 2008.
26. *Wilmington Gazette*, July 24, 1804; *Raleigh Register*, August 27, 1804; Gilpatrick, *Jeffersonian Democracy in North Carolina*, 242.
27. Senate Journal, 1804, [1], 2, 3, 12, 13, 19, 26; Journal of the House of Commons of North Carolina, 1804, 4–6, microfilm, Office of State Archives.
28. Senate Journal, 1804, 9; *Laws, 1804*, ch. 44.
29. Senate Journal, 1804, 34; *Laws, 1804*, ch. 58.
30. Senate Journal, 1804, 31, 41.
31. Wagstaff, *Steele Papers*, 1, 440–442; Senate Journal, 1804, 11, 16.
32. *Laws*, 1801, ch. 9; *1803*, ch. 11; *1804*, ch. 110; *Wilmington Gazette*, April 16, 1801; September 6, 1803.
33. *Laws, 1804*, chs. 21, 22; Gilpatrick, *Jeffersonian Democracy in North Carolina*, 149–151. See also Robert S. Neale, *The Bank of Cape Fear of Wilmington, North Carolina* (Wilmington, NC: Lower Cape Fear Historical Society and the author, 1999).
34. Peterkin, "'Lux, Libertas, and Learning,'" 63–64; *Laws, 1801*, ch. 8.
35. *North Carolina Journal* (Halifax), March 18, 1802; Battle, *History of the University of North Carolina*, I: 126–128; Gavin Alves, Account for Lottery No. 1 and No. 2, Walter Alves Papers, Southern Historical Collection; Benjamin Smith to John Haywood, October 3, 1803, Ernest Haywood Collection of Haywood Family Papers.
36. Minutes of the Trustees of the University of North Carolina, November 26, December 3, 4, 8, 1804, Vol. 3; House of Commons Journal, 1804, 27, 43; *Raleigh Register*, December 10, 13, 1804; Gilpatrick, *Jeffersonian Democracy in North Carolina*, 143.
37. Battle, *History of the University of North Carolina*, 1: 830–831; William D. Snider, *Light on the Hill: A History of the University of North Carolina at Chapel Hill* (Chapel Hill: University of North Carolina Press, 1992), 39, 41.
38. Senate Journal, 1804, 40–43, 49.
39. *Ibid.*, 52; House of Commons Journal, 1804, 55–56.

Chapter 11

1. Minutes of the Brunswick County Court of Pleas and Quarter Sessions, January, April 1805, microfilm, Office of Archives and History, Raleigh, NC.
2. New Hanover County, Deed Book, O, 527, microfilm, Office of Archives and History.
3. Joseph Gardner Swift, *The Memoirs of Gen. Joseph Gardner Swift* (Boston: Privately printed, 1890), 58.
4. Ron Chernow, *Alexander Hamilton* (New York: Penguin Press, 2004), 117–118; Joanne B. Freeman, *Affairs of Honor: National Politics in the New Republic* (New Haven, CT: Yale University Press, 2001), xv; Jack K. Williams, *Dueling in the Old South: Vignettes of Social History* (College Station: Texas A&M University Press, 1980), 6; Kenneth Roberts and Anna M. Roberts, eds., *Moreau de St. Mery's American Journal [1793–1798]* (Garden City, NY: Doubleday, 329.
5. S. Sidney Ulmer, "Some Eighteenth Century South Carolinians and the Duel," *South Carolina Historical and Genealogical Magazine*, 60 (January 1959): 1–2.
6. Joseph J. Ellis, *American Creation: Triumphs and Tragedies at the Founding of the Republic* (New York: Knopf, 2007), 69–70; Williams, *Dueling in the Old South*, 27; Bertram Wyatt-Brown, *Honor and Violence in the Old South* (New York: Oxford University Press, 1986), 146–147; Clement Eaton, *A History of the Old South*, 3rd ed. (New York: Macmillan, 1975), 3, 110, 396–397.
7. Richard Rankin, *Ambivalent Churchmen and Evangelical Churchwomen: The Religion of the Episcopal Elite in North Carolina, 1800–1860* (Columbia, SC: University of South Carolina Press, 1993), 4–5; Williams, *Dueling in the Old South*, xvi, 14. Actually, genteel women accepted, and by so doing, encouraged the code of honor. In fact, they too embraced a code among themselves, a controlling ethic based on standards of fashion. Rankin, *Ambivalent Churchmen and Evangelical Churchwomen*, 5.
8. Delbert Harold Gilpatrick, *Jeffersonian Democracy in North Carolina, 1789–1816* (New York: Columbia University Press, 1931), 143; William D. Snider, *Light on a Hill: A History of the University of North Carolina at Chapel Hill* (Chapel Hill: University of North Carolina Press, 1982), 31; Freeman, *Affairs of Honor*, xv, xvii; Ulmer, "Some Eighteenth Century South Carolinians and the Duel," 8–9.
9. Chernow, *Alexander Hamilton*, 143; Freeman, *Affairs of Honor*, 159–198 and passim; W. J. Rorabaugh, "The Political Duel in the Early Republic: Burr v. Hamilton," *Journal of the Early Republic*, 15 (Spring 1995): 1–23.
10. Don Higginbotham, Donna Kelly, and Lang Baradell, eds., *The Papers of James Iredell*, 3 vols. (Raleigh: Office of Archives and History, North Carolina Department of Cultural Resources, 1976,

2003), 3: 290 n. 5; *Wilmington Chronicle and North-Carolina Weekly Advertiser*, January 21, 1796; Wyatt-Brown, *Honor and Violence on the Old South*, 146–147. For a slightly different version of the Bradley-Swann duel, see Louis T. Moore, *Stories Old and New of the Cape Fear Region* (Wilmington, NC: Broadfoot, 1999), 90–94.

11. Alan D. Watson, *A History of New Bern and Craven County* (New Bern: Tryon Palace Commission, 1987), 109–111.

12. *Laws and Resolutions of the State of North Carolina, 1802*, ch. 5; Watson, *History of New Bern and Craven County*, 111.

13. Watson, *History of New Bern and Craven County*, 149, 317.

14. *Wilmington Gazette*, February 28, 1804.

15. Alfred Moore, Jr., to "My Dr Friend," August 5, 1805, Ernest Haywood Collection of Haywood Family Papers, Southern Historical Collection, University of North Carolina, Chapel Hill, NC; Swift, *Memoirs of Gen. Joseph Gardner Swift*, 59; Kemp P. Battle, *History of the University of North Carolina*, 2 vols. (Raleigh: Edwards & Broughton, 1907), 1:119–120; Alfred Moore Waddell, *Some Memories of My Life* (Raleigh: Edwards & Broughton, 1908), 146.

16. *Dictionary of North Carolina Biography*, s.v. "Moore, Alfred."

17. Waddell, *Some Memories of My Life*, 146.

18. *Ibid*.

19. Alfred Moore, Jr., to "My Dr Friend," August 5, 1805, Ernest Haywood Collection of Haywood Family Papers.

20. Grady L. E. Carroll, ed., *Francis Asbury in North Carolina: The North Carolina Portions of the Journal of Francis Asbury* (Nashville, TN: Parthenon Press, 1964), 138–139; Bradford J. Wood, *This Remote Part of the World: Regional Formation in the Lower Cape Fear, North Carolina, 1725–1775* (Columbia, SC: University of South Carolina Press, 2004), 1–3.

21. Alfred Moore, Jr., to "My Dr Friend," August 5, 1805, Ernest Haywood Collection of Haywood Family Papers.

22. *Ibid*.; Waddell, *Some Memories of My Life*, 149.

23. Waddell, *Some Memories of My Life*, 152; Battle, *History of the University of North Carolina*, 1: 120.

24. Waddell, *Some Memories of My Life*, 152–153.

25. Alfred Moore, Jr., to "My Dr Friend," August 5, 1805, Ernest Haywood Collection of Haywood Family Papers; Waddell, *Some Memories of My Life*, 154.

26. Waddell, *Some Memories of My Life*, 154; Swift, *Memoirs of Gen. Joseph Gardner Swift*, 58–59.

27. Swift, *Memoirs of Gen. Joseph Gardner Swift*, 59; *Wilmington Gazette*, July 2, 9, 1805.

28. Swift, *Memoirs of Gen. Joseph Gardner Swift*, 59; *Wilmington Gazette*, July 9, 1805.

Chapter 12

1. *Raleigh Register*, August 19, 1805; *Dictionary of North Carolina Biography*, s.v. "Kenan, Thomas."

2. Brunswick County Court Minutes of Pleas and Quarter Sessions, July, October 1805, microfilm, Office of Archives and History, Raleigh, NC.

3. Journal of the Senate of North Carolina, 1805, [1], 18, 22, microfilm, Office of Archives and History.

4. William D. Snider, *Light on a Hill: A History of the University of North Carolina at Chapel Hill* (Chapel Hill: University of North Carolina Press, 1992), 35, 41–43; Darryl Lynn Peterkin, "'Lux, Libertas, and Learning': The First State University and the Transformation of North Carolina, 1789–1816," Ph.D. diss., Princeton University, 1995, 69–73; J. G. de Roulhac Hamilton, ed., *William Richardson Davie: A Memoir, Followed by His Letters and Notes by Kemp P. Battle* (Chapel Hill: The University, 1907), 57.

5. Peterkin, "'Lux, Libertas, and Learning,'" 204–207. The decision was *Trustees of the University of North Carolina vs. Foy* (1805).

6. *Laws and Resolutions of the State of North Carolina, 1804*, ch. 5; *1805*, chs. 4, 7; Snider, *Light on a Hill*, 35, 41; Peterkin, "'Lux, Libertas, and Liberty,'" 78–82.

7. Senate Journal, 1805, 31–32; Journal of the House of Commons of North Carolina, 1805, 55, microfilm, Office of Archives and History.

8. *Laws, 1805*, ch. 23; *1811*, ch. 29.

9. Senate Journal, 1805, 22, [54].

10. Brunswick County Court Minutes, January, April, July, October 1806.

11. *Wilmington Gazette*, May 6, 13, 1806.

12. *Raleigh Register*, September 8, 1806.

13. *Wilmington Gazette*, September 16, 1806; Senate Journal, 1806, [1], 8, 11; Senate Committee Reports, 1806, General Assembly Session Records, 1806, Office of Archives and History; *Dictionary of North Carolina Biography*, s.v. "Franklin, Jesse."

14. Minutes of the Board of Trustees of the University of North Carolina, 1806, Vol. 3: 156, 160–166, typescript, North Carolina Collection, University of North Carolina, Chapel Hill, NC.

15. Senate Journal, 1806, 9, 17, 29, 41, 42.

16. *Ibid*., 18–19.

17. Brunswick County Court Minutes, January, May 1807; Nathaniel Alexander to Benjamin Smith, February 10, 1807, Governor's Papers, Nathaniel Alexander, microfilm, Office of Archives and History.

18. Henry Dearborn to Governor of North Carolina, March 25, 1807; Nathaniel Alexander to Benjamin Smith, April 8, 1807; John Winslow to [Nathaniel Alexander], April 9, 1807; Benjamin Smith to Governor Alexander, April 14, 1807, Governor's Papers, Nathaniel Alexander.

19. *Wilmington Gazette*, July 21, 1807.

20. *Wilmington Gazette*, July 7, 14, 1807; Delbert H. Gilpatrick, *Jeffersonian Democracy in North Carolina, 1789–1816* (New York: Columbia University Press, 1931), 158. Alan D. Watson, *Wilmington, Port of North Carolina* (Columbia: University of South Carolina Press, 1992), 42. Quickly, the committee obtained some twenty cannon and considered throwing up breastworks to protect Wilmington. *Wilmington Gazette*, July 21, 1807.

21. *Raleigh Register*, September 10, 1807; Marshall Smelser, *The Democratic Republic, 1801–1815* (New York: Harper & Row, 1968), 160, 161 n. 28.

22. Gov. Nathaniel Alexander to Benjamin Smith, July 15, 20, 1807; Smith to Alexander, July 22, 1807, Governor's Papers, Nathaniel Alexander.

23. Smith's orders to Major Generals, July 25, 1807, Governor's Papers, Nathaniel Alexander.

24. Benjamin Smith to Nathaniel Alexander, August 13, 1807, Governor's Papers, Nathaniel Alexander; *Raleigh Register*, August 27, 1807.

25. Benjamin Smith to Nathaniel Alexander, July 28, August 11, 13, September 3, 1807, Governor's Papers, Nathaniel Alexander.

26. *Raleigh Register*, July 30, August 6, 1807; Benjamin Smith to Nathaniel Alexander, Governor's Papers, Nathaniel Alexander.

27. Henry Dearborn to the Governor of North Carolina, October 22, 1807; Nathaniel Alexander to Benjamin Smith, October 31, 1807, Governor's Papers, Nathaniel Alexander.

28. Senate Journal, 1807, [1], 4, 25, 26, 31, 37, 46, 47.

29. Minutes of the Trustees of the University of North Carolina, 1807, Vol. 3: 183.

30. Return of the militia and the adjutant general's report, 1807, Miscellaneous Papers, General Assembly Session Records, 1807, Office of Archives and History.

31. Return of the militia and the adjutant general's report, 1807, Miscellaneous Papers, General Assembly Session Records, 1807.

32. Senate Journal, 1807, 30, 49; *Laws, 1807*, chs. 6, 23, 24.

33. E. T. Dupont de Nemours & Co., to Messrs. Perry[,] Ferguson & Co., Merchants, Fayetteville, NC, September 11, 1807; Committee on Militia Laws, House of Commons, December 16, 1807, House Committee Reports, General Assembly Session Records, 1807.

34. *Raleigh Register*, December 17, 24, 1807; Senate Journal, 1807, 36, 52.

35. A. D. Schenck, "The History of Fort Johnston, North Carolina, 1745–1879," 39–40. A. D. Schenck Paper, Office of Archives and History; Wilson Angley, *A History of Fort Johnston on the Lower Cape Fear* (Wilmington, NC: Broadfoot, 1996), 45–48; Ethel Herring and Carolee Williams, *Fort Caswell in War and Peace* (Wendell, NC: Broadfoot's Bookmark, 1983).

36. *Laws, 1807*, ch. 17; *1809*, ch. 18; Schenck, "History of Fort Johnston, North Carolina, 1745–1879," 40–41; Angley, *History of Fort Johnston*, 48–49.

37. *Raleigh Register*, December 24, 31, 1807; Senate Journal, 1807, 42; House of Commons Journal, 1807, 40–42; Gilpatrick, *Jeffersonian Democracy in North Carolina*, 160 n. 1.

38. Benjamin Smith to Gov. Benjamin Williams, December 29, 1807, Governor's Papers, Benjamin Williams.

39. Brunswick Court Minutes, January 1805; May 1807; February, July 1808.

40. Watson, *Wilmington: Port of North Carolina*, 42.

41. House of Commons Journal, 1808, 6.

42. Gilpatrick, *Jeffersonian Democracy in North Carolina*, 181; Benjamin Smith to Thomas Jefferson, April 19, 1808; Jefferson to Smith, May 20, 1808, Thomas Jefferson Papers, Series, 1, General Correspondence, 1651–1827, Library of Congress, Washington, DC. http://memory.loc.gov/service/mss/mtj1/041/0300/0390.gif; http://memory.loc.gov/service/mss/mtj1/041/0600/0630.gif, accessed April 17, 2008.

43. Senate Journal, 1808, 2, 7, 21.

44. House of Commons Journal, 1808, 6; Senate Journal, 1808, 29–30; *Raleigh Register*, January 9, 1809.

45. Senate Journal, 1808, 3, 40; Lawrence Lee, *The History of Brunswick County* (Charlotte, NC: Heritage Press, 1980), 91–92.

46. Senate Journal, 1808, 3; *Laws*, 1808, ch. 64; David Leroy Corbitt, ed., *The Formation of the North Carolina Counties* (Raleigh: State Department of Archives and History, 1950), 36.

47. Lee, *Brunswick County*, 92–93, 231–232.

48. Bill Reaves, *Southport (Smithville): A Chronology*, 4 vols. (N.p.: Southport Historical Society, 1978–1999), 1:14; *Laws, 1808*, ch. 64; Brunswick County Court Minutes, April, October-November 1809.

49. *Star* (Raleigh), February 9, 1809; *Edenton Gazette*, December 9, 1808; *Raleigh Register*, February 2, 1809.

50. Earley Winfred Bridges, *The Masonic Governors of North Carolina: Their Masonic Records and Orations; Newspaper Articles of Events Pertaining to the Craft, and Other Information of Interest to Masonry About the Governors of North Carolina* (Greensboro: n.p., 1937), 134–136.

51. Bridges, *Masonic Governors*, 187.

52. Senate Journal, 1809, page, 2, 10, 12, 15, 32, 38, 41, 52; Minutes of the Trustees of the University of North Carolina, 1809, 216–225; *Star*, November 30, 1809.

53. Senate Journal, 1809, 34; *Raleigh Register*, December 21, 1809.

54. Senate Journal, 1809, 15, 38, 44–45; *Laws, 1809*, chs. 1, 25, 29–36. In all the instances of promoting manufacturing, navigability of watercourses, and turnpikes, the legislature did not commit public money but relied upon private enterprise.

55. Senate Journal, 1809, 30; *Laws, 1809*, ch. 24.
56. Senate Journal, 1809, 52.

Chapter 13

1. *Brunswick County, North Carolina, 1810 & 1820 Federal Censuses*, abs. by Delmas D. Haskett (Wilmington, NC: The Old New Hanover Genealogy Society and The North Carolina Room, New Hanover County Public Library, 1995), *1810*, 1, 13.
2. *Wilmington Gazette*, June 26, 1810; *Raleigh Register*, January 3, 1811.
3. *Wilmington Gazette*, April 15, 1806; H. M. Wagstaff, ed., *The Papers of John Steele*, 2 vols. (Raleigh: Edwards & Broughton, 1924), 2: 632. Smith later dismissed his overseer, and attempted to direct operations on his own, but with no evident success. Benjamin Smith to John Haywood, March 27, 1813, Ernest Haywood Collection of Haywood Family Papers, Southern Historical Collection, University of North Carolina, Chapel Hill, NC.
4. *Wilmington Gazette*, January 2, 1810; Joseph Gardner Swift, *The Memoirs of Gen. Joseph Gardner Swift* (Boston: Privately printed, 1890), 89.
5. A. D. Schenck, "The History of Fort Johnston, North Carolina, 1745–1879," A. D. Schenck Paper, Office of Archives and History, Raleigh, NC; Wilson Angley, *A History of Fort Johnston on the Lower Cape Fear* (Wilmington, NC: Broadfoot, 1996), 49.
6. Swift, *Memoirs of Gen. Joseph Gardner Swift*, 90; Angley, *History of Fort Johnston*, 49–50; *Star-News* (Wilmington), August, November 19, 2006. The house served as a residence for a series of commanders of Military Ocean Terminal, Sunny Point, the largest ammunition depot in the United States, which is located five miles north of Southport on the Cape Fear River.
7. Journal of the Senate of North Carolina, 1809, 10, 44, microfilm, Office of Archives and History; David Stone to "Sir" [Benjamin Smith], February 3, 1810; Smith to "Sir" (Stone), February 13, 1810, Governor's Letter Books, David Stone, microfilm, Office of Archives and History.
8. David Stone to "Sir" (Smith), February 3, 1810; Smith to "Sir" (Stone), February 13, 1810, Governor's Letter Books, David Stone.
9. Minutes of the Brunswick County Court of Pleas and Quarter Sessions, January 1810, microfilm, Office of Archives and History.
10. Smith to "Sir" (William Eustis), April 4, 1810, Enc.; W. Eustis to "Sir" (Benjamin Smith), April 6, 1810, Enc., Benjamin Smith to "Sir" (David Stone), July 13, 1810, Governor's Letter Books, David Stone.
11. Lawrence Lee, *The History of Brunswick County* (Charlotte, NC: Heritage Press, 1980), 93; Brunswick County Court Minutes, April-May 1810.
12. David Stone to "Sir" (Benjamin Smith), June 18, 1810; Smith to "Sir" (David Stone), July 13, 1810, Governor's Letter Books, David Stone. Late in 1810, Wilmingtonians expected the receipt of their cannon, but in both Wilmington and New Bern delivery was contingent upon the organization of a company to accept and maintain the weapons. The cannon apparently found their way to Edenton. *Star* (Raleigh), November 29, 1810; Sarah McCulloh Lemmon, *Frustrated Patriots: North Carolina and the War of 1812* (Chapel Hill: University of North Carolina Press, 1973), 137.
13. *Wilmington Gazette*, July 17, 1810; Swift, *Memoirs of Gen. Joseph Gardner Swift*, 91.
14. Brunswick County Court Minutes, July 1810.
15. Swift, *Memoirs of Gen. Joseph Gardner Swift*, 91.
16. Journal of the Senate of North Carolina, 1809, 30; Bill Reaves, *Southport (Smithville): A Chronology*. 4 vols. (N.p.: Southport Historical Society, 1978–1999), 1:15; Swift, *Memoirs of Gen. Joseph Gardner Swift*, 93.
17. Swift, *Memoirs of Gen. Joseph Gardner Swift*, 91–92.
18. Earley Winfred Bridges, *The Masonic Governors of North Carolina: Their Masonic Records and Orations; Newspaper Articles of Events Pertaining to the Craft, and Other Information of Interest to Masonry About the Governors of North Carolina* (Greensboro, NC: n.p., 1937), 137–139; *Star*, February 4, 1811.
19. *Raleigh Register*, November 22, 1810; *North-Carolina Minerva* (Raleigh), November 29, 1810.
20. Senate Journal, 1810, 2, 3, 5, 14.
21. *Minerva*, December 6, 1810; Senate Journal, 1810, 21; Journal of the House of Commons of North Carolina, 1810, 23, microfilm, Office of Archives and History.
22. The governor received £650 or approximately $1,300 at the time of Smith's tenure. The governor's private secretary subsisted on £150, or approximately $300, and fees. *Laws and Resolutions of the State of North Carolina, 1799*, ch. 25; *1806*, ch. 10.
23. Senate Journal, 1810, 43; *Laws, 1810*, ch. 2; John Smith to your Excellency the Governor (Benjamin Smith), March 30, 1811, Governor's Papers, Benjamin Smith, State Archives.
24. Senate Journal, 1810, 38; House of Commons Journal, 1810, 6; Lemmon, *Frustrated Patriots*, 137, 139.
25. *Laws, 1805*, ch. 7; William Henry Hoyt, ed., *The Papers of Archibald D. Murphey*, 2 vols. (Raleigh: Uzzell, 1914), 1: 27; Darryl Lynn Peterkin, "'Lux, Libertas, and Learning': The First State University and the Transformation of North Carolina, 1789–1816," Ph.D. diss., Princeton University, 1995, 88.
26. House of Commons Journal, 1810, 48;

Minutes of the Board of Trustees of the University of North Carolina, December 1, 1810 – December 20, 1810, Vol. 3: 247, typescript, North Carolina Collection, University of North Carolina, Chapel Hill, NC.

27. Minutes of the Board of Trustees of the University of North Carolina, 3: 255–256.

28. Minutes of the Board of Trustees of the University of North Carolina, 3: 248, 251, 253, 257, 259–260, 266–267.

29. *Star*, October 4, 1810.

30. *Star*, September 20, 1810; *Raleigh Register*, November 15, 1810; Elizabeth Reid Murray, *Wake: Capital County of North Carolina*, Vol. I (Raleigh: Capital County, 1983), 117.

31. *Laws, 1792*, ch. 14; 1794–1795, ch. 8; *North-Carolina Gazette* (New Bern), February 24, 1798.

32. *Laws, 1797*, ch. 27; *1802*, ch. 25; *Raleigh Register*, December 2, 1805; Gilpatrick, *Jeffersonian Democracy in North Carolina*, 146.

33. *Minerva*, December 27, 1810; March 14, May 17, 24, November 21, 1811; *Star*, March 7, 1811.

34. *Minerva*, January 24, February 7, 1811.

35. Governor Smith to General Wellborn, July 12, 1811, Governor's Papers, Benjamin Smith.

36. Benjamin Smith to John Haywood, September 30, 1811, Ernest Haywood Collection of Haywood Family Papers. The Rev. Joseph Travis, a Methodist minister, was asked in 1812 by Smith to visit Sarah, who was "supposed to be unbalanced in her mind" and growing worse. Physicians were at a loss. The minister prescribed "instruction and prayer," which offered an immediate cure. The account not only reflects the mental suffering of Sarah but may explain the sympathy of Benjamin and Sarah for Methodism in their later years, though both remained attached to the Episcopal Church. *Autobiography of the Rev. Joseph Travis, A. M., a Member of the Memphis Annual Conference* (Nashville, TN: Stevenson & Owen, 1856), 80–81. For the appeal of Methodism to upper class women of the Episcopal Church, including those in the Wilmington region, see Richard Rankin, *Ambivalent Churchmen and Evangelical Churchwomen: The Religion of the Episcopal Elite in North Carolina, 1800–1860* (Columbia: University of South Carolina Press, 1993), 28–48.

37. Governor Smith to General Wellborn, July 12, 1811, Governor's Papers, Benjamin Smith; Smith to John Haywood, September 30, October 31, 1811, Ernest Haywood Collection of Haywood Family Papers.

38. *Minerva*, January 24, 1811.

39. *Star*, March 7, 1811.

40. *Minerva*, January 24, 31, 1811.

41. Swift, *Memoirs of Gen. Joseph Gardner Swift*, 92, 94, 96.

42. Governor's Papers, Benjamin Smith, passim.

43. John L. Cheney, Jr., ed., *North Carolina Government, 1585–1979: A Narrative and Statistical History* (Raleigh: North Carolina Department of the Secretary of State, 1981), 360, 367 n. 22; J. C. Swift to His Excellency, Benjamin Smith, Governor of North Carolina, May 20, 1811; Joshua Wright to "Sir" (Benjamin Smith), May 7, 1811, Governor's Papers, Benjamin Smith.

44. *Laws, 1799*, ch. 15; *Star*, March 7, 1811; Cheney, *North Carolina Government*, 813. Robert Williams, treasurer of the board of trustees of the university designated Smith to act in his stead in voting the shares stock held by the trustees in the Bank of Cape Fear. "Declaration of Robert Williams," April 4, 1811, University Papers, Southern Historical Collection.

45. *Star*, July 5, 1811.

46. *Ibid.*, July 12, 1811; *Dictionary of North Carolina Biography*, s.v. "Seawell, Henry." In a close contest in 1811, the General Assembly failed to confirm Seawell but instead elected Edward Harris of Craven County to succeed Wright. Harris died in 1813. At that juncture, Seawell received another interim appointment, which was upheld by the General Assembly later in the year, and proceeded to serve on the superior court until 1819.

47. *Star*, July 12, 1811; Governor Smith to General Wellborn, July 12, 1811, Governors Papers, Benjamin Smith. For the Georgia border, see Marvin Lucian Skaggs, *North Carolina Boundary Disputes Involving Her Southern Line* (Chapel Hill: University of North Carolina Press, 1941), 191–205.

48. Minutes of the Board of Trustees of the University of North Carolina, Vol. 4, July 6, 1811–December 20, 1822, 1–2; Governor Smith to General Wellborn, July 12, 1811, Governor's Papers, Benjamin Smith.

49. *Star*, August 9, September 13, November 29, 1811; Governor Smith to General Wellborn, July 12, 1811, Governor's Papers, Benjamin Smith.

50. Minutes of the Board of Trustees of the University of North Carolina, Vol. 4: 3–10.

51. House of Commons Journal, 1811, 4–5.

52. *Ibid.*, 1811, 5.

53. *Ibid.*, 1811.

54. Senate Journal, 1809, 36; *Star*, January 12, 1809; *Raleigh Register*, December 6, 1810; Delbert H. Gilpatrick, *Jeffersonian Democracy in North Carolina, 1789–1816* New York: Columbia University Press, 1931), 176. The General Assembly in 1809 and 1810 incorporated manufacturing companies in Bertie and Randolph counties respectively, and in the latter year authorized Alexander Smith of Ashe County to hold a lottery to raise $1,500 to undertake the manufacturing of steel and nails. *Laws, 1809*, ch. 29; *1810*, chs. 48, 126.

55. *Star*, June 7, 1811. As usual, many regiments failed to make returns.

56. *Ibid.*, May 10, June 7 (quotation), 1811.

57. House of Commons Journal, 1811, 5.

58. *Ibid.*, 1811, 5–6; Luke, 10: 41, 42.
59. *Ibid.*, 1811, 27–28, 62.
60. *Laws, 1811*, ch. 12; House Committee Reports, [1811]; Senate Resolutions, December 9 and action by the House, December 12, 1811, General Assembly Session Records, 1811, Office of Archives and History; *Star*, December 6, 1811; Cheney, *North Carolina Government*, 360.
61. Senate Journal, 1811, 26; House of Commons Journal, 1811, 40, 46.
62. *Laws*, 1811, ch. 4; Senate Journal, 1811, 54; House of Commons Journal, 1811, 65; Gilpatrick, *Jeffersonian Democracy in North Carolina*, 186–192.
63. Senate Resolutions, December 12, 1811, and concurrence by the House, December 14, 1811, General Assembly Session Records, 1811. The legislative burden of private legislation was one of the factors that led to the Constitutional Convention of 1835, whose reforms placed some restrictions on private bills.
64. *Star*, December 6, 13, 1811; Senate Journal, 1811, 17, 20, 25; House of Commons Journal, 1811, 28, 29, 30.
65. House of Commons Journal, 1811, 28.
66. Benjamin Smith to the House of Commons, December 14, 1811, Governor's Message, General Assembly Session Records, 1811.

Chapter 14

1. Sarah McCulloh Lemmon, *Frustrated Patriots: North Carolina and the War of 1812* (Chapel Hill: University of North Carolina Press, 1973), 41–42, 125.
2. Lemmon, *Frustrated Patriots*, 130; *Raleigh Register*, June 3, 1814.
3. Bill Reaves, *Southport (Smithville): A Chronology*, 4 vols. (N.p.: Southport Historical Society, 1978–1999), 1:16; Lemmon, *Frustrated Patriots*, 124, 138.
4. Journal of the House of Commons of North Carolina, 1815, 9; 1816, 4–5, microfilm, Office of Archives and History, Raleigh, NC.
5. Minutes of the Brunswick County Court of Pleas and Quarter Sessions, January 1812; April 1814, microfilm, Office of Archives and History.
6. *Ibid.*, July 1812; July–August 1815.
7. *Ibid.*, April 1812; October 1813; July, October/November 1814; October 1815.
8. *Ibid.*, April 12, 1812; January 1816; January, July 1817; July, October 1819.
9. Joshua G. Wright to "Sir" [David Stone], January 2, 1809, Governor's Letter Books, David Stone, Office of Archives and History; Benjamin Smith to John Haywood, September 30, 1811, Ernest Haywood Collection of Haywood Family Papers, Southern Historical Collection, University of North Carolina, Chapel Hill, NC.
10. Journal of the Senate of North Carolina, 1805, 33, microfilm, Office of Archives and History; *Raleigh Register*, November 29, 1811; James Broussard, *The Southern Federalists, 1800–1816* (Baton Rouge: Louisiana State University Press, 1978), 341–344.
11. Benjamin Smith to John Haywood, March 31, 1812; Benjamin Smith to Judge Potter, March 7, 1817, Ernest Haywood Collection of Haywood Family Papers.
12. Benjamin Smith to [John Haywood], March 31, 1812, Ernest Haywood Collection of Haywood Family Papers.
13. Benjamin Smith to "Dear Sir" [John Haywood], March 27, 1813, Ernest Haywood Collection of Haywood Family Papers.
14. Benjamin Smith to "Dear Sir" [John Haywood], March 27, 1813, Ernest Haywood Collection of Haywood Family Papers; Kate Stuart to "My Dear Mr. Sprunt, January 1, 1921, Alexander Sprunt & Son, Inc., Papers, Rare Book, Manuscript, & Special Collections Library, Duke University, Durham, NC; *Southport Leader*, April 23, 1896.
15. Benjamin Smith to "Dear Sir" [John Haywood], March 27, 1813, Ernest Haywood Collection of Haywood Family Papers.
16. New Hanover County, Deed Book, O, 441, microfilm, Office of Archives and History; Brunswick County, Deed Book, F, 139–141, microfilm, Office of Archives and History; *Wilmington Gazette*, April 27, 1815.
17. Benjamin Smith to "Dear Sir" [John Haywood], April 8, May 4, September 20, 1814, Ernest Haywood Collection of Haywood Family Papers.
18. Benjamin Smith to "Dear Sir" [John Haywood], February 5, 1815, Ernest Haywood Collection of Haywood Family Papers.
19. Smith to "Dear Sir" [John Haywood], February 5, 1815, Ernest Haywood Collection of Haywood Family Papers.
20. Benjamin Smith to "Dear Sir" [John Haywood], July 1, 1816, Ernest Haywood Collection of Haywood Family Papers.
21. Wm. Watts Jones to "Dear Sir," April 21, 1816; June 17, 1818, University Papers, Southern Historical Collection.
22. Benjamin Smith to William Miller, December ?, 1816, University Papers.
23. Senate Journal, 1816, 2.
24. *Ibid.*, 1816, 8; House of Commons Journal, 1816, 10–11.
25. *Ibid.*, 1816, 30.
26. *Ibid.*, 1816, 15.
27. *Ibid.*, 1816, 11, 12.
28. *Ibid.*, 1816, 15, 31, 39.
29. *Ibid.*, 1816, 16, 29; *Laws and Resolutions of the State of North Carolina, 1816*, chs. 3, 4, 7.
30. Senate Journal, 1816, 13, 16, 46; *Laws*, 1816, ch. 131; John Hope Franklin, *The Free Negro in North Carolina, 1790–1860* (Chapel Hill: University of North Carolina Press, 1943), 58–120.

31. Senate Journal, 1816, 17, 18; *Laws, 1817,* ch. 68.
32. Senate Journal, 1816, 9; *Laws, 1816,* ch. 44; Charles L. Coon, ed., *North Carolina Schools and Academies, 1790–1840,* 2 vols. (Raleigh, NC: Edwards & Broughton, 1915), 1: 167–169.
33. Senate Journal, 1816, 23; *Laws, 1817,* ch. 25.
34. Minutes of the Board of Trustees of the University of North Carolina, July 6, 1811–December 20, 1822, Vol. 4: 83, typescript, North Carolina Collection, University of North Carolina, Chapel Hill, NC; Wm. Watts Jones to "Dear Sir," March 6, 16, 1817; Benjamin Smith to [Judge Potter], March 15, 1817, University Papers; Benjamin Smith to "Dear Sir," March 15, 1817, Ernest Haywood Collection of Haywood Family Papers.
35. Wm. Watts Jones to "Dear Sir," March 16, 1817; March 17, 1818, University Papers; Minutes of the Trustees of the University of North Carolina, 4: 101.
36. Wm. Watts Jones to "Dear Sir," March 17, June 17, 1818, University Papers.
37. Benjamin Smith to Judge Henderson, November 18, 1819, Ernest Haywood Collection of Haywood Family Papers, quoted in Donald R. Lennon, "The Political Views and Public Activities of Benjamin Smith of Brunswick County (1783–1816), master's thesis, East Carolina University, 1961, 70; Kemp P. Battle, *History of the University of North Carolina,* 2 vols. (Raleigh: Edwards & Broughton, 1907, 1912), 1: 821.
38. New Hanover County, Deed Book, R, 328–332; Joseph Gardner Swift, *The Memoirs of Gen. Joseph Gardner Swift* (Boston: Privately printed, 1890), 167–168, 187. According to the agreement, Swift held the lands in trust for the United States. If any money remained after their sale to satisfy Smith's debts, Swift retained the funds in trust for Sarah during her marriage, "free from the Controls or debts of her husband."
39. Swift, *Memoirs of Gen. Joseph Gardner Swift,* 172; James Sprunt, *Chronicles of the Cape Fear River,* 2nd ed. (Raleigh: Edwards & Broughton, 1916), 634–635.
40. Sarah [Smith] to "Dear Sir" [John Haywood], August 30, 1811, Ernest Haywood Collection of Haywood Family Papers; Benjamin Smith to "Dear Nephew" [Thomas S. Grimke], November 9, 1819, Grimke Papers, South Caroliniana Library, University of South Carolina, Columbia, SC.
41. Benjamin Smith to "My dear Nephew" [Thomas S. Grimke], January 5, 1813; June 1, 1819, Grimke Family Papers, Rare Book, Manuscript, and Special Collections Library, Duke University; Thomas S. Grimke to "Dear Uncle" [Benjamin Smith], September 22, 1818, Grimke Papers, South Caroliniana Library, University of South Carolina, Columbia, SC.
42. Grace H. Long, "The Grimkes, Southern Iconoclasts," *Peabody Journal of Education,* 20 (May 1943): 359–364; *Dictionary of American Biography,* s.v. "Grimke, Thomas Smith."
43. Benjamin Smith to "Dear Nephew" [Thomas S. Grimke], November 9, 1819, Grimke Papers, South Caroliniana Library.
44. Will of Benjamin Smith, November 21, 1825, Brunswick County, Deed Book, B, 137.
45. *Laws, 1816,* ch. 44; Lawrence Lee, *The History of Brunswick County, North Carolina* (Charlotte, NC: Heritage Press, 1980), 133 (quotation).
46. "Topographical and Historical. Description of the County of Brunswick, in North-Carolina," *National Register,* 1 (1816): 341; Reaves, *Southport (Smithville): A Chronology,* Vol. I, 19–20.
47. Reaves, *Southport (Smithville): A Chronology,* Vol. I, 19; Alan D. Watson, *Internal Improvements in Antebellum North Carolina* (Raleigh: Office of Archives and History, North Carolina Department of Cultural Resources, 2002), 129–130.
48. Eliza Carolina (Burgwin) Clitherall, "Autobiography and Diary of Mrs. Eliza Clitherall," 17 vols., Clitherall Books, 6: 53–54, Southern Historical Collection.
49. Clitherall, "Autobiography and Diary," 6: 55–56.
50. *Ibid.*
51. *Ibid.,* 7: 3–4.
52. Will of Sarah Dry Smith, January 17, 1818, Brunswick County, Deed Book, B, 127; Job, 3: 17.
53. Benjamin Smith to Thomas S. Grimke, June 12, 1822, Benjamin Smith Papers, Southern Historical Collection.
54. Benjamin Smith to Thomas S. Grimke, June 12, 1822, Benjamin Smith Papers, Southern Historical Collection.
55. Brunswick County Court Minutes, July-August 1820; April-May 1821; July 1822; July 1824; Sprunt, *Chronicles of the Cape Fear River,* 58; A. S. Salley, Jr., "Historical Notes. More on Landgrave Smith's Family," *South Carolina Historical and Genealogical Magazine,* 30 (October 1929): 257–258.
56. *Laws, 1813,* ch. 110; Brunswick Court Minutes, July-August 1821.
57. Benjamin Smith to "Dear Sir" [John Haywood], January 15, 1825, Ernest Haywood Collection of Haywood Family Papers.
58. Donna Star Pope, "'Has Troubles Never Come Singly': A Biographical Sketch of Eliza Burgwin Clitherall, honor's thesis, University of North Carolina Wilmington, 1986, 20–21, 23, 25, 29–31.
59. *Wilmington Gazette,* April 16, 1805; Pope, "'Has Troubles Never Come Singly,'" 10–12, 25–28; Lee, *History of Brunswick County,* 137.
60. Clitherall, "Autobiography and Diary," 7: 4–5; *Cape-Fear Recorder* (Wilmington), October 16, 1824. The Census of 1820 listed forty-one

slaves in the possession of Smith, but most were mortgaged and eventually lost to satisfy the General's numerous creditors. Dorothy Williams Potter, comp. and ed., *1820 Federal Census. North Carolina. Supplemented with Tax Lists*, 2nd ed. (Nashville, TN: n.p., 1993), 420.

61. Clitherall, "Autobiography and Diary," 7: 5–6.

62. *Ibid.*, 7: 6–7; George C. Clitherall to John G. Bee, January 30, 1826, University Papers.

63. Clitherall, "Autobiography and Diary," 7: 7; George Clitherall to John G. Bee, January 30, 1826, University Papers. Historians have differed not only over the birth date of Smith but also that of his death, although it often is cited as January 10, 1826. See, for example, among many sources, Lee, *History of Brunswick County*, 141, and Smith's tombstone, laid in 1929, in the Brunswick Town–Fort Anderson State Historic Site. *Appletons' Cyclopedia of American Biography*, 6 vols. (New York: Appleton, 1886–1889), 5: 557, listed the year as 1829. A recent source has taken advantage of the George Clitherall letter as a corrective. Robert Sobel and John Raimo, eds., *Biographical Directory of the Governors of the United States, 1789–1978*, reprint, four volumes in one (Westport, CT: Meckler, 1978), 1119.

Chapter 15

1. Eliza Carolina (Burgwin) Clitherall, "Autobiography and Diary of Mrs. Eliza Clitherall," 17 vols. Clitherall Books, 7: 8, Southern Historical Collection, University of North Carolina at Chapel Hill, Chapel Hill, NC; Will of Benjamin Smith, Brunswick County, Deed Book, B, 137, microfilm, Office of Archives and History, Raleigh, NC.

2. Brunswick County, Deed Book B, 137–138.

3. George C. Clitherall to John G. Bee, January 30, 1826, University Papers, Southern Historical Collection; Thomas S. Grimke to G. C. Clitherall, February 22, 1826; Thomas S. Grimke to ? Walker, May 4, 1826; ? to Robert Howe, June 22, 1826; Thomas S. Grimke to G. C. Clitherall, June 10, 1826; Alfred Moore to [Thomas S. Grimke ?], n.d., Grimke Family Papers, South Caroliniana Library, University of South Carolina, Columbia, SC.

4. William Henry Hoyt, ed., *The Papers of Archibald D. Murphey*, 2 vols. (Raleigh: Uzzell, 1914), 1: 329; H. G. Jones, *For History's Sake: The Preservation and Publication of North Carolina History, 1663–1903* (Chapel Hill: University of North Carolina Press, 1966), 145–157. Smith earlier had shown his appreciation of the need for a history of the state when a member of the Senate in 1807. The General had proposed to allow Francois Xavier Martin, New Bern newspaper publisher, attorney, and legislator, access to the records of the secretary of state for purposes of writing a history of North Carolina. That work eventually emerged in two volumes in 1829. Journal of the Senate of North Carolina, 1807, 47, microfilm, Office of State Archives, Raleigh, NC.

5. Jones, *For History's Sake*, 138–145, 148–154, 157–181. An attempt in the early twentieth century to locate the materials sent by Smith proved fruitless. J. G. deRoulhac Hamilton to "My Dear Mr. Sprunt," September 17, 1921, Alexander Sprunt & Son, Inc., Papers, Rare Book, Manuscript, & Special Collections Library, Duke University, Durham, NC.

6. Hoyt, *Papers of Archibald D. Murphey*, 1: 288; 2: 74; Jay Feldman, *When the Mississippi River Ran Backwards: Empire, Intrigue, Murder, and the New Madrid Earthquakes* (New York: Free Press, 2005), 135–182; Kemp P. Battle, *History of the University of North Carolina*, 2 vols. (Raleigh: Edwards & Broughton, 1907, 1912), 1: 378–404.

7. Battle, *History of the University of North Carolina*, 1: 408, 409, 617; Archibald Henderson, *The Campus of the First State University* (Chapel Hill: University of North Carolina Press, 1949), 118, 134, 143, 147, 184, 249; William Snider, *Light on the Hill: A History of the University of North Carolina at Chapel Hill* (Chapel Hill: University of North Carolina Press, 1992), 64, 108, 181; "Building Notes. University of North Carolina at Chapel Hill," Compiled Fall of 1984. Updated and Revised Fall of 1993 by Rachael Long (N.p., 1993), 506–510, courtesy of the North Carolina Collection, University of North Carolina at Chapel Hill, Chapel Hill, NC.

8. Brooks Newton Preik, "Kate Stuart: Legendary Lady of the Lower Cape Fear," Lower Cape Fear Historical *Bulletin*, 49 (October 2005): [1]; Louis T. Moore, *Stories Old and New of the Cape Fear Region* (Wilmington: Broadfoot, 1999), 117; Joseph G. Swift, *The Memoirs of Gen. Joseph Gardner Swift* (Boston: Privately printed, 1890), 271.

9. John Hill Wheeler, *Historical Sketches of North Carolina; From 1584 to 1851*, 2 vols. in 1. (Philadelphia: Lippincott, Gramno, 1851), 2: 49.

10. John W. Moore, *History of North Carolina; From the Earliest Discoveries to the Present Time*, 2 vols. (Raleigh, NC: Williams, 1880), 1: 458.

11. *Appleton's Cyclopedia of American Biography*, s.v. "Smith, Benjamin."

12. *Laws and Resolutions of the State of North Carolina, 1887*, ch. 76; Lawrence Lee, *The History of Brunswick County, North Carolina* (Charlotte, NC: Heritage Press, 1980), 188–190, 192.

13. Battle, *History of the University of North Carolina*, 1: 119.

14. *Southport Leader*, April 30, 1896; *Hamlet*, Act 5, Scene 1.

15. *Southport Leader*, March 26, April 2, 9, 16, 23, 30, 1896.

16. *Ibid.*, April 30, 1896.

17. *Morning Star* (Wilmington), November 7, 1926; Moore, *Stories Old and New of the Cape Fear Region*, 113; Bill Sharpe, "From Manteo to Murphey," *The State*, 23 (May 19, 1956): 31; Billy Arthur, "The Tragedy of Benjamin Smith," *Our State*, 65 (February 1998): 16.

18. Kate Stuart to "My Dear Mr. Sprunt, January 1, 1921, Alexander Sprunt & Son, Inc., Papers; Moore, *Stories Old and New of the Cape Fear Region*, 115; John D. Bellamy, *Memoirs of an Octogenarian* (Charlotte, NC: Observer Printing House, 1942), 3–4.

19. Samuel Willis and Walter Moxon, *Lectures on Pathological Anatomy* (Philadelphia: Lindsay and Blakiston, 1875), 629; Alfred L. Loomis, *A Textbook of Practical Medicine: Designed for the Use of Students and Practitioners of Medicine* (New York: Wood, 1892), 753.

20. Vern Countryman, "Bankruptcy and the Individual Debtor—and a Modest Proposal to Return to the Seventeenth Century," *Catholic University Law Review*, 32 (Summer 1983): 2; J. F. H., "The Nature of Rights in a Dead Body," *University of Pennsylvania Law Review*, 74 (February 1926): 404–405; Anne Reichman Schiff, "Arising from the Dead: Challenges of Posthumous Procreation," *North Carolina Law Review*, 75 (March 1997): 7.

21. Collier Cobb, "Governor Benjamin Smith," *North Carolina Booklet*, 11 (January 1912): 158–168; Samuel A. Ashe, ed., *Biographical History of North Carolina*, 8 vols. (Greensboro, NC: Charles L. Van Noppen, 1905–1917), 2: 401–405.

22. *Rockingham Post-Dispatch* (Wentworth, NC), January 23, 1919; Cobb, "Governor Benjamin Smith," 158.

23. *Morning Star*, November 21, 1926; *News & Observer* (Raleigh), December 25, 1926; *Sunday Star* (Wilmington), July 13, 1929 (articles written by Louis T. Moore).

24. *Southport Leader*, April 30, 1896; Cobb, "Governor Benjamin Smith," 167; Bill Sharpe, "From Murphey to Manteo," *The State*, 23 (May 19, 1956): 31.

25. "List of the Granite Memorials Erected by the New Hanover Historical Commissi [on]," n.d.; "Marker Found," n.d., Folder entitled "Historical Markers," Louis T. Moore Collection, New Hanover County Library, Wilmington, NC.

26. "The Orphans Friend and Masonic Journal" (Oxford, NC), August 1, 1929, 6–7, Louis T. Moore Collection.

27. Ralph Scott, *The Wilmington Shipyard: Welding a Fleet for Victory in World War II* (Charleston: History Press, 2007), 67–74, 104; John Gorley Bunker, *Liberty Ships: The Ugly Ducklings of World War II* (Annapolis, MD: Naval Institute Press, 1972), 6–7; Joseph F. Nolen, "The Torpedoing of the SS Benjamin Smith," AMMV, St. Johns River Chapter, Jacksonville, Florida, *Newsletter* (June 2004), http://www.armed-guard.com/louv.html, accessed September 22, 2008. The author is indebted to Sue Cody, Randall Library, University of North Carolina Wilmington, for the last reference.

28. Smith had previously received attention in the inscription on two markers for Orton Plantation and the marker for St. Philips Church in Brunswick Town. Michael Hill, ed., *Guide to North Carolina Highway Historical Markers*, 9th ed. (Raleigh: Division of Archives and History, Department of Cultural Resources, 2001), Introduction, 29, 30, 31, 32; *Session Laws, and Resolutions Passed by the 1991 General Assembly at Its Extra Session 1991 ... and Its Regular Session 1992*, Resolution 63.

Bibliography

Manuscripts

Library of Congress, Washington, DC:
  Thomas Jefferson Papers, Series 1. General Correspondence, 1651–1827.
Massachusetts Historical Society, Boston, MA:
  Smith-Carter Family Papers.
National Archives, College Park, MD:
  Miscellaneous Letters Received, 1789–1906.
New Hanover County Public Library, Wilmington, NC:
  Louis T. Moore Collection.
North Carolina Collection, University of North Carolina at Chapel Hill, Chapel Hill, NC:
  Minutes of the Trustees of the University of North Carolina.
Office of Archives and History, State of North Carolina, Raleigh, NC:
  A. D. Schenck Paper.
  Benjamin Smith Papers.
  Slave Collection.
Rare Books, Manuscript, and Special Collections Department, Duke University, Durham, NC:
  Alexander Sprunt & Son, Inc., Papers.
  Grimke Family Papers.
South Carolina Department of Archives and History, Columbia, SC:
  Charleston County Wills.
South Caroliniana Library, University of South Carolina, Columbia, SC:
  Grimke Papers.
Southern Historical Collection, University of North Carolina at Chapel Hill, Chapel Hill, NC:
  Benjamin Smith Papers.
  Clitherall Books.
  Ernest Haywood Collection of Haywood Family Papers.
  Preston Davie Collection.
  Stephen Beauregard Weeks Collection.
  University Papers.

Newspapers

American Agriculturalist (New York)
Cape-Fear Mercury (Wilmington)
Cape-Fear Recorder (Wilmington)
Edenton Gazette
Hall's Wilmington Gazette
Morning Star (Wilmington)
Newbern Spectator
News & Observer (Raleigh)
North Carolina Chronicle; or Fayetteville Gazette
North-Carolina Gazette (New Bern)
North Carolina Gazette or Impartial Intelligencer, and Weekly General Advertiser (New Bern)
North Carolina Journal (Halifax, NC)
North-Carolina Minerva (Raleigh)
Raleigh Register
Rockingham Post-Dispatch (Wentworth, NC)
South-Carolina Gazette (Charles Town)
South-Carolina American and General Gazette (Charles Town)
Southport Leader
Star (Raleigh)
State-Gazette of North Carolina (Edenton)
Sunday Star (Wilmington)
Wilmington Centinel, and General Advertiser
Wilmington Chronicle; and North-Carolina Weekly Advertiser
Wilmington Gazette

Unpublished Public and Official Records

Office of Archives and History, Raleigh, NC:
Brunswick County Deed Books.
General Assembly Session Records.
Governors Letter Books.
Governors Papers.
Journal of the House of Commons of North Carolina.
Journal of the Senate of North Carolina.
Minutes of the Brunswick County Court of Pleas and Quarter Sessions.
Minutes of the Craven County Court of Pleas and Quarter Sessions.
New Hanover County Deed Books.

Published Letters, Memoirs, Travel Accounts, and Other Miscellaneous Sources

Bellamy, John D. *Memoirs of an Octogenarian.* Charlotte, NC: Observer, 1942.
Brickell, John. *The Natural History of North Carolina.* Murfreesboro, NC: Johnson, 1968.
Brunswick County, North Carolina, 1810 & 1820 Federal Censuses. Abs. by Delmar D. Haskett. Wilmington: Old New Hanover Genealogy Society and the North Carolina Room, New Hanover County Public Library, 1995.
"Building Notes. University of North Carolina Chapel Hill." Fall 1984. Updated and Revised Fall 1993 by Rachel Long. N.p., 1993.
Carroll, Grady L. E., ed. *Francis Asbury in North Carolina: The North Carolina Portions of the Journal of Francis Asbury.* Nashville, TN: Parthenon Press, 1964.
Clark, Walter, ed. *The State Records of North Carolina.* 16 vols. (11–26) Raleigh: State of North Carolina, 1895–1906.
Collet, John. "A Compleat Map of North-Carolina from an Actual Survey (1770)." Office of Archives and History, Department of Cultural Resources, Raleigh, NC.
Connor, R. D. W., ed. *A Documentary History of the University of North Carolina, 1776–1799.* 2 vols. Chapel Hill: University of North Carolina Press, 1953.
Coon, Charles L., ed. *North Carolina Schools and Academies, 1790–1840.* 2 vols. Raleigh: Edwards & Broughton, 1915.

"Correspondence of Hon. Arthur Middleton." *South Carolina Magazine of History and Genealogy,* 27 (January 1926): 1–29.
Curtis, Walter G. *Reminiscences, 1848–1900.* 2nd ed. Southport, NC: Southport Historical Society, 1999.
Elliot, Jonathan, ed. *The Debates of the Several State Conventions on the Adoption of the Federal Constitution as Recommended by the General Convention at Philadelphia in 1787.* 5 vols. New York: Franklin, 1968.
Finlay, Hugh. *Journal kept by Hugh Finlay, Surveyor of the Post Roads on the Continent of North America.* Brooklyn: Norton, 1867.
Frohnen, Bruce, ed. *The American Republic: Primary Sources.* Indianapolis: Liberty Fund, 2002.
Griffey, Irene M. *John Armstrong's Entry Book, October 21, 1783–May 25, 1784.* Vol. 11. Clarksville, TN: privately printed, 1993.
Heads of Families at the First Census Taken of the United States in the Year 1790. Baltimore: Genealogical, 1966.
Higginbotham, Don, Donna Kelly, and Lang Baradell, eds. *The Papers of James Iredell.* 3 vols. Raleigh: Office of Archives and History, North Carolina Department of Cultural Resources, 1976, 2003.
Holcomb, Brent H. *South Carolina Marriages, 1688–1799.* Baltimore: Genealogical, 1980.
Howe, Mark A. DeWolfe, ed. "Journal of Josiah Quincy, Junior, 1773." *Massachusetts Historical Society Proceedings* 49 (June 1916): 424–481.
Hoyt, William Henry, ed. *The Papers of Archibald D. Murphey.* 2 vols. Raleigh: Uzzell, 1914.
"Inscriptions of Tablets over Graves in St. Philips Churchyard, Brunswick." Brunswick Town/Fort Anderson State Historic Site, NC.
Jackson, Donald, and Dorothy Twohig, eds. *The Diaries of George Washington.* 6 vols. Charlottesville: University of Virginia Press, 1976–1979.
Johnson, William Perry, and Dorothy Williams Potter. *1800 North Carolina Census. Brunswick County.* N.p.: privately printed, 1975.
Johnston, Hugh B., ed. "The Journal of Ebenezer Hazard in North Carolina in 1777 and 1778." *North Carolina Historical Review* 36 (July 1959): 358–381.
Kellam, Ida Brooks, and Elizabeth Francenia McKoy. *St. James Church, Wilmington,*

North Carolina, Historical Records, 1737–1852. N.p.; privately printed, 1965.

Laws and Resolutions of the State of North Carolina.

Lemmon, Sarah McCulloh, ed., *The Pettigrew Papers.* 2 vols. Raleigh: North Carolina Department of Cultural Resources, Division of Archives and History, 1971, 1988.

Lennon, Donald R., and Kellam, Ida B., eds. *The Wilmington Town Book, 1743–1778.* Raleigh: Division of Archives and History, Department of Cultural Resources, 1973.

McRee, Griffeth J., ed. *Life and Correspondence of James Iredell, One of the Associate Justices of the Supreme Court of the United States.* 2 vols. in 1. New York: Peter Smith, 1949.

Meredith, Hugh. *An Account of the Cape Fear Country.* Earl Gregg Swem, ed. Perth Amboy, NJ: Charles F. Heartman, 1912.

Mereness, Newton D., ed. "Journal of an Officer Who Travelled in America and the West Indies in 1764 and 1765." *Travels in the American Colonies.* New York: Antiquarian Press, 1961.

Merrens, H. Roy, ed. *The Colonial South Carolina Scene: Contemporary Views, 1697–1774.* Columbia: University of South Carolina Press, 1977.

Miranda, Francisco de. *The New Democracy in America: Travels of Francisco de Miranda in the United States, 1783–1784.* John S. Ezell, ed. Norman: University of Oklahoma Press, 1963.

Morse, Jedidiah. *The American Geography.* London: John Stockdale, 1792.

Moultrie, William. *Memoirs of the American Revolution.* 2 vols. New York: New York Times and Arno Press, 1968.

Mouzon, Henry, et al. "An Accurate Map of North and South Carolina (1775)." Office of Archives and History, Department of Cultural Resources, Raleigh, NC.

A New Voyage to Georgia. By a young Gentleman. Giving an Account of His Travels to North Carolina and a Part of South Carolina. 2nd ed. London: Printed for J. Wilford, 1737.

Parker, Mattie Erma Edwards, ed. *North Carolina Charters and Constitutions, 1578–1698.* Raleigh: Carolina Charter Tercentenary Commission, 1963.

Potter, Dorothy Williams, comp. and ed. *1820 Federal Census, North Carolina. Supplemented with Tax Lists.* 2nd ed. Nashville, TN: n.p., 1993.

Potts, Joshua. "The Location of Smithville." *Letters and Documents, Relating to the Early History of the Lower Cape Fear.* James Sprunt Historical Monographs. No. 4. Chapel Hill: University of North Carolina Press, 1904.

Powell, William S., ed. *The Correspondence of William Tryon and Other Selected Papers.* 2 vols. Raleigh: Division of Archives and History, Department of Cultural Resources, 1980, 1981.

Pruitt, A. B. "Land Grants in Tennessee by North Carolina." 1998. www.tngenweb.org/tnland/pruitt2htm.

Ramsay, David. *History of South Carolina, from Its First Settlement in 1670 to the Year 1808.* 2 vols. Newberry, SC: W. J. Duffie, 1858.

Reaves, Bill. *Southport (Smithville): A Chronology.* 4 vols. N.p.: Southport Historical Society, 1978–1999.

Roberts, Kenneth, and Anna M. Roberts, trans. and eds. *Moreau de St. Mery's American Journal [1793–1798].* Garden City, NY: Doubleday, 1947.

Salley, A. S., ed. "Diary of William Dillwyn During a Visit to Charles Town in 1772–1773." *South Carolina Historical and Genealogical Magazine* 36 (October 1935): 107–110.

Saunders, William L., ed. *The Colonial Records of North Carolina.* 10 vols. Raleigh: State of North Carolina, 1886–1890.

Schaw, Janet. *Journal of a Lady of Quality; Being the Narrative of a Journey from Scotland to the West Indies, North Carolina, and Portugal, in the Years 1774 to 1776.* Evangeline Walker Andrews and Charles McLean Andrews, eds. New Haven: Yale University Press, 1921.

Schoepf, Johann David. *Travels in the Confederation [1783–1784].* 2 vols. Alfred J. Morrison, trans. and ed. Philadelphia: Campbell, 1911.

Seeber, Edward D., trans. *On the Threshold of Liberty: Journal of a Frenchman's Tour of the American Colonies in 1777.* Bloomington: Indiana University Press, 1959.

Smith, D. E. Huger, and A. S. Salley Jr., eds. *Register of St. Philip's Parish, Charles Town, or Charleston, S. C., 1754–1810.* Columbia: University of South Carolina Press, 1971.

Smith, Paul, ed. *Letters of Delegates to Con-*

gress, 1774–1789. 26 vols. Washington, DC: Library of Congress, 1976–2000.

Steuben, Baron von. *Regulations for the Order and Discipline of the Troops of the United States: to Which is Added an Appendix Containing the United States Militia Act, Passed by Congress, May 1792.* Boston: Thomas and Andrews, 1794.

Swift, Joseph Gardner. *The Memoirs of Gen. Joseph Gardner Swift.* Boston: Privately printed, 1890.

"Topographical and Historical. Description of the County of Brunswick in North Carolina." *National Register* 1 (July 1816): 340–342.

Travis, Joseph. *Autobiography of the Rev. Joseph Travis, A.M., a Member of the Memphis Annual Conference.* Nashville, TN: Stevenson and Owen, 1856.

Waddell, Alfred Moore. *Some Memories of My Life.* Raleigh: Edwards & Broughton, 1908.

Wagstaff, H. M., ed. *The Harrington Letters.* James Sprunt Historical Publications. Vol. 13, no. 2. Chapel Hill: Published by the University Press, 1914.

———. *The Harris Letters.* James Sprunt Historical Publications. Vol. 14. Durham, NC: Seeman, 1916.

———. *The Papers of John Steele.* 2 vols. Raleigh: Edwards & Broughton, 1924.

Watson, Alan D., ed. *An Index to North Carolina Newspapers, 1784–1789.* Raleigh: Division of Archives and History, Department of Cultural Resources, 1992.

Watson, Winslow C., ed. *Men and Times of the Revolution; or Memoirs of Elkanah Watson.* New York: Dana, 1856.

Webber, Mabel L., comp. "The First Governor Moore and His Children." *South Carolina Historical and Genealogical Magazine,* 37 (January 1936): 1–23.

Monographs and Compilations

Abernethy, Thomas P. *From Frontier to Plantation in Tennessee: A Study in Frontier Democracy.* Chapel Hill: University of North Carolina Press, 1932.

Anderson, Fred. *Crucible of War: The Seven Years War and the Fate of Empire in British North America, 1754–1766.* New York: Knopf, 2000.

Angley, Wilson. *A History of Fort Johnston on the Lower Cape Fear.* Southport, NC: Southport Historical Society, 1996.

Appleton's Cyclopedia of American Biography.

Ashe, Samuel A., ed. *Biographical History of North Carolina.* 8 vols. Greensboro, NC: Van Noppen, 1905–1917.

Bailyn, Bernard. *Voyagers to the West. A Passage in the Peopling of America on the Eve of the Revolution.* New York: Knopf, 1986.

Baldwin, Agnes Leland. *First Settlers of South Carolina, 1670–1680.* Columbia: University of South Carolina Press, 1969.

Battle, Kemp P. *History of the University of North Carolina.* 2 vols. Raleigh: Edwards & Broughton, 1907, 1912.

Bishir, Catherine W., and Michael T. Southern. *A Guide to the Historic Architecture of Piedmont North Carolina.* Chapel Hill: University of North Carolina Press, 2005.

Block, Susan Taylor. *Temple of Our Fathers: St. James Church.* Wilmington: Artspeaks, 2004.

Borick, Carl. *A Gallant Defense: The Siege of Charleston, 1780.* Columbia: University of South Carolina Press, 2003.

Bridenbaugh, Carl. *Cities in Revolt: Urban Life in America, 1743–1776.* New York: Capricorn Books 1964.

———, and Jessica Bridenbaugh. *Rebels and Gentlemen: Philadelphia in the Age of Franklin.* New York: Oxford University Press, 1962.

Bridges, Earley Winfred. *The Masonic Governors of North Carolina. Their Masonic Records and Orations; Newspaper Articles of Events Pertaining to Their Craft, and Other Information of Interest to Masonry About the Governors of North Carolina.* Greensboro, NC: N.p., 1937.

Broussard, James H. *The Southern Federalists, 1800–1816.* Baton Rouge: Louisiana State University Press, 1978.

Bullock, Steven C. *Revolutionary Brotherhood: Freemasonry and the Transformation of the American Social Order, 1730–1840.* Chapel Hill: University of North Carolina Press, 1996.

Bunker, John Gorley. *Liberty Ships: The Ugly Ducklings of World War II.* Annapolis, MD: Naval Institute Press, 1972.

Burnett, Edmund C. *The Continental Congress.* New York: Norton, 1964.

Cavanaugh, John C. *Decision at Fayetteville: The North Carolina Ratification Convention and General Assembly of 1789.* Raleigh: Division of Archives and History, Department of Cultural Resources, 1989.

Censer, Jane Turner. *North Carolina Planters and Their Children, 1800–1860.* Baton Rouge: Louisiana State University Press, 1984.

Chaplin, Joyce E. *An Anxious Pursuit: Agricultural Innovation and the Modernity in the Lower South, 1730–1815.* Chapel Hill: University of North Carolina Press, 1993.

Cheney, John L., Jr., ed. *North Carolina Government, 1585–1979: A Narrative and Statistical History.* Raleigh: North Carolina Department of the Secretary of State, 1981.

Chernow, Ron. *Alexander Hamilton.* New York: Penguin Press, 2004.

Connor, R. D. W. *Cornelius Harnett: An Essay in North Carolina History.* Raleigh: Edwards & Broughton, 1909.

Corbitt, David Leroy, ed. *The Formation of the North Carolina Counties, 1663–1943.* Raleigh: State Department of Archives and History, 1950.

Cress, Lawrence Delbert. *Citizens in Arms: The Army and the Militia in American Society to the War of 1812.* Chapel Hill: University of North Carolina Press, 1982.

Dickerson, Oliver M. *The Navigation Acts and the American Revolution.* Philadelphia: University of Pennsylvania Press, 1951.

Dictionary of American Biography.

Dictionary of North Carolina Biography.

Driver, Carl. *John Sevier: Pioneer of the Old Southwest.* Chapel Hill: University of North Carolina Press, 1932.

Easterby, J. H. *A History of the College of Charleston, Founded in 1770.* Charleston, SC: N.p., 1935.

Eaton, Clement. *A History of the Old South.* 3rd ed. New York: Macmillan, 1975.

Edgar, Walter. *South Carolina: A History.* Columbia: University of South Carolina Press, 1998.

Edgar, Walter, and N. Louise Bailey, eds. *Biographical Directory of the South Carolina House of Representatives.* 5 vols. Columbia: University of South Carolina Press, 1974–1992.

Ellis, Joseph J. *American Creation: Triumph and Tragedies at the Founding of the Republic.* New York: Knopf, 2007.

Feldman, Jay. *When the Mississippi River Ran Backwards: Empire, Intrigue, Murder, and the New Madrid Earthquakes.* New York: The Free Press, 2005.

Fischer, David Hackett. *Washington's Crossing.* New York: Oxford University Press, 2004.

Fowler, William N., Jr. *Empires at War: The French and Indian War and the Struggle for North America, 1754–1763.* New York: Walker, 2005.

Franklin, John Hope. *The Free Negro in North Carolina, 1790–1860.* Chapel Hill: University of North Carolina Press, 1943.

Freeman, Joanne B. *Affairs of Honor. National Politics in the New Republic.* New Haven, CT: Yale University Press, 2001.

Gilpatrick, Delbert H. *Jeffersonian Democracy in North Carolina, 1789–1816.* New York: Columbia University Press, 1931.

Gohdes, Clarence. *Scuppernong: North Carolina's Grape and Its Wine.* Durham, NC: Duke University Press, 1982.

Gordon, John W. *South Carolina and the American Revolution: A Battlefield History.* Columbia: University of South Carolina Press, 2003.

Grill, C. Franklin. *Methodism in the Upper Cape Fear Valley.* Nashville, TN: Parthenon Press, 1966.

Haw, James. *John & Edward Rutledge of South Carolina.* Athens: University of Georgia Press, 1997.

Henderson, Archibald. *The Campus of the First State University.* Chapel Hill: University of North Carolina Press, 1949.

———. *Washington's Southern Tour, 1791.* Boston and New York: Houghton Mifflin, 1923.

Herring, Ethel, and Carolee Williams. *Fort Caswell in War and Peace.* Wendell, NC: Broadfoot's Bookmark, 1983.

Hill, Michael, ed. *Guide to North Carolina Highway Historical Markers.* 9th ed. Raleigh: Division of Archives and History, Department of Cultural Resources, 2001.

Hofstadter, Richard. *America at 1750: A Social Portrait.* New York: Knopf, 1971.

Illick, Joseph E. *Colonial Pennsylvania: A History.* New York: Charles Scribner's Sons, 1976.

Jackson, Claude V., III. *A Maritime History of the Cape Fear and Northeast Cape Fear Rivers, Wilmington Harbor, N.C.* Vol. 1. Edited by Jack E. Fryar, Jr., as *The Big Book of the Cape Fear River.* Wilmington: Dram Tree Books, 2008.

Johnson, Guion Griffis. *Ante-Bellum North Carolina: A Social History*. Chapel Hill: University of North Carolina Press, 1937.

Jones, H. G. *For History's Sake: The Preservation and Publication of North Carolina History, 1663-1903*. Chapel Hill: University of North Carolina Press, 1966.

Jordan, Winthrop. *White over Black: American Attitudes Toward the Negro, 1550-1812*. Baltimore: Penguin Books, 1969.

Kay, Marvin L. Michael, and Lorin Lee Cary. *Slavery in North Carolina, 1748-1775*. Chapel Hill: University of North Carolina Press, 1995.

Lee, Lawrence. *The History of Brunswick County, North Carolina*. Charlotte, NC: Heritage Press, 1980.

_____. *The Lower Cape Fear in Colonial Days*. Chapel Hill: University of North Carolina Press, 1965.

Lemmon, Sarah McCulloh. *Frustrated Patriots: North Carolina and the War of 1812*. Chapel Hill: University of North Carolina Press, 1973.

Lesser, Charles S. *South Carolina Begins: The Records of a Proprietary Colony, 1663-1721*. Columbia: University of South Carolina Press, 1995.

Lester, William Stewart. *The Transylvania Company*. Spencer, IN: Guard, 1935.

Loomis, Alfred L. *A Textbook of Practical Medicine: Designed for the Use of Students and Practitioners of Medicine*. New York: Wood, 1892.

Lumpkin, Henry. *From Savannah to Yorktown: The American Revolution in the South*. Columbia: University of South Carolina Press, 1981.

Mahon, John K. *The American Militia: Decade of Decision, 1789-1800*. Jacksonville, FL: Miller Press, 1960.

Main, Jackson T. *Political Parties before the Constitution*. Chapel Hill: University of North Carolina Press, 1973.

Masterson, William H. *William Blount*. Baton Route: Louisiana State University Press, 1954.

Matthews, Alice E. *Society in Revolutionary North Carolina*. Raleigh: North Carolina Department of Cultural Resources, Division of Archives and History, 1976.

McCrady, Edward. *The History of South Carolina in the Revolution, 1775-1780*. New York: Macmillan, 1901.

Merrens, H. Roy. *Colonial North Carolina in the Eighteenth Century: A Historical Geography*. Chapel Hill: University of North Carolina Press, 1964.

Moore, John W. *History of North Carolina; From the Earliest Discoveries to the Present Time*. 2 vols. Raleigh: Williams, 1880.

Moore, Louis T. *Stories Old and New of the Cape Fear Region*. Wilmington: Broadfoot, 1999.

Morrill, Dan L. *Southern Campaigns of the American Revolution*. Mount Pleasant, SC: Nautical and Aviation Publishing Company of America, 1993.

Morrill, James R. *The Practice and Politics of Fiat Finance: North Carolina in the Confederation, 1783-1789*. Chapel Hill: University of North Carolina Press, 1969.

Murray, Elizabeth Reid. *Wake: Capital County of North Carolina*. Vol. 1. Raleigh: Capital County, 1983.

Mygroves, J. H. *Short History of Cumberland County and the Cape Fear Section*. Fayetteville, NC: North Carolina Baptist, 1905.

Neale, Robert S. *The Bank of Cape Fear of Wilmington, North Carolina*. Wilmington: Lower Cape Fear Historical Society and the author, 1999.

Pancake, John. *This Destructive War: The British Campaign in the Carolinas, 1780-1782*. University: University of Alabama Press, 1985.

Parker, Elmer O. *Roster: Fort Sullivan (Later Fort Moultrie), 1776-1780*. N.p., n.d.

Parker, Roy. *Cumberland County: A Brief History*. Raleigh: Division of Archives and History, Department of Cultural Resources, 1990.

Parramore, Thomas C. *Launching the Craft: The First Half-Century of Freemasonry in North Carolina*. Raleigh: Litho Industries, 1975.

Powell, William S., ed. *The North Carolina Gazetteer*. Chapel Hill: University of North Carolina Press, 1968.

_____. *North Carolina Through Four Centuries*. Chapel Hill: University of North Carolina Press, 1989.

Prince, William Robert, and William Prince. *A Treatise on the Vine*. New York: Swords, Carvill, Collins, 1830.

Rankin, Richard. *Ambivalent Churchmen and Evangelical Churchwomen: The Religion of the Episcopal Church in North Carolina, 1800-1860*. Columbia: University of South Carolina Press, 1993.

Risjord, Norman, K. *Chesapeake Politics, 1781-1800*. New York: Columbia University Press, 1978.

Robinson, Blackwell P. *The History of Escheats*. Chapel Hill: University of North Carolina Press, 1955.

———. *William R. Davie*. Chapel Hill: University of North Carolina Press, 1957.

Rodenbough, Charles D. *Governor Alexander Martin: Biography of a North Carolina Revolutionary War Statesman*. Jefferson, NC: McFarland, 2004.

Rogers, George C., Jr. *Charleston in the Age of the Pinckneys*. Norman: University of Oklahoma Press, 1969.

———. *Evolution of a Federalist: William Loughton Smith of Charleston (1758-1812)*. Columbia: University of South Carolina Press, 1962.

Rose, Lisle A. *Prologue to Democracy: The Federalists in the South, 1789-1800*. Lexington: University of Kentucky Press, 1968.

Rowland, Lawrence S., Alexander Moore, and George C. Rogers, Jr. *The History of Beaufort County, South Carolina*, Vol. 1. *1514-1861*. Columbia: University of South Carolina Press, 1996.

Schechter, Barnet. *Battle for New York: The City at the Heart of the American Revolution*. New York: Walker, 2002.

Scott, Ralph. *The Wilmington Shipyard: Welding a Fleet for Victory in World War II*. Charleston: History Press, 2007.

Seapker, Janet, ed. *Time, Talent, and Tradition: Five Essays in the Cultural History of the Lower Cape Fear Region of North Carolina*. Wilmington: n.p., 1995.

Sirmans, M. Eugene. *Colonial South Carolina: A Political History*. Chapel Hill: University of North Carolina Press, 1966.

Skaggs, Marvin Lucian. *North Carolina Boundary Disputes Involving Her Southern Line*. Chapel Hill: University of North Carolina Press, 1941.

Smelser, Martin. *The Democratic Republic, 1801-1815*. New York: Harper & Row, 1968.

Snider, William. *Light on the Hill: A History of the University of North Carolina at Chapel Hill*. Chapel Hill: University of North Carolina Press, 1982.

Sobel, Robert, and John Raimo, eds. *Biographical Directory of the Governors of the United States, 1789-1978*. 4 vols. in 1. Westport, CT: Merkler, 1988.

Sprunt, James. *Chronicles of the Cape Fear River*. 2nd ed. Raleigh: Edwards & Broughton, 1916.

———. *Tales and Traditions of the Lower Cape Fear, 1661-1896*. Wilmington: LeGwin Brothers, 1896.

Sprunt, James Laurence. *The Story of Orton Plantation*. Wilmington: N.p., 1958.

Stick, David. *Bald Head. A History of Smith Island and the Cape Fear*. Wendell, NC: Broadfoot, 1985.

Trenholme, Louis I. *The Ratification of the Federal Constitution in North Carolina*. New York: AMS Press, 1967.

Waddell, Alfred Moore. *A History of New Hanover County and the Lower Cape Fear Region*. Wilmington: N. p., 1909.

Watson, Alan D. *A History of New Bern and Craven County*. New Bern: Tryon Palace Commission, 1987.

———. *Internal Improvements in Antebellum North Carolina*. Raleigh: Office of Archives and History, North Carolina Department of Cultural Resources, 2002.

———. *Society in Colonial North Carolina*. Rev. ed. Raleigh: Office of Archives and History, State Department of Cultural Resources, 1996.

———. *Wilmington, North Carolina, to 1861*. Jefferson, NC: McFarland, 2003.

———. *Wilmington: Port of North Carolina*. Columbia: University of South Carolina Press, 1992.

Wheeler, John Hill. *Historical Sketches of North Carolina; from 1584 to 1851*. 2 vols. in 1. Philadelphia: Lippincott, Grammo, 1851.

Whichard, Willis P. *Justice James Iredell*. Durham, NC: Carolina Academic Press, 2000.

Williams, Jack K. *Dueling in the Old South: Vignettes of Social History*. College Station: Texas A&M University Press, 1980.

Williams, Samuel C. *History of the Lost State of Franklin*. Johnson City, TN: Watauga Press, 1924.

Willis, Samuel, and Walter Moxon. *Lectures on Pathological Anatomy*. Philadelphia: Lindsay and Blakiston, 1875.

Wood, Bradford J. *This Remote Part of the World: Regional Formation in the Lower Cape Fear, North Carolina, 1725-1775*. Columbia: University of South Carolina Press, 2004.

Wyatt-Brown, Bertram. *Honor and Violence*

in the Old South. New York: Oxford University Press, 1986.
Zahniser, Martin R. *Charles Cotesworth Pinckney: Founding Father.* Chapel Hill: University of North Carolina Press, 1967.

Articles and Essays

Arthur, Billy. "The Tragedy of Benjamin Smith." *Our State* 65 (February 1998): 15–16.
Bishir, Catherine W. " 'The Unpainted Aristocracy': The Beach Cottages of Old Nags Head." *North Carolina Historical Review* 54 (October 1977): 367–392.
Broussard, James. "The North Carolina Federalists, 1800–1816." *North Carolina Historical Review* 55 (Winter 1978): 18–41.
Cannon, Walter F. "Four Interpretations of the History of the State of Franklin." *East Tennessee Historical Society Publications* 22 (1930): 3–18.
Clifton, James M. " 'Golden Grains of White': Rice Planting on the Lower Cape Fear." *North Carolina Historical Review* 50 (October 1973): 365–393.
Cobb, Collier. "Governor Benjamin Smith." *North Carolina Booklet* 11 (January 1912): 158–168.
Crow, Jeffery J. "The Whiskey Rebellion in North Carolina." *North Carolina Historical Review* 66 (January 1989): 1–28.
Countryman, Vern. "Bankruptcy and the Individual Debtor — and a Modest Proposal to Return to the Seventeenth Century." *Catholic University Law Review* 32 (Summer 1983): 809–827.
Gallman, James M. "Determinants of Age at Marriage: Colonial Perquimans County, North Carolina." *William and Mary Quarterly*, 3rd Series, 39 (January 1982): 176–191.
Gallman, James Matthew. "Relative Ages of Colonial Marriages." *Journal of Interdisciplinary History* 14 (Winter 1984): 609–617.
Ganyard, Robert L. "Radicals and Conservatives in Revolutionary North Carolina: A Point at Issue, the October Election, 1776," *William and Mary Quarterly*, 3rd Series, 24 (October 1967): 568–587.
H., J. F. "The Nature of Rights in a Dead Body." *University of Pennsylvania Law Review*, 74 (February 1926): 404–407.
Hamilton, J. G. de Roulhac. "Southern Members of the Inns of Court." *North Carolina Historical Review* 10 (October 1933): 273–286.
Kay, Marvin L. Michael, and Lorin Lee Cary. "A Demographic Analysis of Colonial North Carolina with Special Emphasis on the Slave and Black Populations," 71–121.
Crow, Jeffrey J., and Flora J. Hatley, eds. *Black Americans in North Carolina and the South.* Chapel Hill: University of North Carolina Press, 1984.
Krebsbach, Suzanne. "The Great Charleston Smallpox Epidemic of 1760." *South Carolina Historical Magazine* 97 (January 1996): 30–37.
Lerche, Charles O. "Jefferson and the Election of 1800: A Case Study in Political Smear." *William and Mary Quarterly*, 3rd Series, 5 (October 1948): 467–491.
Long, Grace H. "The Grimkes, Southern Iconclasts." *Peabody Journal of Education* 20 (May 1943): 359–364.
Morgan, Philip D. "Work and Culture: The Task System and the World of Lowcountry Blacks, 1700–1880." *William and Mary Quarterly*, 3rd Series, 39 (October 1982): 563–599.
Nash, Gary B. "The Transformation of Urban Politics." *Journal of American History* 60 (December 1973): 605–632.
Nolen, Joseph F. "The Torpedoeing of the S.S. Benjamin Smith," AMMV, St. John's River Chapter, Jacksonville, Florida *Newsletter* (June 2004). http://www.armed-guard.com/louv.html.
Outland, Robert B., III. "Slavery, Work, and the Geography of the North Carolina Naval Stores Industry, 1835–1860.*"Journal of Southern History* 62 (February 1996): 27–56.
Preik, Brooks Newton. "Kate Stuart: Legendary Lady of the Lower Cape Fear." *Lower Cape Fear Historical Society Bulletin* 49 (October 2005): [1]–7.
Ratchford, U. B. "An International Debt Settlement: The North Carolina Debt to France." *American Historical Review* 40 (October 1934): 63–69.
Rhett, Robert Barnwell, "The Descendants of Col. William Rhett, of South Carolina." *South Carolina Historical and Genealogical Magazine* 4 (January 1903): 36–74.
Rorabaugh, W. J. "The Political Duel in the Early Republic: Burr v. Hamilton," *Journal of the Early Republic* 15 (Spring 1995): 1–23.

Salley, A. S., Jr. "Historical Notes. More on Landgrave Smith's Family." *South Carolina Historical and Genealogical Magazine* 30 (October 1929): 255–258.

Schiff, Anne Reichman. "Arising from the Dead: Challenges of Posthumous Procreation." *North Carolina Law Review* 75 (March 1997): 1–48.

Seapker, Janet K. "St. John's Masonic Lodge, Part I." Lower Cape Fear Historical Society *Bulletin* 50 (January 2006): 1–7.

Sharpe, Bill. "From Manteo to Murphy." *The State* 23 (May 19, 1956): 28–33.

Smith, Mary Phlegar. "Borough Representation in North Carolina." *North Carolina Historical Review* 7 (April 1930): 177–191.

South, Stanley A. "'Russellborough': Two Royal Governors' Mansion at Brunswick Town." *North Carolina Historical Review* 44 (October 1967): 360–372.

Spalding, James C. "Loyalist as Royalist, Patriot as Puritan: The American Revolution as a Repetition of the English Civil War." *Church History* 45 (September 1976): 329–340.

Thornton, Mary Lindsay. "The Price and Strother *First Actual Survey of State of North Carolina*." *North Carolina Historical Review* 41 (October 1964): 477–483.

Tinkcom, Henry M. "The Revolutionary City, 1765–1783," in Russell F. Weigley, ed., *Philadelphia: A 300-Year History*. New York: Norton, 1982.

Ulmer, Sidney S. "Some Eighteenth Century South Carolinians and the Duel." *South Carolina Magazine of History and Biography* 60 (January 1959): 1–9.

Watson, Alan D. "Cornelius Harnett," in Alan D. Watson, Dennis R. Lawson, and Donald R. Lennon, eds., *Harnett, Hooper & Howe: Revolutionary Leaders of the Lower Cape Fear*. Wilmington: Wilmington, 1979.

———. "The Constitution and North Carolina: Rebellion, Rights, and Ratification, 1776–1789," in Patrick T. Conley and John P. Kaminski, eds., *The Constitution and the States: The Role of the Original Thirteen States in the Framing and Adoption of the Federal Constitution*. Madison, WI: Madison House, 1988.

———. "The Lottery in Early North Carolina." *North Carolina Historical Review* 69 (October 1992): 373–387.

———. "Timothy Bloodworth." Lower Cape Fear Historical Society *Bulletin* 29 (February 1986): 1–[6].

———. "William Dry: Passive Patriot." Lower Cape Fear Historical Society *Bulletin* 17 (October 1973), unpaginated.

Weir, Robert M. "'The Harmony We Were Famous For': An Interpretation of Pre-Revolutionary South Carolina Politics." *William and Mary Quarterly*, 3rd Series, 26 (October 1969): 473–501.

Theses, Dissertations, and Reports

Angley, Wilson. "A Brief History of the Eagles Plantation and Mill Facility in Brunswick County." Research report, 1989. Office of Archives and History, Raleigh, NC.

Cross, Jerry. "St. Philip's Church, Brunswick County, North Carolina." Research report, 1975. Office of Archives and History, Raleigh, NC.

Hill, Michael. "Historical Overview of Smith Island (Bald Head Island), Brunswick County, North Carolina," Research report, 1984. Office of Archives and History, Raleigh, NC.

King-Owen, Scott. "North Carolina Federalists in an Evolving Public Sphere, 1790–1810." Master's thesis, University of North Carolina Wilmington, 2006.

Koonts, Russell. "An Angel Has Fallen! The Glasgow Land Frauds and the Establishment of the North Carolina Supreme Court." Master's thesis, North Carolina State University, 1995.

Lennon, Donald R. "The Political Views and Public Activities of Benjamin Smith of Brunswick County (1783–1816)." Master's thesis, East Carolina University, 1961.

Peterkin, Darryl Lynn. "'Lux, Libertas, and Learning': The First State University and the Transformation of North Carolina." Ph.D. dissertation, Princeton University, 1995.

Pope, Donna Star. "'Has Troubles Never Come Singly': A Biographical Sketch of Eliza Burgwin Clitherall." Honors thesis, University of North Carolina Wilmington, 1986.

Web Sites

www.archives.upenn.edu/people/1700s/duche_jacob.html.

www.tngenweb.org/tnfirst/chicksaw/treaties.htm.

INDEX

academies 105, 106
Adams, John 70, 89, 102, 107, 110, 112, 133, 140, 142, 198
Adams, Samuel 139
African Americans 90; *see also* slavery
Alexander, Nathaniel 147, 149, 151, 152, 153, 154
Alien and Sedition Acts 103
Alves, William 64, 131, 169
American Revolution 16–17, 20–22
Appleton's Cyclopedia of American Biography 201, 202
Armstrong, John 46, 113
Articles of Confederation 48, 49
Asbury, Francis 68, 93, 116, 143
Ashe, Samuel 93, 103, 104
Ashe, Samuel A. 204

Baker, Abraham 149
Bald Head Island 44–45, 58, 74, 93, 124, 160, 166–167, 190, 196
Bald Head Island Lighthouse 44–45, 58, 82–83, 167
Bank of Cape Fear 123, 135, 174, 184, 185, 186, 187, 196
Bank of Newbern 135, 174, 184
Barron, James 150
Battle, Kemp P. 69, 73, 87, 204, 205
Battle of Guilford Court House 101
Battle of Long Island 17, 109
Battle of Port Royal Island 20–21, 109
Battle of Sullivan's Island 17, 143
Beaufort, S.C. 160
Bee, Thomas 23
Bell, John 43
Bell, Robert 43
Bellfont 31–32; *see also* Russellborough
Bellune, Daniel 102
Belvedere (house) 36

Belvedere Plantation 28, 36–37, 44, 61, 67, 74, 77, 92, 99, 117, 122, 138, 142, 145, 148, 156, 163, 164, 171, 172, 173, 186, 190
Belville, N.C. 36
Belville Plantation 28
SS *Benjamin Smith* 206
Benton, Samuel 153
Benvenuto Plantation 157, 196
Berringer, Margaret 7
Bessent, Abraham 98
Binford, John 146
Blake, Joseph 19
Bloodworth, Timothy 49, 63, 133, 134
Blount, John Gray 42, 95, 113, 125
Blount, Reading 42
Blount, Thomas 42, 111, 113, 135, 149
Blount, William 42, 50, 113
Blue Banks Plantation 20, 23, 29, 31, 34, 37, 190
Bob (slave) 98, 102
Bolivia, N.C. 159
Bonnet, Stede 8
borough representation 56
Boston Massacre 14
Boston Tea Party 16
Boundary House 29, 143, 144
Bradley, John 140, 141
Braswell, Catty 102
Braswell, Robert 102
Brice, Francis 37
Brickell, John 30, 200
Brooklyn 124
Broom Hall Plantation 9, 23
Broussard, James 132
Brown, Thomas 152–153
Brunswick County 27, 28, 37, 158–159; Court of Pleas and Quarter Sessions 37–39, 51, 69–70, 74–75, 80–81, 92, 97–98, 102, 138, 148, 149, 156–157, 159, 164–165,

166, 167, 183–184, 195–196; courthouse 165; seat of government 43–44, 158–159, 165
Brunswick Town 18, 19, 25, 26, 27–28, 43, 90, 194, 194, 196, 197, 205, 206
Bryan, Nathan 86
Buchoi Plantation 28, 142
Burgwin, Eliza 92, 93; see also Clitherall, Eliza Burgwin
Burgwin, John 92
Burns, Otway 193
Burr, Aaron 140, 150
Burrington, George 25

Caldwell, David 105
Caldwell, Joseph 112, 136, 169, 170
Campbell, Samuel 36
Campbell William 16
Campbell and Hogg 36
Cape Fear Company 86–87
Carolina Playmakers 201
Casso, Mrs. (Margaret) 170, 174
Casso's Tavern 170
Caswell, Richard 41, 49, 57, 168
Charles Town (Charleston), S.C. 5, 9, 10–11, 12, 16, 21, 22, 23, 76, 125, 162, 165, 166, 191, 192, 193, 195
Charles-Town Library Society 5, 11
Chatham Plantation 97
Chavis, Temperance 165
Chesapeake affair 150–152, 155–156, 182
Cheves, Langdon 191
Chisholm v Georgia 79
Clark, Richard 6
Clark Island 182
Clarke, Richard 6
Clinton, DeWitt 176
Clinton, George 70
Clinton, Henry 21
Clitherall, Eliza Burgwin 92, 93, 116, 184, 192, 193, 194, 196, 197, 200, 203; see also Burgwin, Eliza
Clitherall, George 92, 93, 118, 194, 196, 197, 200
Cobb, Collier 204
Cochrane, Robert 166
College of Charleston 13
College of Philadelphia 12, 14
Colonial Dames 205
Compton, Spencer, Earl of Wilmington 26
Constitutional Convention 50
Cooper, Anthony Ashley 6
corn 123
Cornwallis, Charles 27
cotton 122–123

Council of State 174, 188
Croom, William 177
Cross Creek 54, 63, 64

Daughters of the American Revolution 205
Davie, William R. 50, 55, 59, 60, 69, 80, 90, 91–92, 94, 104, 106, 110, 111, 113, 147, 168
Davis, Andrew Jackson 200
Davis, John 95
Davis, Justina 30
Dawson, William J. 53
Dearborn, Henry 150, 151, 153
debtor's prison 189, 203, 204
de Chanla, Monsieur 196
Dickerson, Oliver M. 12
Dillard, Joseph 170
Dismal Swamp Canal 65, 66, 68
Dobbs, Arthur 19, 30, 31
Dorchester, S.C. 124
Dry, Mary Jane 17, 19–20, 30, 32, 34
Dry, Rebecca 30
Dry, Sarah 17, 18, 19, 20, 90; see also Smith, Sarah Dry
Dry, William, I 18
Dry, William, II 18, 19, 25
Dry, William, III 17, 18, 19, 30, 31, 32, 34, 35, 36, 39, 51, 74, 95, 96, 97, 102, 205
Dry, William, Jr. 39
Dry(e), Robert 18
Drysborough 96
Duche, Jacob 14
dueling 120, 138–145

Eagles, Joseph 101
Eagles Island 24, 28, 35–36, 38, 44, 67–68, 102, 160, 205
East India Company 16
Eaton, Clement 139
Edenton, N.C. 26; cannon in 154, 163–164, 165–166, 169
Eleventh Amendment 79
Ellsworth, Oliver 110
Erie Canal 176
E.T. Dupont de Nemours & Co. 154
Eustis, William 164, 165

Fayetteville, N.C. 41, 52, 53, 54, 55–60, 61, 116, 122, 150
Fayetteville Convention 55–56
Ferry Plantation 36; see also Belvedere
Finlay, Hugh 35–36
The Forks Plantation 28
fornication 39
Forster, Alexus 196

Fort Caswell 155
Fort Hampton 82
Fort Johnston 71, 82, 92, 97, 101, 106, 119, 120, 121, 155, 163, 167, 173, 178, 182, 194, 196, 199, 203
Fort Lyttelton 20, 21
Fourth of July observance 92, 119, 133, 145, 150–151, 166
Franklin, Benjamin 13, 45
Franklin, Jesse 104, 135, 149
Franklin, State of 45, 46
Freeman, Joanne 140
Freemasonry 56–57, 90–92, 159–160, 163, 167, 205
French and Indian War 5
Fundamental Constitutions 6

Gadsden, Christopher 139
Gales, Joseph 140
Gallaway, James 56
Gamache, David 98
Garrison House, Fort Johnston 163
Gause, John, Jr. 183
Genet, Edmond 75, 76
Georgetown, S.C. 29, 59
Gibbs, Isabella 124
Gillespie, James 112, 133, 134, 146
Glasgow, James 112, 113
Goose Creek, S.C. 7, 9, 18, 22, 23
Gordon, John 5
Grange, Jack 139, 141–142, 143–144
granite markers 205
Gray, Tom (slave) 98
Green Swamp 58–59, 95, 99, 168
Greene, Nathanael 101
Griffin, John Lightfoot 115–116, 119, 120, 144, 145
Grimke, Angelina 192
Grimke, John Faucheraud 191
Grimke, Mary 191, 200
Grimke, Sarah 192
Grimke, Thomas S. 191, 192, 195, 200
grist mills 122
Grove, William Barry 54, 63, 64

Halifax, N.C. 76
Hall, Allmand 108
Hamilton, Alexander 62, 82, 140, 144
Hamilton, John 153
Harmar, Josiah 81
Harnett, Cornelius 32, 34–35, 39, 48
Harrington, Henry William 123, 124, 127
Harris, Charles 100
Haselton, John, Jr. 51
Hawkins, Benjamin 57

Hawkins, William 179, 180
Hayne, Robert Y. 191
Haywood, John 42, 84, 87, 90, 93, 103, 113, 117, 128, 136, 185, 186, 187, 188, 190, 196
Haywood Hall 84
Henderson, Richard 45, 95
Henry, Patrick 95, 110
Hervieux, François Henri 76, 77
Hill, William H. 133
Hillsborough 40, 41, 52, 100, 118
Hillsborough Convention 50–55, 59
Hinton, James 77
Historical Sketches of North Carolina 201
History of North Carolina 201
Hofstadter, Richard 9
Hogg, James 36, 41, 45, 54, 64, 65, 73, 95, 96, 115, 131, 132
Hogg, Robert 36
Hooper, George 82
Hooper, William 40, 41
Hopton & Smith 9
Howe, Baalam 188
Howe, Richard 17
Howe, Robert (1732–1786) 27, 45, 139
Howe, Robert (the younger) 197
Howe, William 17
Hunter, Isaac 54, 55
Huske, John 72

Indian Queen Tavern 170, 172
Inns of Court 15, 16, 23, 30
internal improvements 58–59, 63–65, 86–87, 147
Intolerable Acts 16
Iredell, James 40, 52, 79, 112, 142
Isabella grape 124

Jamaica 94
James, Hinton 87
Jay, John 79
Jay-Gardoqui Treaty 49
Jay Treaty 88, 102
Jefferson, Thomas 89, 127, 133–134, 140, 150, 198
Johnston, Gabriel 26
Johnston, John 57
Johnston, Samuel 41, 52, 55, 57, 70, 103, 111, 114, 168
Jones, William Watts 186, 187, 189, 190
Jones, Willie 41, 52

Kenan, Thomas 146, 157
Kendal Plantation 7, 27, 28, 45, 156, 195
King, William R. 181

King George's War 19, 72, 106
King's Highway 28–29
Kitchen, Claude 204
Knox, Henry 71, 76, 81, 82

Lane, Joel 84
Larry (slave) 126
Laura (slave) 200
Laurens, Henry 11, 12, 14–15, 139
Lawson, John 200
Lenoir, William 55
Lexington and Concord 16
Liberty Hall Academy 105
Liberty ships 205–206
Lilliput Plantation 28
Lincoln, Benjamin 21
Livingston Creek 75
Lloyd, David 184
Locke, John 6
Lockwoods Folly 27, 28, 43–44, 72, 81, 138, 149, 158, 164
Log College 105
Lord, Elizabeth 116, 120, 193, 194
Lord, John 120 163
lotteries 106, 135–136
Louisiana Territory 137
Lucetta (slave) 194

Maclaine, Archibald 36, 46, 47, 58, 61
Madison, James 157, 159, 161, 178, 181, 182
Mallory Plantation 28, 97, 190
Margaret (slave) 126
Marion, Francis 23
Martin, Alexander 43, 46, 50, 60, 63, 66, 70–71, 90, 104, 111, 168
Martinique 43
Martinon, Nicholas Francis 82
Mat[t]hew (slave) 99
McCall, Alexander 106
McDowell, Joseph 52
McGuire, Rebecca Dry 30
McGuire, Thomas 30, 31, 32, 34, 36
McKoy, W.B. 202, 203, 205
Mebane, James 168, 180
Mercury (slave) 126
Merino sheep 167
Methodist Church 116–117, 192
Middleton, Mary 22
militia 71, 76, 78–79, 81, 86, 98, 128, 151–152, 153, 154, 159, 175, 177, 178
Miller, Phineas 122
Miller, William 182, 188
Miranda, Francisco de 40
Monroe, James 193
Moore, Alexander Duncan 133, 134

Moore, Alfred 28, 98, 103, 112, 118, 142–143
Moore, Catherine Rhett 8
Moore, Duncan 143, 144
Moore, George 31
Moore, James 7, 18
Moore, John Wheeler 201
Moore, Junius A. 200
Moore, Louis T. 201, 203, 204–205
Moore, Maurice (1682?–1743) 7, 25, 97
Moore, Maurice (son of Alfred Moore) 138, 139, 141, 142, 143, 144, 148, 160, 201
Moore, Nathaniel 7
Moore, Rebecca 18
Moore, Roger 7, 18, 19, 25, 31, 97
Mooresfield Plantation 97
Morrill, James R. 43
Morse, Jedidiah 40
Moultrie, William 20, 21, 108
Murphey, Archibald D. 131, 169, 200
Murray, William Vans 110

Nanny (slave) 126
Napoleon Bonaparte 150
Nash, Francis 72
naval stores 124
New Bern, N.C. 26, 40, 52, 96, 101, 141, 160, 165, 169
New Hanover Historical Commission 205
New Madrid earthquakes 200
Newton 26
Ninety-Six, S.C. 16
Norman, Jeremiah 117
North Carolina: and Articles of Confederation 48–49; banking in 135, 184–185; capital 51–55, 59, 68–69, 70–71, 83–85; capitol 84–85; cession of Tennessee by 45–46, 112; and *Chesapeake* affair 150–152; defense 78, 81–82, 106–108, 155; 181–182; economy 182–183; education in 105; and federal Constitution 46, 50, 51, 52, 55–56; Freemasonry in 159–160, 167; General Assembly 39–46, 56–60, 61, 62, 63–65, 68–69, 70–73, 77, 80, 81, 85–87, 93, 94–95, 98–99, 102, 103–104, 105, 111–114, 128–130, 134–135, 136, 137, 146–148, 148–149, 153–156, 157–158, 159, 160–161, 167–180, 182, 188–189; geography 7, 24–25, 26, 28, 33; health in 117–118; opportunities for education in 105; politics in 47, 48–49, 50, 51–53, 55–56, 60, 61, 62–63, 70, 88–89, 101–102, 103–104, 127–128, 132–134, 157, 183; relations with France 76–78, 100–102, 103, 106–108; residence of governors 170–172; resolution of General Assembly 206; state

constitution 47–48; travel in 28–29, 41, 66–68
North Carolina Booklet 204
North Carolina Court of Conference 147
North Carolina Highway Historical Marker 206
North Carolina Medical Society 112
North Carolina Shipbuilding Company 206
North Carolina State Historic Site 206
Nova Scotia 167

Obion County 200
Ocracoke Inlet 169
Orton Plantation 7, 28, 97, 102, 122, 123, 186, 189, 190, 192, 194, 196

Person, Thomas 44, 170
Peterkin, Darryl 131
Philadelphia 12, 13–14
Pickering, Timothy 110
Pilkinton, Seth 31
Pinckney, Charles C. 102
Pitt, William 5
Pitt County 160
Pleasant Oaks Plantation 28
Polk, William 128
Pollock, Cullen 62
Potter, Robert 148, 149
Potter, Samuel 166
Potts, Joshua 72, 120, 163
Price, Jonathan 99
Proclamation of 1763 42, 45
Prometheus 193
Protestant Episcopal Church 51, 90, 116

Quasi-War 103, 106–107
Queen's Museum 105
Quince, Richard 97
Quincy, Josiah, Jr. 31

Raleigh, N.C. 83–85, 92, 98, 103, 111, 153, 160, 170, 188
Raleigh, Walter 83
Ramsay, David 6
Rankin, Richard 140
Read, James 101
Rhett, Catherine 7
Rhett, Mary Jane 19–20
Rhett, Robert Barnwell 195
Rhett, William (1666–1723) 7–8, 18, 19
Rhett, William (1695–1729) 19
rice 121–122
Richard Henderson Company 69
Riddick, Joseph 168, 180
Roberts, Robert 163

Robertson, James 41, 42
Rogers, George C., Jr. 9
Roosevelt, Franklin D. 206
Rowan, John 51, 96, 115
Rowan, Mary 96, 194, 197, 200
Rowan, Robert 42
Russellborough 31, 97; *see also* Bellfont
Rutherford, Griffith 41, 45
Rutledge, Edward 16, 21, 22, 23, 111, 127, 139
Rutledge, John 21, 139

St. Augustine 7
St. Cecelia Society 11
St. Clair, Arthur 71, 81
St. James Church 90
St. John's Lodge 91, 104, 159, 163
St. Philip's Church (Brunswick Town) 18, 27, 30, 32, 90, 194, 201, 205
St. Philip's Church (Charleston) 6, 18, 192, 199
St. Tammany's Lodge 91
Sainte Domingue 62, 94
Sam (slave) 194
Scott, Andrew 144, 145
Scott, William 170
Scull, John G. 146, 148, 149, 155, 160, 166
Sea Castle 74, 77, 93, 99
Seawell, Henry 168, 174
Sevier, John 45, 46
Shallotte, N.C. 27
shipbuilding 124–125
Silbey, John 62
Sirmans, Eugene 25
Sitgreaves, John 49
slavery 26–27, 61–62, 94–95, 99, 125–126, 162
Smelser, Marshall 151
Smith, Ann 6
Smith, Benjamin (1717–1770) 8, 9, 12, 90
Smith, Benjamin (1757–1826): as acting governor 110–111; agricultural operations 121–124; as aide-de-camp to Washington 17; appointment as Adjutant General 149; appointment as justice of the peace 46; and Articles of Confederation 49–50; burial 199–200; character 37, 74, 92–93, 94, 143, 144, 172–173, 185–186, 198, 199, 201–205; death 197; and debtor's prison 189, 203–204; duels 138–139, 141–145; early years 10–16; education 12, 14, 15; elected brigadier general 80; elected colonel 57–58; elected governor 168; elected major general 155; elected speaker of the Senate 93, 98, 102, 103, 111; endowment of UNC by 59–60; as Grand Master of

North Carolina Freemasons 159–160, 167; health 117, 191, 192; hosts George Washington 67–68; marriage 17–18; named trustee of UNC 59; newspaper attacks on 108–110; political conversion 133–134; reinterment 201; Revolutionary experience 17, 20–23; Smithville residence 118–119; surrender letter 21–22; Wilmington residence 138, 172, 186; *see also* Bald Head Island; Bald Head Island Lighthouse; Belvedere Plantation; Blue Banks Plantation; Brunswick County Court of Pleas and Quarter Sessions; Fayetteville Convention; Hillsborough Convention; North Carolina General Assembly; slavery; Smithville Academy; University of North Carolina Board of Trustees

Smith, Benjamin (English shipwright) 125
Smith, Isaac 12
Smith, James 6, 23, 156, 157, 159, 162, 166, 183, 195
Smith, Mary 6
Smith, Peter 6, 14, 22, 23, 195
Smith, Roger 5, 9, 11, 12, 13, 14, 16, 23
Smith, Sabina 6
Smith, Sarah (1752–?) 6
Smith, Sarah Dry 28, 29–30, 34, 90, 92, 115–116, 117, 138, 145, 171–172, 185–186, 189, 190–191, 194; *see also* Dry, Sarah
Smith, Sarah Moore 5, 8
Smith, Thomas (1648–1694) 6
Smith, Thomas (1664?–1738) 6
Smith, Thomas (1691–1724) 6, 7
Smith, Thomas (1720–1790) 5, 7, 8, 9–10, 11, 13, 14, 15, 22, 23, 62
Smith, Thomas (residence on the Bay in Charleston) 8
Smith Hall 200, 201
Smithfield 40, 53
Smithville 28, 40, 53, 71–72, 82, 92, 105, 116, 117, 118, 119, 124, 125, 138, 145, 151, 158, 159, 163, 165, 166, 171, 184, 189, 192–193, 194, 196, 197, 201; incorporation 71–72
Smithville Academy 105, 106, 189
Smithville Canal Company 147
Snider, William D. 69
Solomon's Lodge 90
Southport, N.C. 163, 202, 206 *see also* Smithville
Spaight, Richard D. 49, 50, 52, 76, 77, 78, 81, 82, 85, 87, 90, 141, 168
Springs, Sedgwick 74, 166
Stamp Act 11, 12

Stamp Act Congress 11
Stanly, John 141
State Bank of North Carolina 185
steamboat 193
Steele, John 162
Steuben, Baron von 71
Stokes, Montfort 135
Stone, David 157, 164, 167, 168, 169
Strother, John 99
Strudwick, Samuel 42
Stuart, Kate 203
Stuart, Mary Elizabeth Bensel 201, 203
Sugar Act 11
Supply, N.C. 159
Swann, John 140, 141
Swansboro, N.C. 193
Swedenborg, Emmanuel 14
Swift, Joseph G. 115, 119–120, 121, 124, 138, 139, 142, 145, 155, 163, 166, 167, 173, 190, 196

Tarboro, N.C. 40, 52, 53
Taylor, John 94
Tea Act 16
Tennessee 45, 46, 49, 59, 112–113
tobacco 53
Toney (slave) 126
Topsail Sound 122
Townshend duties 12, 14
Transylvania (Louisa) Company 45, 80, 95, 132, 191
Treaty of Hopewell 46, 69, 80
Treaty of Paris, 1763 5
Treaty of Paris, 1783 47
Trott, Mary 19
Trott, Nicholas 19
Troy, Matthew 149
Tryon, William 31
Turner, James 167

United States: foreign affairs 75–76, 100, 103, 106–107, 110, 150–153, 159; *see also Chesapeake* affair
University of North Carolina 59–60, 72, 91–92, 129–130, 147; Board of Trustees 65–66, 69, 72–73, 79–80, 87, 93–94, 103, 111–112, 130–131, 135–136, 149, 153–154, 169–170, 175, 185–187, 189–190; critics 129–130, 147; incorporation 59–60; opening 87

Van Myddagh, Anna Cornelia 6

Walker, Carleton 185
Walkersburg 72

Walpole, Robert 26
War of 1812 181–182
Ward, Thomas 98
Warrenton, N.C. 76
Washington, D.C. 121, 151, 160, 164, 165, 190
Washington, George 17, 42, 53, 55, 66–68, 70, 71, 75, 76, 81, 82, 89, 101, 109, 127, 129, 179
Washington, N.C. 101, 160
Wayne, Anthony 81
Wheeler, John H. 201
Whiskey Rebellion 62, 88
White, William 84, 176, 179
White-Holman House 84
Whitney, Eli 122
Williams, Benjamin 41, 111, 112, 141, 156
Williams, John 93
Williams, Philip 105

Williamson, Hugh 49, 50
Wilmington, N.C. 25, 26, 27, 53, 54, 66–67, 74, 78, 83, 96, 100–101, 104–105, 106, 116, 117, 118, 119, 133, 140, 141, 145, 147, 150, 151, 165, 166, 169, 171, 173, 183, 206
Wilmington Children's Museum 91
Wilson, Thomas 73
wine 124
Winston, Francis D. 205
wood products 124
World War II 205–206
Wright, Joshua G. 173, 174, 176, 179
Wright, Thomas 76

XYZ affair 103

Yeamans, John 7

www.ingramcontent.com/pod-product-compliance
Ingram Content Group UK Ltd.
Pitfield, Milton Keynes, MK11 3LW, UK
UKHW041937140426
5217IPUK00014B/532